First published 1991
Reprinted 1992

Blackwell Publishers Ltd
108 Cowley Road
Oxford OX4 1JF
UK

Three Cambridge Center
Cambridge, Massachusetts 02142
USA

A CIP catalogue record for this book is available from
the British Library.

Library of Congress Cataloging-in-Publication Data
Pettigrew, Andrew M.
Managing change for competitive success / Andrew Pettigrew and
Richard Whipp.
p.   cm.
Includes bibliographical references and index.
ISBN 0–631–18241–1
1. Organizational change.   I. Whipp, Richard.   II. Title.
HD58.8.P49 1991   91–22958
658.4'06—dc20   CIP

Typeset in 11 on 13 pt Sabon
by Pentacor plc
Printed in Great Britain by TJ Press Ltd, Padstow, Cornwall
This book is printed on acid-free paper.

Managing Change for Competitive Success

Andrew Pettigrew and Richard Whipp

Contents

List of figures

List of tables

Acknowledgements

We are indebted to a great many people for their generous and constructive assistance in the development of this book.

The research underpinning the manuscript was financed by the Economic and Social Research Council as part of a broader ESRC initiative on the competitiveness of UK industry. Arthur Francis of Imperial College, London University, was co-ordinator of the ESRC Competitiveness Initiative and we are grateful to him for organizing many conferences and workshops where we were able to discuss our early findings and ideas with him and the various research teams engaged in the initiative. Subsequent correspondence with John Stopford, Charles Baden-Fuller and Malcolm Cunningham proved helpful.

The project team consisted of Andrew Pettigrew, Richard Whipp and Robert Rosenfeld at the Centre for Corporate Strategy and Change, Warwick Business School. The fieldwork for the project began in late 1985 and continued into 1990, although Robert Rosenfeld left the team in October 1988. Robert Rosenfeld played an important part in the data collection and early case study writing in the project (particularly with our financial services work) and his contribution is reflected in many of the articles and conference papers derived from the project.

While this project on Strategic Change and Competition was developing at the Centre for Corporate Strategy and Change, so other related large projects on corporate strategy change and human resource management, and strategic service change in the NHS were also getting off the ground. We are grateful to our Centre colleagues, and particularly to Ewan Ferlie, Chris Hendry, Lorna McKee, and Paul Sparrow for many discussions of themes common to our related projects.

At various times we have also benefited from conversations and correspondence with colleagues from our international network. Thanks are due to Leif Melin in Sweden; John Kimberly, Alan Meyer, Mike Tushman, Andrew Van de Ven and Richard Walton in the United States; Royston Greenwood and Bob Hinings in Canada; Armand Hatchuel in Paris; and Brian Loasby in Scotland.

The media have shown a constructive interest in the findings of this research some time before the publication of this book. We would like to acknowledge the support of Christopher Lorenz and Ian Hamilton Fazey of the *Financial Times*. Brian Morris of Data Television has also worked with the authors in the production of the BBC television documentary on the findings to be shown in the Business Matters Series in August 1991.

The kind of research documented in this book requires the considerable long-term support and co-operation of the participating firms. We are deeply indebted to all the individuals who helped us carry out the research in our seven firms. It is certainly invidious to mention only a few names for each company, but nevertheless we thank: David Evans and Michael Turner at Associated Book Publishers; Christopher Castleman, Sir Robert Clark, David Longridge and Sir Richard Lloyd at Hill Samuel Bank; Sir John Egan, Ken Edwards and Mike Kinski at Jaguar Cars; Michael Hawkes and David Peake at Kleinwort Benson; Sir Brian Corby, Geoffrey Haslam and Geoff Keeys at the Prudential Corporation; Paula Kahn, Tim Rix and John Robinson at Longman; and Mike Judge, Terry Neesham, Dick Parham and Geoffrey Whalen at Peugeot Talbot.

The Centre for Corporate Strategy and Change has been blessed with strong administrative support and we would like to express our appreciation to Liz Cameron, Gill Drakeley, Ann Jackson and Jeanette Whitmore.

The authors are grateful to the *Financial Times* for kind permission to use the material which appears in Figure 2.1 and Table 2.4; to *Management Today* for permission to use material which appears in Table 2.5; and Macmillan Publishers Ltd for permission to adapt material from R. Kellet's *The Merchant Banking Arena* (1967), p.95, which appears in Table 2.6, and from D. Channon's *The Service Industries* (1978), p.97, which appears in Table 2.9.

In spite of all this help, we, the authors, are entirely responsible for the accuracy of our data and the soundness of our conclusions.

Andrew Pettigrew
Richard Whipp
April 1991

Introduction

An instructive example

In 1980 Jaguar was given a year's notice of closure by British Leyland. Only if it broke even would the threat be lifted. In one sense Jaguar was fortunate to be given the chance denied many other UK manufacturing companies at that time. The 'story' of Jaguar since then is of course well known. The Coventry car maker is almost perfectly suited as *the* company example to illustrate the challenges faced by British industry in the 1980s. And yet how poorly are such instances used. Even in the professional financial press it is the shallowness of the commentary on Jaguar which stands out. Such accounts demonstrate the limitations of our understanding of the way firms have responded to competitive circumstances and managed the consequent changes.

Jaguar's period under the spotlight of intense public attention is symmetrical with the past decade: from its parlous state in 1980, to its much-lauded success in the mid–1980s, down to the controversial acquisition by Ford at the end of 1989. Jaguar has never been short of attention.

The company entered 1980 in disarray. The 1979 Series III model was riddled with quality and reliability defects. Production had fallen to 14,000 vehicles a year from its 1974 peak of 32,000. Losses were running at £4 million a month. The turnaround of Jaguar, led by the new chairman and managing director John Egan, was hailed as a remarkable feat. Sales recovered so that the past record was surpassed in 1984. Between 1981 and 1985 pre-tax profits leapt to £107 million. Productivity more than doubled. After a successful flotation in 1984, Jaguar became a glamour stock in the City: its shares moved from the 170p offer price to 630p before 'Black Monday' in October 1987. The management's internal initiatives in training, for example, were the subject of widespread interest (Simpson 1986). In the words of industry commentators, the company was 'transformed into a profitable symbol of Britain's economic resurgence' (Cassidy and Williams 1988).

The same people, including many City analysts, were quick to reverse their opinions after profits fell in 1987 and 1988. Previous adulation turned to sharp criticism. The principal charge was that the success of Jaguar was reliant on a £/$ exchange rate windfall and that the management had ignored fundamental problems. As one commentator put it:

> Sir John cannot complain too much about all this, since his company (and himself as its very public figurehead) did so well out of the pound's fall in the mid–1980s. Now the hype is over. Sir John, his company and its shareholders have been brought down to earth. (Cowe 1989: 19)

Such reporting has not served Jaguar nor the public well. Some have taken the trouble to account for the company's performance a little more closely. Mention is made of changing consumer demand, the need of new managerial blood and reference to uneven product quality (see Williams, K. and Barber as cited in Cassidy and Williams, I. 1988). In 1988 Egan attacked the short-term views among financial analysts, retorting that 'lunch is long-term planning to them'.

Exceptions to such commentary have been rare. Kevin Done has been one of the few to recognize the depth of the problems faced by the company (Done 1989). He has indicated the onerous investment burden faced by Jaguar as it tried to remedy the omissions of the 1970s and before. In 1984, for example, the average age of Jaguar's machine tools was 25 years. He has also indicated the daunting task which faced Jaguar given the problems of building a 'world-class car company' in a 'non-world-class economy'.

Criticizing Jaguar from a distance is easy. Providing a robust explanation of the performance of this company and others is far more demanding. In short, that is the purpose of this book. The aim is not to concentrate only on performance outcomes but to engage with the range of contributory forces which produce them. Our point of entry to the problem is through the relationship between the management of strategic and operational change and competitive performance. Such an issue opens up many questions which simply are not addressed in current discussions of competition. Closer inspection of the way firms had to manage change in order to compete in the 1980s shows the challenge to have been awesome.

Jaguar is a clear illustration. To ascribe the company's performance merely to the movement in exchange rates ignores more than it explains. Even if the £/$ ratio of 1983–5 made Jaguars cheaper in the USA, that still does not explain why North American customers were prepared to purchase the car in the first place. The answer lay in the ability of the company to transform its product. Yet that in turn relied on the management of an extensive set of interrelated changes.

As subsequent chapters will show, these early changes in just the four years to 1984 included: the total restructuring of Jaguar's retail operation; a protracted process of negotiation with corporate, Department of Trade and Industry and government bodies; a new senior management team involving the re-creation of finance, sales and marketing and purchasing departments; the completion of an 'action programme' which reduced operating costs, raised standards of quality and reliability, reduced head count from 10,000 to 7,000 and set up company-wide task forces to tackle a list of 150 problems. How such changes are managed are vital to understanding the ability of firms to compete. Concentrating exclusively on business policy decisions and their ultimate outcome avoids some of the most formidable problems management face.

An appropriate moment

A brief reflection on the upheavals managers have encountered in the 1980s leads to but one conclusion: one could hardly have picked a better time to study competition and change. The concentrated sequence of European geo-political shifts at the end of 1989 have been truly epoch-making. The unthinkable has almost become commonplace in this 'age of surprises'.

Restricting one's attention to the economic sphere only reveals the depth of the changes in the 1980s. In the UK the growth of credit was remarkable. In 1980 new bank and building society lending was £15.7 billion, by 1988 it had reached £82 billion. The funds unlocked by new forms of finance made unprecedented takeover activity possible. Sir James Goldsmith's 1989 £13 billion offer for BAT would have seemed impossible in 1980. Now such acts slot comfortably within the decade's cast list of 'mega-mergers'. These have included the disconcerting fall of national symbols. Sony's acquisition of Columbia Pictures for $3.4 billion in 1989 is perhaps the most vivid example. A scheme was even put together in 1988 for a $40 billion takeover of General Motors (Brummer 1989: 7).

No company could assume its safety from predators who stalked under-performing assets. Yet equally nobody has been left untouched by the wholesale alterations in work, technology, company form or industry structure (see Lloyd and Leadbeater 1986).

Calculations for the UK have suggested that 342,000 jobs were lost through machines displacing labour in the 1980s. Conversely, 175,000 may have been won back through the effect of new technology lowering costs and prices and thus leading to higher real demand. In France it is thought that one million workers needed retraining in 1989 because of technological change. At the same time, in West Germany it was estimated that a quarter of all office tasks would soon be completely automated. International evidence from OECD countries also points to the major impact of the growth in small businesses. Small firm employment in the UK rose from 13.5 per cent of total employment in 1968 to 21.1 per cent in 1982. At the same time the number of large firms (employing more than 1,000) fell by one million to six million between 1976 and 1989. Parallel with these changes has been the marked rise in unemployment and the reduction in trade union membership. One of the most evocative UK statistics to emerge from these dislocations of the 1980s came in 1987: by then 20 per cent of the work-force was accounted for by part-time workers. Sectors based on the new technology grew by staggering proportions. By 1986 the $31 billion world telecommunications industry had grown by 233 per cent in six years (DTI 1989).

It is interesting that in spite of the enormity of such alterations to the fabric of British and other national economies, to some their significance has already begun to fade. The redrawing of the European political map and the prospect of what has been dubbed a 'post-post-war' period, rightly claim attention. Yet while projections for the 1990s are quite naturally on everyone's lips, it is worth stopping to consider how far we understand the 1980s.

A new mode of thought

It is not the intention of this book to cover such an extensive terrain. The purpose is more specific. Our concern in terms of the UK economy is with an age-old problem but looked at in a novel way. As will be shown in chapters 1 and 2, the head scratching over the relative decline of the British economy has become something of a habit over the past 100 years. It continues into the 1990s (Keegan 1990: 11). Differing interpretations abound. Yet little space is found in such explanations for the capacities of companies to handle the demands of given periods or the role of management in creating and sustaining such abilities. The power to assess, formulate and implement strategies is more often assumed than scrutinized. The research on which this book is based makes the generation of such capacities and the contexts in which they are developed over time its centre-piece. In the area of management we are, to paraphrase Oscar Wilde, trying to move beyond the narrow concern for the price of everything to a concern of the value of much wider managerial actions. These issues are dealt with at length in chapter 1.

The apparent transformations of political, commercial and social life in the 1980s provide an exceptional opportunity to explore such issues. Yet it is abundantly evident that one cannot understand the performance of given industries or companies in the 1980s by reference to that decade alone. Our aim therefore has been to take a long-term perspective in order to provide a distinctive insight into such problems. We have found it necessary to examine the linked changes at the level of the firm, sector and economy over the past three decades. At the same time, that process of inquiry has been informed by knowledge of the whole life-course of the companies and sectors in question.

The following chapters will demonstrate the potency of such an approach. A simple illustration, however, will help to make the point by way of introduction. Companies in the otherwise widely contrasting sectors of merchant banking and auto manufacture shared a common trait. It is impossible to appreciate their competitive performance in the early 1980s without recognizing the composite problems they faced. As the businesses in our sample show, both bankers and auto makers alike were forced to deal with the consequences of unresolved issues from the previous decades as much as the demands of deregulation or foreign competition. Their neglect of human resources in the 1970s, for instance, required major remedial action. The use of a longitudinal perspective will also confront the received notion of recent years which regards the 1970s as an almost wholly negative period for British management.

The twin sister of relative economic decline in Britain and the USA has been the problem of industry maturity in the West. The difficulties facing mature industries have been well catalogued. Foremost among them are slower growth with greater competition for market share.

New products and applications become scarce yet buyer sophistication increases. The attention given to resuscitating such industries has been extensive. Advice has been forthcoming from government commissions on the one hand, to international research programmes on the other (Scott and Lodge 1985). Indeed the needs of the mature industries can be said to have fuelled the rise of the international market for management texts, as well as expanding the bank accounts of a new generation of management gurus (Dodsworth 1986).

This book does not offer the advice for government action which has come from the commissions, nor does it have to sell any of the wonder cures favoured by the guru best-sellers. In sharp contrast to both, it concentrates on the extent of the complex adjustment process required of individual businesses. We do not believe that this process has been anything like fully appreciated in business, policy or academic debates of the late 1980s. The purpose of the subsequent chapters therefore is to suggest a different 'processual' way of thinking about the problem.

The research project

This book reports the outcomes of a research project which began at the end of 1985 and finished in 1989. The intention was to examine in detail the ability of UK firms to manage strategic change and to assess the outcome for competitive performance.

The study investigated the process of assessment, formulation and implementation of strategic and operational change in four mature industry and service sectors: automobile manufacture, book publishing, merchant banking and life assurance. An outline of the major changes in these sectors and their competitive conditions is given in chapter 2. The goal was to discover:

- why firms operating in the same industry and markets should produce such different performances across time, and
- what had been the contribution of the way they managed strategic change?

The results from looking in detail at seven firms from across the four sectors are reported in this book.

The main conclusion to be drawn from examining the four sectors is twofold. First, that a common pattern emerges from the key features of managing strategic and operational change among the firms.

Second, that there is an observable difference in the way the higher performing firms manage change from their counterparts over time. That pattern is best represented by a model composed of five inter-related factors. The five central factors are:

- environmental assessment
- leading change
- linking strategic and operational change
- human resources as assets and liabilities
- coherence.

The relevance of these five factors is examined in detail in chapters 3 to 7. Those chapters do not set out to provide a prescriptive manual or a textbook. Rather, the intention is to combine theory and practice to their mutual benefit – to engage in a number of mainstream academic debates yet at the same time deal with a wide range of practical managerial concerns which emerge naturally from the research. The subject of leading change in chapter 3 is a good example. Leadership has been an established area of academic inquiry since the specialist psychological studies of the 1950s (Bass 1981). It has, however, never been far from the attention of the business press (*The Economist* 1989a). The hope is that this book will interest both academic and practitioner alike.

None the less one feels obliged to declare *caveat emptor*. There is no assumption of a single best-practice in managing change here, and certainly no prospect of a simple 'quick-fix' is being offered. Quite the reverse. As chapters 3 to 7 show, the ability to create a capacity to manage change around the five central factors is not produced over-night. The capacity is not easily generated nor sustained.

Each of the five factors is built upon a combination of conditioning features and secondary mechanisms. The conditioning features and secondary mechanisms gain their power from being developed in combined form. Their potency is built up through repeated application and across differing circumstances. This building process is measured in years rather than months. The keynote of the research is that in terms of competitive success, the management of strategic change is the result of an uncertain, emergent and iterative process. That process relies on the development of less immediately visible organizational capacities, what might be called 'intangible assets'. Managing such an uncertain process places heavy demands on the ability of firms to learn and adapt in relation to all five areas.

The core interest of this study in the relation between managing strategic change and competition has clear relevance for the 1990s. However, there are a number of further potential attractions for the specialist and informed lay reader alike.

First, there has been a concerted attempt to explore a wide range of literatures and different modes of thinking. The aim has been to offer a constructive, critical synthesis of the fields of strategic change and competition. This has been vital given the broadening scope of the developments in the area; it also helps to specify the contribution which this study seeks to make to understanding managing change and competition in the broadest sense. The synthesis and our own position is laid out in chapter 1.

Second, so vast is this field that it was decided to present our position in relation to the separate bodies of writing which have grown up around certain problems in managing strategic change. Each of the five chapters dealing with the main factors in the book's model begins in a challenging way. In other words, a digest of relevant, often isolated, work done elsewhere is given, as well as an attempt to bring together differing, hitherto unrelated approaches. The guiding notion here has been pluralism: to use the insights of both the more traditional academic orientations and the less conventional (yet often equally robust) thinking of managerialists. Nor have we sought disciplinary exclusivity. The book has proved a crucible for mixing the strengths of more than a single view. Help in illuminating the problems of competition and change has been derived from historical, economic and sociological modes of thinking. Chapter 3, 'Understanding the Environment', draws, for example, on the work of the industrial organization economists, planning experts and anthropologists. This in turn facilitates the development of our own conception of 'action and interpretation' in understanding the competitive environment.

Third, the understanding of change built around multiple contexts and a multi-level approach to competition on which this study has been based had important implications for the format of this book. Chapter 2 therefore presents an overview of the political and economic changes in the UK centred on the 1960s, 1970s and 1980s. The account does not aspire to completeness. None the less, the bullet has been bitten to make an informed judgement of what has generally been claimed to be an exceptional period. Without such a judgement the nature of the competitive forces which have operated within the sectors of the UK economy is unintelligible.

Chapter 2 goes on to survey the character of the four sectors studied during this research. Chapter 2 and chapters 3 to 7 are intended to make both an analytical and empirical contribution to the body of knowledge on these sectors. The centrality of these sectors to the changes in the British economy require little emphasis given:

- the continuing significance of the auto industry in employment, balance of payments or stark political terms
- the under-studied yet universally known revolution in merchant banking and life assurance following the de/re-regulation of the financial services sector
- the allegedly total redefinition of book publishing in the face of new product technology, retailing and patterns of ownership.

Above all, the unusual spread from the industrial to the service sector was chosen to provide a singular test of the research's findings: if there did prove to be a pattern in the way higher performers managed strategic change, did it hold across such very different sectors?

Fourth, the subsequent sections try to weave a strand of comparisons between the empirical results of this study and relevant work elsewhere. Kipling cautioned against narrow introversion in his observation that 'how little they know of England who only England know'. The same is true by analogy of industry and firm-based studies.

As a result, pertinent contrasts and comparisons are made throughout the book with the experience of organizations in not only other sectors but also other countries. The claims made on behalf of US or Japanese companies in linking strategic and operational change are set against our UK evidence in chapter 5, for example. By the same token implicit use has been made of the feedback on the research's interim results received from scholarly and practitioner audiences, not to mention the detailed observations of those responsible for managing change and meeting the competitive challenges in the sectors and firms being studied. The use of such diverse sources is as uncommon in the empirical as it is in the conceptual domain. Such a combination has the potential to make a telling contribution to the field of strategy and competition.

In the closing year of the 1980s some commentators argued that the events of 1989 signalled the 'end of history'. Francis Fukuyama coined this polemical phrase (Fukuyama 1989) to denote the final and irrevocable triumph of the liberal ideals of democracy and market economies. While one welcomes his bravery, his assertion sits uneasily with our findings.

The conceptual apparatus assembled in this research is based on the inherent instability and turbulence of social and economic relations.

Fukuyama's finality, therefore, seems premature if not dangerous. In the commercial and industrial sphere the motive forces for change appear in lusty health, to the extent that they endlessly reproduce themselves. Understanding that reproduction has a long way to go. In many ways the chapters which follow are a partial demonstration not of the end of history or change but rather its ironic permanence. This book is testimony to the difficulty man has in controlling change, matched only by his unquenchable need to do so.

1

Competitiveness and Managing Change

The novelist Malcolm Bradbury has turned his critical gaze to the character of the 1980s. As an academic he naturally looked to his students as indicators of the generation growing up in that decade. He summarizes the distinctiveness of the 1980s in the following way: from the 1960s to the mid–1970s his charges assumed 'never trust anyone over 30'. In the 1980s they began saying 'I want to be a millionaire by 30' (Bradbury 1989).

Such commercial values point to the way some of the most powerful images of Britain in the 1980s relate to the changes in its economy. Everyday speech accepts as commonplace not only the VDU, the Filofax or 'Big Bang' but also such terms as competitive edge, leverage and innovation. Popular English has become coated with a managerial varnish. And therein lies a problem. In order to understand the nature of competition and managing change in sectors of the UK economy, those concepts require careful specification.

A clear demonstration of how one understands the relationship between competition and strategic change becomes imperative when the literature on management is considered. The fashion in 'airport bookstall' or instant management texts has not helped. The concepts of competition and strategy have become diluted with familiarity. No positive correlation has emerged between understanding and the volume of print on these subjects.

Any study of the nature of competition and managing strategic change is obliged therefore to do two things at the outset: first, lay out the major approaches to these issues, and second, make clear the understanding of competition and change on which this book is based. The following two sections of this chapter are devoted to that task.

The third sets out the goals of the study derived from our particular approach to the problem.

A review of the main analysts of competition (see figure. 1.1 for the major schools of thought with indicative authors shown in brackets) will reveal the parentage of their ideas, the family connections among them, the family friends and the black sheep. At the same time this will show why our approach to competition is constructed as it is and hence our place in this extended kin network.

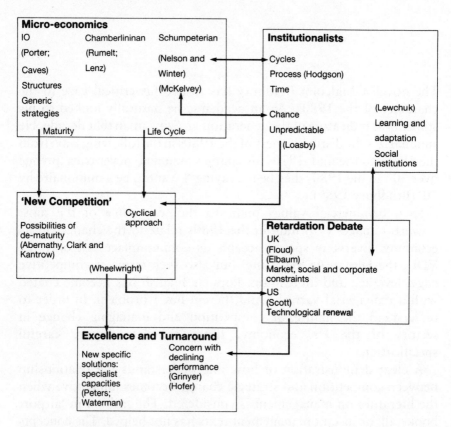

Figure 1.1 The strategy and competition literatures

Competition

If the family of students of competition have a religion then it is surely housed in a 'broad church'. Without any claims to recording every conceivable sect there are perhaps five major groups of believers: the industrial organization specialists; the related break-away group of 'new competition' writers; the deviant 'institutionalists'; the many generations who have participated in the retardation debate; and most recently, the prophets of business turnaround. As in many religious movements all the groups share certain common assumptions yet can diverge widely in their interpretation of key ideas. Taking each in the order indicated will make their particular contributions clear.

Microeconomics and the industrial organization (IO) tradition

Established economic theory has provided a number of basic models of competition related to specific market structures. These well-known models (see Jain 1985; Call and Holahan 1983), built upon the nature of demand, include: monopoly, oligopoly and perfect competition. Each relies, however, on assumptions about the products of a firm, the firm's knowledge of the market, the mobility of resources and the information levels of consumers. Thus under conditions of 'perfect competition' the number of firms is infinite, consumers respond only to price, the demand curve is perfectly elastic and product homogeneity and resource mobility are complete.

Although these models offer general concepts of competitive market structures their assumptions reduce their usefulness. They say little about understanding competitor behaviour. More fundamental problems arise in the way such theory is predicated on rational, maximizing behaviour by all economic agents and the absence of chronic information problems. There is little space in the traditional economic theories for the real-world ignorance displayed by firms and consumers alike. Above all, these approaches to competition seem preoccupied with movement towards equilibrium states of rest (Hodgson 1988: 4–21).

Research on British business in the twentieth-century highlights the blind spots of traditional economic theory. It shows how the survival of firms has been secured by non-rational means and how inefficient management has not necessarily been ejected by optimizing market mechanisms. A well-documented example is provided by the original Rover company in the early twentieth century. In the 1920s there was a sharp transformation in the size and composition of the UK car market. Annual sales increased from under 100,000 to more than 400,000. A new market for cheap, lightweight vehicles, such as the Austin 7, emerged. Rover's specialist models and lack of innovation in production meant it was unable to match Morris' and Austin's exploitation of US technology and work organization. From 1925 Rover suffered substantial losses and by 1929 was technically bankrupt. Yet the company did not go out of business. Lucas, a major supplier, and Lloyds Bank, through family and personal connections, were persuaded to provide financial support. The help was sufficient to enable Rover to return to its speciality car production (Whipp and Clark 1986: ch. 3; Foreman-Peck 1981).

The development of different streams of microeconomics has proved to be of more direct relevance to strategy scholars. Three core conceptions of competition stand out in this respect: 'Chamberlinian' (Chamberlin 1933) views (Barney 1986b); the 'industrial organization' or IO approach (Bain 1956); and the Schumpeterian (Schumpeter 1950).

Chamberlinian economics has as its starting point the unique capabilities of the firm. Competition necessarily unfolds between firms with distinctive resources. Firms are said to differ in key ways, such as their technological know-how, product reputation and so on. The logical imperative for management is to create strategies which exploit a firm's uniqueness (Lenz 1980; Kotler 1984).

In the IO model of competition the relationship between the firm and the industry is central. Returns to the firm are determined by the structure of the industry of which it is a part. The key features of that structure include not only the number and relative size of firms but also the existence of barriers to entry. Firm conduct and performance are said to follow directly from these structural characteristics hence the 'structure, conduct, performance' paradigm which has been developed from this approach.

The implication for strategy at firm level is clear. Enterprises should seek to alter the structure of their industry so that it favours high returns. By this argument firms would create high barriers to entry, increase product differentiation, reduce demand elasticity and the number of firms in the industry. Some have combined the implications of the Chamberlin concern with uniqueness and the IO school's industry concern to produce the SWOT (strengths, weaknesses, opportunities and threats) analysis of strategy. IO writers have also suggested that firms can combine to alter industry structure to their joint benefit by acting in 'strategic groups' (Harrigan 1985).

The Schumpeterian model is altogether more esoteric and is not so easily applied to strategy. Schumpeter did not share the assumptions of other economists who presumed a degree of stability in the competitive forces confronting a firm, and that strategic planning models are therefore able to respond to those forces. On the contrary, for Schumpeter, instability and uncertainty are the keynotes of his view of competition. In truth Schumpeter's main concern was to understand the economic development of Western capitalist economies. The mainspring of this process was the revolutionary technological and product market upheavals of the past 200 years: for him the essential fact of capitalism was this process of 'creative destruction' (Schumpeter 1950: 82–3). The implication was that firms could only imperfectly anticipate such revolutionary innovations.

Schumpeter's insights have been developed by a number of authors seeking to describe the way firms react to competitive uncertainty derived from revolutionary technological and product market change (Nelson and Winter 1973). Few have tried to extend the implications to strategic management (Barney 1986a). Nelson and Winter (1982) point to the benefits and costs associated with product innovation policies and the way firms can attempt to initiate revolutionary changes to their advantage. The irreducible uncertainty which still remains in the firm's environment, however, introduces the notion of luck into competition. This is to the ultimate discomfort of both the IO or Chamberlinian specialists and of course strategic planners.

The IO approach to competition has been applied extensively to strategy issues by Porter. Both Porter and Caves (Caves 1980; Porter 1981) have created a more elaborate model of competition within the conceptual boundaries of the IO tradition. They give full recognition to the role of markets which make up a given industry and hence identify a fuller range of forces which may influence the intensity of competition. Central to these forces is the concept of rivalry among companies who contest the same area of business and are therefore incompatible. Porter extended this view of rivalry among competing firms in a critical way to include the role of potential competitors, suppliers of substitute products, suppliers of inputs, and buyers in the industry. Changes in any area can have dramatic results. The bargaining power of suppliers of raw materials or components to the industry can lead, for example, to higher input costs and final product prices.

Porter went on to classify the different types of strategies which firms might pursue within the competitive conditions of an industry. He argues that a firm's strategy will fall into three broad generic types based on cost leadership, differentiation or focus. Cost leadership seeks to achieve lower costs than competitors but without reducing product or service quality. Uniqueness is the goal of differentiation with the anticipated advantages of brand loyalty and insulation from rivals. A focus strategy seeks to concentrate on a specific market segment, product type or geographical area. Many others have extended the application of these generic strategies such as Gerstein's (1987) work on technology strategies .

An important strain of Porter's work following from his IO perspective is his attempt to order industries into types according to their competitive environment. The resulting classification includes fragmented, emerging, mature, declining and global industries (Porter 1980; see also Gilbert and Strebel 1988).

In fragmented industries the large number of firms means that no competitor has sufficient market share to influence the competitive conditions. The emerging industries appear to produce the conditions of Schumpeter's revolutionary competition. They come into existence as a result of new customer needs or innovations; knowledge of the shape and change in the market or the likely participants is difficult to establish. The mature and declining industry states have their own competitive demands. Maturity, with slow growth yet sustained demand, means that companies can achieve increased sales only through taking market share from competitors. These competitive features become even more pronounced in a declining industry where all participants experience a sustained fall in the total volume of sales they are able to achieve. Companies active in global industries operate in markets which are world-wide in nature with a correspondingly international set of national markets and competitors (see, for example, Doz 1986).

Traditional economics has therefore provided some of the essential ways in which competition is both conceived and operationalized in the area of strategy at firm level. Yet in spite of the strength of the contribution of IO to the understanding of competition it is by no means complete or without its limitations. There are three important deficiencies.

Above all, each of the IO schools confines itself to the firm/industry levels of analysis. The contribution of the national economy and its attendant social formations is never tackled directly. (For a move in this direction based on the clustering of successful firms in certain countries see Porter 1989.)

Second, even where the IO instruments are handled with great sensitivity the underlying rationale is still one of *homo economicus* with all the assumptions of rationality and the primacy of neo-classical economic relations which that implies. Competition is seldom conceived here to be the result of the collision of less rational motivations, unintended consequences and pure chance.

Third, although the various microeconomics schools recognize the relevance of transition states from one competitive condition to another, or the importance of revolutionary competition, the dynamics of the process of competition (especially within the firm) always remain richly implicit but never explored in their work (for the attempts of game theory to capture dynamic relationships see Leibenstein 1976; Schotter 1981). Consequently their appreciation of time and their concept of competition as a process has remained stunted (see Barney 1986b for an attempt to resolve some of the differences between the three main schools by the use of a developmental model).

The new competition

In the space of a year, two short but timely articles appeared in the *Harvard Business Review*. The first was by Robert Hayes and Bill Abernathy (Hayes and Abernathy 1980) entitled 'Managing our way to industrial decline'. The second was by Abernathy, Clark and Kantrow (1981) and dealt with the issue of 'The new industrial competition'. In those pages the Abernathy team set out a biting critique of the shortcomings of US industry and the orthodoxies which had resulted in its failure to match international standards of competition. The authors also argued that a qualitatively new type of competition now confronted the main industries of the United States.

The main blame for the deterioration in the competitive strength of US business was placed at the doors of the executive suite. The strict application of short-term returns, return on investment-based financial controls and portfolio management concepts by senior management meant that they had refused to bear the risks of long-run product and market innovation. The cult of quantification, allied to the primacy of financial and legal skills, left little space or influence for technological ideas. By contrast, the Harvard group saw overseas competitors' growing superiority arising directly from their strengths in technological innovation. In the Schumpeterian sense they saw a series of revolutionary changes emanating most especially from the ability of Asian companies to link high levels of innovation in not only product but production and management systems. The implications for US managers in the 1980s was clear. They predicted that 'the basis of competition will have changed to reflect the now crucial importance of technology-driven strategies' (Abernathy, Clark and Kantrow 1981: 79). In a later work (Abernathy, Clark and Kantrow 1983) the trio went on to challenge some of the accepted notions of industry life cycles and maturity, within the IO literature (Porter 1980). As the title of their book *Industrial Renaissance* implies, Abernathy, Clark and Kantrow did not accept that the room for strategic manoeuvre had to be so limited.

Instead they argued that maturity was not inevitable, that industry evolution is not fixed but can be altered and indeed reversed. Moreover, by combining technological and market changes the problems of rigid product designs and the dead weight of elaborate production processes could be overcome. In questioning basic design concepts and setting off searches for new technological solutions, such innovations could create revised options for consumers. Thereby fresh demand could result, triggering new cycles of industry development (Abernathy, Clark and Kantrow 1983: ch. 2). Perhaps the most vivid example of the possibilities of renewal in the 1980s was in the consumer electronics industry (Gerstein 1987).

The group and their disciples clearly directed their attention at management and the scope for action in tackling the immediate problem of competitive performance (as distinct from the government intervention stance of Lawrence 1987). In the words of Jones and Womack (1986) they saw the need for not only technological hardware but also managerial software. The appreciation of the long-term processes of technological change together with the relevance of radical short-term upheavals leads to a rare appreciation of the extent of managerial action needed to change competitive positions of the firm. Steven Wheelwright (1987) sees the problems this creates in manufacturing alone as it shifts from the 'static optimization' mode of the post-war years. He recognizes:

> It is not a matter of simply changing a few *decisions* or even making one major issue or event the focal point for change. Rather it requires a change in the process of management, encompassing a broad range of behaviours, practices, and decisions as well as philosophies and values. Fundamental changes such as this can be accomplished only over years of sustained effort. (Wheelwright 1987:99)

The new competition writers do provide a great service. They highlight the importance of specific technological bases of competition, the potential role of management and some of the key temporal frameworks for analysing competition in industry. The approach, however, has a number of gaps. In common with the IO specialists the important contribution of the political and social environment is not covered. Given their backgrounds the authors have concentrated on manufacturing and engineering industry at the expense of the service sector. There is also a danger in the way their work has given such prominence to technology. As the experience of General Motors and the Saturn project shows, an over-reliance on technology as the means to competitive salvation can be highly dangerous. It is noticeable, too, how in spite of identifying the key role of management in effecting technological and related changes, the new competition writers have not pursued the issue. Consequently they say little on how such processes of change are to be managed within the firm or what less tangible assets might be necessary.

Institutional economists

The 'institutionalists' have appeared from within the mainstream of traditional economics. Yet they differ from the neo-classical understanding of economic relations in a number of fundamental ways. The institutional approach has been greatly influenced by Schumpeter (1950), the Austrian school (Hayek 1967) and the transaction cost models of Williamson (1975). It has also produced an attractive conception of competition.

The prime objection of the institutionalists to the neo-classical tradition has been the over-rational qualities which it ascribes to economic agents and the static nature of its analysis. Institutionalists do not assume that such agents are rational in the sense of maximizing their resources within a framework of known alternatives. Instead, economic relations are in large measure the result of experience and learning over time. Economic explanation should therefore be a dynamic exercise. Economic activity is not co-ordinated simply through price-mediated transactions. It is informed by a range of social institutions which are themselves a worthy topic of inquiry (for a detailed account see Langlois 1986; Hodgson 1988).

Schotter (1981: 11) defines a social institution as 'a regularity in social behaviour that is agreed to by all members of society' and which specifies behaviour in specific recurrent situations. Examples taken from the work of institutional economists include property rights or other forms of contract.

One of the sharpest differences between the institutionalists and the neo-classicists arises over the issue of competition. The former sees competition as a process, the latter regard it as a state. In other words, the traditional view conceives of competition as a timeless, equilibrium state – a condition of logical consistency among a group of mathematical relations. By contrast, an institutionalist is concerned with explaining a sequence of events taking place in real time. The institutional orientation attempts to develop its model of competition from observation of real life. As a result the model places great emphasis on the way competition as a process moves forward through people's day-to-day learning. This learning consists of economic agents discovering the data (e.g. costs) that are assumed to be already in their possession by traditional IO writers.

The most realistic conclusion of the institutionalists, which is seldom acknowledged by others writing on competition, is its impermanence. As Hayek (1978: 181) argues, competition implies a method of discovering particular facts relevant to the achievement of temporary purposes, the benefits of which are in large measure transitory.

The institutional perspective on competition has been well demonstrated on a number of occasions and its explanatory power amply displayed. Two appropriate examples come from the work of Lewchuk (1987) and Nelson (1986).

Wayne Lewchuk explains the major differences between the technological base of competition in the US and British motor industries. He does so by reference to the social institutions related to the effort bargain. In other words, the ability of American employers to control effort norms allowed the greater control over the productivity of capital equipment. It also motivated them to develop capital intensive methods of production. In the UK, employers were less successful in reducing labour's control over effort norms. Instead they relied on the indirect control of incentive payment systems. In broad terms therefore British management's lack of control over effort levels made investing in capital intensive production methods a highly risky activity. Innovation was retarded. Moreover Lewchuk, by adopting a long-term view of the processes involved, is able to show how important are the states of crisis and disequilibrium.

In a similar way Richard Nelson has demonstrated the vital role of crisis or disequilibria in the institutional approach. In an essay (Nelson 1986) he examines productivity performance in the 1970s specifically so that he can show the relevance of social institutions and learning. He thereby reveals the complex influence of energy price shocks which knocked the economy out of equilibrium and forced firms to substitute energy intensive inputs and rendered obsolete their R&D experience.

Firms had to learn the extent of their inadequacies and how to adjust their efforts if, for example, R&D effort was to pay off in successful innovation. He goes on to build up a truly synthetic account by reference to institutional changes and their impact on firm performance. Thus he weaves in the intrusive role of government in the industrial economies which made the advance of productivity more costly and structural adjustments to shocks more difficult. Most importantly he draws the reader's attention to how the explanation 'is about process. Also, to come to grips with this story requires paying attention to institutional detail and changes in institutions' (Nelson 1986: 140). The institutionalists' concern with the dynamics of the competitive process and the contribution of learning (cf. Pucik 1988) and uncertainty is well received. Yet there is a noticeable gap in the way they have applied their analytical tools. The process of strategic management is hardly covered. Yet, as will become clear, the process of managing strategic change is particularly suited to such an inspection. A later section,'Competition and strategic change', will suggest how some of the concerns of the institutionalists can fruitfully be met in the study of strategic change.

The economic retardation debate

The arguments over the relative economic decline of the British economy have been some of the most long-running. Since the Royal Commissions and government inquiries occasioned by the 'Great Depression of the 1880s', successive generations have attempted to explain the way the UK has lagged behind other advanced industrial nations in productivity growth, competitiveness and relative level of per capita income.

Indications of the malady come from the reports of the National Economic Development Council (NEDC 1985). The report suggests the depth of the problem. It outlines the impact of poor rates of investment on cultural factors over the long term; in the medium term it highlights failings of demand. As regards the early 1980s the authors pointed to the impact of North Sea oil together with government financial and exchange policies.

The literature devoted to explaining the 'British disease' is voluminous. A wide range of contributory factors have been blamed. Among the most prominent have been cultural conservatism and the resulting entrepreneurial shortcomings (Weiner 1981). Also included is the relative inability of UK firms to convert product inventions into marketable innovations and appropriate manufacturing systems. In terms of cost reduction, British management performed acceptably given the constraints which they faced. Institutional analysts maintain, however, that it was the inability to change the social institutional limitations of UK business which was critical to its poor performance.

Elbaum and Lazonick (1986) group together some of the most recent work on such constraints. They argue that Britain failed to develop the mass production techniques and corporate forms of managerial co-ordination on which the successful economic development of the USA, Germany and Japan was based. These technological and organizational innovations were unable to flourish because of the deeply embedded restrictions associated with the UK's atomistic nineteenth-century economic organization.

The set of interlocking constraints were considerable. Britain failed to match the form of corporate capitalism epitomized by its competitors. In other words, UK industry remained in its fragmented nineteenth-century pattern. It therefore missed out on the advantages of oligopoly, hierarchical managerial control, vertical integration of production and distribution, the linkages of financial and industrial capital, or the benefits of systematic research and development. Vested interests in the old structures provided major obstacles to transformation.

Instead of developing corporate management skills British industrialists remained wedded to family control. Bankers lacked direct involvement in industry and did not use their positions to facilitate changes in industrial structures. Successive education systems were ill-placed to provide managers and applied scientists who might accomplish the task. Elbaum and Lazonick (1986:6) maintain that even middle-class businessmen sent their sons to elite public schools 'to partake in aristocratic culture rather than to challenge it' . Unable to create a corporate enterprise structure, UK management was unable to secure shop-floor control from trade unions. Innovations in costly mass production systems were therefore avoided. Market linkages were left unchanged. Manufacturers did not produce in anticipation of demand but to order and for sale to merchants for distribution.

One of the strengths of the retardation literature is its concerns with state intervention. As Feinstein (1983) shows, by the inter-war period the British state played a direct role in the industrial and social arenas even if it moved only slowly from its well-established nineteenth-century traditions of *laissez-faire*. The problems stemmed from the hesitancy and lack of coherence in government action in the mid-twentieth century. Government-sponsored research was unable to make up for the deficiencies in the in-house facilities of British companies. The protection of the pound, allied with weak domestic demand exacerbated the problems of excess capacity, declining profit margins and the scale of the debt burden. The opportunity to rationalize industries was missed. Instead trade associations were encouraged. The public funds devoted to rationalization schemes were small and the government failed to use regional policy as a systematic means of industrial restructuring.

The retardation debate is to be commended for the range of contributory influences on competition which it has uncovered. Its main drawback has been its overwhelming concentration on national competitive performance. Specialist studies within this debate have dwelt on the industry and the firm. The concept of industry used is also somewhat rigid (see the next section on competition and strategic change). Key features of management have also been scrutinized in order to discover the contribution of businessmen to the national competitive condition. What is missing are studies of the ability of British firms to comprehend their competitive environment and to explain how they managed the necessary processes of change. Most noticeable is the lack of intensive comparative studies which explore the role of strategic management across different industries (cf. Gospel's forthcoming study related to labour management).

The same point could be made of the growth of a similar retardation literature in the USA as its laggardly productivity performance and the failure of its hitherto successful staple industries became all too apparent in the 1980s. As in the UK, discrete aspects of US management and institutional structures have been inspected but seldom are the subjects of competition and the ability to accomplish strategic change combined (see Scott and Lodge 1985).

Excellence and turnaround

The shock which US industry experienced at the hands of overseas competitors in the early 1980s motivated a number of commentators to specify what the appropriate response of management should be. Following the lead of Peters and Waterman (1982) a multi-million dollar international industry has grown up as others attempt to prescribe the rules of excellence (see, for example, Clifford and Cavanagh 1985; Goldsmith and Clutterbuck 1984).

The approach of these writers is by now well known. The authors

specify generic recipes based on the experience of apparently successful companies. Peters and Waterman's (1982) eight rules of
excellence is perhaps the most famous example. The effect on the
academic world has been interesting, as some scholars have sought
to move from the descriptive to the prescriptive. A heavy reliance
has been placed by some on the methods of management which
apparently underlie the outstanding record of Japanese management
(Pascale and Athos 1981). The result has been a noticeable increase
in the claims made for the impact of specialist techniques on
competitive performance.

Marketing and technology are two obvious examples. A paper
(Wong, Saunders and Doyle 1989: 1) by a group of academic marketing specialists is able to claim therefore how 'poor marketing has been
the single most important constraint on British companies' domestic
and overseas market shares'. They go on to argue that British firms
need to pay more attention to the structural barriers to integrating
marketing with other key functions, the narrow financial focus of
management and the need to overcome functional compartmentaliz-
ation. A similar advisory style is used by those who place great faith
in the transforming power of technology. Quinn (1988) catches the
tone perfectly in the results of his study of highly innovative US,
Japanese and European companies. Thus the manager is told to: be
oriented to the market, develop flat organizations, structure for innovation, and allow chaos within guidelines.

A close relation of the excellence genre is the body of writing devoted
to the issue of company turnarounds. This subject has received increasing attention in the light of the severe dislocation to companies'
existence provided by the recession of the early 1980s. Some analysts
have generated very precise checklists to follow in helping a business
to recover. Taylor (1983), for example, contends that a firm should
shift to new areas of business by: mergers and co-operative supply
agreements; sales of assets and reduction of overheads; tight budgetary
control; and pruning the product line. Some MBA students now almost
consider turnaround techniques as straightforward as learning how to
calculate a discounted cash flow.

Others within the turnaround genre see the problem as more
complex and are more descriptive. The study of crises and the reasons
for company failure has produced a fruitful crop of insights. They have
also directed attention to the uncompetitive firm. Grinyer, Mayes and
McKiernan (1988) show how inadequate financial control and the
failure of giant projects appear as common features which have

undermined performance across industries. Recovery is said to rely on not only immediate actions to ensure the survival of the firm but also on linking the strategic and operational spheres (Hofer 1980; Melin 1985), using the crisis period 'space' to effect a re-orientation of the firm's strategy, and thoroughly exploiting the luck or windfall gains which appear (Grinyer, Mayes and McKiernan 1988).

The drawbacks of the excellence and turnaround school for the study of competition are readily apparent. The concern with managerial remedies necessarily has led to an over-emphasis on the firm at the expense of the competitive environment. The problem of competition is immanent within their accounts. Seldom are the firm's competitors dealt with directly or the concept of competition addressed. The urge to prescribe sometimes seems to have overcome the need to show how the data were collected. There is of course the danger of reductionism, since the impression is often left that successful management can be encapsulated in neat laundry lists.

If the preceding pages offer a rudimentary SWOT analysis on the main schools of thought on competition, then what sort of an analytical framework might utilize the identifiable strengths, make good the apparent weaknesses and exploit the many opportunities? A possible answer is provided in the next section.

Competition and strategic change: an integrated approach

The distinctive characteristics of this study of competition are manifold. The primary feature is that it sees competition and strategic change as intimately linked.

It regards strategic change and competition as joint and inseparable processes. In particular the research contends that these processes occur at multiple levels across time. In other words, these processes move forward within their firm, sector and national contexts. The study's framework is also unusual to the extent that it pays due regard to the way such processes are structured by a trinity of forces. These include not only the objective decisions of managers using information derived from their competitive environment, but they also embrace the subjective learning and political dimensions which operate both in and outside the firm.

These features can best be understood by first examining an outline of the framework and then considering its more unusual attributes in close-up.

The central aim of this book is to link the competitive performance of British firms to their ability to adapt to major changes in their environment. This motivation stems from the way the existing literatures appeared to have minimized the role of management in the debates over competition. Even allowing for the popular handbooks on business success little analytical weight in the prevailing accounts of competition has been attributed to the capacity of management to adjust to external change. In spite of the recent speculation on supply side improvements in the UK economy most policy discussion of competition has concentrated on policies at the expense of processes. Extensive coverage is given to what firm level policies should be adopted. Comparatively little is said of how such policies should be carried out or in what way the changes which they require might be managed. Too often these processes are assumed to follow. In practice the situation is far less straightforward.

The overriding intention of the framework used in this book is to capture strategic change and competition as holistically as possible. Figures 1.2 and 1.3 set out the main constituents of that framework. This implies major judgements about the nature of these twin processes. These have been described at length elsewhere (Pettigrew, Whipp and Rosenfeld 1989). Here it is important to explain the central features.

The purpose of figure 1.2 is to communicate the three essential dimensions necessary to an understanding of strategic change. In short, strategic change should be regarded as a continuous process which

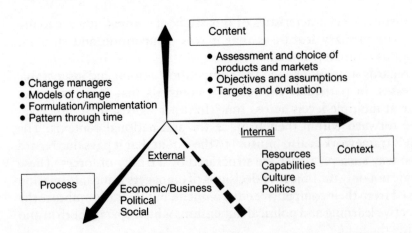

Figure 1.2 Understanding strategic change: three essential dimensions

occurs in given contexts (Pettigrew 1985b). We find it impossible to comprehend such changes as separate episodes divorced from their historical, organizational and economic circumstances from which they emerge (Pettigrew, Whipp and Rosenfeld 1989: 121–8). The point to appreciate is the richness of these contexts and their simultaneous shaping of strategic change. The hallmark of the processual dimension is that strategy does not move forward in a direct, linear way nor through easily identifiable sequential phases. Quite the reverse, the pattern is much more appropriately seen as continuous, iterative and uncertain.

Competition, similarly, is best appreciated in a multi-dimensional way (Whipp, Rosenfeld and Pettigrew 1989a). Two dimensions stand out: the levels at which competition operates and the element of time as indicated in figure 1.3. Along the vertical axis are the three major levels with their associated characteristics and measures. The competitive performance of a firm hinges therefore on the recognition that businesses compete not merely against one another but *at the same time* within the sectoral and national/international structures and relationships.

A number of differences will already be apparent between this framework and those presented earlier, including the composite dimensions of strategic change and competition. One of the most critical contrasts is with the way traditional economics concentrates

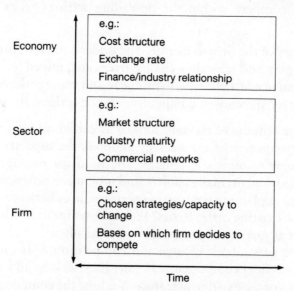

Figure 1.3   Competition: three levels across time

on the singular competitive traits of a firm. Even the new competition writers emphasize one key base of competition related to technology. We argue that the competitive performance of an enterprise is the result of a collection of abilities and modes of action. One must appreciate therefore the bases on which a firm competes and above all their process of creation. Rarely is there a single base. Most firms develop many layers of competences and advantages which explain their overall competitive strength. These may combine both price and non-price characteristics, with assumptions about quality, production efficiency and distribution networks. Every aspect of the value chain is implicated.

As the horizontal axis suggests, the sectoral and national conditions in which a firm operates and hence the bases on which it competes are quintessentially unstable. They are never static. It is to these changes that management has to respond continuously and which provides part of the major external impulsions for strategic change (see chapter 2). Yet there is a critical differential. The ability to perceive those changes and to take necessary action diverges considerably between and within firms. It is those divergences of choice and execution which interest us.

This multi-level and dynamic view of competition is greatly strengthened by uniting it with a contextually and processually sensitive understanding of strategic change. Put simply, the ability of an enterprise to compete within the prevailing settings relies on two qualities:

- the capacity of the firm to identify and understand the competitive forces in play and how they change over time, linked to
- the competence of a business to mobilize and manage the resources necessary for the chosen competitive response through time.

None of the schools of thought looked at earlier address this core point. Yet, irrespective of the strategy adopted, the capacity to carry out the changes it implies is critical. The need for management to assess the environment, make choices and mount the necessary alterations is vital to explaining contrasting performances between firms. In the light of the existing orthodoxies, such an attempt to combine these dimensions is as analytically unusual as it is timely.

This linking of strategic change and competition rests on a set of distinctive analytical components. In part they seek to address some of the concerns of the existing literature. Yet how the components have been conceived and assembled has resulted in something quite different from the prevailing schools of thought. A closer look at the analytical foundations of the research framework will make the point clear.

Three aspects of this analytical approach deserve highlighting:

- the distinctive view of strategy used
- the levels of analysis employed
- seeing the ability to manage the compound process of competition and strategic change as an asset in its own right.

Strategy

We have already outlined the powerful impact of microeconomics on competition and strategy. The influence of the IO specialists has been pervasive. Their classification of industries and generic strategies has proved of enormous value in mapping out the competitive environment of the firm and indicating the variety of strategic options. The problem is that this widely held view of strategy (see Greenley 1989: ch. 1) is unbalanced. As with others in the microeconomics tradition, it is the assumptions of rationality and abstract clarity which are most dangerous.

The IO tradition has given rise to battalions of strategy writers who wear the common badge of rationalism (see Chaffee 1985). Throughout the late 1960s and the 1970s an essentially linear orientation to strategy held sway (see Evered 1983 on the influence of the military origins of strategy). The essence of strategy was taken to be the direct, linear sequence of goal-setting and resource allocation set out by Chandler (1962: 13) in his classic formulation 'Strategy is the determination of the basic long-term goals of an enterprise, and the adoption of courses of action and the allocation of resources necessary for carrying out these goals.'

Senior managers are assumed to have wide discretion in changing the organization to match the strategy. Strategy is synonymous virtually with planning. Decisions taken 'on the 14th floor' are assumed to be implemented throughout the firm. Whether one takes the earlier version (Andrews 1971) or the later more sophisticated format (Porter 1980) the linkage between competition and strategy is regarded as self-evident. Clarity of vision concerning the competitive environment is vital. In Andrews' (1971) words, strategy is 'rivalry amongst peers, for prizes in a defined and shared game'.

As has already been noted, our framework departs from this linear model in a number of ways. It regards the linear, rational model of strategy as at best providing a single probe. Yet in reality managers do not have the privilege of the comprehensive information such models assume. Even if they did, the way they would understand and use it would vary markedly (see chapter 3). The competitive game, including the 'peers', is by no means clearly 'defined' nor 'shared'. On a broader front the rationalism of the IO and linear conception of strategy is compounded by its determinism. The problems of strategy and competition are over-simplified. In its extreme form it not only reduces the richness of the variables in play, it also ignores their reciprocal effect (cf. the criticisms by Bourgeois and Brodwin 1984). Managers tend to be allotted a passive role, acting only on the constraints of their environment.

The major problems of the IO and linear views of strategy is the way they (1) underestimate the importance of the internal operation of the firm, and (2) ignore the critical dimension of process. Our approach to strategy raises both of these aspects to the first order of importance.

Rather than equating strategic management with planning, the analytical framework adopted here sees it as a far more complex activity. The assumption is not made that strategic intentions are translated directly into action; quite the reverse. Our own research (Pettigrew 1985a, 1987a; Whipp, Rosenfeld and Pettigrew 1987, 1989a, 1989b) allied with the evidence of others (Ginter and White 1982; Lewis 1988) suggests a more adaptive and interpretative perspective is required.

How strategy arises, what conditions its formation and above all how it is carried out are non-trivial issues. Apparently objective technical decisions over markets, finance or products are deeply influenced by the social and political texture of the firm (Whipp 1988). Business strategy, far from being a straightforward rational phenomenon, is in fact interpreted by managers according to their own frames of reference, their particular motivations and information (Chaffee 1985; Johnson 1987; Whipp, Rosenfeld and Pettigrew 1989a). Strategy in practice is an organization-wide activity, it does not just concern senior management. Analyses of strategic management should be oriented accordingly. In our view it is the limits to managerial action which are as telling in understanding the outcome of strategic changes rather than the assumed width of their discretion. Many views of strategy and competition emphasize the complexity of the firm's environment. We give equal emphasis to the intricacy not only of the environment but also of the firm itself.

Figure 1.2 indicates the main constituents of that complexity within the firm. Hence one is concerned with both the intended content of a given strategy and the way it is shaped by the interior forces of the firm – the inner context. We see that content as made up of not only overt, immediate commercial and financial objectives but also the accumulated, less obvious knowledge and success formulae of the decision makers. These vital personal or group frames of reference are in part derived from the internal life of the firm, including the historical development of its structure, culture and politics. Such features do not only inform the actions of management. As the subsequent chapters will show, managers in turn can use them when attempting major strategic changes (Pettigrew 1985a; Whipp, Rosenfeld and Pettigrew 1989b).

The ability to see strategy in terms of a process cannot be emphasized too strongly. The major deficiency of the strategy theorists who come from the microeconomics background is their inability to study strategy in such a way. They analyse snapshots of the firm. An attempt is being made here to study motion pictures. The aim is to use the video recorder rather than the pocket camera.

Our own previous work (Pettigrew 1985a; Whipp 1986, 1987) had already suggested that the process of strategic change involved streams of activity across time. Even single strategic decisions over, say, a major project or product change, are not translated into action immediately. In practice that translation extends from the formulation of the strategy right through to its implementation. The research reported in the following chapters has uncovered a number of further key properties of this process.

The processes by which strategic changes are made seldom move directly through neat, successive stages of analysis, choice and implementation. Given the powerful internal characteristics of the firm it would be unusual if they did not affect the process: more often they transform it. Changes in the firm's environment persistently threaten the course and logic of strategic changes: dilemma abounds. Along with other researchers (Mintzberg 1978; Quinn 1988; Frederickson 1983; Hampden-Turner and Baden-Fuller 1989) we conclude that one of the defining features of the process, in so far as managerial action is concerned, is ambiguity. Seldom is there an easily isolated logic to strategic change. Instead, that process may derive its motive force from an amalgam of economic, personal and political imperatives. Their interaction through time requires that those responsible for managing that process make continual assessments, repeated choices and multiple adjustments.

Confronting strategic change adequately as a process implies a dialectical orientation. It is a live, difficult, creative process whose complexity cannot be avoided. As figure 1.2 tries to show it is the reciprocal effects between the key dimensions which make the process so demanding both to analyse and to conduct. It is the pattern of this interaction which will concern this book throughout. The institutional economists have drawn attention to the impermanence of competitive performance. It is this pervasive degree of difficulty and unpredictability which heightens the need for managing those interactions within the process of strategic change, as the successive chapters will show. Such skills are essential to understanding how competitive performance is not merely achieved in the immediate snap-shot sense but sustained and reinforced over time. Given these characteristics the process of strategic change cannot be likened to a linear, sequentially ordered industrial production line. A more faithful analogy would be the process of fermentation with all its connotations of volatility.

Levels of analysis

An essential part of our framework is its multi-level concept of competition encompassing the firm, sector and the national economy (see figure 1.3). Businesses compete within an overlapping set of relationships related to the sector and the economy. It is the appreciation of the combined relevance of these domains of action and how they are constituted which sets the framework apart from the main approaches to competition and strategic change.

The combined effect of these levels of activity is quickly demonstrated. Government intervention can have direct effects on industries through, for example, demand management, or indirect effects in the form of purchasing, licensing or standard-setting. Perhaps the most graphic instance of the impact of the national economy on firm performance has been the exchange rate. The effect on UK businesses in general has been clear. When the effective exchange rate was low during the mid–1970s Britain's competitiveness overall rose. When the exchange rate moved sharply upwards from 1978 to 1981, 'the effect on competitiveness was catastrophic' (Fay and Knightley 1986).

It is the sector level though where existing approaches to competition are found wanting. The work on identifying the participants in the competitive relations of an industry have been greatly advanced by both the IO tradition and those who espouse an adaptive orientation to strategy and environment (see Chaffee 1985). However, their common weakness is the restrictive notion of the relations in play. The key point to note is the existence of jointly economic and social relationships in a given sector. The term sector is used since it includes both the population of organizations providing similar goods and services *together* with the other organizations which regularly transact with them in a supplying, servicing or regulatory role (see Whipp and Clark 1986: ch. 1; Rasanen 1989).

The grid of relations between such organizations within a sector are under-researched. Apparently direct competitors within a sector still operate according to common cognitive fields (Huff 1982). Often it is the shared beliefs and assumptions within a sector which may explain the inability of their constituent members even to consider certain strategic paths (Whipp 1990b). Researchers at the University of Wisconsin show in their work on US industries how the market, hierarchical and associational mechanisms of industries differ widely in their operation. The reason lies precisely in the fact that 'each of these mechanisms . . . operates according to different logics' and 'shared norms' held by the actors (Hollingsworth and Lindberg 1985: 4–6).

It is also useful to bear in mind the way such features of sectors are influenced by national cultures (Lodge and Vogel 1987; Commission of the European Communities 1986). Yet the relationship here is two-way: enterprises both absorb and contribute to the generation of the wider culture. The result is that firms and industries display differing versions of national cultural traits.

The competitive and strategic behaviour of a firm cannot therefore be understood solely by reference to the industry structure model (Ballance and Sinclair 1983). The role of the national economy and a wider conception of the social and economic relations of the sector are vital. Such a perspective has two considerable benefits in the exploration of competition and strategic change.

First, attention to these economic and social relations can clarify the otherwise opaque behaviour of management. As will be shown in chapter 3, it is through these grids of relations that managers make sense of (in Weick's (1987) words 'enact') their environment. The modes of thought and language by which such relations exist also act as fine mesh filters of external signals.

Second, employing multiple levels of analysis has a further advantage. It would appear that the more successful companies are able to understand and manage both these economic and social relations and at each appropriate level of their operation. More than that, they then go on to develop the bases on which their firms compete accordingly. The result is the construction not of a single comparative advantage but the creation of 'layers of advantage' linked to each level (cf. Hamel and Prahalad 1989: 69).

Managing a compound process: an invisible strategic asset?

One implication of this framework is overwhelming. Competition and strategic change must be seen together as a compound process. Analysis of competitive forces and strategic management should not be presented as separate activities. The consistent picture which emerges from our research is that in practice management deals with both at the same time. Even when apparently implementing only part of a given strategy, management still has to assess and respond to the perpetual changes in the environment.

An apt example comes from Chrysler UK in 1970. Chrysler Corporation of the US acquired the UK-based Rootes Group in 1964. The new senior management brought in from Detroit to head what was renamed Chrysler UK in 1970, found itself faced by fundamental problems. The Linwood plant was operating at half capacity. The Imp and Hunter models had failed against the equivalent products of Ford, BMC and Vauxhall. In the words of one senior executive they had the task of mounting:

> two simultaneous programmes. On the one hand we are retrenching, making economies, cutting costs and reshaping our structure. On the other hand, we are re-equipping our plants to meet new programmes and to arrange our manufacturing capabilities to match the best techniques. (Interview)

Processes such as these require simultaneous and continuous action; analysis should attempt to match that fact of commercial life.

A helpful way of capturing this compound nature of strategic change and competition is to regard it as a hologram (cf. Van de Ven 1986: 599). The visual complexity of the hologram seems an apt representation of the way the key dimensions of strategic change and competition combine. The process of strategic change and competition is not to be likened to a linear, sequential assembly line of investigation, choice and implementation. In practice, knowledge, decisions and actions are simultaneously linked. Just as when looking at a hologram one can observe more than one dimension at any one moment, so with strategic change and competition. Thoughts, choices and outcomes co-exist and are observable at any given point in time.

Indeed, it is the capacity of a firm to accommodate and manage this compound process, to manipulate the hologram, which appears as *the* decisive strategic asset. Nor is this finding the figment of an over-heated academic imagination. The weight of evidence from this project can be added to the conclusions of a number of others. A consistent line runs through the work of: Gilbert and Strebel (1988) on the 'creative and innovative combination of several activities' which form the basis of successful strategies; Winter's (1987) view of the structures of managerial knowledge and competence underlying competitive advantage; Rumelt's (1988) highlighting of the need for firms to develop 'co-specialised assets'; and similarly Teece's (1987) discovery of the role of 'complementarity' between a plurality of such assets (for a full account see Whipp, Pettigrew and Sparrow 1989).

The management of this compound process of competition and strategic change is a vital asset in its own right. In practice this asset of handling the demands of simultaneity and continuity must be done in such a way that it cannot be copied or easily appropriated by competitors. This of course raises problems for those trying to study such processes. To the outsider these assets may be 'invisible' (Pucik 1988). The hologram may be out of focus to the untutored eye.

The next section outlines a research design which was developed with two ends in mind: (1) to maximize the analytical power of the framework described in this section, and (2) to help uncover the intangible assets on which the process of managing competition and strategic change relies.

Study goals and research sites

The project has centred on the transformation processes of firms as they were faced with the twin dilemma of survival and regeneration in the 1980s.

The study has examined the process of managing strategic and operational change in four mature industry and service sectors of the UK economy: automobile manufacture, book publishing, merchant banking and life assurance. All the sectors had reached stages in their life cycles where established products, markets and relationships were undergoing marked alterations. A major benefit of the chosen industries is their range and most especially the way they extend from manufacturing to service. (For a more detailed account see Pettigrew, Whipp and Rosenfeld 1989.)

A pair of firms was chosen for study in the automobile manufacture, book publishing and merchant banking sectors, with an extra financial services example drawn from life assurance. All the firms have exhibited varying and contrasting performances over time. The list of firms involved is as follows:

- Automobiles: Jaguar, Peugeot Talbot
- Merchant Banking: Kleinwort Benson, Hill Samuel
- Book Publishing: Longman, ABP
- Life Assurance: Prudential.

The objective has been to discover:

- why firms operating in the same industry, country and product markets should record such varying performances, and
- what has been the contribution of the way they manage strategic change?

An important advantage of examining contrasting performances is the avoidance of the general bias in the business literature towards successful organizations.

Longitudinal data have been collected covering the firms' activities in detail over the 1970s and 1980s guided by a detailed question *pro forma* (see Pettigrew, Whipp and Rosenfeld, 1989: Appendix). The sources of data were threefold:

- semi-structured tape-recorded interviews conducted extensively in each firm and related organizations (e.g. government and industry bodies, competitors)
- primary documentary evidence from within the firm, such as board and departmental records and internal reports
- secondary published material ranging from official HMSO documents to standard book publications.

In excess of 350 recorded interviews, conducted at all levels of the firms and sectors involved over a three-year period, is an indication of the scale and intensity of the research.

Above all, the standard of the data collection has rested on the uniformly high quality of access which has been negotiated with the firms under study. Close working relationships for three years with major organizations undergoing marked changes cannot be taken for granted. Such access was secured in part by the relevance of our central study questions.

Deciding on the comparative companies to be studied rested on a combined approach to performance. In other words, reliance on a single indicator, such as profitability or market share, was rejected. Such single indicators can be misleading. Market share can be bought by price cutting in the short term, while profitability in one year can be inflated by the use of exceptional balance sheet items. Problems over the confused state of balance sheet conventions (Waters 1989) make the use of a broader approach vital. The same is also true of the flawed condition of many sets of aggregate statistics in the UK (Yamazaki 1989: 18). In this study, therefore, a group of appropriate general and specific measures have been employed in each sector. Equal emphasis is given to the performance of companies in the sense of creating the relevant bases, which will enable them to compete in their sector (see chapter 2).

Great emphasis therefore has been placed on indicators which relate to the sectors concerned. Turnover is included in book publishing, since it discriminates immediately between the top six large, international houses, the medium sized independents and the other 20,000 registered yet often inactive publishers in the UK. Longman and ABP were chosen for study on the basis of their performance within the top six who account for 70 per cent of sales. Equally, the comparisons have been spread over time in order that eccentric one or two year windfalls do not mislead the identification of performance.

Similarly, careful attention was paid to the perceived performance of firms by others in each industry. In the book publishing example, therefore, those who work in the industry were able to qualify or underwrite the objective measures of performance. In ABP's case, in spite of its position within the top six, it soon became clear that ABP's ranking was heavily reliant on its dominance with Butterworth in the area of legal publishing. Building up such a composite picture of performance is the first step in uncovering the critical bases on which individual firms compete.

The result has been a set of firms which do not represent extreme 'outliers' of performance but which instead display relative differences over time. As a result, the match within the three pairs is not perfect in all cases across time. In this sense the research has the virtue of reflecting commercial reality. More importantly such historical profiles and variations in performance enable the study to capture the way losses (Ouchi 1980) and gains in competitive performance occur and how they relate to managerial action (see, for example, Peugeot Talbot). As will become clear in the following chapters, this provides the opportunity to validate our broad framework of how competitive performance is linked to the management of strategic and operational change over time.

All the organizations studied here have been at the heart of the upheavals in their respective sectors. Chapter 2 examines the character of those sectors. The subsequent chapters explore, in detail, the comparative ability of the companies to handle those upheavals. First though, it is necessary to establish an outline of the firms studied and their overall records.

The profile presented by the two auto industry examples has, to say the least, been volatile. Peugeot Talbot, and its forerunners, make the point well. The differences between the Rootes, Chrysler and Peugeot Talbot operations are immediately apparent.

The origins of the Rootes group can be traced to the establishment of William Rootes' car sales business in Hawkhurst, Kent, in 1898. In 1926 his company began a series of acquisitions as it moved from servicing the industry to manufacturing cars and commercial vehicles. Up to 1939, Rootes was able to buy into manufacturing relatively cheaply through the purchase of the virtually bankrupt Humber-Hillman, Karrier Motors and Sunbeam-Talbot. By the Second World War, the Rootes Group accounted for 10 per cent of the UK car market.

During the post-war replacement demand, Rootes embarked on a second phase of acquisition in the 1950s. Uneven cyclical demand and increased competition led to problems. The company had to rationalize a diverse mixture of plants and sales networks. Yet Rootes could not achieve the sales levels that would allow it to benefit from such a re-organization (see chapter 2, figure 2.4). The difficulties faced by the Linwood plant in Scotland in 1963 were a graphic example of Rootes' inability to move from being a producer of medium size/speciality cars to a volume manufacturer.

Between 1964 and 1967, Chrysler Corporation bought control of Rootes. While tackling the problems inherited from Rootes, Chrysler UK (CUK) was overwhelmed by the worsening position of the British motor industry and economy and a sharp decline in the fortunes of Chrysler Corporation in the USA. Losses mounted (see figure 1.4a). After a threat by Chrysler Corporation to shut down the UK operation, an agreement was signed at the end of 1975 with the UK government. Both underwrote Chrysler UK's losses for four years and provided loans of the order of £121 million. Against continuing losses, Chrysler Corporation sold its European operations in France, Britain and Spain to Peugeot SA in August 1978.

The character of Peugeot Talbot UK has to be understood through three phases. Between 1978 and 1980, a new managing director and his colleagues were allowed to mount their own attempt at solving the problems of CUK, in particular low productivity, weak products and poor industrial relations. Less than two years into tackling these issues the company was engulfed by the second oil crisis and the effects of world recession (see figure 1.4b). Drastic action was taken, including the closure of the Linwood plant and the sale of the commercial vehicle operation to Renault. The result was a reduction in size commensurate with the production of three French-developed cars. A work-force which had been 31,000 in 1974, stood at a fifth of that number by 1983.

The 1983–9 period witnessed the return to profit of Peugeot Talbot UK and its establishment as one of the strongest parts of the Peugeot SA group (see figure 1.4b). The financial performance would have been even stronger had it not been for the effects of an uncertain Iranian contract. After 1989 the bases on which Peugeot Talbot UK competed in the UK and European market were transformed. Product quality and productivity (see chapter 6, figure 6.1) were raised to the highest in Peugeot SA. This action was supported by major changes in industrial relations, supplier links and management approach. The following chapters will seek to explain therefore why it was that Rootes and Chrysler UK failed to develop the capacities to match the competitive demands of the 1960s and 1970s. Those chapters will also have the interesting task of demonstrating how Peugeot Talbot was able to meet the equally formidable challenges of the 1980s.

As the Introduction showed, the experience of Jaguar Cars has been

Figure 1.4   Profitability of Chrysler UK and Peugeot Talbot 1965–1989
Source: Peugeot Talbot

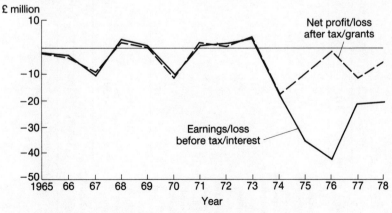

(a) Chrysler UK profitability 1965–1978 (unadjusted)

(b) Peugeot Talbot Motor Company Limited: turnover & profit/(loss) performance (£000s)

	1975	1976	1977	1978	1979	1980	1981	1982	1983	1984	1985	1986	1987	1988	1989
Sales	351,105	331,575	457,983	610,176	575,210	487,883	496,095	417,574	558,744	502,414	516,456	639,767	749,152	1,153,747	1,481,925
Operating profit/(loss)	(25,147)	(32,714)	(8,340)	(6,103)	(22,107)	(41,380)	(63,963)	(25,654)	17,987	12,378	2,633	(4,846)	24,310	93,462	108,055
Interest	(7,817)	(10,029)	(13,418)	(14,720)	(19,142)	(26,150)	(24,151)	(20,921)	(10,566)	(11,651)	(15,470)	(10,086)	(6,072)	1,174	15,019
Exceptional/ non-operating items	(2,489)	144	286	619	107	(7,541)	(2,934)	(8,340)	(4,360)	–	–	–	–	–	–
Taxation	(3)	(264)	(65)	40	13	11,922	–	105	18	–	–	–	–	–	–
Minority interest in subsidiaries	(63)	(28)	–	–	–	–	–	–	–	–	–	–	137	53	(127)
Dividend received	–	–	–	–	–	–	44	62	63	–	–	–	–	–	–
Extraordinary item*	–	–	–	–	–	(39,200)	–	–	–	–	–	–	(5,228)	12,013	12,319
Profit/(Loss) before grants	(35,519)	(42,891)	(21,537)	(20,164)	(41,129)	(102,349)	(91,004)	(54,748)	3,142	727	(12,837)	(14,932)	13,147	106,702	135,266
Tax	–	–	–	–	–	–	–	–	–	–	–	–	–	(450)	(30,469)
Grants	–	41,501	10,000	15,000	10,000	35,000	89,189	55,000	–	–	16,502	15,000	–	(60,000)	(30,000)
Net Profit/ (Loss)	(35,519)	(1,390)	(11,537)	(5,164)	(31,129)	(67,349)	(1,815)	252	3,142	727	3,665	68	13,147	46,252	74,797

* Provision for Linwood closure

no less volatile. That experience falls into three main periods. From 1945 to 1968, domestic market dominance in luxury saloon and sports class cars was matched by a consistent record of 50 per cent of output being exported (see figure 1.5a). In spite of suspect product reliability, Jaguar's performance was underlain by incremental engineering innovation linked to an obsessive concern for costs and fiercely competitive pricing by the founder and chief executive William Lyons. The height of this achievement came in the E-Type model of 1964 and the award-winning XJ6 of 1968.

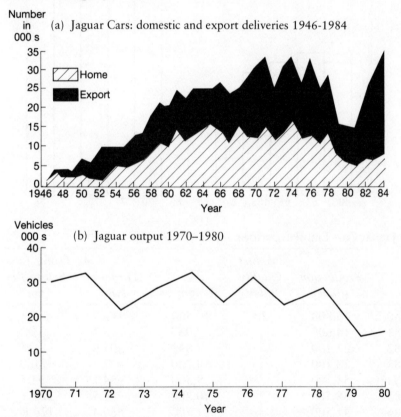

Figure 1.5 Jaguar Cars: domestic and export deliveries 1946–1984 and output 1970–1980
Source: Jaguar Cars

The reversal of this record between 1972 and 1980, when Jaguar was owned by British Leyland (BL), was severe. The 1979 Series III XJ6 was riddled with quality and reliability defects. Production plummeted from 32,000 to 14,000 between 1974 and 1979 (see figure 1.5b). Although Jaguar was still profitable in 1974 (the last year

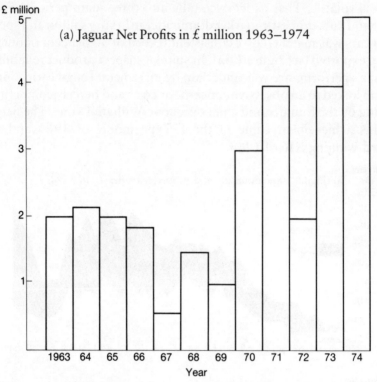

(a) Jaguar Net Profits in £ million 1963–1974

(b) Jaguar Cars Limited: performance indicators 1980–1988

	Production (units)	Product Quality Index[a]	Manpower	Turnover (£m)	Profit/(Loss) Before Tax (£m)
1980	13,800	20	10,500	166.4	(47.3)
1981	14,600		7,067	195.2	(31.7)
1982	22,100		7,849	305.6	9.6
1983	28,100		8,700	472.6	50.0
1984	33,500		9,500	634.1	91.5
1985	38,500		10,200	746.5	121.3
1986	41,500		11,500	830.4	120.8
1987	48,000	70	12,500	1,002.0	97.0
1988	51,939	▼	12,611	1,075.5	47.5

[a]The Quality Index is based on a demerit system, i.e. 100 QI is a perfect car and a 0 QI is a very poor car. Demerits are taken off for faults found during sample audits of cars as they come off the tracks. Value of demerit points are based on customer perceived quality faults not our own.

Figure 1.6 Jaguar Cars: net profits 1963–1974 and performance indicators 1980–1987 *Source:* Jaguar Cars

separate accounts were published – see figure 1.6a) by the end of 1979 losses were calculated internally to be running at £4 million per month. In 1980 Jaguar was given a year's notice of closure by BL unless the unit broke even. A new managing director, John Egan, was appointed in the same year. The turnaround in Jaguar's performance was exceptional (see figure 1.6b). What stands out is the extent of the transformation across virtually every aspect of the company's operation. Jaguar was successfully floated on the Stock Exchange in 1984.

Survival and regeneration were secured. Problems for the company occurred during the attempt to grow and remain independent. Turnover continued to rise but profits fell from £97 million in 1987 to £47.5 million in 1988. Having only just rebuilt the company after a decade of neglect to meet the competitive bases of the 1980s, Jaguar simply did not have the resources necessary for the 1990s. The management's attempt to find a 'protective' buyer of their choice, in late 1989, before the government's 'Golden Share' expired, was pre-empted by the Department of Trade and Industry. The DTI waived its Golden Share which allowed Ford to mount a successful, hostile £1.6 billion bid in November 1989. The challenge which Jaguar sets us is a clear one. Why was it that an apparently exceptional post-war company lost its ability to innovate and adapt in the 1970s? Equally, how was it that this ability could be rebuilt to produce such a marked recovery in the exceptionally difficult period of the early 1980s? The answers to these questions may suggest why the growth and independence ambitions of the late 1980s could be thwarted so swiftly.

The experience of the two book publishers, Associated Book Publishers (ABP) and Longman presents an intriguing comparison. Although both have been well known as leading UK publishing houses, closer inspection reveals differing competitive strengths.

The book market has rightly been likened to a honeycomb. It is remarkably difficult to compare the activities of book publishers. Each publisher categorizes their products differently. Meaningful statistics covering book publishing have been slow to emerge. Even those that exist at an industry level are challenged by individual publishers. Reliance on reporting schemes in such a diffuse industry, with so many small houses and non-members of the Publishers Association (PA), makes the compilation of national figures a problem. The number of unquoted companies and those which are part of larger groups (and therefore do not disclose the results of their book publishing activities) make it difficult to compare company results. On trying to survey business activity in the industry in 1986 one of stockbroker Capel's analysts concluded that 'the industry is not well served by up-to-date quantitative information' (interview).

With these caveats in mind one can begin to create a competitive profile for ABP and Longman which combines a range of measures.

In terms of market share ABP has occupied a middle place in the top ten publishers with around 5 per cent (see chapter 2, table 2.3b). Longman has around double that figure. If one then breaks that figure down into specialist market share positions then ABP's base is revealed to be somewhat narrower. Longman can rightly claim to be among the leaders in each of the specialist product areas in which it competes and in fact the dominant force in almost all (see figure 1.7).

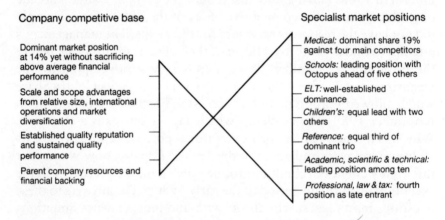

Company competitive base

Dominant market position at 14% yet without sacrificing above average financial performance

Scale and scope advantages from relative size, international operations and market diversification

Established quality reputation and sustained quality performance

Parent company resources and financial backing

Specialist market positions

Medical: dominant share 19% against four main competitors

Schools: leading position with Octopus ahead of five others

ELT: well-established dominance

Children's: equal lead with two others

Reference: equal third of dominant trio

Academic, scientific & technical: leading position among ten

Professional, law & tax: fourth position as late entrant

Figure 1.7 Longman Group UK: composite competitive position

ABP comes second to Butterworth in the law and professional market at 25 per cent and 30 per cent respectively. ABP's academic and scientific divisions combined (and after the acquisition of Routledge & Kegan Paul PLC (RKP) and Croom Helm) is one of ten main publishers in the area. ABP is one of the main publishers in the specialist children and medical areas.

While market share is a good indicator of competitive strength it is not conclusive and must be combined with other indicators. The turnover figures for the main UK publishers confirm ABP as one of the largest, but by the early 1980s a little behind outright leaders. In 1985, before acquisitions totally distort the picture (see chapter 2, table 2.4) Longman recorded a turnover of £122 million, Collins £120 million and ABP £76 million (see figure 1.8a). In other words, the figures reflect the expansion of Longman in the 1970s and 1980s, and ABP's more modest growth of the 1980s.

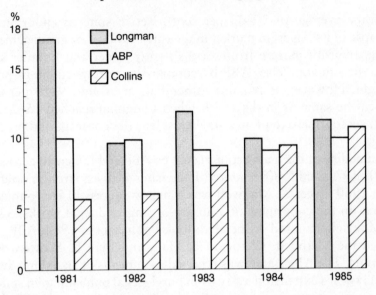

(a) Profit margin: trading profit as a % of turnover

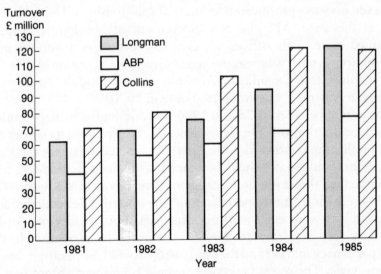

(b) Turnover

Figure 1.8 Turnover and profit margin of Longman, ABP and Collins 1981–1985
Source: Annual Reports

However, if profitability is then assessed together with market share and turnover the general picture is confirmed. As figure 1.8b shows, Longman's profitability is hit by its international exposure from 1982 (Longman exported 60 per cent of its production compared to an industry average of 20–43 per cent). Yet in spite of enduring the collapse of its Nigerian market in the early 1980s, Longman achieved a higher profit margin from a consistently larger and broader sales base than anyone else. ABP by comparison is respectable in profit margin. However, it remains rather flat, at around 9–10 per cent (much the same as in the 1970s when Longman reached 15–25 per cent) yet to some extent on a smaller, safer sales coverage and product range.

An outline of the main actions taken by ABP and Longman across the 1960s, 1970s and 1980s reinforces Longman's relatively stronger position.

In 1960 Sweet & Maxwell was a highly successful law publisher reliant on the copyrights of a library of standard legal works. Sweet & Maxwell acquired Associated Book Publishers in 1964. ABP contained the Methuen, Chapman & Hall, and Eyre & Spottiswoode imprints. The ABP name was retained as a means of signalling Sweet & Maxwell's expansion away from purely legal publishing. In spite of an attempt to create three publishing divisions down to 1973 (law, trade and academic) specialisms remained in place. By the early 1970s the trade division produced five internal sub-divisions. Unlike Longman at this time, ABP did not relocate out of London. Instead, it remained close to its offices adjacent to the Inns of Court. A new distribution centre was established in Andover. Linking ABP's inherited interests in Canada and Australia proved difficult. The merger process in Australia was completed only in 1970.

The period between 1973 and 1980 was dominated by fire-fighting in the face of inflation. The dependence of the group on its successful legal publishing continued. Other parts of ABP came to see the legal imprint as a 'lifeboat' when they faced difficulties. Expanding and strengthening the trade and academic divisions was not easy. The 1973–4 recession hit the specialist publishing hard. The academic and scientific lists were cut by 40 per cent. Attempts to respond to the economic recovery from 1976 were seen in the form of entry to the mass paperback market and the establishment of a US operation, based in New York. The second oil crisis brought both to an abrupt halt.

The 1980s for ABP were dominated by three main episodes. First was the appointment of an outsider to head the UK operations. Alan Miles, from Weidenfeld & Nicolson, was able to supply a vital internal restructuring and much-needed financial controls. Together with the up-turn in demand for consumer goods in the mid–1980s, these actions led to a clear improvement in short-term performance (see chapter 4, figure 4.1). The second episode of the 1980s began in 1985 when ABP acquired RKP, Croom Helm Ltd and Pitkin Pictorial. ABP's long-term problem of developing wider successful publishing to match its legal division's strength remained. RKP and Croom Helm were both within established areas of ABP's publishing.

As the search for increased international market domination by an emerging group of major world publishers became intense during 1985–7, interest in ABP grew. The Bahamas-based trust set up to benefit the seven grandchildren of Sir Oliver Crosthwaite-Eyre held 36.65 per cent of ABP's shares. Not only did this provide an effective block to takeover, it also meant that the shares were therefore a very inactive stock. Yet while the trust secured the independence of ABP it could not play the same funding role of Pearson at Longman or Penguin, or Murdoch at Collins.

It was the historically high premium prices which bidding companies were paying for publishers in 1986–7 which proved decisive. The readiness of international publishers to pay such prices was confirmed in the competitive bidding for ABP. By 17 June, International Thomson's bid had been accepted. The 730p a share cash offer represented a total cash price of £210 million. The grim irony for ABP was that International Thomson's motivation in bidding so high was for ABP's core non-renewable assets of its legal publishing. The acquisition made Thomson one of the world's leading law book publishers and improved the geographical spread of its markets. Like other world publishers International Thomson had been trying for ten years to expand its publishing in North America, Britain and Europe.

The house of Longman had developed a strong reputation in commercial publishing across two centuries. A library of publishing classics appeared in print at the 'sign of the ship' – Longman's colophon. These included: *Gray's Anatomy* (1863), Disraeli's *Lothair* (1870), Trevelyan's *English Social History* (1942) through to *Longman's Dictionary of Contemporary English* (1978) and *Dictionary of the English Language* (1984). Charles Longman was the first president of the Publishers Association in 1896 and in conjunction with other major publishers pioneered the UK Net Book Agreement in 1901.

The series of Education and Public Libraries Acts from 1870 brought a new public demand for mass-produced books. The average price of a book fell by half. Longman developed a leading profile in not only the trade and general areas but also in education, reference and journal publishing. The company's recovery after the Second World War was based largely on the exploitation of the rapid growth in state educational provision shaped by the major reports of Crowther, Newsom, Robbins and Plowden.

More generally the international position of the business, even if it was heavily linked to the colonial/Commonwealth trade, laid the foundations for future market growth. The major change came in the 1960s. Longman therefore was a truly international company of long-standing by the 1970s and 1980s. There were companies from Hong Kong to the Caribbean and Latin America, from west, east and southern Africa and across the Arab world to Malaysia, Singapore, Australia and New Zealand. Joint publishing companies were also established in a number of European countries. It was much easier for Longman to adapt to the marked changes in world markets in the 1980s than some of those houses, such as ABP, who had only limited previous exposure to international publishing.

In 1966 Longman had changed its name to the Longman Group of Publishing Companies to reflect the outcome of the process of internationalization. Unlike ABP, Longman did not choose to rely on its family shareholding. Two years later Longman became part of S. Pearson & Son Ltd, the engineering, publishing and energy group. Pearson already owned the well-known medical publishers J. & A. Churchill, E. & S. Livingstone, and Oliver & Boyd the Scottish educational publishing house. These were now incorporated into Longman. Also in 1968, Longman moved from Grosvenor Street to a new building at Burnt Mill, Harlow.

Mark Longman explained his decision to join Pearson in terms of finding an acceptable home for Longman rather than be swallowed by a hostile publishing house. Penguin's union with Pearson shortly after was also motivated by the desire to elude McGraw Hill. Specific assurances were given, and subsequently honoured, that Longman's publishing activities would continue without undue interference.

The move into the US market gathered pace in the 1970s as Longman went from being just an import operation to publishing first British and then American authors in the United States. Entry to the US market was on three fronts: medical, university and higher education ('college' in the USA), and English language teaching. In spite of the difficulties encountered in the US market Longman was able to sustain its efforts more consistently than many other UK publishers. The reasons for Longman's persistence were twofold: the need to find substitutes for threatened Third World markets, and the backing of Pearson. The long-term benefits of remaining in the USA were to be fully realized in the 1980s.

As at ABP, the problem of inflation uniquely combined with two major recessions wrought havoc with publishers' costs. Print material costs rose 29 per cent from 1970 to 1974. Longman had to centralize its rather fragmented print buying operations and establish competitive tender arrangements for supply. From 1975 to 1978 40 per cent of Longman's UK printing and binding needs were transferred to the Far East.

The world recession of 1979–81, triggered by the rise in oil prices following the outbreak of the Gulf War and deepened by the tightening of monetary controls in the Western economies, formed a painful break-point for most publishers. Longman's discomfort was increased by the collapse of the Nigerian market in 1982. It lost $7 million worth of sales per annum as the fall in the price of Nigerian oil precipitated an economic crisis and the abrupt termination of import purchases. Yet as figure 1.7 shows, the breadth of Longman's strength has meant that it has been able to combine growth (a doubling of its business) and internationalism (expanding into Europe and the Far East) across the 1980s. Longman has gone on to deepen its competitive base (compare figure 1.7 with table 2.10). Between 1982 and 1988 Longman made 19 US and UK acquisitions.

Both Longman and ABP have been in the leading group of UK-based book publishers and set many of the standards which others have followed. Both generated international reputations for their editorial strength and integrity of their staff. The essential aim of chapters 3 to 7 is therefore to uncover why, given their leading positions, Longman was able to develop further in the 1980s; in other words, through new publishing areas, deepen its international spread of operations and re-create itself over the long term.

Among the merchant banks, Hill Samuel and Kleinwort Benson have been leading houses in much the same way as have Longman and ABP in book publishing. The main activities of the two banks have provided some of the key events for the whole merchant banking sector.

The Hill Samuel Group was created in 1965 by the merger of a traditional family-owned banking firm, M. Samuel, with one of the more aggressive issuing houses, specializing in corporate finance work, Philip Hill, Higginson, Erlangers (see chapter 4, table 4.1). The latter saw the merger as an expansion and a means of entry into the established league of merchant banks. Further expansion followed. In 1968, Hill Samuel purchased Lambert Brothers Limited, a specialist insurance broking company and von Ernst & Cie, a small Swiss bank.

In 1969, Noble Lowndes, an employee benefits consultancy, was acquired. In 1971, Hamilton Smith, a firm of Lloyds brokers, was purchased along with L. Hammond & Co., a ship broking firm. As the markets for financial services remained good, assets and earnings were maintained.

However, as the economic climate changed in the mid–1970s, Hill Samuel was forced on to a more defensive footing. Profits were flat. The failure of the Herstatt Bank in West Germany in 1976 resulted in a large foreign exchange loss of £9 million (ultimately reduced to a net £1 million). From being one of the front-rank merchant banks in the 1960s, Hill Samuel fell behind Kleinwort Benson, Warburg and Morgan Grenfell.

In 1980, a new chief executive, Christopher Castleman, was appointed with a view to revitalizing the organization. He attacked the problems of a weakened financial position and loss of managerial self-confidence, for example, through tough budgetary controls yet combined with innovations in reward systems. The Hill Samuel group was no longer felt to be the banking operation surrounded by diverse subsidiaries. None the less, these changes could not prevent the resignation of Castleman in August 1987 over his disagreement with his board colleagues' acceptance of the bid for Hill Samuel by the Union Bank of Switzerland. The bid fell through and TSB made a successful offer to acquire the group in October 1987.

Kleinwort Benson, like Hill Samuel, was one of the select group of institutions who was a member of the Accepting House Committee of the Bank of England. Kleinwort Benson was formed in 1961 following the merger of the premier accepting house, Kleinwort & Sons, with one of the leading issuing houses, Robert Benson Lonsdale. Kleinwort & Sons' traditional strength lay in the provision of acceptance credits (commercial loans) to foreign clients and UK exporters. The 1960s saw the relaxation of foreign exchange regulations by the British government. Kleinwort moved to exploit the benefits of the Common Market and established offices in Jersey (1962), Brussels (1964) and Geneva (1964). The bank's corporate finance division also entered the new Eurobond market. In spite of the difficulties of the 1970s, Kleinwort Benson expanded their international commercial business incrementally. Joint ventures were created with the Bank of America in 1971 and Fuji Bank of Japan in 1974, in order to exploit the demand from those countries' multinationals.

At the start of the 1980s Kleinwort Benson was well placed to respond to the heightened importance of international markets in the wake of deregulation. Management sought to re-position the bank as a 'global investment bank'. This involved a switch of emphasis from commercial lending to cover the markets for international as well as domestic borrowers and investors. The bank placed emphasis on the interest rate swap markets (already a speciality of Hill Samuel), international government securities and the domestic equity and gilt trading markets. Kleinwort purchased Grieveson Grant, the UK stockbroker which accounted for 10 per cent of the UK gilt market.

As in the case of book publishing, one has to be careful with any figures used as a basis for judging performance in this sector. Many of the merchant banks have been reluctant to provide accurate public breakdowns of results. Until recently, most merchant banks provided only overall profit figures without information on how they were generated. Hill Samuel and Kleinwort Benson adopted full disclosure in the mid–1980s. In the case of Hill Samuel and Kleinwort Benson, a portrait of their performance can be constructed over the long term. In the 1960s, both did tolerably well in the circumstances of expansion. The creation of both groups (see chapter 4, table 4.1) was an indication of the two merchant banks' ability to acquire and integrate an issuing house within their activities. As table 2.6 shows, the traditional indicators of the time for Accepting House Committee members (deposits and after-tax profits) put both banks in healthy positions.

The 1970s present a different picture. As we have seen, both Hill Samuel and Kleinwort Benson sought to expand early on. Both had to be more cautious after the dislocations of 1973–5. Yet as table 1.1 and figure 1.9 indicate, Hill Samuel lost out in the 1970s, relative to Kleinwort Benson, in the sense that it lost clients for merger and acquisition activity (see table 1.1 and chapter 2, table 2.7) as its corporate finance strength was reduced. Hill Samuel's equity base growth did not keep pace with Kleinwort Benson's; its return on equity (ROE) and management profit fell in the second half of the 1970s, while Kleinwort's grew markedly (see figure 1.9a).

The relative positions of the two banks in the 1980s are more difficult to summarize. In terms of size and independence, at first sight Kleinwort Benson appears more successful. Kleinwort Benson emerges not only as one of the largest UK merchant bank groups in respect of asset size (see table 1.1), it also increases its equity to a much higher level (see figure 1.9b). Hill Samuel became part of the TSB group in 1987 while Kleinwort remained a separate entity. In 1988, some regarded Hill Samuel as one of the 'losers' from the era of deregulation. Hill Samuel was said to have found the post–1986 securities market

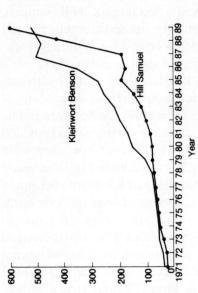

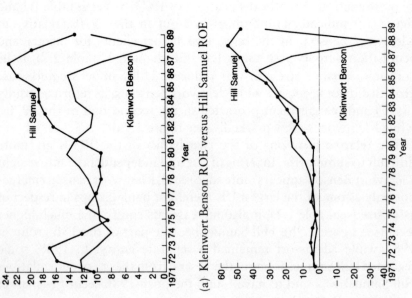

(a) Kleinwort Benson ROE versus Hill Samuel ROE

(b) Kleinwort Benson equity versus Hill Samuel equity

(c) Kleinwort Benson and Hill Samuel management profit

Figure 1.9 Kleinwort Benson and Hill Samuel: equity, ROE and management profit 1971–1989

Source: Kleinwort Benson and Hill Samuel

Note: management profit represents pre-tax contribution before income implicit in investing capital of each bank. Arrived at by taking each year's profit from annual accounts, grossing up to pre-tax using standard corporation tax rate of 35 per cent, and then deducting assumed income on investment capital of 10 per cent of average shareholders funds (equity).

Table 1.1 UK merchant banks: asset size and client lists

Asset size of merchant banks

	1988–1989
Kleinwort Benson	8,028,470
Morgan Grenfell	5,932,329
S. G. Warburg	3,372,019
Samuel Montagu	3,179,971
Hambros	3,178,414
Hill Samuel	2,875,100
N. M. Rothschild	2,849,392
Schroders	2,720,066
Baring	2,358,842
Robert Fleming	1,911,180
Lazards	1,364,917
Charterhouse	1,297,100
Brown Shipley	800,113
Guinness Mahon	766,696
Singer & Friedlander	499,026
Rea Brothers	215,948

Source: The Times 1000 – 1989

Financial adviser client lists

	1981	1987	1989
Hill Samuel	150	162	120
Kleinwort Benson	108	157	128
Morgan Grenfell	99	149	112
S. G. Warburg	133	135	155
County Bank	113	114	90
N. M. Rothschild	71	112	113
Schroders	103	108	112
Samuel Montagu	70	89	85
Hambros	87	86	70
BZW	87	85	93
Robert Fleming	63	75	61
Baring	68	64	63
Lazard	42	55	96
Brown Shipley	24	42	41
Charterhouse	49	42	57
Lloyds Merchant Bank	9	42	35
Singer & Friedlander	47	23	30
Henry Ansbacher	8	12	13
Guinness Mahon	16	11	8
Rea Brothers	18	10	7
Arbuthnot Latham	18	5	7

Source: Crawford Directory of City Connections (1982, 1988 and 1990)

too crowded and was forced to find a larger partner with adequate capital (see figure 1.9b for the increase in equity from 1987). The result of the merger was that Hill Samuel withdrew from the securities trading business. It concentrated instead on its historic strengths of corporate finance and commercial lending.

Others argued that Hill Samuel was taking the action necessary for longer-term survival; this was thought especially so in the way it had the courage to alter its strategic viewpoint on the securities world and exit in advance of significant losses – choices which others might face in due course. The bank maintained that its own brand of simple 'hands-on' management in the mid 1980s was particularly effective, as the results appeared to improve. This picture is not confirmed by Hill Samuel's partial improvement in management profit and ROE in the late 1980s (see figure 1.9c and a) and its £40 million loss in 1990.

Meanwhile, Kleinwort Benson's apparent success in growth is no more straightforward. Kleinwort's early emphasis on diversification and growth through international operations looked to many in the first half of the 1980s to be appropriate to the expanded opportunities in London and elsewhere (Lascelles 1990). Yet in the attempt to become large, offering a wide range of services (as in US investment banks) Kleinwort Benson has incurred major risks. The result has been: lower returns on equity than Hill Samuel; broadly similar management profit down to 1987 followed by a sharp dip; an exposure to greater risks, such as the agonizing loss associated with Kleinwort's market-making position with Premier Consolidated Oilfields' shares in the face of the Gulf crisis in 1990.

In the central pages of the book, the aim will be to explain why the two banks diverged in their performance from the 1970s: how Kleinwort chose an expansion strategy through an international network, and sought to remain independent and develop a capacity to handle change; and conversely why Hill Samuel after its diversification was more cautious in the face of the rigours of the new market forms in the early 1980s and sought security through merger and specialization.

The Prudential was formed in 1848. As a loan and assurance association it grew through its attention to industrial life assurance and the use of a distinctive field staff. By 1915 the Prudential expanded into general insurance (fire, motor and accident). Agencies were set up abroad in the 1920s. Although all the life offices were held back by government wartime legislation, the Prudential developed an enviable reputation for stability. By the 1960s, the Prudential and its sales-force of 14,000 dominated the supply of life assurance to the mass of the population in the UK. During the 1960s the company became the market leader in the provision of group pension plans and acquired a majority interest in the Mercantile & General Re-Insurance Company. The Prudential remained the largest life assurance company, aided by its considerable fieldstaff advantage. Profits grew in line with market growth. Meanwhile, smaller unit-trust-linked life assurance providers made substantial inroads into the market (see chapter 2, table 2.9).

In the 1970s, management responded directly to both internal problems and to the new demands for life assurance and related products. The crash of 1973–4 depressed profits (see figure 1.10a) and made for caution, as we saw in the merchant banks. The losses sustained by M&G in 1978 hit profits only slightly. Yet as figure 1.10b shows, the Prudential did diversify its customer base by reducing dependence on its industrial life business, introducing new unit-linked products from 1973, and placing greater emphasis on investment management. In 1978 the Prudential Corporation, a holding company form, was created which increased the financial flexibility of the subsidiary businesses.

Figure 1.10 Prudential Assurance Company: profit and loss account 1970–1980 and new business premiums 1980–1986. *Source:* Prudential

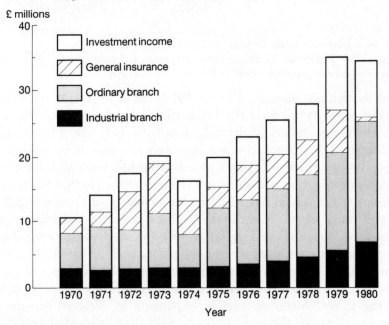

(a) Profit and loss account 1970–1980

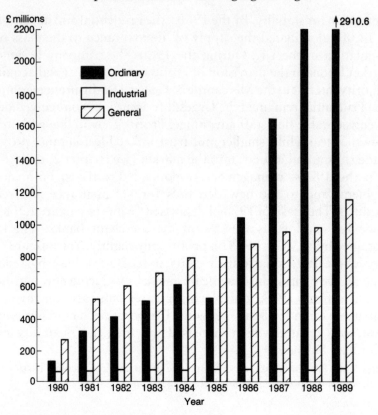

(b) New business premiums written 1980–1989

Figure 1.10 Prudential Assurance Company: profit and loss account 1970–1980 and new business premiums 1980–1989

Although not unscathed in the 1980s (as in the losses in 1989–90 in the property market) the Prudential is seen as one of the more successful performers of the old life offices. As figure 1.10 and table 1.2 suggest, the corporation has been able to maintain profitability in the diversity of its ordinary and industrial life areas and sustain the success of its group pension work (Nisbet 1990: 28–9). On the other hand, the Prudential has made major strides in offering a 'cradle to grave' range of products; these included the early expansion of its unit-trust business, and re-organizing its investment management operation. An increasing weight was placed on internationalization in the 1980s as shown by the acquisition of Jackson National of the US in 1987. Prudential's relative success is confirmed by expert opinion in the sector. Although further expansion in Western Europe has currently ceased, the view strongly held that Prudential could join

Table 1.2 Prudential selected ratios

(a) *New business to life funds*	*Prudential*
1972	81.6
1973	91.6
1974	94.2
1975	91.3
1976	165.9
1977	174.3
1978	210.4
1979	205.1
1980	188.0

Note: 'New business' figures are no longer reported by Prudential in the 1980s. 'Premium Income' and 'Gross Investment Income' are reported from 1982, as follows:

(b) *Premium income to life funds*	
1982	16.3
1983	15.9
1984	15.4
1985	16.1
1986	14.5
1987	n.g.
1988	10.5
1989	13.1

(c) *Gross investment income to life funds*	
1982	9.4
1983	9.8
1984	9.1
1985	9.3
1986	9.1
1987	n.g.
1988	5.2
1989	5.2

Source: The Times 1000 1972–1990

Allianz of West Germany, Generali of Italy and Winterthur of Switzerland as major multinational insurers in post–1992 Europe.

Prudential is an excellent illustration of the competitive challenges which faced the life assurance houses and the need to develop multiple bases of competition. Chapters 3 to 7 will try to show how the

Prudential's strong performance was underpinned by a growing capacity for managing strategic change in the 1970s which was not overtaken by events in the 1980s.

This broad sketch of the companies studied only introduces them. The main chapters of the book will examine the reasons behind these profiles in detail. The first step towards that explanation is to explore the environment in which these firms have operated; that is, the nature of the four sectors, their changing bases of competition and the impact of the political and economic alterations in the UK during that time. That step is taken in the chapter which follows.

2

A Changing Backcloth: New Rules and Relationships

If Malcolm Bradbury is right about the reversal in social values over the past decade (see chapter 1), then clearly this must be linked in some way to wider shifts in the character of Britain. A fierce debate now rages over both the nature and significance of such changes (see, for example, Skidelsky 1988; Hoover and Plant 1988). However, the outcomes of these real world processes for individual firms has been vital in the true sense of the word.

The framework described in chapter 1 (see figure 1.3) provides a means of encompassing such broad alterations and appreciating their relevance at company level. Certain national programmes represent true break-points with the past. Yet there is a need to understand the parallel and linked changes at the level of the economy and the sector. Together they frame the context in which managerial action takes place. This chapter therefore provides a critical account of the generally acknowledged transformation of the UK economy since the 1960s, its expression within four of its major sectors, and the demands this has placed on the firms concerned.

Political and economic change

The changes in the political and economic complexion of Britain in the 1980s has been the subject of extensive reportage. The actions of three successive Conservative governments are widely seen as having effected a break with the assumptions which lay behind its post-war predecessors. Yet the political phenomenon known as Thatcherism is often inaccurately portrayed and its real impact confused with the rhetoric of its proponents. In practice the degree of continuity with past policies has been higher than most people realize. Looking back over the 1970s and 1980s it is the unevenness of the impact of the Thatcher administrations which stands out. Managers at firm level have had to cope with the challenges posed by continuity or the lack of change as much as those which arise from radical innovation.

Political change

That Thatcherism is one of the few 'isms' named after a British Prime Minister speaks volumes for its political and wider significance. It is the unquestionable starting point for considering the political and economic profile of the UK in the 1980s. Yet to see the so-called 'Thatcher revolution' as having wrought a thoroughgoing reformulation of British politics would be misguided. On closer inspection the record on change is far more uneven. Like many governments before them the Conservative administrations from 1979 have been forced to combine undoubtedly novel initiatives with more humdrum compromises. The verdicts of the headline writers notwithstanding, the outcome has been a distinctly mixed record of political change. The Conservatives' revolutionary zeal has been diluted by not only timely opportunism but a good deal of pragmatism. Decision makers in each sector of the economy have had to cope therefore with the problems of inertia just as much as the opportunities which have resulted from the central political change agent.

The aims of Conservative governments in the 1980s were made abundantly clear. The party's election manifesto in 1979 was different from all the previous post-war governments in one essential respect. The promise was not to modernize or improve the existing economic and welfare system. Rather there was an explicit pledge to reverse Britain's long-term decline and effect a shift in the balance between the state and the individual as a central means of doing so. The corporatist state was to be if not removed then emasculated. This was to be achieved by a series of measures built around: monetary control as a means to mastering inflation; deregulation; the return of nationalized industries to the private sector; the diminution of state responsibility in key areas; and union reform.

The advent of a world recession at the start of the first Thatcher government, together with three million unemployed and the deficiencies of Britain in the 1970s, gave ministers a major advantage (Skidelsky 1988; Phelps-Brown 1988). They were able to drive home the message that, individually or nationally, no one was 'owed a living' more successfully than any other administration since the war. Armed with a set of new labels supplied by the thinking of the 'New Right' the government was able to exploit the setting where cherished beliefs could be truly challenged in the quest for efficiency. David Henderson in his 1986 Reith lectures drew attention to three central tenets (Brittan 1987) which had been directly confronted in Thatcherite policies:

- centralism – the received idea that government should decide on what industries and services a country supports;
- structurism – the notion that services are inherently inferior to manufacturing
- mercantilism – the assumption that government should encourage exports but not imports.

The loosening of the bonds of such assumed wisdom has proved vital in supplying alternatives for those faced with the need to respond to acute pressures for economic change.

Yet in spite of the radical colouring of the Tory aims, in practice the colours have been shown to be less than fast and often to fade. This is hardly surprising when some of the main features of the 'Thatcher experiment' were rooted in the policies of earlier governments. Money supply controls, targets for reduced government borrowing and attempts to stabilize the share of public spending in GNP all date from the Labour administration of 1975–6. It was, after all, the Labour chancellor, Denis Healey, who remarked at the time, 'we're all monetarists now'.

Others point to how little has been done to dismantle the post-war settlement (Middlemas 1990) in the NHS or social benefits and the high degree of political caution over union reform and privatization when judged against the rhetoric of Thatcherism. As the political analyst/commentator Ivor Crewe put it, Keynes has been rejected, Beveridge has not. The centre-piece of monetary targets, principally sterling M3, was abandoned after 1982. After that time, the supposedly free movement in exchange rates became subjected to an unpublished target range. Ministers increasingly attempted to intervene by 'talking down' pay settlements. The government's supporters also drew attention to the absence of deregulation outside the showcase examples of financial services. The political veto was used over the proposed purchase of UK companies by overseas interests. Quotas on certain imports continued. Major tax subsidies on home ownership and restrictions on land use persisted. In 1987–8 the DTI planned to spend £417 million on industrial support programmes. Not only had some of the bright colours of the free market come out in the wash, in the case of monetarism the fabric had even shrunk.

The practical importance to industry of such a mixed government record should not be underestimated. Examples taken from our own research support this view of an uneven impact of a Thatcherite transformation based on free-market operation. Peugeot Talbot's experience provides a clear instance of the way firms in the auto industry must continue to take account of the action of government besides more conventional market forces. In practice Peugeot Talbot's rationalization programme in the 1980s involved the DTI in a number of ways. The government extended the repayment period on an outstanding loan of £28 million made to the previous owners, Chrysler, in 1969. Assistance was also given including the £2.25 million for the 309 project and £1.5 million for the introduction of the 405. Besides haranguing Ford and Vauxhall on foreign sourcing of components the DTI looked for similar action on local content from Peugeot Talbot. Far from ushering in a completely new free market situation, past forms of government intervention were perpetuated.

Irrespective of political affiliation the posture of the Conservative governments of the 1980s is an interesting example of an attempt to manage change. This effort at the national level has parallels with the path taken by certain managers within their firms (see chapter 3). What becomes apparent is the combination employed of broad, imprecise and potent visionary appeals, which give considerable room for tactical adjustment in practice and as circumstances alter. Mrs Thatcher's famous 'political luck' may be largely explained by such a combined approach to managing her political change agenda in the first two administrations of the 1980s.

Some commentators see nothing exceptional in this dilution of the full force of the radical intentions of the government. Riddell (1987) sees Thatcherism essentially as an instinct rather than a fully worked out ideology. It is not synonymous with monetarism nor a pure free-market approach. Meanwhile Rogaly (1989) maintains that Thatcherism was always based politically on an appeal to an individual, moral spirit which has therefore permitted shifts or trimming in its detailed application. In particular it is very difficult to establish how far this appeal has been taken up nationally. Public expenditure may be under strict control, producing a budget surplus. Yet aggregate data indicates that the quantity of national wealth spent by government or by private individuals shows no great historical discontinuity. The available evidence would suggest that in the south-east of England many of the assumptions behind the corporate state have disappeared. The same cannot be said of the north, Scotland or Wales. It is hardly surprising that many government policies should be reshaped during their implementation in such inhospitable terrain. The Conservatives won a third of the possible vote in 1979 and just over 30 per cent in 1983 and 1987, all in the face of a divided opposition.

The limitations on the Thatcher project have to an extent come from its internal contradictions and unforeseen consequences. Thus the creation of new private monopolies, in the utilities for example, has required the formation of new regulatory organizations such as Ofgas or the National Rivers Authority. Paradoxically for a government which was to 'roll-back the frontiers of the state', the powers of ministers and civil servants have been greatly strengthened by the flow of legislation.

It remains to be seen therefore whether 1979 will be regarded as a watershed in British history comparable in importance to 1945. After more than a decade of Thatcherism, it is still not possible to tell conclusively if 1979 set in motion a fundamental alteration in the relationship between state and society, voting patterns and the character of the UK economy. Perhaps the greatest threat to achieving a more permanent shift would be the failure to sustain a full economic restructuring beyond the short-term recovery of the mid-1980s. In order to appreciate the relevance of the economic dimension and its impact at firm level, a closer look is required at the record of the UK post-war economy.

Economic change

Lasting judgements about the long-term significance of the recovery – some might say miracle – of the UK economy in the 1980s are not easy (cf. Ball 1989). At the time of writing, the current account deficit stands at 4 per cent of GDP and inflation is 8 per cent. Does this denote a familiar reprise of the 'stop–go' cycles of the post-war era? Prophecy apart, marked changes have occurred at the level of the economy compared to the two preceding decades. The period contains both unprecedented contraction followed by accelerated expansion. The position of UK firms in general has altered dramatically for the better but the depth of their recovery is more questionable.

The UK economy in the 1970s and 1980s can be fully understood only through a long-term perspective. Britain's record has been one of consistent relative economic decline. The economy continued to grow yet those of other countries, notably Western Europe, grew faster still (see chapter 1, 'Economic retardation'). Measures of productivity (real GDP per hour worked) show how the USA overtook the UK in the 1880s, followed by Sweden in the 1940s, the Netherlands in the 1950s, and West Germany, France and Belgium in the late 1960s (*Oxford Review of Economic Policy* 1988). In the three decades after the Second World War, the British economy showed the lowest rate of growth of the major industrialized countries (an average of 2.5 per cent per annum). The UK slipped from being one of the wealthiest countries in the world to a position of nineteenth in terms of per capita income (Thirlwall 1989).

The problems associated with this fall form a dismal litany. Investment levels were poor by international standards. The growth of exports was the slowest of all OECD countries. The balance of payments problem was intractable. Inflation overcame price stability. Industrial relations were appalling, the management performance was weak. The penalty paid in industrial failure was the loss of over three million manufacturing jobs between 1966 and 1979 (Wolf 1988).

As the aggregate indicators show, no government was able to supply conclusive answers to these deep-seated problems in spite of a range of policy action. Under the Macmillan administrations from 1951 to 1964 consumption took precedence over investment and foreign trade and growth rates were still half of the UK's European neighbours. The dash for growth in 1963 led to one of the worst balance of payment crises of all time. The Labour governments of 1964–70 attempted a form of national planning with target growth rates, yet were overcome by the need to deflate in the face of a persistent balance of payments problem. Inflation appeared as a major problem in the late 1960s and grew in the following decade; it was abetted by the sterling devaluation of 1967, the failure of price and wage controls, and the commodity price boom of the early 1970s.

The jury is still out over the ultimate political impact of the Tory governments in the 1980s. This cannot be said of the economic consequences of its policies in its first three years. In spite of the cushion of North Sea oil revenue the government created one of the deepest recessions of the century. The application of an extremely severe monetary and fiscal policy meant that firms faced the nightmarish combination of rising oil prices and commodity prices, high interest rates, and a grossly over-valued pound (the effective exchange rate rose by over 20 per cent). The result was a fall in total output by 3 per cent, a rise in unemployment from 1 to 2.5 million and the extinction of considerable parts of British industry as manufacturing output fell by 15 per cent (Godley 1989).

The recovery of the UK economy from 1982 is less easily described. Some argue that Britain is no longer an industrial museum. Nor does its economy provide easy fodder for the satirists. To those responsible for effecting this recovery in their sectors of the economy their efforts have been exceptional. Many indicators are testimony to the extent of the adjustments which have been made (Maynard 1988). In the post-war period the growth in the UK of real GDP was below the rate of most of the OECD countries. Between 1979 and 1988 the reverse was true. In the period 1973–9 real GDP grew 1.5 per cent a year in the UK, 2.4 per cent in the USA, and 2.4 per cent in the EC. From 1979–88 the growth rate of the British economy registered 2 per cent, the USA 2.5 per cent and the EC 1.8 per cent. Output and productivity gains have been accompanied by rising corporate profitability (see figure 2.1). The annual growth rate of productivity in manufacturing has risen to 4 per cent (typical of the 1960s) in the 1980s against the 1 per cent of the 1970s. The rate of return on industry's capital, which hit a low of 4 per cent in 1974, averaged 8.5 per cent in 1988. This compared favourably with West Germany and the USA. Abysmally low investment in the early 1980s has now recovered to its 1979 level .

These impressive figures need to be handled especially carefully. Unemployment is double what it was in 1979 (see figure 2.1c). Earnings are running ahead of an inflation rate already above that of competitor countries. Wage inflation has been stuck at around 7.5 per cent, a rate much faster than in the USA, Japan or West Germany. Economic growth, which has been reliant on rapid increases in consumption, has led to a record trade imbalance of £14.3 billion a year (see figure 2.1d) by 1989 (equivalent to 3 per cent of GDP). Critics see the deficit as a sign that many sectors of the UK economy remain uncompetitive. They are, therefore, seen to be unable to produce and sell enough at home or abroad to maintain steady growth in a fully employed economy (Gamble 1988). International and historical comparisons are required. The efforts to survive and recover from the 1979–81 recession were heroic. Yet in some respects these actions represent the progress of someone who, to use Thirlwall's image, has fallen off a cliff and then climbed back to the top. The performance of the economy in the 1980s may have improved vastly on the previous decade but it has not been that much better than in the 1960s. At the same time the other European countries have performed relatively poorly, remaining at their levels of the 1970s.

Other weaknesses have continued. Rates of return in UK manufacturing are still low by international standards (UK 10 per cent against 20 per cent in the USA and Japan, 15 per cent in West Germany and 13 per cent in France). The manufacturing sector's recovery has been weaker than in other countries (see figure 2.2). The National Economic Development Office (NEDO) has drawn attention to the slow growth in the 'high research intensity' sector of manufacturing including data processing and electronics. Without them other sectors are vulnerable while the whole economy loses the benefit of their high value-added

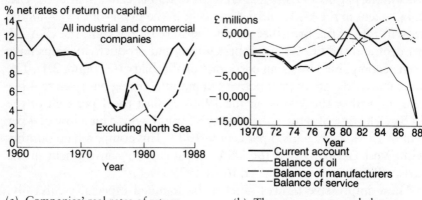

(a) Companies' real rates of return

(b) The current account balance
      and its main components

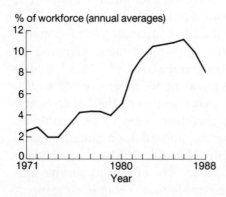

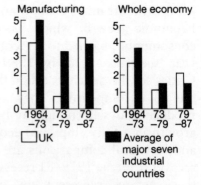

(c) Unemployment

(d) Growth of output per head
      (average annual % changes)

Figure 2.1 UK economic indicators: rate of return, current account balance, unemployment and growth of output per head.
Source: Financial Times, 16 June 1988, p.27

products. On the basis of real average annual growth in value-added, the UK achieved faster growth during the 1980s in agriculture and energy compared with its main European competitors, but manufacturing trailed behind (NEDO 1985).

The relative weakness of UK manufacturing becomes even more critical in relation to the problem of the trade deficit. The hope that services will be an adequate replacement for the loss to the economy of manufacturing is thrown into sharp doubt when it is realized that in Japan and West Germany the share of manufacturing in GNP is still around 30 per cent – the proportion of manufacturing in the British economy in the 1960s. In addition, the balance of trade in services actually fell by around 40 per cent between 1985 and 1988 (Godley 1989).

Certain problems which have emerged during the 1980s present considerable challenges to British management. The problems of the balance of payments will have to be faced without the benefit of North

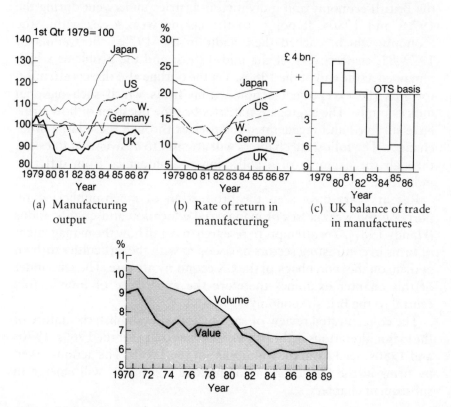

(a) Manufacturing output   (b) Rate of return in manufacturing   (c) UK balance of trade in manufactures

Figure 2.2 UK manufacturing: output, rate of return and balance of trade
Source: Financial Times, 30 March 1987, p.12

Sea oil. The continuing decline in investment in R&D is alarming to some (Crafts 1988). There is a suggestion that some of the productivity gains of the decade are underpinned by changes in the conduct of wage bargaining, not by any major alteration in the structure of the industrial relations system. Skill shortages may well become acute, sufficient to undermine sector competitiveness. In spite of high unemployment, skill shortages increased in the 1980s. Work by the Manpower Services Commission and the National Institute of Economic Research brought into sharp relief the UK's unenviable record on training. Britain compares badly with all her main competitors in terms of proportion of turnover devoted to training, the narrowness of the approaches to skill generation at all levels (especially youth), and the amount of post-school training. Chris Hayes (NEDO 1985) summarizes the position well when he says: 'most of our companies are having to make good what their competitors take as given'.

This profile gives some idea of the enormous changes which both the British economy and individual industries underwent during the 1970s and 1980s. It points to the lasting weaknesses within the economy which reached their nadir in the 1970s; the trauma of 1979–81; the recovery of the mid–1980s; and the problems which remained at the end of the 1980s. Yet the outline also directs attention towards the exceptional action within firms which such national indices imply. The aggregate statistics beg the question of how firms have survived and regenerated themselves through these large order changes. The following chapters will attempt to answer that question through the example of a collection of companies from different industries.

Recent years have seen the production of much-publicized reports on the weaknesses of managerial education and qualifications (Handy 1987). Yet attempts to research in detail how the management of firms in contrasting sectors have coped with the difficulties thrown at them on the switchback of the UK economy are rare. The remainder of this chapter examines therefore the experience of four sectors central to the British economy.

The concentrated review of each sector will establish the nature of the major alterations in the bases of competition over the 1960s, 1970s and 1980s, seen from the standpoint of the 1980s. The actions taken by firms in the face of such competitive conditions will emerge in subsequent chapters.

Automobiles

The transition from the post-war decades of replacement demand to the turbulence of the 1970s irrevocably altered the character of competition in the UK auto industry. Car production increased by a factor of 4.5 in the 1950s. By contrast the following two decades were characterized by market dislocation and a redefinition of the bases of competition. The UK producers were ill-equipped to meet the challenge. The period 1979–87 in the UK car industry witnessed a gradual, painful recovery from the combined onslaught of two bouts of contraction in demand and the establishment of radically new performance standards by other international volume producers. At the same time changes in the European and world auto industry called into question almost every accepted notion of the business of car manufacture developed during the preceding decades of US domination.

To a world industry which had increased annual output from 16.2 million in 1960 to 93.1 million in 1973 the twin oil shocks of 1973–4 and 1979 were traumatic; for the British automobile industry they were devastating. Demand for cars fell, depending on market segment, by between 25 and 40 per cent. UK auto makers were still dealing with unresolved, long-term weaknesses when the shock waves hit them. The set of deficiencies is by now well known: unrationalized company form (BL had 30 constituent parts in 1968), lack of investment, underdeveloped production automation and marketing (see Whipp 1990a). The resulting problems were weak products, indifferent quality, outdated distribution, high manufacturing costs and poor labour relations of the domestic producers. Foreign producers, without those drawbacks were able to enter the UK market as tariff barriers fell. The results were devastating. Import penetration rose from 6 per cent in the late 1960s to 40 per cent by 1975. The US-owned producers in the UK, Ford and Vauxhall, brought in tied imports from their European plants as they sought to overcome the unfavourable cost climate of the British auto industry.

The 1980s opened with the British auto industry in a depressing state. 1982 saw the lowest level of car production since the late 1950s. Spain's output of cars exceeded the UK's in 1980. The first efforts of the UK industry to improve its crippling weaknesses, exposed in the early 1970s, were therefore dashed by the contraction in demand from 1979. The second attempt was more successful but still incomplete down to 1984. By that date quality and the high cost base were still acting as brakes on the industry's competitiveness. Sterling's status as a petrocurrency made it more difficult to export. The multinational producers (Ford and GM) were forced to switch their sourcing of products to other European plants even more. In this period Britain's cost competitiveness deteriorated by 35–55 per cent compared to the other major European currencies. Nor were the lower wage rates in the UK industry (20 per cent cheaper than in Europe) of help since productivity was still lower.

The improvement in the overall position of the British auto industry can be seen in the course of the car production figures (see table 2.1). In the medium term the levels recovered somewhat unevenly from the low points of 1980–2. Yet in the long-term sense the whole sector, including parts, was still below the 1972 output level of 1.92 million cars during the mid–1980s. Car manufacturing also fell in output terms well below the general trend of the index for total manufacturing industries in the early 1980s. Moreover, the recovery in output between 1986 and 1989 must be put into perspective. It was boosted by record domestic demand and the build-up of production at the new Nissan plant in Sunderland. Above all the rising output was accompanied by record annual trade deficits in cars from 1982 (see figure 2.3). The figure stood at £6.11 billion in 1988 (56 per cent of the market was taken up by imports) – 30 per cent of the UK's total visible trade deficit.

The improvement in the overall performance of the industry has therefore been modest in the 1980s. Two main causes stand out: strengthened company competitive bases, and the fall of the pound against other main currencies in the mid–1980s.

The second is more clearly demonstrated than the first. A general

Table 2.1 UK motor vehicle registrations 1980–1989

	Number of passenger cars
1980	1,513,761
1981	1,484,622
1982	1,555,027
1983	1,791,698
1984	1,749,650
1985	1,832,408
1986	1,882,474
1987	2,013,693
1988	2,215,574
1989	2,300,944

Source: SMMT Annual Reports

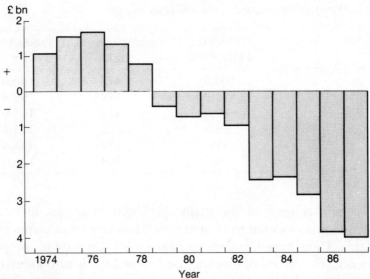

Figure 2.3 Britain's balance of trade in motor products
Source: SMMT

'surge' was evident across all manufacturing industries after the depreciation of sterling (notably in comparison to the Deutschmark) in the middle of the decade. There was a beneficial effect on the UK cost base, from the autumn of 1986 to the end of 1987. Yet as the car industry shows, an upturn was apparent prior to that date. If the recovery was to be more than a devaluation-led 'bounce' then it had to be underpinned by more permanent supply-side improvements. In 1989 there were indications that this had begun to occur in automobiles.

According to general measures of output and employment, the UK industry has seen a marked upturn in productivity, particularly in the early 1980s (see table 2.2).

It is of course immensely difficult to attribute the contribution of work-force reduction (150,000 jobs disappeared in 1981–6) versus improved techniques across the whole industry. However, changes in industrial relations and technology have been significant on a wide scale. Key indicators include: days lost per employee through strikes fell from 6.7 in 1979 to 3.7 in 1984; output per head in the industry increased by 21 per cent. Wage settlements were below the rate of inflation 1979–84. In the leading plants productivity increased from 5 cars per man in 1979 to 14 in 1984. Automobiles used more robots and computers than any other manufacturing industry, spending £250 million per annum for this purpose in the mid–1980s.

These figures confirm the immense efforts the industry made not

Table 2.2 Productivity record of the UK auto industry

	Output 1980 = 100	Employment 000s	Productivity 1980 = 100
1980	100.0	415	100.0
1981	82.9	359	95.8
1982	79.6	321	103.0
1983	83.9	307	113.4
1984	81.3	292	115.6
1985	86.5	284	126.0

Source: SMMT

only to gain control of the major problems in its products and production processes but to re-orient itself to a new set of competitive standards. These improvements conceal a wide variation in company experience. The record of market share in the British auto industry is shown in figure 2.4.

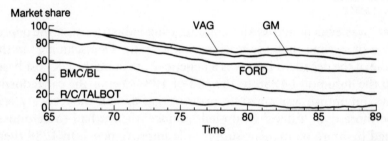

Figure 2.4 Market share of major producers in the UK auto industry 1965–1989
Source: SMMT

Output has also been boosted by the introduction of new producers. Nissan developed a greenfield plant at Washington in Tyne and Wear, in the north-east of Britain in 1986. Initial production was 24,000 car kits in that year. The plan was to raise annual output to 100,000 cars with a high European content by 1991, with market share set to rise from 6 to 10 per cent. The impact on the rest of the industry has been electrifying. The selected use of Japanese techniques unfettered by traditional practices further raised the pressure on the existing producers' efficiency. The comparison between Nissan and Vauxhall in the UK is instructive. In 1989 Vauxhall made 200,000 cars a year with 12,500 workers. Nissan planned to build 100,000 cars with less than 3,000 people.

In 1989 Japanese investment in the UK auto industry was running at £1.81 billion. At that time, Honda aimed to produce 100,000 units at Swindon by 1994, and Toyota 200,000 units per annum at Burnaston, near Derby. It was expected that by the mid–1990s Japanese car makers would account for around a third of UK car output.

The world car industry

A record production figure of 11.6 million in 1986 moved Europe ahead of both the US and Japanese auto industries in terms of output. The pressures on UK operations to rationalize and develop new standards of quality and production have come from the intense competition in the European market. Since 1978 six main producers have been locked in a struggle for leadership with hardly a few percentage points between them. In 1987 the market percentage shares were: VW 15, Fiat 14.2, Peugeot 12.1, Ford 12, GM 10.7 and Renault 10.6. Some experts felt at the end of the 1980s that the car market was more competitive than at any time since the 1920s. Why was this so?

The intensity of the competition has been the result of over-capacity and the way national governments have withdrawn from direct subsidies. At the end of the 1980s the car industry in Europe could make about 13 million vehicles instead of the 10–11 million that was previously achieved. The resulting pressure for rationalization was immense. In the latter part of the 1980s 130,000 jobs were lost in Italy, 55,000 in France and 150,000 in the UK industries. A more sophisticated consumer plus the new product/price standards set by the Japanese proved difficult to meet.

Most of the specialist producers (BMW, Mercedes, Volvo and Saab) had remained profitable during the price wars of the early 1980s. By 1986 the volume producers were recovering. Peugeot was a conspicuous example which joined Fiat, Ford and Volkswagen-Audi. Renault and GM aimed to break even around 1988. The improvement of the industry in the mid–1980s was aided by Ford and GM easing back from their market share at all costs approach, together with lower energy prices (which account for a large proportion of production costs), and lower interest rates, which lessened the burden created by the companies' massive inherited debts. Lower oil prices also increased real income and therefore the spending of consumers.

In 1989 the position of the European industry and its prospects point one inevitably to the USA and Japan. All world producers have had to face two major upheavals since the 1970s: the rise of the Japanese and fundamental changes in management practice and technology.

The radical transformation of the world car industry in the 1970s and 1980s centred on the rise of the Japanese car industry. A post-war government policy of developing a Japanese automobile industry behind protective tariffs and the prohibition of foreign ownership worked well. US management practices were combined with European product technology to meet the local priorities of limited space, materials and energy. The result has been a unique synthesis of 'just in time' production with 'total quality control'. When combined with the national structure of suppliers and producers within a single group the result has been truly revolutionary: much cheaper products but at a higher quality than other national car industries. The Japanese management paradigm has come to dominate the world industry. The resolution of this competitive disparity between the Japanese producers and the rest of the world is expected to be one of the dominant factors within the industry in the 1990s.

The impact of these new technologies, organization and market structures has undermined Western managerial assumptions. Major changes in production technology since 1970 have made the dedicated production lines developed by the US giants less appropriate. Greater flexibility and new economies of scale are offered by the use of computer controlled production lines together with the more versatile form of automation seen in robotics, automated handling and machining cells. This flexibility will be vital as models change at a faster rate given the immense product innovations emerging in the 1990s.

The Japanese goal of a continuous flow from foundry to customer without the conventional buffers or inventories, the elimination of costly defects, and the cross-ownership between producers and suppliers are incompatible with the past US-based methods of mass-production. Collaboration between Japanese industrial groups and the imaginative use of joint ventures to produce inside the USA and Europe also have pointed the way forward for other producers faced with the problems of intense competition and insurmountable short-term problems due to the cost and degree of change involved. The intimate linkage between such methods of production and product innovation suggest much wider possibilities for car makers than appeared possible in the 1970s.

The established view in the 1970s was that markets in the OECD countries were now saturated. At the end of the 1980s it appeared that demand was not converging between countries. Patterns of demand amongst the main Western producers have remained quite different. The segmentation of the market has become more complex. The resulting divergence confirms the move away from easy world domination by a handful of producers. Instead it points to the potential of the larger group of volume manufacturers exploiting the more fragmented market and the variety of niches it will contain.

In this period of flux or 'de-maturity', survival will not depend solely on economies of scale or market domination but on the identification of distinctive capabilities and strengths which can be traded with others in order to cover weaknesses and maximize potential. Given the vast amounts of capital required for product and process innovation and their increasing speed, single producers need to hone their skills of joint development, buying in of necessary components and the acquisition of technical knowledge from other manufacturers. The retention of a strong engineering capability will be crucial in order to make the technical choices, absorb the inputs from others and combine the new knowledge. Above all the key will be flexible and robust managerial capacity to combine with this technical base.

This need is all the more pressing in the light of international comparisons. Jones and Womack (1986) note how:

- the average car plant in Japan can produce a comparable car to European-owned plants in Europe with half the human effort
- European technology leaders' (VW and Daimler-Benz) spending on R&D only matches that of the third-ranked Japanese producer
- the Japanese need 43 months to move a new model from concept to consumer versus the USA's and Europeans' 62 months.

Book publishing

It has been suggested that the small size of UK book publishing accounts for the slowness in compiling complete and accurate statistics for the industry (Curwen 1981). However, some of the broad dimensions of the industry emerge from existing records.

The small size of the industry is seen in both employment (41,000 were engaged directly in printing and publishing in 1985 – around 1 per cent of those employed in the manufacturing industry) and in terms of consumer spending (0.4 per cent of total consumer spending). The importance of the industry comes in the significance of its product both internationally and in the way books are one of the major bearers of the cultural record of society. According to the Publishers Association estimates, around 685 million books are sold each year.

In 1989 Whitaker listed more than 20,000 publishers in the UK, of which only 9,500 were classified as active. However, there are only 200 publishers whose principal business is book publishing. There is a pattern of concentration amongst those 200. Prior to the series of mergers and take-overs of the mid–1980s (see below) the top 20 publishers in 1984 accounted for 22.6 per cent of titles produced in 1984 of which the top five took just under 9 per cent (see table 2.3a). At the same time the top 11 book publishers accounted for 62 per cent of the market (see table 2.3b). In the latter part of the 1980s the concentration increased with acquisitions among the top set. Publishing is not a capital-intensive industry and hence it is comparatively simple for an individual to set up in business. Smallness even brings its own advantages, including low overheads, specialization and the opportunity to omit some of the links in the production chain. Size can confer the major benefits of bulk purchase of materials, easier access to exports and a range of product types which spread risk.

Notwithstanding its small size the British book industry has a high level of output by international standards as table 2.3c shows. The figure understates the position of the UK in so far as countries such as the USA include theses, for example, whereas Britain does not. New title output stood at just under 50,000 in 1985 and has grown considerably from the 25,000 level of the 1970s.

Growth in sales has been more problematic. Book sales have increased sevenfold from 1969 to 1985, reaching £1 billion for the first time in 1985. In cash terms this represented an annual increase of 12 per cent. In real terms the picture is less outstanding, as figure 2.5a shows. The real value of sales declined in eight years between 1970 and 1982 (1970, 1973, 1975, 1977, 1979, 1980, 1981 and 1982) although the fall was disguised by rising cash values. The impact of the recessions of 1973 and 1979 on consumer demand is particularly noticeable. The book-buying appetite of the British has long been thought to be lower than in other Western countries. Buying levels remained virtually static in the UK when compared to the growth in demand for other consumer goods. The UK industry's emphasis on exports is wholly understandable in such circumstances. Over 30 per cent of the industry's output was exported by the end of the 1980s.

In real terms, school books reached a plateau in the mid–1970s but fell back to their 1969 level in 1985(see figure 2.5b). The technical and scientific category has moved in the opposite direction down to 1979; thereafter it has experienced a strong recovery and expansion beyond its previous highest points. Fiction and children's books have both remained much the same as a proportion of total book sales, although

Table 2.3 UK book publishing: concentration, market share and national output

(a) *Concentration ratios by titles published 1984*	
Imprints by size	*Cumulative % of total titles produced*
top 5	8.9
top 10	14.6
top 20	22.6
top 30	28.0
top 40	32.4

Source: The Bookseller

(b) *Market share of largest publishers 1983*	
Pearson Longman	10%
BPCC/Pergamon	8
Collins (excluding Granada)	8
OUP	8
Macmillan	6
ABP	5
IPC	5
Pitman	4
Heinemann	3
Octopus	3
Thomson	2
Others	38

Source: Jordan's Dataquest

(c) *International output of new books*	
USA	72,382
USSR	58,372
West Germany	48,900
Great Britain	44,482
Japan	42,217
South Korea	33,321
China	31,784
France	27,152
Spain	26,964
Canada	13,954
Italy	11,140

Source: Britannica World Data Annual 1986

their sales have struggled to recover from their highest demand in the mid–1970s. The segment which has experienced marked growth has been that of 'other' which has increased its sales value and proportion of total books sold. The increase in this segment's adult non-fiction books appears to have been the result of the demand for books related to new leisure activities, linked publication with television series and home study material.

Figure 2.5b shows the movement in the various categories of books over the 1970s and 1980s; it also illustrates the highly fragmented nature of the industry's output and, as will become apparent, the difficulty of establishing the nature of competition on an industry-wide basis. Longman's or Octopus's shift away from the reliance on traditional product areas is fully justified by reference to the nature of demand in the UK over those two decades.

Longman for example, would seem to exemplify the UK book industry's high levels of exports given the narrow sales base offered by only the domestic market. More precisely, Longman appears to have been in the vanguard of the movement to follow the markets with growth potential in Western Europe and the USA. The wider book industry appears to have caught up later. UK book exports to Europe increased by 57 per cent from 1981 to 1985 and by 86 per cent to the USA in the same period. Longman was thus able to plan for a third of its business being in the USA in the 1990s. In 1985 only 22 per cent of British book exports were to the USA. ABP would also seem to illustrate the UK book industry's high levels of exports given the narrow sales base offered by the domestic market alone. In 1983, 31 per cent of ABP's sales came from exports against a figure of 35 per cent for the whole industry.

Although ABP and others have not engineered the same kind of movement in its coverage of world markets as Longman and Collins there has been an advantage. Undoubtedly ABP and others have been faced with the difficulties posed by the strength of sterling and the weakness of the dollar in the early 1980s. However, the reliance on long-standing Commonwealth operations and the absence of such a range of new subsidiaries elsewhere has been helpful in one sense: although ABP has not been as adventurous as Longman (similar to Hill Samuel and Kleinwort Benson), neither has it been exposed to the same degree of risks.

The recent alterations in the character of UK and foreign booksellers is also worth noting. The resulting impact on distribution has been marked. Bookselling has been caught up in the consumer boom of the

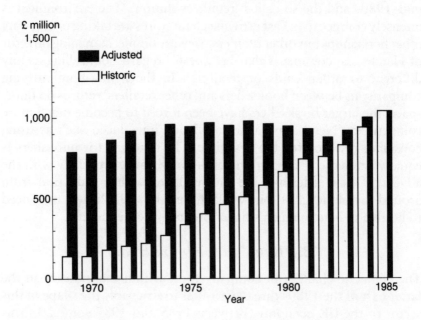

(a) Total turnover

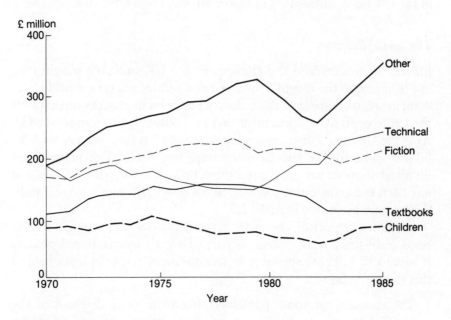

(b) Sales of book by category
Figure 2.5 UK book publishers' turnover and sales of book by category
Source: Publishers' Association

mid–1980s and the so-called 'retail revolution'. The environment is intensely competitive. Fast growing chain stores are taking on not only other bookshops but other retailers. Stewart Binnie, managing director of Hatchards, comments that he 'doesn't regard bookselling as any different to other kinds of retailing'. In the light of unflattering comparisons between booksellers and other retailers' returns on floor-space, the larger booksellers have been forced to become much more competitive. 'New' approaches are being introduced such as using consumer research for the first time. The outcome for publishers is equally dramatic. Expectations of delivery times, especially with the advent of 'tele-ordering', are much higher with a reduction from around the old level of four weeks to ten days. Publishers now need to be able to handle much smaller orders more frequently.

'Big Bang' in the book trade?

The climactic changes in company form within the industry in the latter part of the 1980s threaten to alter irretrievably the shape of this sector of the UK economy. Between 1985 and 1987 some 20 firms merged or were taken over in the UK industry. The major acquisitions in the UK book publishing industry are shown in table 2.4.

The world industry

Indeed, to understand the changes in the UK industry requires an appreciation of the recent course of book publishing on a world scale. A major restructuring of the industry has been in process throughout the 1980s centred on concentration of corporate form (Snoddy 1988). As in the UK, acquisition and merger activity has been intense with $3 billion spent by US and British companies alone. The process has involved some of the most prominent houses in the trade. The result has been the creation of a group of six dominant international pub-lishing groups shown in table 2.5.

On closer inspection the shifts in company size and scope in British book publishing now emerge as part of a truly international process (Calder 1987). There appear to be five dominant forces at work behind this restructuring:

1 The recovery of some publishers from the poor demand of the 1970–82 period clearly made them attractive to would-be purchasers.
2 European groups, as in the case of the UK, faced flat demand for

Table 2.4 Major acquisitions in UK book publishing

Date	Purchaser	Purchased	Approx price £m
1985	Century merged with Hutchinson		
1985	W. H. Smith	Webster Books (off Octopus)	5–6
1985	Associated Book Publishers	Routledge & Kegan Paul	9
1985	Penguin (Pearson)	International Thomson UK Books	4–5
1985	Longman (Pearson)	Pitman	21
1985	Reed International	R. R. Bowker (USA)	18
1985	Octopus	Heinemann (off BTR)	64
1985	St Ives	Richard Clay	100
1986	Octopus	Hamlyn Books (from Reed)	19
1986	Associated Book Publishers	Croom Helm and Pitkin Pictorial	10
1986	Macmillan/Octopus	Collins ⅓ share in Pan	5.7
1986	Penguin (Pearson)	New American Library (USA)	10
1986	Hodder & Stoughton	Dormac Inc (USA)	50
1986	Norton Opex	McCorquodale	1.8
1987	Octopus	Mitchell Beazley	160
1987	Random House	Chatto, Virago, Bodley Head and Jonathan Cape	4.8
			17–20
1987	News Corporation including 40% of Collins	Harper & Row	$300m

Source: Snoddy 1988

Table 2.5 The six largest international publishers

Parent company (country)	Book-publishing subsidiaries (country)	Parent sales 1986 $m	Publishing subsidiaries (% change on previous yr) 1986 $m	
			Sales	Net profit
Bertelsmann (W Germany)	Bertelsmann (W Germany), Bantam (US), Plaza Janes (Spain), Doubleday (US)	3,033.0	459.5 (+24.6)	n.a.
Gulf Western (US)	Simon & Schuster (US) Prentice-Hall (US)	3,781.1	949.0 (+18.9)	140.5 (+35.5)
International Thomson (Canada)	International Thomson Publishing (Britain, Canada and US) Associated Book Publishers (Britain)	2,508.6	1,019.6 (−2.5)	127.6 (+40.2)
Newhouse (US)	Random House (US) Cape Group (Britain)	2,030.0	n.a.	n.a.
News Corporation (Australia)	Collins (Britain) Harper & Row (US)	2,672.8	n.a.	n.a.
Pearson (Britain)	Penguin (Britain and US) Longman (Britain) New American Library (US)	1,397.5	404.3 (+32.1)	36.5 (+8.6)

Source: Calder 1987

some of their traditional products due to the negative movement of demographic and public spending factors. The need to gain access to growth markets abroad grew accordingly.

3 The scale opportunities involved were considerable. America and Britain combined publish around 100,000 titles each year; ten times that figure are in print. The $10 billion US market consumes four times as many as the Commonwealth nations. Hardback and paperback rights can be controlled and the marketing and distribution organized accordingly rather than having to sell or buy paperback rights separately.

4 As the pace of internationalization has increased, acquisition also has become the means of raising potential strength and profitability. Specialist publishers outside the trade area are particularly desirable given their profitable backlists and the stock of books which will remain in print over a long period; they generate sales while allowing the development of new lists alongside them.

5 As Longman's strategy demonstrates, the aim of many leading publishers, from within their national base, has been to establish a dominant position in their specialist fields. As the internationalization of book publishing increases in line with the spread of the English language, such dominance can only be judged in world terms.

The process of restructuring in book publishing has continued beyond the October 'crash' of 1987. The $1.65 billion struggle for the independent US text and general book publisher Macmillan (no connection to the UK house of that name) which began in May 1988 is one of the most recent instances.

Yet a parallel sequence of change has occurred alongside the alterations in corporate form. The source of this second process has come from a combination of the publishers themselves and those in hitherto separate industries. As in the automobile industry this is still in its early stages. Yet the changes in product and production offered by new technology could lead to the reworking of the boundaries of book publishing.

The potential for using new electronic-based technology to extend the sales of information previously contained only in book form is in theory almost limitless. That potential has clearly lain behind the acquisition programmes of communications specialists such as News Corporation and MCC. The new technological challenges which publishers now face fall into two broad categories of innovation: those that are related to production and those that offer possible new products.

The application of computing power, with ever more sophisticated word processing software, has already had an impact on the traditional publishing process. OUP, for example, in 1989 had around 20 per cent of its new titles arrive from the author on disk. Efficiencies can be gained at the manuscript, copy-editing, mark-up, printer's key-boarding and proof-reading stages. Desk top publishing (DTP) systems in the 1980s have been developed which promise the production of small scale, non-hardback manuscripts. Broadly speaking, DTP systems mean that computer-assisted publishing and printing is no longer the sole preserve of professional printers. The growth in the US DTP market rose from $0.8 billion in 1986 to $2 billion in 1988 with projections that it would double again by 1991. The possibilities for large, technical publications are especially exciting.

The production advantages are clearly startling. Yet it is the product innovations which micro-electronic text processing offer which are equally important. Product innovations for publishers have appeared around the use of databases and new electronic-based media. It is here that book publishers are facing a direct threat to some of their products from competitors outside the industry. Linking database software with DTP systems means that new output can be distilled from across the existing publications of a publishing house. Equally, other institutions could use the DTP technology to publish the information contained within their own commercial databases if there is a ready market. The accountants Deloitte, Haskins & Sells began such a venture in February of 1988 in the UK, publishing specialized financial products through book shops.

New electronic media such as video and computer software have more recently been joined by compact disc interactive (CD-I) and compact disc read only memory (CD-ROM). Major producers in the electronics industry such as Philips, Sony and Hitachi are developing a form of compact disc which captures data, video and audio information all in one.

The keynote of such innovations in the media by which publishers' traditional products could be carried is in its highly infant state. The same is broadly true of the methods of text processing. In many ways the confluence of such a range of information technology has pro-duced a highly immature set of products and processes with no obvious dominant design. The application of some of the technological possibilities, such as DTP, has gone furthest in the USA with its larger market. The entry of communications specialists such as Warner Bros, News Corporation and MCC into publishing is highly significant. Their expertise in cable, satellite and optics could lead to radical transformations in the means of disseminating publishers' works. Similarly, the increasing amount of collaboration between publishers, computer producers, software houses and academic and private consultants necessary for the development of such technology already poses interesting questions of organization and management. Chapters 3 to 7 will explore these demands in closer detail.

Merchant banking

The changes in merchant banking in the 1980s alone have been among the most colourful of any sector of the UK economy. Yet behind those highly visible recent innovations lies a more complicated sequence of alterations from the 1960s. The bases of competition have been built up in the face of a series of challenges posed by the combined impact of government intervention, new market opportunities and the action of foreign finance houses. Different bases of competition have applied at each stage.

The 1960s were a period of fundamental change for the merchant banks. The result was a major shift in the balance of the three main areas of merchant bank activity – accepting house, issuing house and investment management work. The title accepting house refers to the traditional commercial banking offered by the original members of the 'Accepting House Committee' of the Bank of England. 'Issuing house' was the label given to the banks who provided corporate finance services. Investment management refers to the work of managing institutional and private client funds. Down to the 1960s these three areas of work had remained separate with finance houses specializing in a particular service.

The recovery of the UK economy in the 1960s from its post-war difficulties (see 'Political and economic change' above) meant that the demand for corporate finance work rose. At the same time, the restrictive legislation governing foreign investment forced the merchant banks to pay greater attention to the domestic market. A clear trend emerged as the banks attempted to meet these opportunities. First, the traditional merchant banks sought to expand into issuing house activity, either by merger or by building up an internal corporate finance function. Most chose the merger route as a means of gaining an immediate market share. Second, this expansion required an extension of the traditional merchant banks' competences beyond commercial lending. Not only did they recruit solicitors and researchers, for example, but their internal organization became more complex, based on functional specialisms. Third, with the entry of traditional merchant banks into the issuing house area competition intensified with great attention paid now to client lists.

Notable mergers of the period (see table 4.1) included J. Henry Schroder & Co. (whose main strength was acceptance banking) with Helbert Wagg & Co. (who specialized in corporate finance) in 1960. The same pattern of linkage was seen in the mergers of Kleinwort & Sons with Lonsdale Investment Trust in 1961 or Philip Hill, Higginson, Erlangers & Co. with M. Samuel & Co. in 1965 (Robinson 1976: 42). The new competitive conditions worked to the advantage of banks such as S. G. Warburg. As a late entrant to London merchant banking, Warburg was outside the family connections which dominated the distribution of accepting house business. Warburg was able to use its European and American connections to build a corporate client list composed of those who were also outside the mainstream of City financing.

As in book publishing, comparative performance in the conditions of the 1960s is difficult to gauge. Until very recently, most merchant banks published only a single overall profit figure with no indication of how it was generated. Moreover, banks differed in the capital requirements of the financial services they offered yet these were not reflected in their reports. However, as Kellet (1967: 95) shows, figures for total deposits and after-tax disclosed profits, point to a leading group of growth-oriented merchant banks who were able to offer a wide range of services; the group included Warburg, Hill Samuel, Schroders, Hambros and Kleinwort Benson (see table 2.6). This group also established new managerial requirements in merchant banking in the 1960s. They marked the beginning of the change from 'gentlemen' to 'players'. Previously, banks such as Kleinwort, Lazards and Morgan Grenfell had been run by the families and associates of the founders. Now professional managers increasingly assumed senior positions after the mergers of the 1960s.

The following decade for the merchant banks was intensely difficult. In common with automobiles and book publishing, the 1970s marked a clear shift in the competitive environment.

Up until 1974 the merchant banks and many of the new secondary

Table 2.6 UK merchant banks 1961: total deposits and after-tax disclosed profits

	Part (a): Total deposits	
1	Schroders	£117 m
2	Hambros	£78 m
3	S. Montagu	£61 m
4	Kleinwort Benson	£42 m
5	Baring	£41 m
6	Brown Shipley	£33 m
7	M. Samuel	£30 m
8	Philip Hill	£24 m
9	Lazards	£23 m
10	Morgan Grenfell	£19 m
11	Warburg	£14 m
12	Singer & Friedlander	£10 m
	Part (b): Total disclosed profits after-tax	
1	Hambros	£655,000
2	Philip Hill	£628,000
3	Kleinwort Benson	£600,000
4	Schroders	£548,000
5	Warburg	£539,000
6	S. Montagu	£268,000
7	Singer & Friedlander	£246,000
8	Brown Shipley	£204,000
9	M. Samuel	£170,000
10	Baring	£159,000
11	Lazards	£124,000
12	Morgan Grenfell	£91,000

Source: Adapted from Kellet 1967: 95

banks took advantage of the booming stock market. They lent heavily on speculative ventures. Ways were found of circumventing the foreign exchange rules by UK merchant banks. This included reinvesting their existing dollar deposits into foreign commercial opportunities (such as oil rig leasing) and to lend to newly developing countries such as Mexico and Brazil. The leading group of the 1960s borrowed to finance their expansion. As will become clear through the experience of Hill Samuel shown in subsequent chapters, the secondary banking crisis of 1973–5 terminated many of these expansion plans. The collapse of the secondary bank fringe brought about a dramatic loss of confidence in the financial sector underlined by the fall in property and share prices.

The major merchant banks were never in serious financial difficulties. Yet aside from their own losses they had to shoulder the financial burden of the weaker banks which did fail as the Bank of England launched a 'lifeboat' – a collective rescue operation of the secondary banks. This entailed a contribution by all the banks to bail out the more imprudent. The resulting alteration in the strategic disposition of the merchant banks was clear-cut. The paramount virtue became conservatism. Clients now valued safety above all else. Previously leading expansionist banks such as Hambros, Hill Samuel and Kleinwort shunned the opportunities which emerged in the commercial lending markets in the second half of the 1970s. The second requirement became diversity. It was clear that those who had failed (Slater Walker, London & County Securities) had concentrated on a narrow range of business. When their specialist markets failed they had no alternative sources of income. The message from those who had survived was the need to maintain a range of businesses. At Kleinwort Benson profit levels were maintained due to the contribution of its gold and commodities trading subsidiary, Sharps Pixley.

Overall, UK merchant banks lost out to international competitors in the 1970s. Opportunities were numerous; these included the abolition of fixed commissions on the New York Stock Exchange and the invitations to prospective purchasers from Dillon Read or Shearson and Lehman Brothers. UK banks also failed to exploit the fast-growing international capital (Euro-dollar) market in the face of overseas competitors. Warburg and Kleinwort Benson's (innovators in the early 1970s) market shares were squeezed by Credit Suisse, Union Bank of Switzerland, Chase Manhattan and Citibank. Meanwhile, in the domestic market competition emerged from the clearing banks who attempted to take up some of the slack in the commercial lending market.

Warburg did especially well out of these new circumstances. It managed to expand its international operations. The expansion included offices in Japan, an alliance with French bank Paribas and the purchase of US investment bank A. G. Becker. Warburg committed more resources than Kleinwort Benson to maintaining a presence in the Euro-dollar market. Morgan Grenfell's new leadership after 1974 mounted an aggressive expansion of its corporate finance work. By contrast extraordinary losses in other UK merchant banks were covered by reserves and did not appear in the published reports. Although none of the merchant banks made official losses in this decade (the reverse of the auto companies) some clearly suffered.

In the 1980s the nature of merchant banking in Britain has undoubtedly been transformed. Yet it was the decisions made by the banks in the previous decades which help to explain the form which that transformation took.

The removal of foreign exchange controls in 1979 by the incoming Conservative government was followed by the announcement that the restrictions which regulated the London Stock Exchange would be lifted. There were three main implications for merchant banks. In dropping exchange controls it now became easier for foreign competitors to enter the London market. Second, the freedom to export and import all forms of currency opened up the possibility of a new type of demand: clients of the merchant banks could now expect a worldwide service in all the main product and geographical markets. Third, the ability of non-stock exchange members to trade in securities meant merchant banks could offer an enlarged investment banking service, that is, from commercial loans through to corporate finance as well as issuing new equity and trading equity.

Most of the UK merchant banks reacted slowly to this unprecedented situation. The difficulties of the mid–1970s had established a high degree of caution among the merchant bankers. The importance of maintaining a solid reputation after the horrors of the secondary banking crisis still dominated their minds. Furthermore the long-established culture of most UK merchant banks put a premium on taking advantage of short-term opportunities using relatively small amounts of capital. The changes of the early 1980s required more formalized planning capacities and a long-term implication for the commitment of human, technological and capital resources.

The UK merchant banks concentrated therefore on the deregulation of the Stock Exchange. The possibility arose of acquiring existing stock jobbers and brokers or to develop such operations from scratch. The acquisition of Hoare Govett by Security Pacific Bank in June 1982 set off two years of negotiations. The merchant banks found themselves competing for stock brokers and jobbers against foreign securities houses (e.g. Merrill Lynch), foreign commercial banks (e.g. Citibank) and domestic clearing banks (e.g. Barclays). However there were great differences in the routes which individual banks pursued. Only Warburg and Kleinwort Benson had the funds to purchase a stock broker and jobber. Others acquired a stock broker and then sought to establish an in-house jobbing function by attracting experienced personnel from other firms.

The UK merchant banks also became aware of the rapid globalization of the financial securities market. Yet they were preoccupied with the implications of entering the domestic securities market. Most chose to delay decisions or downplay international opportunities. Only Warburg and Kleinwort Benson developed an early international and domestic strategy, combining London and expanded US and Far Eastern operations. After the 'Big Bang' in October 1986, when the deregulation of the London Stock Exchange took effect, the other merchant banks began to establish a stronger presence in the USA and Japan. By the end of the 1980s most had scaled down such operations following the collapse of the securities markets after 1987.

The alterations in the UK market for financial services, its mode of regulation and the internationalization of its operators has led to the reworking of the bases of competition and therefore what constitutes a merchant bank. The members of the Accepting House Committee no longer form a single group. Instead three different types of merchant bank have emerged as a result of the wider changes within the sector competing on very different strengths. The first category is filled by those merchant banks which have sought to become global investment banks, offering a complete range of financial services. In the second comes the merchant banks who had entered the domestic securities market hesitantly and defensively but who did not have the resources to operate on an international scale. The third category covers the small Accepting House Committee members who did not even try to enter the global securities market. Instead they confined their existing business to the provision of bespoke financial advice and limited capital to established clients. Table 2.7 indicates the spread of such activities by showing the scale of activity in: (a) the traditional acceptances market, and (b) total clients per merchant bank in mergers and acquisitions activity – essentially corporate finance strength and securities operations.

The turbulence in the financial services sector of the 1980s has left few unscathed. Kleinwort Grieveson for example had difficulties coping with processing the paperwork involved and were forced to spend large amounts in order to meet Stock Exchange regulations. Hill Samuel was acquired by the TSB Group in 1987. The stock market crash of October 1987 highlighted the very thin layers of profitability on which the new securities trading firms were operating. The major firms of County Natwest, Barclays de Zoete Wedd and Warburg are all understood to have suffered substantial losses due to the equities they were holding on their books. The unpredictable nature of the changes in the rejuvenated financial services sector is illustrated by

Table 2.7 UK merchant banks: total acceptances and mergers and acquisitions transactions

	(a) Ranking by total acceptances ('000)	
		1986
1	Kleinwort Benson	£702,444
2	Hambros	£549,611
3	Morgan Grenfell	£413,833
4	N. M. Rothschild	£356,643
5	Samuel Montagu	£346,182
6	S. G. Warburg	£321,655
7	Baring	£242,823
8	Schroders	£165,832
9	Hill Samuel	£136,800
10	Charterhouse	£126,939
11	Lazards	£124,584
12	Singer & Friedlander	£120,511
13	Brown Shipley	£72,122
14	Robert Fleming	£39,450
15	Rea Brothers	£33,595
16	Guinness Mahon	£16,976

Source: The Times 1000 – 1986–7

	(b) Mergers & acquisitions activity rankings: 1974–1986 (by number of transactions)			
		1974	*1986*	*Percent change*
1	Kleinwort Benson	37	60	+62.16%
2	Morgan Grenfell	36	51	+41.66%
3	Hill Samuel	55	39	−29.09%
4	Warburg	35	34	−2.85%
5	Hambros	22	26	+18.18%
6	Robert Fleming	16	25	+56.25%
7	Schroder	23	24	+4.35%
8	N. M. Rothschild	25	20	−20.00%
9	Baring	18	20	+11.11%
10	Charterhouse	25	20	−20.00%
11	County Bank	13	19	+46.15%
12	S. Montagu	51	16	−68.62%
13	Lazards	24	13	−45.83%
14	Barclays	6	11	+83.33%

Source: The Times 1000 – 1974–75 and *Acquisitions Monthly*, January 1987

Kleinwort Grieveson. Although making deep losses in 1988, they suffered negligible losses at the time of the crash since their paperwork backlog limited their ability to take large lines of equities.

Few beyond Warburg among the London firms have established the reputation of having made a success of the opportunities presented by the 'Big Bang'. Warburg have been able to manage and control a securities operation in conjunction with a full range of merchant banking functions. In spite of their success, important questions still remain, as in both the auto and book publishing industries. The long-term survival even of houses such as Warburg is still in doubt in a market dominated by the financial giants such as Citibank, Nomura and Deutsche Bank.

Life assurance

In many ways the life assurance sector has paralleled the developments in merchant banking during the 1960s, 1970s and 1980s. A well-defined market with clear specializations and a general stability of relations between long-established participants in 1960, has since been completely overturned. As in the case of merchant banking many of the changes of the 1980s had their roots in the 1960s.

The major assurance companies in the 1960s had established reputations in many cases going back over a century. The largest (Prudential, Britannic, Pearl, Refuge and Royal London) had developed strong emphases on the two main life assurance products: ordinary life assurance (directed at the middle-class market) and industrial life assurance (sold mainly to the working-class customers), as shown in table 2.8. The industrial working class grew in number up to the Second World War. They lacked a comprehensive state welfare system, which meant that family security depended largely on maintaining a basic life assurance. The industrial policies supplied to meet this need generally required premiums to be paid in cash on a weekly or fortnightly basis. By contrast, ordinary life policies required the payment of a year's premium in advance. Industrial life assurance was sold through a large salesforce which also collected premiums in cash; they were employed directly by the life assurance companies. Ordinary life assurance was sold through a variety of distribution channels which included insurance brokers, independent financial intermediaries and tied salesforces.

The traditional life assurers in the 1960s saw their capacity to innovate, and in particular diversify, constrained by a combination of government restrictions and customer expectations. Financial institutions, in the words of Brian Corby (appointed general manager of the Prudential in 1979), 'stuck to their own lines of business'. Established pre-war markets in the USA and the Commonwealth still supplied the majority of overseas non-life business.

However, as table 2.8 shows, ordinary life policies increased at a faster pace than industrial life assurance from 1950. The largest life assurance firms have devoted greater resources to the provision of industrial life assurance. Between 1950 and 1972 almost half their market share was taken up by the providers of unit-trust linked life assurance (see table 2.9). By 1967 ordinary life policies amounted to almost two-thirds of all life and annuity business in the UK (Channon 1978: 103).

The established participants in the life assurance market were able

Table 2.8 Analysis of premium income among selected life assurance companies 1950–1970

	1950			1960			1970		
	O	I	G	O	I	G	O	I	G
Prudential									
%	40	50	10	48	39	13	53	29	18
£	32.6	40.1	8.1	70.9	58.2	18.8	161.9	88.2	54.4
Britannic									
%	31	64	5	30	62	7	27	65	7
£	3.3	6.7	0.5	5.1	10.3	1.2	7.8	18.6	2.0
Pearl									
%	29	51	20	33	49	18	39	44	17
£	8.2	14.5	5.5	15.4	22.4	8.3	22.6	29.0	14.1
Refuge									
%	42	57	–	43	55	2	41	55	4
£	6.5	8.7	–	9.3	11.7	0.5	12.6	17.2	1.3
Royal London									
%	28	68	4	28	66	6	30	62	8
£	3.4	8.3	0.5	4.8	11.5	1.1	7.6	15.4	2.0

Source: Annual Reports
O: Ordinary life assurance
I: Industrial life assurance
G: General insurance business
(% = percentage of total premium income   £ = millions of £)

Table 2.9 Concentration of market share (by premium income) among UK life assurance companies 1950–1972 (*percentages*)

	1950	1960	1965	1970	1972
Largest Company	24.3	17.6	16.4	15.5	12.6
Largest 2	32.0	25.4	24.6	23.1	18.4
Largest 3	39.6	30.9	30.2	28.7	23.4
Largest 5	49.3	40.8	38.7	38.1	31.8
Largest 10	65.7	54.5	50.7	52.0	45.8

Source: Channon 1978: 97

to take advantage of particularly strong barriers to entry. The major obstacle to new entrants was the widespread distribution networks, built up over decades, of the existing life assurance companies. To compete along the same lines would oblige the new entrant to start a salesforce from scratch at great expense. The independent intermediaries used by the suppliers of ordinary life assurance, were no less easy to break into. An additional difficulty was posed by the generally held assumption that in order to attract customers, a life assurance provider must enjoy a clear reputation for declaring bonus payments on their 'with profits' life policies.

During the 1960s, new competitors were able to circumvent some of these barriers. One means was by using a sound reputation in another market. Life insurers from Canada, for example, such as Sun Life and Canada Life expanded into the UK. The large resources of the parent firms were used by their UK subsidiaries to create salesforces. Another approach was to offer an identifiably new product which was, say, less dependent on a bonus payments record. The main form which these new products took was the 'unit-linked life assurance'. This type of product was based on the future performance of a selected set of investments. The implications for the life assurance sector were far-reaching. As the unit-linked assurance products grew in popularity, their existence questioned the long-standing distinction between life assurance and other forms of consumer savings and investment.

As in the merchant banks the events of the 1970s posed serious problems for the life assurance sector. By 1974 most of the major companies were forced to curtail the expansion and diversification programmes they had begun in response to the new entrants and product forms of the previous decade. They were confronted by three main forces.

First, the stock market crash of 1973–4 and the difficulties of the more aggressive unit-linked life assurance companies made the major companies reconsider their positions. Conservatism became the watchword. Second, in spite of the setbacks to the unit-linked products around 1973–4 the nature of demand shifted in the later 1970s. Consumers from the lower social strata became relatively more sophisticated in their financial service requirements. Alternative sources of advice to the insurance agent, such as banks, building societies and independent brokers, were increasingly consulted. Having drawn back from the new unit-linked products in the mid-1970s, the established life assurance companies were confronted with their renewed popularity by the end of the decade. Unit-linked products were based on the value of the linked investments performance on the stock market. Stock market values recovered and rose through the late 1970s faster than the conservative valuation of traditional life assurance profits. Unit-linked policies therefore grew in their appeal. At the same time, the boom in the late 1970s in unit trusts led to important in-roads being made into the markets which had hitherto been the preserve of the main life assurance companies.

The evident decline in the size of the industrial life assurance business in contrast to the ordinary life area created further problems for the established UK companies. Given the scale of the resources devoted to supporting industrial life business, these organizations soon became vulnerable to rising costs. Yet this occurred in the face of shrinking demand. Cost control became imperative rather than expansion of the product range. This was clearly demonstrated in the energy devoted to the reorganization of field staff, the reduction of employee numbers and the schemes introduced which linked pay to productivity.

As in the case of the merchant banks, the 1980s clearly mark a break point in the history of the life assurance sector. Yet both show how the legislation of that decade only partly explains their new form. Government intervention combined with, and in some cases extended, the changes already in progress in financial services. The ideological conviction that above all controls should be radically loosened in the City did not become reality. The government in practice brought in changes in a rather measured way. As the effects of one act of de- or, more properly, re-regulation was introduced so another was announced, forming a sequence over nine years.

As was shown in the previous section, the first major change was the government's abolition in 1979 of foreign exchange controls. Prior to this date the City had, in effect, been divided between firms who dealt solely with foreign currency denominated assets (e.g. Eurobonds) and those who engaged only in domestic finance. The life assurance companies fell mainly into the second category since they had been required by previous administrations to reinvest their sterling inflows in UK gilts and equities. The abolition of foreign exchange controls posed enormous questions for the main UK life assurance companies. The main problem centred on how to develop techniques appropriate to foreign investment in a much larger, more complex market.

The influx of wealth from North Sea oil and the recovery of parts of the UK economy from 1982 had a sharp impact on the life assurance companies. Increases in disposable income, a rising stock market and the government's privatization programme all heightened consumers' awareness of the potential investment returns available. Comparisons were made between the returns on life assurance *vis-à-vis* unit trusts and direct investment in the stock market. As will become clear in chapter 3, quick decisions were required of the life assurance companies in order to accommodate the new demand. Almost in unison, the life assurance companies which had held back from the unit trust market in the 1970s now sought to compete for unit trust business. The traditional demarcations of the retail financial services and the separation of the skills involved could no longer hold. The dramatic increase in funds under management in the mid–1980s pointed to greater potential profits and therefore intensified competition further.

The budget speech of March 1984 included the immediate withdrawal of tax relief on life assurance premiums. The argument behind the act was that the tax advantage which life assurance premiums enjoyed was an unfair advantage over other forms of investment. The life assurance sector was shocked. A serious reduction in new business was predicted. In reality the effect was slight. Consumers saw life assurance products as complementary to other forms of investment rather than direct substitutes. The withdrawal of tax relief had much greater effect on the comparative financial position of the life assurance companies and the unit trust firms. It led to an unequal tax situation. In the case of life assurance, tax is paid by the assurer with profits distributed after tax. The tax on the gains achieved by alternative forms of investment, such as unit trusts, is paid by the consumer/investor. The unequal tax situation and the lead which the unit trust firms had taken in energetic marketing techniques meant that the old life assurance companies had to move quickly and establish a position in these new areas.

The effect of the 'Big Bang' in 1986 on the life assurance companies was less than at first supposed. Contrary to the beliefs of the merchant banks the deregulation of the Stock Exchange was not 'put on for the sake of the Prudential, Legal & General and others like them' (interview) although the commissions charged to them on equity dealing fell. This area was only one part of the life assurance companies' activities. More important were the Financial Services Act and the Building Societies Act. The government in 1985 was quite clear in its intentions: in the retail end of the financial services sector the inability of clearing banks, life assurance companies, building societies and unit trust/investment firms to compete should end. Instead they should be able to compete directly by offering similar products if they wished. The two Acts meant that banks, building societies, unit trust firms and life assurance companies could all now offer deposit taking, life assurance, mortgages and other investment products.

The effects of the Acts have destabilized the competitive environment of the life assurance specialists in a number of ways. The Financial Services Act altered many of the established working practices of the traditional providers of life assurance. Clearing banks could set up their own life assurance company and sell their products directly to their banking customers, thus bypassing the need to create the costly sales network of Prudential, Legal & General or Pearl. Information on commissions paid to the selling agent had now to be made available to consumers.

A further piece of legislation changed the Social Securities Act and effected the very lucrative pension fund management business of the traditional life companies. The reform of the Act allowed employees to transfer their pension plans from their employer's company plan into one of their own choosing. The dominant effect of the apparent portability of pension contributions has been to force the companies who provided pension plans to ensure that the returns on the pensions they offered were high enough to maintain their market share. At the same time an improved marketing effort was required in order to attract employees contemplating leaving other pension plans.

The full effect of the regulatory changes in the retail financial services sector has yet to take complete effect. None the less, the outcome of these changes in the 1980s is clear: as in the merchant banking sector, none of the established providers of financial services can guarantee their survival in the new conditions of severe competition. The alterations in the traditional life assurance houses market in the preceding two decades had already undermined their stability. The upheavals of the 1980s threaten to destroy the remnants of that balance completely. It would appear that the firms with the greatest chance of survival are those who are able to provide a wide range of products which can command competitive prices in each of the relevant markets.

Conclusion

The central aim of this chapter has been to identify and explain the dominant shifts in both the immediate competitive environment of the four sectors under study, together with the broader political and economic context which they all inhabit. Four outcomes of this task deserve highlighting, namely: the depth of the common problems posed to all four sectors; the insights derived from using an appropriate time-scale; the variety of ways in which maturity can break down; and the linkages between the political and sectoral levels which suggest the differences in reported and actual change.

The first point to emphasize from the experience of the sectors is the emergence of a formidable set of common problems at firm level. Long-standing post-war nostrums and company taboos have collapsed in all the industries. Such rules simply could not survive the massive alterations in markets. Every firm in these sectors has had to contend with new entrants. This included the auto industry, which had supposedly reached its final form of oligopoly in the 1960s. In all the sectors, the new entrants included global operators who then have established international performance standards. All the firms have had to adjust to assessments of their operations based on new definitions of being world-class.

Combined with the impact of macroeconomic dislocation has been the appearance of unprecedented productivity and efficiency requirements. Simultaneously, all the managers involved have had to confront the issues of: first, contraction/survival (in 1973 and 1979–81 especially), and then growth from the mid–1980s, and latterly contraction once again. Equally, those managers found that they also had to solve the nest of problems which a new generation of technology introduced. This applied not only in product and production areas but across every element of the organization. The enhanced speed of change such technology offered confronted all the sectors. This high density of common problems underscores therefore the emphasis placed in chapter 1 on the need for firms to create a compound capacity to manage change.

Secondly, the use of a time-scale which covers the 1960s, 1970s and 1980s has been critical to understanding both the nature of competition in given sectors and as means of gauging the significance of supposedly epoch-making national political acts. Above all, the bases on which firms compete in all four sectors under study have changed profoundly in that time; these changes are summarized in table 2.10. Yet as table 2.10 indicates, rarely has there been a simple break from one period to another with a new set of requirements replacing the existing bases. Rather, bases of competition in one era become the essential prerequisites for new company capacities in the next.

In the case of automobiles the price competition and quality standards of the mid–1970s with their requirements for production efficiency and engineering capacity did not somehow disappear after 1979. They intensified in the conditions of over-supply, new consumer demands and new market entrants. Similarly in life assurance, the bases of reputation or effective distribution channels remained as relevant in the 1980s as they had done twenty years previously. The critical point was that these had to be maintained alongside the provision of an extended product range. The keynote for the firms involved in all the sectors was that in order to compete they had to be able to raise the standards of their existing competences while also augmenting those with genuinely new strengths. This account therefore underscores the need for companies to develop not merely single 'winning' or 'excellent' strengths but something far more demanding: layers of competences which are built up and, equally important, sustained over the long term (for a summary across the four sectors see table 2.10).

The third insight which deserves separate attention is the way the mature state of these sectors has broken down. Some might argue that the radical possibilities of new technology or decisive government intervention in the 1980s is a sufficient explanation of the widely noted onset of dematurity (Hamel and Prahalad 1989) in such industries. In our view these forces indicate the immediate trigger of that process but they do not fully explain it. As the previous sections have shown, in all four sectors, fundamental challenges to the nature of products, alternative production processes and new forms of demand were already apparent. In many cases the impact of the two oil crises or the stock market crash of 1974 had already greatly disturbed established patterns of competition. It was their combination with key political acts or developments in information technology, for example, which enhanced their impact in the 1980s.

Table 2.10 Bases of competition in the UK automobile, book publishing, merchant banking and life assurance sectors

Automobiles

1960s	1970s	1980s
1 Production capacity	1 Production capacity and efficiency	All intensify plus greater interdependency and greater speed of impact in the 1980s
2 Base price	2 Growing price competition	
3 Base quality	3 Increasing universal quality standards related to consumer education	
4 Engineering capability	4 Engineering capability increasingly vital	*The new bases are:*
5 Specialist producers (relative price competition)	5 Above now also applies to specialist producers	6 Requirements for new business organization and networks
		7 Applying new technologies to current problems
		8 Flexibility of manufacture and economies of scope not scale
		9 New knowledge bases become critical e.g. marketing organization and human resources and increasing commercial requirements

Book Publishing

1960s	1970s	1980s
1 Attracting best authors	5 Internationalize 1: change to local house publishing and ability to attract local authors	8 Internationalize 2: USA, Western Europe and Far East
2 Editorial and production process	6 Managerial competence marketing and financial skills	9 Foreign currency management
3 Price understood against range of product	7 Price now becomes increasingly important	10 Production and distribution competence
4 Ability to export		11 Managerial competence to meet above changes critical
		12 Technological changes in product and production becoming important
		13 Size

Merchant Banks

1960s

1 Diversification into wider range of services

2 Asset growth

3 Corporate finance client list

4 Quality and nature of relationships with clients

5 Changing human resource base

1970s

6 Operational implementation of 1960s' strategic changes

7 Adaptation capacity in a more punishing environment

1980s

8 Performance in global financial markets

9 Performance in UK securities

10 Corporate finance capacity to meet industrial expansion

Life Assurance

1960s

1 Bonus declarations

2 Reputation

3 Effectiveness of distribution channels

4 Investment performance (cost control)

1970s

5 Limited product adaptation and innovation

1980s

6 Diversification of product range

7 New distribution channels

8 Changes in knowledge base

9 Innovative response capability

Moreover, this chapter gives a full empirical challenge, for the sectors concerned, to the nostrum that change at the level of the industry has been exceptional in the 1980s. In our view the pace of change began to accelerate in the 1970s, an increase that has been maintained, and its impact deepened, in the 1980s.

The fourth general feature of note from the chapter is the importance of linking the political and the economic. In the simplest sense the way government intervention has altered both market form or company action is easily demonstrated. The examples of 1986 in financial services, state funding in the auto industry or the decision to leave untouched the Net Book Agreement in publishing in 1989 come readily to mind. More complex however is judging the significance of the character of the so-called Thatcher revolution in the 1980s. Some of the more extreme claims relating to macroeconomic performance were shown to be overstated at the beginning of the chapter. Even with regard to the ark of the covenant, monetarism, the Conservative administrations from 1979 cannot argue they were innovators. What stands out instead is the consistently turbulent profile of the national economy across a succession of administrations of all colours.

The critical difference lies at the level of political rhetoric. What has been substantially new in the 1980s has been the combination of a qualified set of government measures with the establishment of possibly the most effective radical political language of the post-war era. In spite of its only partial foundation in the economic record, Thatcherism has had an enormous impact on the way business and people in general think, as Bradbury (1989) perceptively notes. In particular the new creed has done two related things: in part it has been the cause of the extreme economic conditions management has faced in the 1980s, yet at the same time it has supplied a key resource when management has tried to cope with the outcome of those changes at the level of the firm. Both government rhetoric and action has created a context in which management has been more prepared to undertake certain fundamental changes. The demonstration effect of truly radical government policy initiatives which paid scant respect to economic and social taboos born of consensus was immensely powerful. The tactical adjustments and impressive ability of the government to survive, though less widely appreciated, also offered an ironic lesson in managing change.

This chapter represents one version of the character of the automobile, book publishing, merchant banking and life assurance sectors of the UK economy and the changing political context during the

1960s, 1970s and 1980s. It represents a benchmark against which one can assess the action of firms operating within those areas. Yet one thing must be made abundantly clear: this in no way makes assumptions about how those involved should have acted – quite the reverse. As chapter 1 pointed out, what is of interest are the differences in the way managers perceive the forces which have made up their environment; in other words the divergent constructions they put on the industry and market patterns outlined here and hence the contrasting paths they subsequently choose. Furthermore one is equally mindful of the way people actively create their own context and through their own actions modify that environment. Nowhere is this more true than in the firm, as the next chapter will demonstrate.

3

Understanding the Environment

The major conclusion to be drawn from examining competition among the firms in the four sectors of automobile manufacture, book publishing, merchant banking and life assurance is that:

- there is an observable difference in the way the higher performing firms manage change from their lesser performing counterparts, and
- a pattern emerges, across the four sectors, from the actions taken by the higher performing organizations.

That pattern is represented in the five interrelated aspects of managing strategic and operational change shown in figure 3.1.

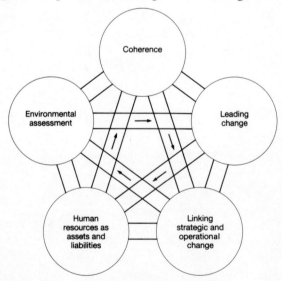

Figure 3.1 Managing change for competitive success: the five central factors

Clearly these five factors require definition and elaboration. The task of this and the following chapters therefore is to explore what the factors mean, how they are constituted and their relevance to the firms across the sectors concerned.

What will become clear is that each factor contains two main components:

1 the primary conditioning features which logically have to exist before
2 the secondary actions and mechanisms can have any meaningful effect.

Figure 3.2 provides a summary of the characteristics of each factor.

The five central factors for managing change

Environmental assessment

The process of competition often begins from the understanding a firm develops of its environment. This research shows that it is not enough for firms to regard judgements of their external competitive world as only a technical procedure. On the contrary, the requirement is for organizations to become open learning systems. In other words, the assessment of the competitive environment cannot be the responsibility of a specialist function. Nor does it happen through neat, separate acts. Strategy creation tends to emerge from the way a company, at all levels, processes information about its environment.

Leading change

The main conclusion with regard to leading change is that there are no universal rules. The opposite is true. Leadership is acutely sensitive to context. The choosing of a leader clearly is affected by those who make the choice and the circumstances in which they do so. The problems faced by the incoming leader are derived from the circumstances which the leader inherits. The areas of manoeuvre available to the new leader in deciding what to change and how to go about it are bounded by the environment within and outside the firm.

The critical leadership tasks in managing change are more incremental and often less spectacular than the prevailing business press images. Leading change involves linking action by people at all levels of the

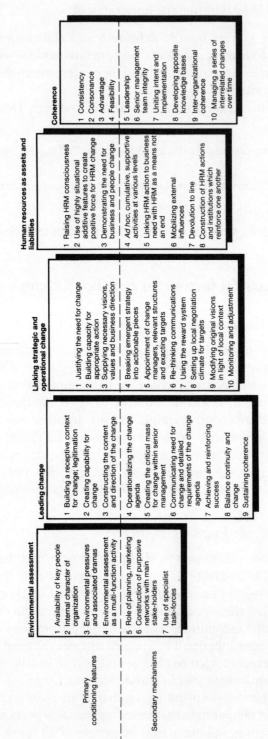

Figure 3.2 Managing change for competitive success: characteristics of the five central factors

The content of the figure is as follows:

Environmental assessment

Primary conditioning features
1 Availability of key people
2 Internal character of organization
3 Environmental pressures and associated dramas
4 Environmental assessment as a multi-function activity

Secondary mechanisms
5 Role of planning, marketing
6 Construction of purposive networks with main stake-holders
7 Use of specialist task-forces

Leading change
1 Building a receptive context for change; legitimation
2 Creating capability for change
3 Constructing the content and direction of the change
4 Operationalizing the change agenda
5 Creating the critical mass for change within senior management
6 Communicating need for change and detailed requirements of the change agenda
7 Achieving and reinforcing success
8 Balance continuity and change
9 Sustaining coherence

Linking strategic and operational change
1 Justifying the need for change
2 Building capacity for appropriate action
3 Supplying necessary visions, values and business direction
4 Breaking emergent strategy into actionable pieces
5 Appointment of change managers, relevant structures and exacting targets
6 Re-thinking communications
7 Using the reward system
8 Setting up local negotiation climate for targets
9 Modifying original visions in light of local context
10 Monitoring and adjustment

Human resources as assets and liabilities
1 Raising HRM consciousness
2 Use of highly situational additive features to create positive force for HRM change
3 Demonstrating the need for business and people change
4 Ad hoc, cumulative, supportive activities at various levels
5 Linking HRM action to business need with HRM as a means not an end
6 Mobilizing external influences
7 Devolution to line
8 Construction of HRM actions and institutions which reinforce one another

Coherence
1 Consistency
2 Consonance
3 Advantage
4 Feasibility
5 Leadership
6 Senior management team integrity
7 Uniting intent and implementation
8 Developing apposite knowledge bases
9 Inter-organizational coherence
10 Managing a series of interrelated changes over time

business. The primary conditioning features are critical. Early and bold actions can be counter-productive. More promising is the construction of a climate for change while at the same time laying out new directions, but prior to precise action being taken.

Linking strategic and operational change

The process of linking strategic and operational change has both an intentional and emergent character. Intentions are implemented and transformed over time. The cumulative effect of separate acts of implementation may be immensely powerful. This may even supply a new context for future strategic choices. Strategies often amount to the after-the-event labelling of such unpredictable sequences of 'successful' operational acts.

Human resources as assets and liabilities

Human resource management (HRM) relates to the total set of knowledge, skills and attitudes that firms need to compete. The differing ability of the firms studied to recognize and carry out a version of human resource management is apparent. As we shall see, this has considerable impact on their relative competitive performance. However, the disparity is less unusual when one considers the time required to create such a fragile capacity. An HRM approach is not amenable to instant construction. A longer-term learning process is involved which requires the creation of successive positive spirals of development.

Coherence in the management of change

This factor in managing change for competitive success is the most complex of the five central factors. In many ways the requirements for coherence arise from the demands of the other four. As in all the other central factors the crucial need is in ensuring that the primary conditioning features are reinforced by a complementary set of mechanisms. It is worthwhile for this factor to consider these subsidiary features more closely.

The conditioning features relate to the formation of strategy. A given strategy should be characterized by: consistency (not present inconsistent goals); consonance (by an adaptive response to its environment); advantage (provide for the maintenance of competitive advantage); and feasibility (the strategy must not create unsolvable problems).

In order for these features to prevail requires a range of secondary, complementary management action to reinforce them. As figure 3.2 indicates, there has to be a coherence of purpose among the senior management, even though individual emphases may differ. HRM activity has to produce a knowledge base which complements the strategic conditioning features. Similarly there must be interorganizational coherence across customers, suppliers, distributors and collaborators. The scope of activity implied by the preceding four factors puts the ability to manage a series of interrelated and emergent changes at a premium.

The subsequent chapters will demonstrate how the significance of the twin set of subsidiary features within each factor lies in their cumulative impact over time. The conditioning features and the secondary mechanisms derive their potency from not only their complementarity but the way they interlock and their being applied in conjunction, with sustained effort and often repeated application. One of the central characteristics of the firms under study, therefore, is that the management of strategic and operational change for competitive success is an uncertain and emergent process. Managing that process places heavy requirements on the ability of companies to adapt in all five areas. Above all it calls into question a firm's ability to create and sustain a collection of 'intangible assets': difficult for the outsider to uncover but essential to the capacity to manage strategic change and competition.

The wider implications of this framework will be assessed in the Conclusion (chapter 8).

Environmental assessment

The undoubted turbulence of the Western economies in the 1970s and 1980s has confirmed the importance of the way a firm understands its environment. Unfortunately for managers the volatile nature of that environment has made its assessment more difficult. And of course just when they were most needed, academic experts have fallen out over the optimum means of comprehending either the firm's environment or the way it might change.

Economic and business commentators, and in particular those associated with the computing and micro-electronics areas, are right to highlight the unique challenges posed by information technology. The ramifications of the use of the microchip are far-reaching and their collective impact has been rightly dubbed revolutionary. Computer-based, information technology looks set to recast the character of society in much the same way as the technologies associated with the agricultural and industrial transformations of previous centuries. Although computer technology has taken virtually the whole twentieth century to develop, its frightening potential became fully apparent during the 1980s.

The use of computer hardware and software has suggested truly epoch-making changes which have already altered the nature of industries and shifted the balance of whole economies. Yet beneath such over-arching movements at the level of society a formidable array of more specific problems have arisen from the baser rumblings of the business cycle, international trading relations or even consumers. As chapter 2 showed, there are truly novel aspects to the character of the environment which business has faced in the 1970s and 1980s. The machinations of politicians and their effects on industry and commerce have always been with us, yet the breaking of the post-war consensus in the 1980s is manifestly clear. In the economic sphere the conjunction of inflation and recession from the early 1970s was a phenomenon unknown to Keynesians and neo-liberals alike; it was even more baffling to those who had the responsibility of managing a business.

Beside the specific movements within the four sectors outlined in chapter 2, all industries and services have experienced major dislocations. The traditional constellation of assumptions of industry boundaries, market mechanisms or commercial relations based on the post-war replacement demand or 1960s growth, have been shattered. In their place have appeared a new, less predictable firmament. This now includes: the management buy-out; the 'junk bond' financed acquisition used by the corporate raiders who stalk underperforming assets; Japanese producers with their own definitions of best practice confirmed by their market shares in Western countries; the penetration of marketing into organizations previously unconcerned with such instruments; and not least the unpredictable nature of international currencies and exchange rates.

Yet if this constellation has altered so dramatically, how are companies to produce accurate celestial maps? What devices are appropriate to assessing the movement of the commercial heavens? Above all, can one suggest means of strategic navigation which go beyond the sextant and the astrolabe? The first step to providing an answer is by inspecting the existing approaches to environmental assessment.

Industrial organization

The industrial organization (IO) economists discussed in chapter 1 have staked a strong claim to expert status in understanding a firm's environment. There now exist well-developed means of identifying competitive structures. These centre on the Porterian industry model, life cycle approaches and strategic group analysis.

As we showed in chapter 1, the hallmark of Porter is the way he addresses not only the 'established combatants in a particular industry', but also the potential entrants or substitutes and the bargaining force of buyers and suppliers. The strategist at company level can use the model to assess, for example, the threat of competition from outside the industry. This would include consideration of economies of scale, capital requirements, access to distribution channels, product differentiation, cost advantages derived from experience.

The model can be readily applied to the economic environment of the four sectors under study. In the car industry the enormous capital requirements of developing totally new models (around £2 billion in the late 1980s) is enough to exclude the new entrants to the ranks of the volume producers. In book publishing, desk top publishing systems have enabled the proliferation of small scale ventures (10,000 were registered in 1989/90), yet their reliance on personal distribution severely limits their impact.

A firm can also locate itself within its environment according to the stage of its industry life cycle. Conditions will vary widely therefore between the early infant phase (with many entrants and products ill-defined) and maturity, with well-established products, saturated markets and immense pressure on margins and market share.

Strategic group analysis has been developed in order to be more precise about the pattern of competitive relations in the view of the difficulty of defining the boundaries and participants of given industries. The approach has been developed in view of the upheavals of the 1970s and 1980s in particular. Applying a simple differentiation between domestic and international producers, or specialist and diversified, allows a more fine-grain map of the competitive environment to emerge. In merchant banking these criteria quickly distinguish those houses such as Warburg who attempt to offer a complete range of services both in the UK and abroad, versus those specializing in, say, corporate finance only within the City of London. Other means of creating such maps include the differences between organizations in size, pricing, ownership, technological leadership and product diversity.

It would be misleading to suggest that the powerful techniques of environmental assessment which have been developed within the IO tradition see the world through an entirely rational lens. Porter's work is often reconstructed around its central elements and simplifying themes – such as the value chain or generic strategies. Yet on closer inspection his work points to the complexities of understanding the environment and the range of possible action. As he stressed in 1987 (Porter 1987), in contrast to the Boston Consulting Group's emphasis on scale and market share leadership, 'there is an infinite number of possible strategies even within the same industry.' He also recognizes in passing how 'no tool can remove the need for creativity in selecting the right strategy. Great companies don't imitate competitors, they act differently . . . we do need to discover how the process of creativity takes place.'

Others who operate mainly within the bounds of IO and neo-classical economics have also come to recognize the limitations of the tools of their craft. Thomas and McGee (1985) in their paper 'Making sense of complex industries' (centred on the reprographics industry) acknowledge the key influence of the changes in industry and market composition in the long term. They highlight the importance of when and how firms enter an industry and the significance this may have subsequently for the way managers in those firms understand their environment. The natural logic of the industry life cycle advocates has shown them the immense difficulties of even conceiving of a firm's environment at certain points. The myriad technological possibilities contained within the period of infancy within a single industry has led them to place greater emphasis on the more subjective judgements of entrepreneurs (see, for example, Wheelwright 1987).

Planning

The first cousins of the industrial economists are the professional business planners. Their rise to prominence, notably in the USA, in the post-war years was founded on the conviction that the environment was amenable to rational observation and reasonably accurate forecasting. Business plans could be formulated accordingly. Company structures could be adjusted to complement those plans. The success of giant US corporations in Western mass markets down to the 1970s confirmed the view as well as providing a role model for some of the larger European companies (Marginson 1985; Gospel forthcoming).

The growth in the extent and depth of planning techniques over the post-war decades was prodigious. Attempts to categorize them agree on the breadth of the field. Pearce and Robinson (1985) distinguish between what they call the 'operating environment', specific to a firm, and the 'remote environment', which is common to most firms. The remote environment refers to national economic variables, social developments, technology, political and legal influences. It is interesting that they regard the marketing function as best-suited to collect and analyse data relating to the operating environment (made up of customers, markets, competitors and industries). A rather different picture will emerge from the evidence of our research companies below.

The major responsibility of the planner has been to link the result of this appraisal of the external environment with the internal abilities of the organization. The most well-known method for supplying that connection is through SWOT analysis. This requires, first, the identification and classification of opportunities and threats and second, the assessment of their relevance to the internal abilities (strengths and weaknesses) of the firm. The means of classifying and linking the two domains has become increasingly elaborate (for an overview see Greenley 1989). The rising popularity of marketing techniques – directed at exploiting the potential of both internal and external market relations – in the UK during the 1980s has added to the planners' SWOT armoury.

Indeed, the armoury is by now crammed full. If one takes the example of forecasting techniques applied to the environment the point is forcibly made. Higgins (1980) uses a three-fold classification embracing economic (e.g. regression analysis), technological (e.g. cross-impact analysis) and social and political (e.g. value profiles) forecasting techniques. His inventory runs to 26 major methods. Some of the methods by now have long pedigrees. Among the most prominent are the Delphi method and scenario analysis (Zenter 1982). The application of computer memory and processing power has added a new dimension to such techniques.

Just as some of the IO economists have found their weapons are not up to the onslaught presented by the 1980s, so this uncertainty has affected the planners. The major problem was that, in spite of this arsenal of forecasting and planning techniques, large parts of Western industry failed badly in the face of the barrage of environmental shifts in the 1980s (Zan 1987). The essential problem was two-fold. Many of the planning techniques assumed that they could (1) mount objective observations of the environment, and (2) plan accordingly.

It is noticeable that the more successful organizations have been much more self-critical of their planning. Above all they questioned its supposed objectivity. Shell International provides an excellent example. The group has made a series of alterations: from its 'comprehensive financial planning system' adopted in 1965, to its pioneering introduction of scenario planning in 1971, through to its total revamp of the system around internal 'strategy consultancy' in the 1980s. Perhaps the essence of their approach has been their refusal to rely on the techniques to supply adequate environmental assessment and planning. Shell instead has devoted enormous energy to discovering how their managers at all levels understand their environment, how that knowledge can be generalized and a 'common understanding' generated as the foundation for action (de Geus 1988).

Industry, culture and perception

Somewhat distant from the front line commercial battle of the planners, other analysts have developed a different way of understanding the environment. It does not constitute a school of thought. What unites these commentators is their willingness to tackle the imperfect and subjective way that managers perceive their environment.

One of the strongest brands of this thinking centres on the notion of industry culture. If an industry is a collective categorization of firms, then it is entirely logical for certain shared beliefs to emerge. Gregory (1982) shows how such a grid of values informed business relations in the development of the English woollen industry. Others have identified the changing pattern of these shared assumptions across the stages of sector life cycles (Shearman and Burrell 1987; Smith, Whipp and Willmott 1988; Huff 1982).

Researchers trying to explain the governance of the US economy have reached similar conclusions. They observe how governance is maintained via a range of mechanisms: markets, hierarchies, 'clan' and 'community' groupings. It appears that 'each of these mechanisms . . . operates according to different logics', where 'shared norms among different actors . . . are alternative mechanisms to markets and hierarchies for governing behaviour'. They conclude that 'non-market forces are far more important in the governance of the American economy than is usually recognised' (Hollingsworth and Lindberg 1985). Firms seldom collect 'clean' data on the environment; it has to be perceived, constructed. How that is done will be affected by the values of those concerned and the pre-existing norms which structures their thought.

Sound examples appear in the work of scholars from different countries. In the USA, Scott-Morton (1986) demonstrates the powerful impact of chief executives' world views on the way a company approaches, engages with and decodes information from its environment. Melin's (1985) study of the Scandinavian television industry in the 1970s and 1980s is equally instructive. The crisis in the industry in the 1970s arose from the demand for colour TV reaching saturation point, rapid changes in product and production technology, and the combination of over-capacity plus new entrants with unique advantages. Melin demonstrates that who was responsible for the unusual version of the environment held by the ailing Tandberg or Luxor companies was vital:

> The power structure, in both Luxor and Tandbergs, was centralised. In this autocratic milieu there was only one person who had the general view of the firm's activities and who monopolised the interpretation of the structural freedom of action for the firm. (Melin, 1985)

Understanding the environment: action and interpretation

The results of our research suggest that the way firms comprehend their environment, including the relevant bases of competition, cannot be encapsulated solely by the structures of the IO economists nor by reference to the tools of the planners alone. In order to appreciate how an organization reaches an understanding of its environment requires consideration of four related aspects:

1 how the process of understanding and assessment combines analysis, judgement and action
2 that the process is shaped jointly by the dominant logics of an industry and the internal features of the firm
3 recognition that environmental assessment occurs across the whole organization
4 above all, analysis, judgement and action seldom reflect the well-ordered progressions of the traditional planning manuals. The problems of recognition, acceptance and contest are legion.

The first point to appreciate about the way a firm assesses its environment is that it does not occur through a single act or at a given point. Instead it arises from a sequence of actions through time (cf. Gilbert and Strebel 1988: 79; Pettigrew 1985b). That process is open to manifold influences. No matter how sophisticated the instruments which a firm uses, they have to be applied by someone. By themselves the techniques can do little. What matters is who uses them and how they are used. Computer networks in some sectors (e.g. travel, retailing – see Earl and Runge 1987) now supply unprecedented amounts of information: they do not tell the recipients what to do with it (Whipp, Pettigrew and Sparrow 1989). This will become clear presently in the case of Chrysler UK in the auto industry. Management failed to appreciate that how the techniques were applied was of immense importance to their effectiveness.

The second key feature of the process of environmental assessment is its lack of innocence or isolation. Even in pure mathematics it is now recognized that the supposedly scientific laws and protocols of proof are not immune from the contexts in which they are produced. In management the link is even stronger. It is not simply that those who assess the firm's environment are influenced to a greater or lesser degree by their 'backgrounds' or personal values. This implies that there exists, external to the firm, an absolute, objective environment which awaits inspection. The problem is much deeper.

The individual or collective beliefs of managers fundamentally affect the way they conceive of the environment in the first place (Whipp 1984). Such beliefs are equally vital to the way they collect and evaluate what they see as relevant data (Grinyer and Spender 1979). But the following case examples will show something more. By the very act of assessment and their subsequent behaviour, managers are in part creating their own environment. As will become clear, the actions of Longman's staff in the book trade in the 1980s has not only altered the shape of the market it has also helped redefine its nature. The major practical issue is that firms differ in the extent to which they recognize both the subjectivity of their understanding of their environment and the consequences of their actions.

In all of the organizations studied, the very attempt by someone to identify the critical components of the firm's competitive context implied judgement and choice between alternatives. Such choices were almost by definition controversial: they conflicted with the world view of certain functions or professional groups. The process of assessment, therefore, cannot be described simply as a technical exercise. In every case, as the process unfolded so it was open to influence. Acts of apparently clinical quantitative judgement (over the future size of the US book market, for example) triggered immense activity within firms; this concerned not only the accuracy of the forecasts but the implications for future resource allocation and power relations. Indeed it is the emphasis on the mode of analysis and the consequent neglect of its political significance which undermines the work of many planners.

The third and arguably the most evident common characteristic of the firms studied is that environmental assessment occurs across the organization, come what may. Each function of an organization engages with some aspect of its environment through its routine activities; distribution through customers or manufacturing with suppliers for example. A critical difference between firms is the extent to which this is realized, built upon and exploited. In other words, to assume that a single specialist planning or marketing function can by itself supply an adequate interpretation of a firm's environment is highly dangerous. In the case of Jaguar the realization was immensely valuable. Its whole turnaround rested on a new-found ability. To use the intelligence not only from its new product planning group from 1982 but also to combine it with the piercing insights which already existed elsewhere in the company. These included the views on product competition and demand from the service engineers or the movements in the industry from the purchasing department's relationships with their suppliers.

Evidence from other industries supports the point. A survey by Deloittes showed that there was no positive correlation between the performance of firms and whether they had a formal planning function (*The Economist* 1989b). It is interesting also that major companies such as General Electric and IBM in the USA have drastically reduced their central planning or marketing functions in the last year and redistributed the staff to business unit level (Lorenz 1988). Conversely, the ability to absorb, process and act upon data from the environment systematically, at all levels of the firm, has of course been demonstrated in the most chilling fashion by certain Japanese companies such as Honda, Cannon or Fujitsu in the 1980s (Hamel and Prahalad 1989).

On the evidence of the firms we have studied, the process of environmental assessment concerns much more than just forecasting or the application of discrete planning techniques. It is an uncertain process, deeply conditioned by the industrial and organizational contexts from which it emerges, and can potentially relate to many parts of an organization. In order for this sort of process to work management has to take appropriate action. As Romme (1989) puts it, there is the problem of not only environmental 'sensing', but also of 'sense-making'. Sensing of a key threat may come from an individual or department. Sense-making is broader and requires a more collective impact. The threat has to be presented so that it makes sense to the company as a whole.

There are a number of ways in which sense-making can be achieved. The effect of task forces or specialist groups at J. C. Penney or Honeywell in the early 1980s was particularly strong (Kanter 1983). The keynote was that they were drawn deliberately from a variety of fields. No single function was given disproportionate power to define the focus of attention. Longman and Jaguar will supply clear instances below. Yet gaining acceptance of such threats or key changes in the environment may be especially difficult. This is particularly true where in-house recipe knowledge cannot decode new market information.

Some management have manufactured a drama or created a quasi-crisis to overcome such obstacles. Komatsu, for example, constructed a budget which deliberately created the problem of an overvalued yen (Hamel and Prahalad 1989: 67). Jaguar constructed a 'black museum' showing poor product quality to break open the complacency of its staff. There is a major need not only to open up but to update the cognitive maps of staff. Management can then monitor the extent to which the firm is (1) sensitive to environmental signals, but (2) can collectively make sense of those signals and act upon them. The huge upheaval in the 1980s caused by changes in demand and available technology has forced these issues to the fore in manufacturing. It is fitting then for a book (Hayes, Wheelwright & Clark 1988) which attempts to summarize these requirements in the production area alone to be entitled *Dynamic Manufacturing*. What is more interesting is the choice of sub-title: *Creating the Learning Organisation*.

The following company examples drawn from four sectors will show how these features of environmental assessment combine in action. At the same time they will highlight the different pattern of activity which distinguishes the higher and lesser performing firms.

Automobiles

The experience of Jaguar and Peugeot Talbot provides a number of telling insights into the problem of environmental assessment. In the 1950s and 1960s their means of understanding the environment were basic yet adequate to the immediate market circumstances. The limitations of such devices were cruelly exposed by the crises of the 1970s. The creation of new instruments and learning how to use them appropriately has been a central feature of both companies in the 1980s.

Rootes had moved in the inter-war years from being Britain's largest car retailer to a manufacturer of medium-sized saloons. The Rootes Group of 1956, as its name suggested, had resulted from the acquisition of eight virtually bankrupt producers. Such a course relied on the accurate view of the UK car market as dominated by a relatively benign post-war replacement demand expansion. Environmental assessment was not catered for by any official department. Instead great reliance was placed on the sales acumen of Bill Rootes within the family-run business.

The attempt to move into the small car, volume market was equally well targeted in the light of changes in demand. The problems for Rootes by the early 1960s lay in the company's inability to match those objectives with its internal capacities. These were most acute in the integration of its acquisitions and the manufacturing area. This resulted in the failure to supply the production engineering base which the competition of the 1960s demanded. The consequent loss of sales and the inability to fund new models led to the purchase of Rootes by Chrysler Corporation in 1964.

The problems of the renamed Chrysler UK (CUK) were linked directly to not only the unusual view of the environment which Chrysler took but also the way that view was constructed. The essence of the Detroit management's perception of the auto industry into the 1970s was one of expansion. In common with the existing preoccupations of the Rootes board the emphasis was on increasing output. Much less concern was given to the emerging requirements in product quality. To be fair, this preoccupation was shared by others in the industry, such as the newly created BL group. Yet at CUK it is the extreme version of expansion which stands out.

This stance flew in the face of economists who foresaw a cyclical downturn in the industry by the early 1970s. The explanation has to be sought not only in the recipe knowledge of the Rootes and Chrysler senior management but also in personal terms. A memo of the Chrysler board in Detroit of 8 June 1964 contended that:

> the activities of the Rootes Group and those of the Chrysler Group, in
> terms of product lines, manufacturing facilities and marketing

organisation, are compatible rather than in conflict and the pattern of the two groups is such that association as provided by the agreement assures the combined strength essential to a strong competitive position in the world market.

What the memo reveals is the strength of Lynn Townsend's (Chrysler Corporation's chief executive) well-known personal ambition to match Ford and GM's foreign expansion. The result is that both the memo and the entire expansion plan ignored the realities of Rootes' situation, let alone the major differences between the North American and European industries. The optimistic view of the environment ran counter to the clear divergence between the Anglo-American market structure, product design, production technology and managerial methods.

Indeed it was the force of the personal motivation behind the view which resulted in the operational contradictions and mounting losses of the 1970s. The practical result was, in the words of a plant manager, that:

> it was all about volume and they couldn't afford to stop the track. So we reached a stage where the quality as well as integrity of management, relationships with the hourly paid, were being sacrificed to volume.
> (Interview)

As figure 3.3 shows, in practice the expansion fell foul of the need to move in two opposite directions at once: retrenching and reshaping the Rootes structure while re-equipping plants for the assumed increase in output. The violent contraction in demand following the oil crisis in 1974 and the incursion of foreign producers who could offer reasonably priced, fuel-efficient cars was disastrous for CUK given the already contradictory path it had chosen.

Equally disastrous were the monumental amounts of rules and procedures (see chapter 5) which accompanied the Detroit-inspired mass market/volume view of the environment. The reliance on multi-volume corporate manuals was obstructive of learning. As a management systems officer observed, ' the whole range of the documentation was never absorbed. Sometimes out of convenience and sometimes out of necessity sections of it obviously were – but as a total concept it never was' (interview).

In spite of the headline-grabbing events of 1975–8 (see chapter 1) the early 1980s for the Talbot operation in the UK represented a more radical attempt to resolve the core contradictory CUK view of the environment. What is remarkable is the long-term significance of the

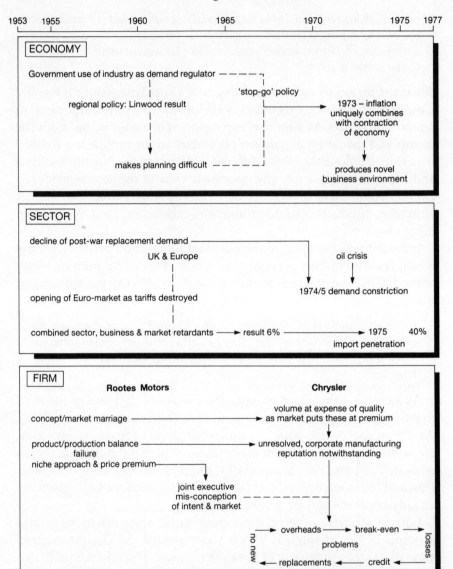

1953   1955   1960   1965   1970   1975   1977

ECONOMY

Government use of industry as demand regulator

'stop-go' policy

regional policy: Linwood result

1973 – inflation uniquely combines with contraction of economy

makes planning difficult

produces novel business environment

SECTOR

decline of post-war replacement demand

UK & Europe

oil crisis

opening of Euro-market as tariffs destroyed

1974/5 demand constriction

combined sector, business & market retardants ⟶ result 6% ⟶ 1975   40% import penetration

FIRM

Rootes Motors   **Chrysler**

concept/market marriage ⟶ volume at expense of quality as market puts these at premium

product/production balance failure ⟶ unresolved, corporate manufacturing reputation notwithstanding

niche approach & price premium

joint executive mis-conception of intent & market

overheads ⟶ break-even ⟶

no new   problems   losses

⟵ replacements ⟵ credit ⟵

Figure 3.3 Rootes and Chrysler UK: dimensions of competitiveness 1953–1977

original position taken by Chrysler Corporation on the European auto industry. Even after the failed rescue attempt by the UK government and the acquisition by Peugeot SA, George Turnbull (the new MD in 1978) was still trying to mount an operation which would compete across Europe. The attempt was ended abruptly by the combined impact of the second oil price jump, a world recession and historic levels of interest rates and sterling in the UK. The implications of Townsend's assessment of the environment had taken 16 years to unravel.

Since 1981 Peugeot Talbot has been able to create a far less distorted version of its environment. Reduced to a UK production and marketing operation it can at last exploit its knowledge of this distinctive national environment. As will become apparent in chapter 5, this strength is very much recognized and used by the Peugeot SA group. It is within this more limited framework that Peugeot Talbot has addressed the competitive requirements of the 1980s head on in a way it never could under Chrysler. The central reason why it has done so far more successfully than in the previous decade is because the company is unencumbered by a grandiose view of its potential position as a volume producer. At the same time, the corporate manuals and formal rules of CUK have been abandoned. In their place, greater reliance has been placed on developing a shared problem-sensing ability amongst senior management. As an assistant MD candidly noted, 'It is a very informal basis . . . I get weeks when we have an executive committee when we are discussing the same [market] problem over and over again. But I have to say it works. People work more closely together with this effort' (interview).

There were immense similarities in the way the senior management of Jaguar and Rootes understood their environment down to the 1960s. Both companies made the most of the high entry barriers in the post-war years. Both relied on high levels of personal responsibility by senior management for major areas, neither developed specialist planning functions. In the case of Jaguar the aversion of Lyons (founder and chief executive) to formal management systems verged on the pathological. Given some of the individuals concerned (Lyons in styling, Heynes and Hassan in product engineering) this resulted in exceptional achievements, notably in engine and model development.

By the same token major weaknesses arose in manufacturing. As with other domestic producers, these shortcomings were not punished by the expanding market. Judgement on the environment was the prerogative of Lyons. Jaguar did without a sales director and Lyons took direct responsibility for the North American market down to the 1960s. Retailers bore a great deal of the burden. In the UK Jaguar apparently 'didn't worry about selling cars. We just made them for Henleys' (interview: ex sales manager). Delays in supplying cars for the market were even encouraged in order to add to the exclusivity.

In a period of overall growth the pursuit of engineering perfection allied to a pronounced cost consciousness were allowed to continue. However the lack of investment in production engineering and the long-term absence of formal management or market intelligence were shown up severely by the conditions of the late 1960s. As in the case of Rootes, Jaguar was unable to finance the rising cost of new model development on its own. Jaguar tried to form its own group of companies, embracing commercial and military vehicles from the late 1950s but to little effect. Jaguar became part of the newly formed BLMC in 1968 and Lyons retired in 1972.

After Lyons' departure the competitive base of Jaguar was almost destroyed by the direction adopted by BL corporate management. As in the case of Chrysler UK, the assessment of the environment by new incoming managers proved decisive. In 1973 John Barber the new MD of BLMC (part of a cohort of ex-Ford managers) sought to emulate the European expansion of Ford. This resulted in a £60 million expansion programme for Jaguar. The intention was to double output to 60,000 units a year. This strong personal view of the potential for Jaguar led to the appointment of the like-minded Geoffrey Robinson as MD of Jaguar in 1974. Serious problems arose as quality suffered at the expense of production targets. A team of fitters had to be sent to the USA to rectify problems with that year's model at a cost of £2,000 per car.

The crux of the problem was the Ford-dominated character of the new corporate management's view of the industry in the 1970s. Irrespective of the validity of the targets, Jaguar was made to run before it could walk. Jaguar production engineers, for example, realized that although targets had been drastically altered, no corresponding shift in the total set of relations on which production relied had occurred. Most important of all, there was no attempt to make good the long-term deficiencies within Jaguar's mode of environmental assessment. New capacities in marketing or product planning were not formed at Jaguar. After the successive corporate reorganizations Jaguar was expected to act on the instructions of the corporate marketing functions.

The result was damaging in two respects. First, it meant Jaguar missed the opportunity to develop these vital instruments of environmental assessment. Jaguar even saw its sales and finance functions transferred to BL headquarters. Second, the assessment that was carried out at corporate level met stiff opposition from Jaguar. Little effort was made to reconcile the two views, to help Jaguar staff 'make sense' (see 'Environmental assessment' earlier in this chapter) of this wholly different approach to the market.

The government's Ryder Committee of inquiry into BL was established after the discovery that the corporation had net liabilities of £43 million in 1974. Its report in April 1975 caused further problems for Jaguar. Overall it accepted the figures supplied by BL and ended up confirming the ambitious BL view of the European car market. Yet by also using Ford advisers, the committee tried to make BL emulate Ford's structure. The result was divisions grouped around product types with a new cars division which combined volume and luxury cars. The two mentalities of the mass market at corporate level and Jaguar's luxury approach clashed from the start. Little remedial help was available. Trench warfare ensued and Jaguar's product quality plummeted. Rather than developing a more sophisticated understanding of the market, senior managers at Browns Lane were 'totally dedicated to getting Jaguar out [of BL]'(interview). The most senior, as in the case of Bob Knight, were noted not for commercial acumen but for corporate street-fighting. The accolade given him by his staff speaks volumes when they concluded that 'history will say that it was almost entirely up to him that Jaguar "stayed out" of British Leyland'.

The central thrust of the recovery which Jaguar mounted in the 1980s has been the creation of what the new MD, John Egan, called 'a grown-up car company'. In other words, the construction of the full set of specialist functions which Jaguar had failed to develop previously. The company's survival and then regeneration rested on the newly found ability to understand its environment. Above all, this required the company to confront its long-held assumptions of the industry, the market and the political milieu. Without doubt the critical contribution of John Egan was to redirect Jaguar's attention to a wholly different conception of its environment. The rather parochial concern with the UK auto industry standards of the 1970s was replaced. The new frame of reference was now the world industry and its competitive bases.

Huge efforts were made therefore between 1980 and 1985 to recruit and resource not only a marketing department but also a fully-fledged product planning function. The marketing staff's world customer survey was decisive. In the short term it demonstrated that there was sufficient demand world-wide for the Jaguar product if only it could be manufactured to meet contemporary quality standards. More fundamentally, the results cut through the many assumptions held by Jaguar engineers. The exercise exposed basic flaws in the company's engineering-led approach. These included the realization of potential customers' rejection of plastic interior trim and the high level of female purchasers of the XJS in North America.

What stands out in the case of Jaguar is the extent of the energy devoted to environmental assessment across the whole organization. Every department has been used to develop as full a picture as possible. The purchasing department has created not only databases covering all its 600 major and potential suppliers but an entirely deeper set of relationships. Instead of the inevitable spot bargaining relations of the 1970s, longer-term collaborative projects have been pursued enabling Jaguar to use the invaluable specialist knowledge of GKN and others. In product engineering, managers have constructed what Rex Marvin (a senior vehicle design engineer) calls 'positive feedback loops' within the department's web of external relations. Dealers from around the world are brought to the Browns Lane plant as those best qualified to point out quality failings in relation to customer needs. A continual dialogue has been established between the vehicle designers and Jaguar's international service managers at quarterly sessions also held on site.

Important action has been taken in ways unheard of to Jaguar in the 1970s. The Manufacturing Technology Centre has extended its knowledge of leading edge developments by joining user and supplier clubs. As a result of the crisis of 1979–80 Jaguar has also forged personal, co-operative links with Mercedes-Benz, its major competitor, in the face of industry changes which confront them both.

These novel techniques of engaging with the environment represent a breakthrough for the company. However, critical to the survival and regeneration of Jaguar has been the extent of the supportive action taken. Trouble was taken to generate a common position between new functions, as the company uncovered unprecedented market knowledge in the early 1980s. The chief executive sums up the resolution of conflicting interpretations of the market thus:

> Typically, when we have a problem between two departments we will get the most outspoken people in that area to give us [the board] a joint report as to how to solve the problem. And they are not allowed to give a minority report. (interview)

Aspects of the way other techniques have been used will be seen in chapter 5, including the care taken in establishing cross-functional teams or wider communication structures. One form of support though was decisive in ensuring that the environmental sensing of the new management in 1980 'made sense' to the Jaguar work-force. In 1979 and 1980 it was immensely difficult to alter the assumptions which staff made of the company's environment and which in turn guided their everyday actions.

The threat of corporate management to shut the plant unless it broke even by itself counted for little. Workers had long been sceptical of an alien corporate management's views. It was not easy to convince staff that the company was in serious financial trouble when the last published accounts in 1974 showed a £12 million profit. Jaguar management were forced to bring the environment into the workplace to dramatize it. In other words, Jaguar's abysmal product quality rating on the J. D. Powers index in the USA was given full exposure in-house; a 'black museum' was set up in the plant to display the worst product defects; and dealers were allowed on to the shop floor to trace the source of faults.

Book publishing

The experience of Longman and Associated Book Publishers reveals how the way a company assesses its environment is constrained by its internal character. In certain respects both organizations made similar diagnoses of the industry in the 1970s and the relevant markets. Yet they diverged in certain ways: they challenged their cherished strategic formulae; they adjusted their structures to open up their businesses to new features of the environment; they ensured the shifts in the environment were understood within the companies; and they developed specific techniques to ensure a more sophisticated understanding was sustained. As a result their ability to comprehend and meet the competitive bases of the 1980s was different.

In the 1960s the two companies were highly representative of the UK book publishing industry. Both could point to a healthy level of exports and overseas publishing, especially in the Commonwealth and related markets. Highly entrepreneurial editorial staff in each house exploited the opportunities provided by the post-war understanding between British and US book publishers not to compete in their respective English language territories. Longman enjoyed success particularly in its educational lists in Africa, the Near and Middle East and the Caribbean. ABP did well out of its legal and educational publishing, more particularly in Australia and Canada. It was in the 1970s that differences within the two companies began to develop in their contrasting assessments of the environment.

The narrowness of demand for books in the UK continued during the 1970s. Yet it was the decision of the US courts to declare the World Book Agreement a restraint of trade in 1974 which upset the international market. US and British publishers were now free to enter each other's markets. The ability to compete internationally (particularly in the USA) now became one of the main bases of competition for UK publishers. Longman was able to respond effectively and has an enviable record of having established itself early and soundly in not only the USA but also Western Europe and the Far East. Michael Wymer, the person responsible for co-ordinating that move, notes:

> Longman saw a need to change the balance of its business really quite significantly. We had been very successful through the 1960s but we realized that we were extremely vulnerable. A lot of our business was in the developing world which was obviously politically and economically very vulnerable. (interview)

In 1987, 50 per cent of Longman's sales were derived from outside the UK. A clear instance of the company's speed of response was shown as print material costs rose 29 per cent between 1970 and 1974. In the face of great hostility from the UK industry, in the three following years Longman transferred 40 per cent of its UK printing and binding needs to the Far East. ABP has been more like the rest of the British book industry. Between 1981 and 1985 UK book exports to the USA, for example, increased by 86 per cent. ABP though was unable to move into the USA in the 1970s in the same way as Longman. Its new office in Boston in the 1980s had difficulty in registering a profit, except in two years, between 1980 and 1985.

There is no better illustration of the relevance of the way the internal character of an organization can condition its environmental assessment capability. In both cases there were key people available in senior positions in the 1970s who saw the international opportunities. The difference was in the way they were able to develop their assessments.

In Longman the evolution of its relationship with its overseas operations and its corporate structure facilitated its new market position. Longman's aim was to be both international and multi-national. In other words, the company sought to export products from the UK but also publish and produce in a wide range of overseas locations. The UK company became but one unit (albeit large) among the collection of international subsidiaries. The strength of local publishing overseas is impressive from which the UK company derives clear benefits, especially in market knowledge. Longman Hong Kong therefore has its own integrated sales and production operation. People from Longman UK's English language teaching division can use such local knowledge in selling their own specialist books in the Far East.

Longman (as will become apparent when dealing with the company's knowledge base in chapter 6) has been able to devote time and resources to creating a set of secondary mechanisms which have extended and deepened its understanding of its environment. This is especially true in the way it has felt confident enough to challenge accepted editorial views of the market by recruiting marketing staff from outside the industry. At the same time it has effected a shift from being purely editorially-led to being market-led: the equivalent of Jaguar's move away from its view of the world being dominated by engineers.

Planning has been developed accordingly in the light of the evolving structure. The movement has been away from the strict financial accounting approach of the 1970s. Full, discursive annual planning in the 1980s reports have replaced the previous slim budgetary exercises. The process of international market diversification, divisionalization and the establishment of profit centres by 1981, led spontaneously to the demand for more planning resources at divisional level. This has resulted in the last four years in: a series of workshops run by the finance function for senior divisional management; staff changes to support the move; and the development of training modules which address the specific skills concerned. The keynote has been the inculcation of greater awareness of the appropriate part of the environment by each division of Longman. This in turn has increased the appetite for more accurate information. In 1987 a publisher in the Longman schools division was aware of the gaps in its market knowledge, for example. As he put it, 'I still don't think we do it as well as we should. We are not as keenly aware as we should be of the book-by-book performance of our competitors' (interview). In some cases, such as Longman's distribution, computing and production services division (LDCPS) since 1983, the move has been more problematic.

In ABP there were many readily apparent strengths. The senior management of ABP was highly distinguished – Michael Turner had negotiated the changes to the World Book Agreement with the USA for the Publishers Association. The excellence of ABP's commissioning editors, especially in the law and academic lists, was widely recognized.

In spite of their efforts it was the composition of ABP which proved a restraint. The company's ability to develop a fuller understanding of its environment, compared to Longman, suffered as a result.

The nagging unresolved problem of the structure of ABP went back to its creation in 1964. The cause lay in the reverse takeover by Sweet & Maxwell (legal specialists) of the larger group containing Methuen (academic, children and general), Eyre & Spottiswoode (general and bible publication) and Chapman & Hall (scientific and technical). Sweet & Maxwell managers supplied the senior positions in the new company, yet were relatively inexperienced in the other three main areas of publishing for which they were now responsible. Three difficulties arose. It proved difficult to re-order the group around three new divisions of law, academic and trade (general) publishing. The words in a paper by a senior academic editor makes clear how:

> the merger with Sweet & Maxwell that brought about the lasting form of Associated Book Publishers made no difference to the organisation of Methuen's publishing. A single editorial board continued to publish all of the imprint's traditional lines.

It was therefore impossible to prevent duplication and overlap of lists.

Second, the linking of the inherited overseas interests of the group was far from straightforward. It took two years of personal intervention by John Burk, the original chief executive down to 1970, to merge the law and other publishing areas in Australia.

The third problem was one of imbalance arising from the success of the legal division. The Sweet & Maxwell imprint and its major rival Butterworth accounted for the vast majority of the standard legal texts and continuation works in British law. The direct costs of this legal publishing was much lower than other types and the result was very high gross profit levels of around 70 per cent. The importance of the division was demonstrated by the way the group's offices were located adjacent to the law courts in the Strand. The problem was that although the legal imprints contributed the majority of ABP's profits, there was little way that it could be copied by the other divisions since its market position was so unique. As an editorial director in the scientific division noted, this meant that the group when contrasted with Longman, did not need to re-examine its relation to its environment as thoroughly as it might have done if Sweet & Maxwell had not existed.

These three main internal problems meant that ABP's environmental assessment capability was conditioned in a number of negative ways that Longman's was not. This meant that ABP was hit by the economic dislocation of the 1970s. Without zero-based accounting the company found it extremely difficult to cope with 26 per cent inflation.

In short, ABP, like many other British companies, was fire-fighting in the second half of the 1970s. As an editor of the time describes:

> You were looking at taking publishing decisions, issuing contracts for a book today where you knew you wouldn't get the manuscript for two years, having no real idea what production costs would be in three years' time or what the market would accept in three years' time. (Interview)

Unlike Longman, many of the secondary mechanisms for environmental assessment, simply did not get a chance to develop. The early attempts at developing full divisional three-year plans were abandoned and even the group did not have a fully worked-out five-year plan until 1981. Merely trying to cope with the ravages of reduced demand and

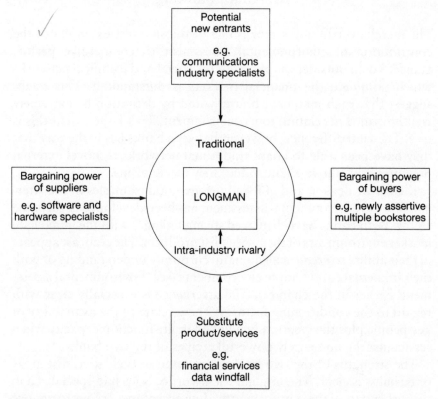

Figure 3.4 Longman and potential competitive forces

unprecedented inflation mean that the inculcation of improved means of understanding the environment fell outside the remit of fire-fighting.

The result was that ABP entered the period of renewed demand in the 1980s, and the external challenges represented by figure 3.4, still needing to restructure and develop new mechanisms of internal control. In contrast to Longman, the ABP 1986 group plan was anticipating opportunities, not only in Europe, but also in the ASEAN region and Japan, through more purposeful planning and marketing operations.

This also meant that ABP was less able to use environmental pressures or crises as means of dramatically demonstrating the need for a new course of action. Longman's planning capacity meant that it both anticipated the effect of the collapse of the Nigerian market in 1982 and used it as a lesson for other divisions.

Merchant banking

The merchant banking sector is one of the sharpest examples of the contribution of environmental assessment to competitive performance. To an outsider the extent of the social and technical networks which dominate the financial markets is outstanding. This might suggest that each merchant house would by definition be extremely well-informed in relation to its environment. To a large extent this is true. The vital difference, however, between banks lies in the way that they have been able to adapt traditional networks to novel external pressures and, above all, introduce new mechanisms.

Kleinwort Benson and Hill Samuel are good examples of the alternative ways environmental assessment has been developed in the same sector. Both banks have displayed strong linkages with the immediate market environments of their specialist products. The contrast appears in their ability to create a meaningful corporate understanding of both their immediate and remote environments (see 'Environmental assessment' earlier in the chapter). The divergence is especially clear with regard to the conditioning features. These relate to the availability of key people plus the creation of a linked multi-function capacity when set against the immensely powerful recipes of the two banks.

The strengths of the two banks in relation to their specialist areas of business is clear. The original Kleinwort & Sons had specialized in the earlier part of the century in providing acceptance credits to finance foreign lending. The firm enjoyed well-established connections with many of the US securities firms such as Goldman Sachs or Lehman Brothers, some stretching as far back as 1900. In the 1950s it was renowned for being 'an old-fashioned firm which depended upon close relations with an excellent and loyal clientele'. Few other UK merchant banks had the will or connections to establish themselves overseas. Without such direct contact with clients the bank had no commercial banking market. A director of the firm puts the point well when he remarked on the 1970s, 'nobody thought the business was about product. They thought it was about relationships . . . the right marketing on the one hand, inviolable relationships on the other' (interview).

These relations were equally important at Hill Samuel. The central moving force within Hill Samuel in the early 1970s, Kenneth Keith, had a background in corporate finance as distinct from the accepting house strength of Kleinwort. None the less his reputation had rested equally on the extensive web of corporate clients for whom he had managed 'deals'. The profiles of Hill Samuel's senior management often reflected the need to maintain appropriate connections. Lord Sherfield, the chairman of Hill Samuel in 1967 had been a fellow of All Souls, head of the Treasury and Ambassador to Washington.

In this sense both banks clearly had, by their very nature, marketing and network connections (in our terms secondary mechanisms) way beyond the thoughts of their counterparts in manufacturing industry. Until the 1980s most of them would have argued that elaborate corporate planning was unnecessary given the short-term, opportunist requirements of their business. It was the assumption of closeness to their environment which meant that the merchant banks in general underestimated the importance of what we have identified as the conditioning features. It is an insight which also helps to explain Kleinwort's success relative to Hill Samuel in the 1970s.

Two very different pictures emerge, therefore, of the core knowledge, main logics of action and their interplay with key individuals/groups responsible for the way the banks interpreted their environment. In Kleinwort Benson there was a stark clarity with regard to the bank's *raison d'être* and the dominant influence of the Kleinwort partners (after the original merger of Kleinwort & Sons with Robert Benson Lonsdale (RBL) in 1961). There was a natural fit between the accepting house strength of Kleinwort with the issuing house specialism of RBL. The key to the integration though was the way the commercial banking world-view of Kleinwort dominated. Meanwhile, the more advanced meritocratic structure and remuneration system of

RBL (needed in their case to retain scarce corporate finance staff) set the tone at the operational level.

Given the inclination of key individuals at a senior level, Kleinwort Benson in the 1960s and 1970s was able to adopt an overall view of its environment. The actions of Sir Mark Turner in the 1960s are a fitting illustration. A non-executive director of a number of companies and a deputy chairman of Commercial Union, he appeared to grasp the full significance of the spate of mergers in the City (similar of course to that of Kleinwort and RBL). Greater clarity was required in what constituted the environment for the whole bank. This was especially true given the naturally centrifugal tendency of the newly arrived deal makers from RBL. Professor Rowland Smith of UMIST as well as psychologists were brought in. The aim was to open the eyes of the senior management to the environment and to adopt a more systematic planning orientation. In spite of the political in-fighting which occurred around the events the demonstration and learning effects were very evident. The irony of the situation was not lost on one of the senior directors since:

> the obvious conclusion was that we were not looking at ourselves in the way that we were constantly advising our clients to look at themselves, in the way of looking at what are we, what do we want to be, where are we going to, what are the impediments, what are the advantages that we have got . . . we were assuming that our business somehow managed itself. (Interview)

Though far from fully developed by comparison to some corporate planning functions in other industries, it was this vital open orientation to its environment at a senior level which stood Kleinwort Benson in such good stead in the upheavals of the early 1980s. In chapter 5 we will deal in more detail with the 'Hermes' operation at Kleinwort. It was no accident though that in 1982 Hermes not only evaluated the nature of the changes in the total financial services sector but drew in contributions from a wide range of backgrounds within the bank. Although some argue that the bank's international operations are unproven, Kleinwort was able to survive the 'Big Bang' (see chapter 2), retain its core commercial banking competence and move into investment banking. A large part of the explanation relates to the way it had adjusted its structure in order to open up its total operations to comparison against the environment.

Hill Samuel approached the environment rather differently. In the 1960s Hill Samuel pursued one of the most active diversification programmes of any of the merchant banks. Although largely successful in the 1960s, Hill Samuel maintained such an approach in the following decade in spite of the changes in the sector which necessitated a more focused approach. The bank was heavily influenced by the regime of Kenneth Keith until his departure to become chairman of Rolls Royce in 1980. The apparently remarkable salesmanship of Keith derived from his corporate finance background at Philip Hill, Higginson, Erlangers and was sustained after their 50/50 merger with M. Samuel in 1965. The acquisition followed therefore of businesses ranging from insurance to ship broking. These included: Lambert Brothers (specialist shipping agents and brokers) in 1968, Noble Lowndes (employee benefits consultancy and insurance company) in 1969, Hamilton Smith in 1971 and L. Hammond & Co. (insurance brokers) in 1972.

In simple terms Hill Samuel was so heavily committed to its growth and diversification path that no alternative view of the sector's condition emerged. Unlike Kleinwort Benson at that time, senior management had neither challenged nor opened up its senior management's assessment of the environment. Nor did it adjust its internal structure to link the immediate environmental sensing of its subsidiaries to a larger sense-making at corporate level. Senior management operated within the expansion philosophy largely as overseers of budgets. Meanwhile within the subsidiaries there was little understanding of any collective environmental sensing.

Given the strength of the system established by Keith, the shocks from the environment in the 1970s had a negative effect on the bank. The secondary banking crisis caused by the steep drop in property values and the fall in share values drastically reduced the earnings of many firms in the financial services industry. In 1976 the Herstatt bank in Germany failed. The result was a foreign exchange loss of £9 million for Hill Samuel (ultimately reduced to a net £1 million). As in the case of ABP's Magnum imprint failure, the reaction was one of defensiveness and insulation at subsidiary level. The opportunity was not taken by group management to use the crises to demonstrate the need for an alternative, fundamentally different way of looking at the bank in relation to the whole sector.

The appointment of Christopher Castleman as group chief executive in 1980 did much in the early 1980s to remedy the immediate problems of flat profits in a growth era for merchant banks, turnover and lack of confidence of staff, and the absence of a clear way forward in an environment which offered many opportunities as Kleinwort showed. Yet the enormous alteration to the whole sector set off by government reregulation meant that the Hill Samuel group was forced to evaluate the environment as a totality at great speed. The resignation of Castleman in 1987 over the board's preference to seek a friendly takeover of the group only highlighted the difficulties the group faced in making sense of its environment in the circumstances of the 1980s.

Life assurance

Evidence from the life assurance sector confirms the importance of the ability to mobilize new mechanisms of environmental assessment. At the same time Prudential drives home the point that such mechanisms can be diluted if attention is not paid to the deeper conditioning features already in existence.

The continued profitability of the Prudential across market cycles since the Second World War meant that the management had become disinclined to embrace major changes by the 1960s. The concern borne of the innately conservative actuarial mentality was with not losing the Prudential's leading position. At an operational level, the dual responsibility of field staff to generate business and administer premium collection further inhibited change.

None the less what distinguishes Prudential was the way critical aspects of its internal character were changed during the 1970s. These alterations enabled the Prudential to take a wholly different view of its sectors' changing bases of competition, and in so doing lay the foundations for the competitive posture required in the 1980s.

The alterations in senior management, the creation of the Prudential corporation and the use of the investment management function to alert the Prudential to wider environmental changes in the 1970s went hand in hand. The appointment of Geoffrey Haslam as the first non-actuary to be general manager was a considerable breakthrough (sustained by the managerial approach of Brian Corby into the 1980s). He did not see the competitive relations outlined in the previous chapter by the conventional view of the actuarial risks involved. Quite the reverse: his work in the new group pensions business had provided him with an understanding of the possibilities of diversification. At the same time, Haslam's period in the organization and methods department convinced him that the Prudential needed to clarify its strategic planning as the activities of the Prudential expanded.

The way in which these alterations were mutually reinforcing is perfectly illustrated by the creation of the 'Prudential Corporation' in 1978. Incorporation meant a financial restructuring which gave Prudential access to both the debt and equity market for financing, the creation of a top level of management which could now divorce itself from the previous heavy operational responsibilities, and not least the opportunity to set up clear signals in-house and to the environment. As one executive concerned put it, 'creating the corporation was a more dramatic gesture to make people realize we were actually making changes, and to ram it home that this is the way we are going to manage' (interview).

Such changes, then, allowed the Prudential to consider the environment in different ways and to innovate accordingly. The role of investment management (not one of Prudential's traditional strengths) is a clear example of the way the new corporation was now opened up to what hitherto had been considered unthinkable. In the 1960s investment management had been traditionally kept separate from the rest of the organization. By the late 1970s it was apparent to the fund managers that investment performance was now growing as a measure of the firm's ability to attract funds in the sector. The previous restrictions on fund managers' decision making, with board members' agreement needed, were jettisoned. An aggressive stance was adopted with relevant performance data and a market rate salaries structure in order to retain a vital resource.

The success of the investment management operation in the 1980s is instructive. Above all it is indicative of the way the Prudential deployed a set of major internal restructurings which then released the full potential of more specialist mechanisms for understanding an environment which then became increasingly turbulent.

Conclusion

The starting point in the process of competition often derives from the understanding a firm develops of its environment. In general terms the research shows that it is insufficient for companies to regard the creation of knowledge and judgements of their external competitive world as simply a technical exercise. Rather the need is for organizations to become open learning systems. In other words, the assessment of the competitive environment does not remain the preserve of a single function nor the sole responsibility of one senior manager. Nor does it occur via isolated acts. Instead strategy creation is seen as emerging from the way a company, at various levels, acquires, interprets and processes information about its environment.

There are four conditioning features which help to explain the degree of openness of an organization to its environment and its receptiveness to the changes in its environment. These are

1 the extent to which there are key actors within the firm who are prepared to champion assessment techniques which increase the openness of the organization
2 the structural and cultural characteristics of the company
3 the extent to which environmental pressures are recognized and their associated dramas develop, and
4 the degree to which assessment occurs as a multi-function activity which is not pursued as an end in itself but which is then linked to the central operation of the business.

However, even if this set of primary conditioning features existed within an enterprise then that would be no guarantee of the survival of its environmental assessment capacity. In order for it to endure, a set of secondary actions are required in order to stabilize and impel the assessment capacity forward. Incorporation of those responsible for planning and marketing is critical, as is the availability of purposive networks which link the firm with key stakeholders and interest groups. The use of specialist task forces or teams, beside their technical relevance, can often reinforce the importance attributed to the assessment process, especially if they are drawn from across functions.

At the start of this chapter we quoted Michael Porter's (1987) imperative 'to discover how the process of creativity takes place' in companies in order to understand the strategies they choose. The evidence from the four sectors considered here suggests that how management combines the range of possible activities within the process of environmental assessment accounts for a substantial part of the answer.

That creativity comes when management goes beyond the skills in acquiring and processing relevant data from the environment. The abiding problem of Chrysler, both in the USA and in the UK, was its prowess at assembling extensive data on its environment but then failing to put that information to effective use within its operations. The evidence used in this chapter points to the need for a much deeper but less immediately tangible strength: the capability for the whole organization to learn from its environment.

The material presented on the life assurance sector underlined the importance of mobilizing new mechanisms of environmental assessment, especially given their lack of development in that sector and elsewhere in the UK. However, Prudential confirms the point that even such sophisticated mechanisms can be rendered virtually useless if deeper conditioning features based on collective learning are ignored. The use of such learning ensures that the full implications of the firm's view of its environment are captured, understood and retained at all levels. This learning can then inform (1) subsequent actions over the long term, and (2) the way in which future shifts in the environment are approached. A large part of the task in leading change therefore becomes clear. Leaders have the responsibility not merely to ensure that the environment is understood; the vital need is to ensure that the organization can learn and act on such analysis over time as the following chapter will show.

4

Leading Change

On 7 January 1989 the 'Business' section of *The Economist* began with an engaging cartoon. Arranged across the top of page 65 was a collection of middle-aged men making energetic use of various pieces of gym equipment. Closer inspection reveals that each figure bears the likeness of the head of a major corporation. Prominent among them are Jack Welch of General Electric and Louis Gerstner, president of American Express. The article is entitled 'A work-out for corporate America'. Because of the new commercial fitness attained by those such as Welch, the piece goes on to exalt the reader not to apply for Japanese citizenship just yet. Why? Because 'there are enough success stories to provide guidance on how best to revitalise an American company. On the way, such successes are revealing a new breed of American chief executives.' Similar articles in the UK and European business press abound.

The profound challenges to the existence of many traditional Western industries in the 1980s has often led to spectacular changes in the businesses which have survived. The chief executive or business leader has been catapulted to the forefront of national attention. In the UK the names of Hanson, Sugar or Branson are as prominent on the front pages as they are in the business sections of newspapers. In the face of epoch-making problems, those who appear able to supply solutions are eagerly lauded. The climate of expectation seemingly has made them into the modern day counterparts of the medieval wizards.

Appreciation of the supposedly magical qualities of such chief executives is by no means universal. Yet most people can appreciate the need for leadership simply from their everyday acquaintance with group activities, be it in their work or social lives. Meanwhile, the image of the leader figure is constantly reinforced. The heads of

government, political parties, sporting organizations and social movements are convenient targets for the analyst, satirist and layman alike.
In times of crisis the leader figure's role becomes the subject of intense
scrutiny. We may not all aspire to the position of leader but it is one
to which most people can relate.

Leadership though has proved to be one of the most appealing and
yet intractable subjects within management. Two immediate difficulties present themselves. First, leadership cannot be equated only with
command and the obedience of followers as some handbooks would
have it. Nor, second, is leadership best understood when it is reduced
to the sweeping prescriptions of the ghost-written businessman's
autobiography. The immense problems which experts have
encountered in trying to teach leadership directly and the lack of
commonality in the routes leaders have taken in reaching their positions, only serve to make the subject more elusive.

But it is this elusiveness which has also given rise to such extensive
commentary on the subject of business leadership. This chapter begins
therefore with a summary of the field. It specifies the contribution of
the management writers and highlights the range of leadership forms
which have been identified. The main conclusion to arise from this
synthesis is that the otherwise valuable managerial literature on leadership contains some substantial defects. Most serious of all is the
relative absence of studies which connect directly leadership and
competitiveness. Comparative studies of leadership in different industries are equally rare. Few have explored the full relevance of process
and context to leadership.

Each of these conceptual issues will be considered next. The rest of
the chapter will then examine the role of leadership in managing change
and competition in the four sectors of the study. The pattern to emerge
from the firms in the study is clear: the problems of dynamics and
constraints are ignored by leaders of change at their peril. In particular
this chapter will show how premature or isolated use of the wealth of
tools which leaders have at their disposal can be disastrous. Honing the
tools in order to match them to the processes and circumstances which
leaders must operate within, appears far more advantageous.

Leaders, heroes and Chief Executive Officers

Recent attempts to survey the extent of the literature on leadership
have reached a common conclusion: its vast scale. Over 100 definitions

exist derived from a wide range of perspectives (Bass 1981). Theories of leadership have proliferated across the social sciences, ranging from trait analysis to ethical assessment approaches. One needs to tread very carefully through the thickets of academic specialization and some brief ground-clearing is required before the contribution of the managerial writers becomes apparent.

Psychologists in the 1950s and 1960s devoted great energy to trying to identify the personality traits of the successful leader (Fiedler 1967). This work saw leadership in terms of authority and follower relationships. The aim was to discover what differentiated leaders from followers. The programme of research at Ohio State University generated broadly defined categories such as 'consideration' and 'initiating behaviour' (Fleishman 1957). Others concentrated on task-oriented and employee-oriented leader behaviour and sought to locate leaders on the 'autocracy–democracy' continuum. Subsequent work has elaborated the theme of behaviour types. These included Bass and Valenzi's (1974) categories of 'direction, delegation, consultation, and manipulation'. One study proposed 19 behaviour types arising out of this field of research.

These attempts at understanding leadership have remained largely unfulfilled. The main problem has been the way they placed undue emphasis on personality at the expense of the situation in which leadership occurs.

However, an entirely different plant has grown lustily away from the academic leadership undergrowth: the leader as hero seen in the pages of the business biography/autobiography. In many ways the general formula used here shares the main assumption of the psychologists – the centrality of the leader's personality. The success of such volumes if measured in sales has on occasions been exceptional (see, for example, Iacocca 1985). The impact of these books on the lay view of leadership is considerable. Apart from simple curiosity fanned by PR hype, the outpourings of business leaders appear to speak to their times. The social and political tastes of the 1980s seem to provide a willing audience. Such figures have in many ways assumed the mantle of the self-improving, Smilesian hero of the high Victorian era. In the USA, academic commentators have drawn attention to the appetite for what they describe as the 'romance of leadership' (Hambrick 1987). In Europe too there seems a ready market for the views of chief executives such as Jan Carlzon of SAS (Edstrom 1986).

It is easy for academics to be dismissive of this genre, often seen through their eyes as representing the collision of the hard sell of Madison Avenue and the literary style of Mills & Boon. Yet even passing acquaintance with this type of book soon suggests that they have a value beyond self-advertisement. In fact the more reflective versions can be extremely illuminating even allowing for the inevitable *post-hoc* rationalizations.

To be sure, Sir John Harvey-Jones' (1988) book *Making it Happen* is heavily prescriptive and dwells on his skills of motivation and leadership. Yet at the same time he alerts the reader to leadership as a process. In his case as chairman of ICI between 1982 and 1987 he highlights the critical part of that process: transforming its top executive team from a collection of rival advocates on behalf of individual businesses into a cohesive body of directors of the group's best interests. One of the results was that greater resources were released for ICI's growth businesses.

Careful reading of the more thoughtful biographies and autobiographies can be rewarding in a further sense. Such accounts offer insights into not just leader personality, but sometimes the wider set of relations which leaders encounter when managing change. It is significant that the discussions which followed Iacocca's (1985) autobiography centred not only on his tempestuous relationship with Henry Ford but also the internal problems he had to solve at Chrysler. Read carefully, these works offer valuable clues not only to the practical difficulties of leading change but they also signal the intricacy of the contexts in which it takes place. In this sense the genre has performed a service: it has popularized and opened up the subject. In revealing the scope of the leadership task the authors have reinforced the recent efforts of business analysts in framing a more faithful model of leadership.

Since the late 1970s a much broader approach has been taken to leadership by management writers. The problem is seen more via the situation in which leadership takes place. Some have drawn attention to the requirement to facilitate the work of other managers – to enable them to influence and direct the activities of personnel (Peters and Waterman 1982). Others have claimed that outstanding companies exhibit leaders who ensure that the work of staff is effective (Walton 1987). New classifications of leadership have therefore replaced the traditional categories based on personality. Bourgeois and Brodwin (1984) place great emphasis on the leadership styles of companies expressed in the way they implement strategy (see also Kanter 1983; Tushman and Romanelli 1985). Their classification extends from the 'commander' (where strategy is forced down to lower levels) to the 'crescive' (where all managers contribute to strategy creation and implementation).

A broader orientation to leadership by management experts is now well established. It is now possible therefore to separate out three models of leadership which have become accepted: transactional, transformational and representational (see Ropo (1989) for a comprehensive overview).

The transactional leader is one who exchanges money, jobs and security for compliance (Burns 1978). The term implies management-by-exception, i.e. the leader only intervenes if standards are not met. The approach is more suited to the accomplishment of routine tasks but is found wanting when the need is for major change.

Transformational leadership is quite different. Here the leader motivates others to strive for higher order goals rather than merely short-term interest (Burns 1978). It involves *inter alia* risk taking, building commitment and the visionary skills of focusing attention and communication. It does not assume individual exchange relations. In Nancy Roberts' (1985: 1024) words: 'the collective action that transforming leadership generates empowers those who participate in the process.' The collective action is often induced as part of the heightened response to a crisis.

The more recent identification of representational leadership arises from an awareness of the multiple constituencies related to a given organization. Representational leadership refers to the requirement for leaders to represent some feature of their organization to those who are by no means their subordinates. This is particularly evident in environmental scanning, resource acquisition and network development (Hunt, Baliga and Peterson 1988).

In spite of this widening of the leadership field, conceptual shortcomings persist. Two linked defects stand out: insufficient attention to (1) leadership as a process (Pettigrew 1987a), and (2) the reciprocal relationship between leadership and context. Above all, nobody has specified what difference leadership can make to competitive performance by comparing firms. Some writers have maintained that situational conditions make leadership irrelevant and unable to effect organizational performance (Pfeffer 1981). The evidence presented in the rest of this chapter will show the opposite to be true.

In our view, leadership cannot be understood outside of a processual perspective. Too often leadership is treated in a unitary way. In other words, it is the action of a leader at a given moment, or through a single episode (albeit a crisis) which claims attention. The changing nature of leadership across time through cycles of radical and incremental change is seldom addressed (cf. Nadler and Tushman 1988). As Ropo (1989) perceptively notes:

> Although an implicit notion of change and flexibility is inherent in most situational leadership models . . . the issues of time and processes have been totally neglected . . . leader behaviour of managers is abstracted from their concrete contextual settings and investigated in reductionist terms as if it had no past or future.

As chapter 8 will show, to comprehend the dynamics of change processes one has to appreciate the role of energy within the process; its source, means of generation and how it is sustained or dissipated. The contribution of leadership to this aspect is a vital one. We agree with Roberts (1985) that leadership is one key way of creating and redirecting energy within the change process. And it is that energy which makes such a difference when comparing the competitive performance of firms. In book publishing, for example, Longman's superior record can be directly related to the way its leadership maintained the level of energy over two decades. That energy level was necessary in order to shift from its editorial preoccupations of the 1960s and 1970s, to the market-oriented competitive bases of the 1980s.

Although this study is at pains to specify how leadership can shape strategic change, one thing should be made quite clear. There is no assumption here of the powerful efficacy of the charismatic leader; no prescriptions being offered for the instant success of the visionary. Quite the reverse, sensitivity to questions of time and process in leadership and change produce the opposite view. It is the unpredictability of the process as it unfolds through time that makes the prospect of control so remote. Assertive action by itself is of limited use and may well be dangerous. Paradoxically this research indicates that the accumulation of more modest preparatory actions is all-important. These might include consideration of the political implications of a given strategy for instance, through problem-sensing and climate setting within the firm (cf. Pettigrew 1987a). The art of leadership in the management field would seem to lie in the ability to shape the process in the long term rather than direct it through a single episode.

One of the keys to understanding the process of leading change is to link that process to its contexts. Chapter 1 showed how the analytical judgments and resulting action from strategic decisions cannot remain separate from the circumstances in which they are taken. Indeed, it is the tension between these forces which impel the process of change. This relationship demands careful attention in understanding the problems of leading change.

The key to understanding those problems is the extent of the shifting contextual pressures which leaders face through time. The main weakness of the earlier approaches to leadership was their search for almost universally applicable leader behaviour. As the evidence from the research companies in the rest of the chapter will show, the flow of alterations in both the organization and the external competitive environment call for varying responses and above all different types of leadership. Leading change requires action appropriate to its contexts. Different eras produce different leadership needs – leaders have to adapt accordingly. In Jaguar, for example, the type of leadership necessary in the survival year of 1980 was wholly different from that required by the problems of growth from 1985. Indeed, from our evidence the solidifying of apparently successful leadership behaviour into a single mould (as happened at Hill Samuel in the 1960s and 1970s) can become a competitive liability.

Supportive evidence of the need for variation in leadership, rather than the adoption of supposedly timeless principles, is available. In the area of technological innovation Manz and colleagues (Manz et al. 1989: 633) point to the existence of 'multiple influence procedures' which may be used in that process. For them 'effective leadership combines different types of leadership influence over time as different needs arise'. This does not mean that the earlier categories of leadership outlined above (e.g. transactional or transformational) are of no use in leading change and managing competition. Rather, any category by itself is of limited value. Instead those alternative types of leadership approaches are better seen as being deployed where and when they best suit the demand (cf. Goold and Campbell 1987: 180). As Nadler and Tushman (1988) argue, 'magical', heroic, visionary leadership has simply been inappropriate when relatively successful companies have undertaken adaptations in order to sustain their performance. Examples include Xerox, Digital Equipment, NCR and Kodak.

Nor should one forget that leading change is not a one-way relationship emanating solely from the leader. Leaders are themselves affected by the forces which they seek to manage. The relationship is more accurately described as reciprocal. Leaders alter as they attempt to handle change. In the case of Tim Rix at Longman, his leadership triggered a substantial personal development. At Hill Samuel the problems of the market in the 1970s compounded certain problematic traits of Kenneth Keith's style. The observation is simple yet penetrating: it cuts across the familiar assumptions made by many management writers. Otherwise respectable accounts which demonstrate the need for varying forms of leadership fall down when they argue for the need to 'fit' leadership to company character (Goold and Campbell 1987: 246). Attempts in practice to achieve such a static, singular fit almost inevitably come undone as both leader and circumstances change.

One of the strongest features of leadership to arise from this research is that leading change should not necessarily imply a single leader. Change may ultimately involve a number of leaders, operating at different levels in the firm. This becomes all the more likely given the need for a variation in leadership styles to match changing circumstances, whether they originate from environmental threats or the particular needs of implementing strategy. No one person can cover all possible situations. It is noticeable how Prudential, Longman, Kleinwort Benson, Jaguar (and Peugeot Talbot in the 1980s) share a common characteristic in this regard. Alongside their assessment of their competitive environments, great emphasis was placed on two things: (1) creating a broader notion of collective leadership at the highest level, and (2) inculcating over time a complementary sense of leadership/responsibility at lower levels (cf. Hambrick 1987; see also the importance of complementarity among multiple stakeholders in the British National Health Service in Pettigrew, McKee and Ferlie 1988a, 1988b). Chapter 5 will show how such an approach is vital in linking strategic and operational change.

The pattern which emerges from the companies in this study is a strong one. Leading change in order to compete is not understood by reference to universal principles carried out by an exceptional individual. More effective in leading change appears to be: the use of varying leadership approaches over time; a combination of practices to address shifting competitive circumstances; the recognition that leader and context will affect each other reciprocally; and the use of operational leaders at all levels in the firm.

In practice, the successful companies studied in this research show that so-called decisive action by their leaders was in many ways more apparent than real. Time and again the companies revealed how extensive preparatory work facilitated such short-term acts. These included the less visible asset in leading change of taking time in fashioning the company's precise competitive choice, creating a capacity for effecting the required changes, and legitimating such acts before undertaking them. These conditioning devices then enabled the full potential of other mechanisms subsequently used by leaders to be released.

In Kleinwort Benson, their seemingly incisive response to deregulation in the City of London in 1987 was not the result of flashes of genius from their leadership. Rather it was the result of a sequence of moves in the 1970s. These had set the tone for diversification, had demonstrated the capacity to do so, especially abroad, and had meant that such moves were already well received at various levels in the bank come 1987. In the less successful companies in our sample, it is noticeable how similar decisive competitive acts were made (the Magnum venture at ABP, or the Avenger project in Chrysler UK). Yet those acts crumbled exactly because they did not have the benefit of such conditioning. Such comparisons require inspection at greater length.

Book publishing

The book publishers ABP and Longman are especially clear examples of the contribution of different styles of leading change to their companies' performance. Useful insights can be derived from the similarity of their intentions yet the contrasts in the means they employed to achieve them.

The aim at ABP, as at Longman, was to secure the benefits of separate divisions devoted to particular types of publishing; in ABP's case, law, academic and trade. Yet as management found in the Rootes Group and in other industries (Gospel forthcoming) the problems of running such structures for the first time were immense. The constraints of previous fragmentation of demand, the slow emergence of mass markets and the avoidance of formal management techniques in favour of devolved control through payment systems are by now well known (Elbaum and Lazonick 1986). These applied especially to book publishing. ABP registered the considerable achievements of physically uniting the group on the New Fetter Lane site in London by 1970 and establishing, like Longman, a purpose-built distribution centre on a greenfield site, in ABP's case at Andover. Book distribution had previously been handled by Book House in Neasden which was part owned by Oxford University Press and Pitman.

The difficulties with the divisional system arose from the way it was conceived in the context of the norms of publishing and the model provided by the rest of British industry. It was entirely logical therefore for the leadership of John Burk and then Peter Allsop from 1972, to concentrate on the most prized asset of any publisher: its editorial strength. This produced a devolved style of leadership. This in turn was reinforced by the problems which arose in the integration of previously distinct businesses in both Canada and Australia and commanded so much of the group executives' attention.

The result was the separation of senior management – to deal mainly with overseas problems. The divisions became the responsibility of management committees. The aim was to give maximum scope for the entrepreneurship of the lists within each division. It was highly indicative that ABP as a corporate entity was not emphasized. Instead, the brand name, that is the imprints of Chapman & Hall or Methuen, were reinforced both internally and to the trade. Imprint boards remained in place.

The type of leadership which emerged was closest to the transactional, leadership-by-exception mould outlined above. Apart from the emphasis on the autonomy of the divisions and lists down to 1974, action was directed towards the divisions more where problems arose. Such a style of leadership was consistent with the values and experience of the senior management. It was also made possible by the enduring profitability of Sweet & Maxwell's legal publishing. ABP did not develop as fast therefore as an international company in the manner of Longman.

The reliance on a devolved transactional style of leadership (through which editorial flair had been given its head) meant that the problems of the 1970s were hard to face. The reliance on editorial entrepreneurship was exposed by the fourfold rise in oil prices in 1973–4.

The outcome for ABP was that the 1970s became dominated by fire-fighting. The company's planning mechanisms, for example, had to deal with the repricing of entire lists every three months as well as fending off the investigations of the Prices Commission. As with Chrysler UK, the leadership and management was pitchforked into a succession of crisis-like responses. They were therefore unable even to consider much beyond the creation at speed of what change was necessary. Given the accumulated and immediate problems there was simply no opportunity to build a more sophisticated capacity for change seen at Longman. The failure of the Magnum mass paperback list from 1976 served to emphasize ABP's difficulties. A new entrant to the company summarized the outcome well in 1986 when he told his colleagues how:

> If you are actually going to be an entrepreneur you are going to reach into things that you are not used to and your cash flows are going to be different. And I don't think yet we had enough nerve to follow this entrepreneur thing the whole way. (Interview)

Understanding the nature of ABP's stance from 1964, the circumstances in which it was formed and the way wider economic upheavals acted as constraints, is illuminating. This perspective throws light on why by the 1980s ABP had been unable to devote as much attention as Longman to building the competitive bases which the market now demanded, notably in the areas of marketing and new technology. This is not to argue that there was no change in leadership approach. ABP is a good illustration of the point made earlier concerning the reciprocal effect between leader and situation. The leadership remained within the transactional mode. They were unable to move as speedily as Longman to a more transformational style.

ABP took decisive action in 1979 by separating out the group from the UK operations and appointing an outsider to head ABP UK. Alan Miles' skills had been amply demonstrated at Weidenfeld & Nicolson where he had been managing director. He had managed an illustrious imprint which none the less relied wholly on the vagaries of trade publishing. His subsequent achievements at ABP were immense. In the short term he established a new system of financial controls and monthly management accounting which enabled managers to monitor and control performance, purchased a new generation computer system to enhance systems capability and distribution effectiveness and made key appointments in the form of a new head of the trade division (a colleague of Miles' from Weidenfeld) and the creation of a group marketing director.

These acts provided a sound base for a series of reforms in the 1981–5 period. The aim here was to preserve the experienced publishing teams, maintain the momentum of successful publishing, improve cash flow and profitability by cutting out unprofitable publishing, develop opportunities where they were manageable within current resources, and step up training of managers and staff. The result was a £10 million reduction in costs, and a decrease in staff of 25 percent. As figure 4.1 shows, ABP's problem divisions recovered with the improvement in demand in the early 1980s. Yet as was shown in chapter 1, ABP's overall performance relative to Longman remained somewhat flat.

The enthusiasm of managers was clear. As one in the legal division put it, 'he introduced all the modern systems, all the proper modern systems a company should have. Everyone had a cost centre, every cost centre had a manager, every manager a reviewer' (interview). In one sense he orchestrated his own set of conditioning devices and secondary, supportive mechanism. What was lacking was the time (see chapter 2 for the pace of acquisitions in the early 1980s) to produce a

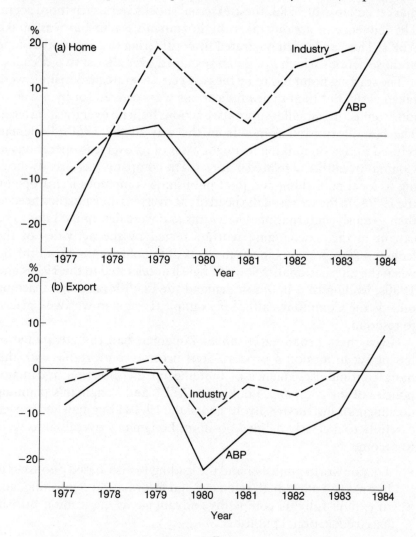

Figure 4.1 ABP and UK book publishing industry: index of home and export sales at constant prices 1977–1984
Source: ABP

new set of such devices linked to a conception of the long-term strategic development which would move ABP beyond its traditional bases.

The contribution of the leadership at Longman was rather different. The core of that difference has been in the way the company's strategic changes since the early 1970s have been matched by a commensurate alteration in its leadership. Longman had to endure the same economic and market challenges as ABP. In some cases, such as the Nigerian market collapse of 1983, these external shocks were even more acute. The sequence of actions taken by Longman's leadership was unlike ABP's. This can be demonstrated by considering the distinctive scope of those actions which Longman sustained over almost two decades.

The starting point has to be the way certain strategic decisions were taken early, but then their implications were catered for by a web of interconnecting, smaller supportive actions built up over the long term. The best illustration comes from the way in the 1960s Longman refused to rely on milking its major asset of its overseas operations in Commonwealth and related markets. The company was already moving to local publishing and joint publishing companies in Europe by the 1970s. In the words of the head of the overseas division they heeded their extensive international networks and were determined not to be caught in the 'unchanging world' created by the activities of the 'colonial entrepreneurs in the markets of the old commonwealth'. So when the internationalization of English accelerated in the 1970s and 1980s, leading to a boom in demand for English language teaching outside the Commonwealth, for example, Longman was well placed to respond.

Given these broad early moves Longman had the advantage of having set in motion a process. Staff became comfortable with this more continuous sequence of building up the direction and major policies of the company. Looking at ABP's and Longman's planning documents is instructive. By the end of the 1970s Longman had moved carefully to a clearly defined position: Longman's overall aims were to become

- a major world publisher and the leading British-based publisher in business, professional, reference and information publishing, and
- to exploit fully its competitive advantage as the leading British-based educational publisher.

ABP by 1985, was still trying to create fully a long-range orientation. As will be shown in detail in the next chapter, Longman was then in a position to develop supportive secondary mechanisms. While building its strategic goals incrementally, Longman's senior management was able, for example, to elaborate and operationalize these aims into a change agenda (e.g. specific targets in North America, or the Third World).

At the same time that Longman built up strategic goals, its leaders were almost equally concerned with fashioning the internal character of the company. Thereby staff might adapt to the implication of such goals more readily. Longman did not try to retain family control and shareholdings as at ABP but sought out a position within the loosely federated Pearson & Son Ltd in 1968. Nor did Longman attempt to establish a new divisional structure in one go. Unlike ABP, Longman had already become a group of companies in 1966 in order to reflect its spread of overseas publishing units. Longman then embarked on what is best described as a progressive divisionalization. The aim was to replace the three existing departments of overseas, home and general publishing, sales and production.

Longman did not opt for a reduction to three divisions as at ABP. Instead it adopted seven product-based divisions and three geographically related. The mix was deliberate; it set up a more tolerable span of financial control without losing the essential small-scale character of the publishing process at imprint level. It also in time liberated group managers, notably sales, to take a much wider view. The important point to note though is that the structure was gradually adjusted both to meet the needs of diversification and to prevent their ossification. As figure 4.2 shows, the new sector format by 1986 had opened up greater flexibility across the company. The sectors brought together some earlier divisions and became homes for new operations which Longman's long-term diversification required.

Moreover, the development of the strategic goals and the preparation of the internal character of the company were not left to operate alone. They were augmented by generation of an appropriate capacity for change within Longman. This entailed parallel shifts effected in the Longman culture. These centred on a refinement of the attitude towards quality, a reworking of the notion of professionalism and a movement in the balance of editorial versus marketing priorities. This has necessitated the recruitment of marketing and personnel experts from outside of book publishing. As important has been the inculcation of specific financial skills of the divisional/sector heads with a view to their identifying and mounting their own acquisitions. It is also worth noting the amount of effort put in over a period of seven years to remoulding the relationship between computing staff and the rest

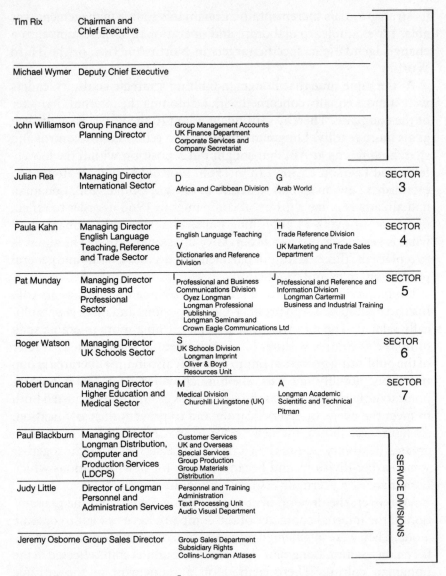

Tim Rix	Chairman and Chief Executive			
Michael Wymer	Deputy Chief Executive			
John Williamson	Group Finance and Planning Director	Group Management Accounts UK Finance Department Corporate Services and Company Secretariat		
Julian Rea	Managing Director International Sector	D Africa and Caribbean Division	G Arab World	SECTOR 3
Paula Kahn	Managing Director English Language Teaching, Reference and Trade Sector	F English Language Teaching V Dictionaries and Reference Division	H Trade Reference Division UK Marketing and Trade Sales Department	SECTOR 4
Pat Munday	Managing Director Business and Professional Sector	I Professional and Business Communications Division Oyez Longman Longman Professional Publishing Longman Seminars and Crown Eagle Communications Ltd	J Professional and Reference and Information Division Longman Cartermill Business and Industrial Training	SECTOR 5
Roger Watson	Managing Director UK Schools Sector	S UK Schools Division Longman Imprint Oliver & Boyd Resources Unit		SECTOR 6
Robert Duncan	Managing Director Higher Education and Medical Sector	M Medical Division Churchill Livingstone (UK)	A Longman Academic Scientific and Technical Pitman	SECTOR 7
Paul Blackburn	Managing Director Longman Distribution, Computer and Production Services (LDCPS)	Customer Services UK and Overseas Special Services Group Production Group Materials Distribution		
Judy Little	Director of Longman Personnel and Administration Services	Personnel and Training Administration Text Processing Unit Audio Visual Department		
Jeremy Osborne	Group Sales Director	Group Sales Department Subsidiary Rights Collins-Longman Atlases		

SERVICE DIVISIONS

Figure 4.2 Longman Group UK structure, 1986
Source: Longman

of the company. Without it, many of the advances in the production process and list development in the 1980s would have been still-born.

The pivotal reason for the adoption of these conditioning features in Longman has been the profound change in the style of leadership. The senior management of Longman represents a shift over time: from a liberal version of transactional leadership in the early 1970s to a flowering of transformational leadership in the 1980s. It was through the personal development of the former chief executive, Tim Rix, that the pitfalls were avoided. Rix came from the powerhouse division of ELT, much as his counterparts at ABP came from their legal division. In the first instance, there were a number of more direct exchange relations which had to be worked on, such as the relationship between the emerging group planning system and the newly created divisions. Yet it has been the progressive movement to a more transformational style from the late 1970s which set Rix and his senior colleagues apart.

It is worthwhile to dwell on the main aspects of the mechanism which have been used. From 1976 he assembled around him a critical mass of the so-called 'finance committee' and divisional directors who made up the UK board. Rix's extensive international publishing experience gave him the advantage of an early insight into the trends and growth possibilities inherent in the USA, Europe and the Far East. His accomplishments of having achieved growth in the area allied to his personality meant that he was able to transfer many of his techniques piloted and proven in the 1960s and early 1970s. He was able therefore to aim for the altogether higher-order goals outlined above. What is commonly referred to as 'Tim's vision' did not appear in response to the fashion for mission state-ments but was forged into a robust form over ten years. Such a vision has then provided the basis for collective action at first board and then divisional level. Robert Duncan, head of the medical division was in

> no doubt that there was a two way movement between Tim Rix and myself . . . It appeared to me that there was a lot we could do outside our traditional markets, a lot of opportunities open to us, particularly in America. His feeling was that we should do something to get us out of the dependence on Africa and therefore he encouraged it. It was undoubtedly me and Tim, a joint version. (Interview)

The board was therefore relatively stable in the 1980s, augmented by key appointments in computer and productions services. The finance committee (Rix and his deputy plus the finance director) grew from its necessary early control and monitoring duties to a position where it performed a constant educative role for the heads and then top teams of each division. Much of the basic communication of the ongoing flow of changes was a mature combination of Rix's regular personal appearance in the divisions, a professional communication apparatus across the company and then the home-grown efforts of the divisions. Sector 4's 1988 divisional conference on 'planning for development' is a case in point. The result according to a sector manager is that 'there are intersectoral problems . . . but it takes time for problem areas to be brought into the open. It's not a secretive culture' (interview).

An easily overlooked yet important mechanism developed under the Rixian mode of leading change has included the balancing of continuity and change. In part this has been accomplished within the interlinked nature of the changes which have been sustained incrementally over a decade and are well expressed in the strategic goals described earlier. The crucial outcome has been that Longman has retained its most basic assets such as its author loyalty. The strongest product areas have not been left to themselves. Perhaps the best illustration of the way this balance has been achieved, and to an extent coherence maintained, has been in the regrouping of lists. Hence in 1987 the ailing trade and reference lists were moved in alongside the vastly successful ELT division, as part of the sectoral arrangement.

Automobiles

The experience of Jaguar Cars and Peugeot Talbot are immensely instructive in respect of leading change and competitive performance. Not only do they expose some of the weaknesses of traditional UK leadership, they also graphically illustrate the interplay of leader and company context. Above all, they demolish any monolithic notion of how to lead change. Both companies demonstrate the wide variation in leadership over the long term and even in the space of two or three years. The variation in leadership style across the existence of first Rootes, then Chrysler UK and lastly Peugeot Talbot has been startling.

The direction of the Rootes group throughout its existence down to 1964 remained heavily dependent on the Rootes family. Billy and Reginald (sons of William Rootes the founder) provided joint leadership until 1939. Billy won a wide reputation as an entrepreneur while Reginald's skills lay in administration and finance. After the Second World War their sons joined them. Geoffrey and Brian, sons of Billy, became MDs of manufacturing and overseas operations. Timothy, son of Reginald, was director of sales and service. These family members controlled the boards of each member of the group. As the current success of many West German family-owned firms shows (including BMW) there is no reason why such enterprises should not succeed. However, in the case of Rootes the perpetuation of family control and executive responsibility resulted in a number of deficiencies. Most important of all, managerial expertise in product planning, finance and training remained underdeveloped by contemporary standards.

In many ways this backwardness provoked the extreme action taken by the new Chrysler UK leadership from 1967. On the other hand such leaps were entirely consistent with Chrysler Corporation's history in the USA of bold innovation and what became known in Detroit as 'panic management'. The response of Chrysler was to import a combination of US managers together with those who had come through a US-inspired system in Ford UK. Great faith was placed in the financial and accounting procedures derived from Detroit. The problem was in the way the new system of divisionalization and procedure manuals was applied. The leadership devoted insufficient time to preparing and conditioning the company for such a massive change. The exasperation of a British project engineer is indicative. As he put it:

> Chrysler came over here and plonked a nine foot high stack of manuals on the desk and said 'apply that'. There was never the manpower to apply that. There was never the experience in a lot of people to apply the things to the letter. It was an attempt to apply certain procedures, certain methods of operating that quite honestly the organization was incapable of responding to. (Interview)

The exceptional actions taken by the new leadership were also undermined by their standing within CUK. The MDs, Hunt (1967–73), Lander (1973–6) and Lacey (1976–8), along with the expatriate US directors of the main functions of CUK, were beset by the common disadvantage of suspicion over their authority. That suspicion was fuelled by their apparent loyalty to those who had appointed them in Detroit, not to mention their intense mode of double reporting to Chrysler Europe and Detroit (a special Atlantic switch had to be installed). The result apparently was:

> a lot of fear in the executive management system. They were very conscious that they were on a month's notice . . . and they were very loyal to their people in Detroit who had put them here in the UK. (Interview)

An additional problem was the feeling that the group of exiles were 'rejects' from Chrysler's debacles of the 1960s. Chrysler's lack of experience as a multinational producer also meant that little attention was paid to adjusting their aim of rapid expansion to the British social or competitive circumstances. A hasty, ill-founded strategy was compounded by the leaders' failure to develop the capacity to change or prepare the setting into which such a strategy was to be launched.

The intriguing profile of leading change presented by Peugeot Talbot could not be more different. The position of chief executive has been occupied by two men: George Turnbull from January 1979 to March 1984, and Geoffrey Whalen, assistant MD from October 1981 and MD from 1984 to date (1989). Once the decision had been taken to scale down the UK operations in 1980, a clear continuity has appeared in the strategic intentions across the two regimes: the essential rebuilding of the competitive bases of the company as a car manufacturer. Yet with hindsight one can see that in order to achieve the sequence of demanding changes the wholly different styles of both men were required.

In many ways Turnbull broke the deadlock imposed by the inherited problems of CUK. Whalen then astutely delivered the changes which logically followed. George Turnbull supplied a determined, combative personal style linked to a clear vision of contemporary international competitive standards. Together these provided the impetus to rework the assumptions which had brought the demise of CUK. His precocious rise to become MD of British Leyland in his forties and his successful stewardship of Hyundai in Korea commanded attention. He rehabilitated the notion of leadership. His manufacturing expertise won him the respect of his staff. A manager of the parts department was clear:

> He knew how to build a car, how to run a manufacturing company, that was his business . . . once he was running the show the meetings for example were very serious, very professional and he was very strong. (Interview)

To outside constituencies he was, in the words of a senior DTI officer, unequivocally

> a first-class car man. He didn't need the money. In other words he could afford to say his mind and stand up for his corner, which he did in a very firm way both with the government and his French masters. (Interview)

Turnbull's re-establishing of managerial authority and basic manufacturing standards was epitomized by his decision to sit out a three-month strike in 1979. In Dick Parham's (deputy MD) view,

> that was a very fundamental point in establishing a new relationship between management and work-force. It allowed the management to manage and the work-force to understand that things had changed, that the era had changed. (Interview)

Of course this is precisely the bold action which was discounted earlier in the chapter. The difference was that having established the legitimacy of the new direction and its standards, his successor had the opportunity to develop the capacity to change more fully. Furthermore, Whalen's method of leading change brought into operation a new style of leadership. In the opinion of the director of manufacturing:

> We have a managing director in Geoff Whalen who is very good at democratic management. It can't all be democratic but he is very good at a relaxed style of management. So I would never get the feeling, and my plant directors wouldn't, as they certainly would have some years ago, that the central operation is god . . . now the central operation is much more like consultants. (interview)

In addition to this he has created a series of supportive secondary mechanisms. These have included:

- the judicious shift to a more open, consultative set of relations within the senior management built around the weekly meeting of the operations committee since 1983
- a vital reshaping of the working and authority relations with Peugeot SA so that it became more symmetrical; PSA now accept the expertise of Peugeot Talbot's entirely native management; for example, over the peculiarities of the 50 per cent of the UK market taken by fleet sale
- rebuilding the confidence of staff (shell-shocked by the horrors of 1975–9) through the necessary contractions which had to occur before the new models and improved standards could bear full fruit from 1983
- operationalizing the strategic programme of regeneration through an incremental adjustment of internal reporting and communications structures – examples include the termination of the Iranian contract and the Triaxle bus project.

The experience of Peugeot Talbot from 1979 is an excellent example of how leading change doesn't have to be associated only with a single leader. The regimes of two very different leaders have combined to produce a transformational leadership. In Jaguar in the 1980s the alteration in performance has pivoted on an individual but one who has had to adapt his leadership over time.

Under William Lyons and British Leyland the problems associated with leadership were almost polar opposites. In the period of post-war growth the system of management at Jaguar relied heavily on Lyons.

He maintained a constant level of intervention exemplified by his two tours of inspection per day around the Browns Lane site, his personal stewardship of the US market, his sole right to make new model decisions and his personal supervision of management salary levels. Lyons' exceptional presence meant that after his absence, and given his distaste for formal management techniques, nobody had been suitably prepared to take his place. 'Lofty' England was MD from 1972 to 1973 and Geoffrey Robinson from 1973 to 1975. Between 1975 and 1980 the Jaguar management board was disbanded and Bob Knight, the head of engineering at Jaguar, was responsible for Browns Lane. Knight had no general management experience. In the light of the confusion within BL after the financial losses and problems high-lighted by the Ryder Report in 1975, Knight and Peter Craig, the plant directors, were forced to devote all their energies to retaining as much as possible of Jaguar's traditional strengths and to thwart the incursions of corporate management.

When John Egan arrived in 1980 leadership had shrunk to this rather negative operational level and was concentrated on survival. One of his main achievements has been the construction of a full version of leadership which was capable of leading strategic change. As with Turnbull at Peugeot Talbot he had to rehabilitate the position of chief executive. His reputation within the industry (after experience at GM, Unipart and Massey Ferguson) and his natural communication skills were combined with a series of initiatives which established him as a solid point of focus for the stand-alone company. Many of the actions were modest but well chosen, such as his move to receive customer complaint calls personally in 1980–1. Equally relevant was his openness at not having the technical knowledge about building cars so that he

> very much had to rely on the knowledge of the people who reported to me. I couldn't invent any of this stuff because I didn't know. So therefore a non-authoritarian regime started immediately simply because the person in charge didn't know the solution. (interview)

In many ways this early orientation to Jaguar's problems was highly indicative of the way the strategic changes at Jaguar were led in the 1980s. Apparently exceptional measures, such as the stripping out of £20 million of costs in 1980–1 were underpinned by vital parallel adjustments. Immense trouble therefore was taken over what we have called the conditioning features of that process. Hence the effort placed in the demonstration effect of the Black Museum and the inviting of

US dealers to the tracks which began to loosen the complacency of the previously engineering-led company. What stands out in the Jaguar case is the time taken between 1981 and 1986 to regenerate Jaguar into a 'fully grown-up car company'. Before the company reintroduced the Series III model in domestic and international markets, for example, care was taken to win back control of Jaguar's sales outlets from BL; to build a new sales and marketing function at Browns Lane virtually from scratch; and to recruit people from outside (as at Longman) who could supply the skills and perspective tuned to the demands of the world car market. This example is indicative of the way the entire change process was approached. In other words as much trouble was taken over creating the capacity to change as in constructing the strategic goals themselves.

Although ultimately baulked in its growth strategy by unpredictable government intervention in 1989 the range of secondary mechanisms which Jaguar mobilized to support its regeneration was formidable. Its methods of communicating the need for the changes in the regeneration programme (such as pay and quality, see chapter 5) and its colourful way of reinforcing success within that programme (e.g. Jaguar national supplier excellence awards) have been widely recognized as establishing new benchmark standards in these areas. The best example of the use of such supportive mechanisms comes in the way a critical mass, which believed in the regeneration, was assembled. To this end a small senior team was brought together by 1981, a team containing complementary skills. They were notable for their untypically wide engineering qualifications, even in the finance position, as much as for the sporting metaphors which Egan employed to structure their approach. Egan also skilfully included a mixture of ex-BL people desperate for Jaguar to survive (Beasley from manufacturing, Ken Edwards from personnel and Johnson from marketing) as well as outsiders who brought approaches which hitherto had been lacking. Those from within BL were essential for their knowledge prior to Jaguar becoming a private company away from BL.

Life assurance

The example of Prudential is particularly revealing of the difficulties in leading change as the environment shifts. The organization almost retained for too long, forms of leadership which had served the business well in one type of market and economic context. Prudential's

improved performance was made possible by the way its new leadership in the 1970s took action which unlocked the latent potential
within the company.

Prudential had its own problems of conservatism within its leadership; the difference from other life assurance houses was in the timing
and extent of the action it took to overcome the restraint. Down to
the 1960s the senior management were reluctant to consider serious
innovations to the established business in the light of their commanding size (twice as big as the nearest competitor). Their role was more
of 'guardianship' than creating new ventures. By the late 1960s the
long-established policy of internal promotion meant that the company
failed to keep pace with the developments elsewhere in marketing,
personnel and data processing. Even where experts were introduced
from outside in the 1970s they were not placed in senior positions and
many left. Leadership was provided by an in-bred management. Until
then the range of businesses was sufficiently small to allow the
actuarially trained senior managers to use their common language of
concepts to embrace the whole organization.

The increasing specialization and diversification of the Prudential
in the 1970s in investment management, group pensions and overseas
meant that this shared understanding could no longer hold. The
Prudential, like Longman, is an excellent illustration of the way
effective change leadership can require a collection of linked long-term
actions. In Prudential the appointment of Geoffey Haslam as the first
non-actuary general manager was vital. Like Egan at Jaguar, he refused
to accept the assumptions behind the established approach to the
business. He brought all the force of his experience in marketing when
he ran the pensions business to begin the process of creating long-term
strategic planning. As with Tim Rix at Longman, in the mid–1970s,
this only meant, at first, the generation of business forecasts and
linking them to budgets. Its value lay in the way it laid the foundations
for (1) the capacity to mount more ambitious commercial innovations,
and (2) the opportunity to lead on to more sophisticated strategic plans
in the context of the problems of the 1980s. The creation of the
Prudential Corporation in 1978 put the seal on the alterations of
Haslam. In particular it liberated the company's finances by providing
access to both debt and equity markets. Furthermore incorporation
secured an executive body which could concentrate on strategic issues.

These actions in the mid–1970s can now be seen to represent the
highly uneven discovery process – a process which conditioned
Prudential for the more momentous challenges which the upheavals

of the market in the 1980s created. Moreover, the actions of Prudential's senior management enabled them to try out certain subsidiary mechanisms which could then be refined and used more expertly after 1979. The incorporation had already begun the creation of a more appropriate executive corp which could sustain the sequence of commercial changes which the removal of foreign exchange restrictions and deregulation in 1986 would require. Haslam's initiatives of the 1970s also triggered indirectly the operation of the mechanisms of communicating the need for change and showing how key changes could be operationalized. The company responded to the increasing centrality of investment management in the industry by encouraging its fund managers to expand, linking that freedom to performance data and in turn breaking tradition by paying salaries to those managers at the market rate.

As will be shown in more detail in the following chapter, the path-breaking moves of Prudential's chief executive in the 1980s, Brian Corby, can be brought into much firmer perspective. Dramatic though they have been, their relative success cannot be understood in isolation. They in fact form a logical part of a pattern of leading change which stretches across two decades. Prudential highlights the need to encompass such fields of vision in comprehending leadership.

Merchant banking

The cases of Hill Samuel and Kleinwort Benson provide some of the more colourful leadership episodes of any of the sectors in this study. In part, their appearance is explained by the norms of a sector which virtually eschewed scientific notions of management, thereby giving greater discretion to some who sought to lead change. At Hill Samuel the contrast in style of leadership was as dramatic as the examples of CUK and Peugeot Talbot. At Kleinwort the opposite has been true.

Kenneth Keith's leadership at Hill Samuel between 1965 and 1980 faithfully reflected his personality and background. His experience in corporate finance was built upon the provision of advice to companies which wished to grow and diversify. He duly turned his advice into practice at Hill Samuel following the merger of M. Samuel with Philip Hill, and Higginson Erlangers (see table 4.1). As we saw in chapter 3 a string of purchases followed, beginning with shipping and employee and insurance interests from 1969. Keith was a pronounced individualist. But in Keith's case the objective was innovation through

Table 4.1 Major merchant bank mergers 1956–1965

Participant	Year	Major services	Accepting houses committee member
S. G. Warburg	1956	CF (✳✳)	No
Seligman Brothers		B (✳✳) CF (✳)	Yes
Philip Hill, Higginson & Co.	1959	B (✳) CF (✳✳✳)	No
Erlangers		B (✳✳) CF (✳)	Yes
J. Henry Schroder & Co.	1960	B (✳✳✳) I (✳) CF (✳)	Yes
Helbert Wagg & Co.		CF (✳✳✳)	No
Lazard Brothers	1960	B (✳✳✳) CF (✳)	Yes
Edward de Stein		CF (✳✳✳)	No
Kleinwort & Sons	1961	B (✳✳✳) I (✳) CF (✳)	Yes
Lonsdale Investment Trust (Robert Benson & Co.)		I (✳) CF (✳✳✳)	No
Philip Hill, Higginson, Erlangers & Co.	1965	B (✳✳) CF (✳✳✳)	Yes
M. Samuel & Co.		B (✳✳) I (✳) CF (✳)	Yes

Key
B: Banking (mainly acceptances)
CF: Corporate finance services in new issues, and advisory services in mergers and acquisitions
I: Investment management
✳: Denotes relative strength

Source: Robinson 1976

expansion not the maintenance of the status quo. Described within the bank as an archetypal 'seat-of-the-pants' manager, Keith personally led the deals which carried the expansion forward. The problems of managerial control and organizational adjustment were left to others to sweep up. One executive colleague summarized the position well. He noted how Keith was an excellent salesman who won the major accounts and deals; these in turn had to be 'landed' by others. At the same time he left the managerial accounting by which such accounts could be administered undeveloped until after the shocks of the mid–1970s.

Kenneth Keith's identification of the need to extend the breadth of the bank's product line was an accurate judgment of the main competitive bases of the 1970s. The problem was the remarkable absence of any newly created conditioning features within his model of leading change. Vivid examples spring readily to mind. Pre-eminent among them were the failures to buy MEPC in 1972 or merge with Slater Walker in 1973, precisely because of the scant attention paid to legitimating the deals even at board level, let alone among shareholders or staff. It comes as no surprise therefore that senior executives (in common with the bid team at TSB in 1988) felt by the close of the 1970s that Hill Samuel had become 'everything but the kitchen sink'.

The secondary banking crisis in 1973 and the sharp fall in share prices in 1974 were followed in 1976 by the Herstatt Bank failure. These shocks exposed the imbalance within Keith's leadership and the weak operational control of the group with a vengeance. It was these issues which Christopher Castleman was brought in to face in 1980. There was one fascinating aspect of the change in leadership. The lack of coherence and control, together with the flattening of profits within Keith's vigorous diversification, indirectly furnished a more receptive context for Castleman and the actions of Hill Samuel's chief executive, Sir Richard Lloyd.

More especially, Castleman was assiduous in piecing together the components of his personal strategy for the bank. This included taking a highly visible year of familiarization followed by creating a set of much-needed guiding principles which were to enable staff to understand necessary operational changes. These were built around the notions of re-affirming the confidence of senior management, motivating staff more directly through divisional and unit incentive schemes and, in contrast to Keith, setting up a personal dialogue with managers over projections. The coincidental removal of foreign exchange restrictions in 1979 plus the improving market for corporate finance aided Castleman's revitalization of Hill Samuel no end. The irony is that in spite of providing a more robust basis for growth than the Keith regime, Castleman was felled by the same problems of board disagreement which Keith had faced. These were most graphically exposed first in the fracturing of the board over the hostile Antipodean stake building, by Adler and others in 1987, and then most of all in the board's collective decision in contradiction of Castleman's wishes, to seek shelter within the Union Bank of Switzerland in the following year. Hill Samuel in the 1980s supplies the clearest evidence that lack of attention to such a vital secondary mechanism of establishing a critical mass for a given strategy, can undermine the most painstaking conditioning work.

The experience of Kleinwort Benson also brings out the role of the indirect conditioning which can facilitate leadership. Beyond that, Kleinwort's competitive strength in leading change has more parallels with the long-term incremental approach found in Longman or Prudential. The indirect conditioning appears at the very outset in the merger of Kleinwort & Sons with Robert Benson Lonsdale. The houses were already interlocked by friendship links at the most senior level. In the 1950s Sir Mark Turner (MD of RBL) and Cyril Kleinwort were both directors of the Commercial Union. Both understood well their respective balance of strengths in corporate finance and banking and most especially the natural ascendancy of Kleinwort's banking in the City. Kleinwort's leadership position was assured from the start.

Much of the strategic development which followed emerged from this sound mutual understanding among the senior management of Kleinwort Benson. Hence the efforts of Sir Mark Turner to create a capacity for future change by inducing directors to think more strategically were respected in the light of his corporate finance knowledge. Kleinwort's expansion and diversification through the 1970s and 1980s was less erratically led and therefore more successful. The best example is the nurturing of the banks' international initiatives which were vital to its performance in the late 1970s and early 1980s. As at Longman, modest but early moves to cover foreign market changes and then incrementally develop them was critical. Thereafter there was less need to undertake enforced, radical changes from scratch. Examples include the establishment of subsidiaries in Brussels and Geneva as early as 1964 on the commercial banking side. This then allowed Kleinwort to expand its international banking as Britain entered the EEC in 1972.

It is crucial to realize that the shared understanding which allowed collective leadership to function at Kleinwort Benson could only have taken the bank so far. It was the broadening of this leadership approach during the 1970s which sustained the flow of strategic changes on which Kleinwort's competitive position came to rely. Similar to Longman, there has been a deliberate effort to retain the collegiate style of the board after the Kleinwort family members retired. This was supported with the development of a management committee (12 people) with executive authority and the formation of a chairman's group similar to Longman's three-man finance committee. The result was the bringing forward in the late 1970s of a set of junior directors (the divisional heads at Longman) who were capable of leading the business in the 1980s under Michael Hawkes. It is noticeable therefore how Kleinwort, in regenerating its capacity to lead change, has been able to respond to the opportunities of deregulation of the London Stock Exchange, even if in due course the bank had to bear the costs of the slump in the securities market of the late 1980s. In sum, the major inherited advantage of certain features which positively conditioned the bank for change in the late 1960s have been actively exploited, not only by their further development but also by the addition of appropriate subsidiary mechanisms.

Conclusion

Our central finding in relation to leading change is that there are no simple universal rules which arise. In fact the reverse is true. Leadership is acutely context sensitive. This is manifested in a number of ways. The very choice of leader clearly relates to the those who make the choice and the circumstances in which they do so. The immediate problems which the incoming leader faces are largely supplied by the situation which the leader inherits. The zones of manoeuvre open to the new leader in deciding what to change and how to go about it are bounded by the context within and outside the firm.

The critical leadership tasks in managing change appear to be much more fragmentary and incremental than the popular images of business heroism allow. Leading change involves action by people at every level of the business. The general preoccupation of the 1980s with the saviours of corporations in crisis has been unfortunate. It has minimized the even more demanding challenge of sustaining effective leadership over time shown in the companies reported in this chapter.

Nowhere among the five central factors is the set of primary conditioning features so important. Moving directly to bold leadership actions can be costly. Instead, the prior need is to build a climate for leading change while at the same time raising energy levels and setting out the new directions to be followed *before* precise action is taken.

The primary conditioning set here includes:

- the building of a climate within the firm which will be receptive to change, which involves justifying why the change should take place
- similarly, there is little point attempting change without first building the capability to mount that change
- equally, establishing a change agenda which not only sets the direction of the business but also establishes the necessary visions and values is by no means simple. It is a process in itself which may take a series of attempts before completion.

Once these conditioning features have been attended to, then a more direct set of mechanisms can be put in place. These extend from the formation of a core of senior managers (and later operational leaders) who are convinced of the need for change, to the reinforcement of successful outcomes in order to build confidence.

The term 'leading change' has been chosen rather than 'leadership'. This seems more appropriate precisely because it suggests the full dimensions of the task facing firms. Leadership, partly for historical reasons, has all the connotations of individualism and, too often, one dimensional heroism. If the companies here show anything, it is the complexity of the demands which confronted them in leading change. Leading change calls for the resolution of not so much great single issues but rather a pattern of interwoven problems. The skill in leading change therefore centres on coping with a series of dualities and dilemmas.

Longman is a clear example. Its management across the 1970s and 1980s had, for example, to: link continuity and change by preserving existing product strengths while moving into totally new markets; reconstituting its centre's role while preparing the case for the consequent restructuring of its divisions; adjusting the Longman culture by both surface interventions in the form of swiftly altering the role of financial reporting, but at the same time devoting seven years to the remoulding of the computing function. The problems of maintaining simultaneous action over a long-term process are at their sharpest in leading change. The need appears to be not boldness or decisiveness as much as a combination of planning, opportunism and the timing of interventions.

The result is that leading change necessitates a leadership which can operate with multiple levers and at multiple levels. Nowhere is this better illustrated than in Peugeot Talbot. From 1983, the regeneration of the company has been founded on a combination of: a new set of open working relations among senior management; a reworking of the authority relations with Peugeot SA; rebuilding the confidence of staff shell-shocked after the contraction of 1975, 1978 and 1981–3; and the progressive elaboration of the new model programme through reworked communications and interdepartmental structures.

As Peugeot Talbot also shows, such breadth of activity cannot be accomplished by one person or through single episodes or programmes. In Peugeot Talbot, the move from survival to regeneration and then growth involved two radically different types of leader in the 1980s, followed by the emergence of complementary leaders of change at lower levels in the company. The example of Jaguar is interesting in that it did not move to a new chief executive in the later 1980s. It also found the development of a capacity to lead change at middle management a problem.

One of the central characteristics of leading change which has arisen from the eight companies under study has been its connectedness; in other words the way leadership style can influence the way an organization handles the other central factors in managing change. Nowhere is this more apparent than in linking strategic and operational change which is the subject of the following chapter.

5

Linking Strategic and Operational Change

The West German power tool maker Bosch supplies one of the more effective examples of a European company's defence of its market position against Japanese competition. It also demonstrates the way sound strategic analysis can be undermined by operational shortcomings.

In 1984 the business had a turnover of DM 1.4 bn (£424 million). The company had 50 years' experience and a high reputation in the industrial power tool business. Bosch's response to the threat from Makita and Hitachi after 1979 rested on the move into the domestic do-it-yourself market. Yet in attempting to translate that strategic intention into practice the company found that its operational skills broke down in use. Consumer marketing was found wanting. The result was a 1.5 hp drill too powerful and unwieldy for the average DIY enthusiast (Parkes 1986).

Bosch's response has been instructive in many ways. In the early 1980s it had to blend newly acquired marketing skills with its traditional design and engineering strengths. Yet that engineering prowess had to be remodelled to include the novelties to Bosch staff of cost engineering which did not adversely affect quality. Techniques of linking the strategic and operational within the company have been created. One example is the appearance of board directors at the weekly brainstorming sessions convened by the 20 people in the research department. Bosch's reaction to the Japanese in Europe has produced steady growth in the company's position in all European countries. Apart from Hilti of Switzerland, Bosch is the only importer with a significant presence in Japan itself. The ability to link strategic and operational change can pay high dividends as the following pages will show.

Elsewhere in Europe, Ladurie's work on French history is suggestive of many of the contemporary issues in understanding strategic and operational change. In his study of the Chouan uprising he demonstrates the need to understand the problem as a process. Examining only the strategic event (in this case the uprising itself) or project is insufficient. The character of change at the operational level over time must be jointly considered. Equally important are the thoughts and actions which pre-date the strategic event. Ladurie is also very clear on the indeterminate nature of the process. His conclusions highlight the 'accidental', the role of 'remote factors' and 'delayed action' (Ladurie 1979: 130). In all, the 'transition from one structure to another, the mutation, often remains, in history as in biology, the most perplexing zone.'

The results of our research have little to add to the history of the Chouan rebellion. On the other hand, the findings can confirm and extend the unintentional insights of Ladurie into strategic and operational change. It is necessary, however, to specify our position in a little more detail for two main reasons. First, the deluge of published opinions on managing operational change has muddied rather than clarified the issue; and second, in spite of many allusions, most writers have not related this particular managerial capacity to competitive performance.

This chapter will investigate these issues by critically appraising the dominant approaches to strategic and operational change and then presenting our own processual conception of the problem. The rest of the chapter is then devoted to the four sectors where the issue has been studied in practice.

The evidence from these companies does not support those who view managing strategic and operational change as totally chaotic and unmanageable. Certainly, the companies studied here do point to the very real confusion which can accompany the range of actions required, their repeated application and the way that implementation may involve the re-creation of strategies. One is also highly aware of the temptation to impose a premature order on such complexity. Our conclusion, however, is that there is pattern in the process, a pattern whose complexity we in no way wish to minimize. Furthermore, it appears that companies can differ markedly in the way they handle such processes; that difference has great relevance to their ability to compete.

Innovators, sceptics and specialists

There are three principal categories of writer who have a bearing on the problem of managing the link between strategic and operational change. They do not constitute well-established schools of thought but within each collection the commentators do share similar assumptions. The first concerns those who are grappling with the demands of managing technological innovation. The second arises from certain management scholars who mistrust overly hygienic accounts of strategy and implementation. The third relates to those who propose specialized strategies for each function within a firm. Let us deal with each in that order.

The growth in the past decade of the uses of computer technology in business has thrust the subject of innovation to the fore. Information technology has been shown to provide powerful advantages in the service sector. Well-researched examples in the UK include Thomson Holidays, Sainsbury or Reuters (Earl and Runge 1987). TOP, the computer-based reservation system developed by Thompson for use by travel agents, revolutionized its distribution channels. It gave Thomson an advantage by leading to reduced costs and enabling the company to undercut rivals' prices. The system also bound agents to Thompson. Comparable cases cited in the USA in the mid–1980s include Merrill Lynch, American Airlines, American Hospital Supply or Mrs Fields Inc. Yet as the recent poor performance of American Airlines or Mrs Fields show, new technology in no way confers a straightforward or permanent advantage on its adopters.

The potential of the new technology is striking. Researchers at MIT observed back in 1983 how new technology raised fundamental questions about strategy, competition and management. Scott-Morton and Rockart (1983: 2) put the point this way:

> Beyond the use of information technology to support the existing business strategy is the opportunity of using information technology, proactively, to create new opportunities for the business. These new strategic opportunities are being created by a broad range of information technologies. They not only lead to new markets and new products but also provide whole new ways to manage the firm.

Taking time to penetrate behind the outlandish claims of those who see the new technology as some sort of corporate patent medicine is worthwhile. The rich bundle of possibilities identified by the MIT group has also attracted the attention of others. Some of the results can be of value to those seeking to comprehend managing change and competition.

Rothwell and Gardiner's (1985) research in the UK has identified a set of demanding requirements for firms wishing to innovate successfully. They argue at the outset for the need for top management commitment, 'long-term corporate strategy in which innovation plays a key role', and the rejection of short-term investment criteria for broader considerations of future market penetration and growth. They go on to argue that the company must adapt itself to suit the requirements of the innovation, accepting risks but backed-up by rational termination criteria (pp. 17–18).

Technology is commonly referred to as providing 'competitive edge'. Technology of itself confers nothing until it is used by somebody. Human choice is central to its development and exploitation (Child 1987). At the same time, each innovation within a firm entails a whole set of supporting less readily observable investments and capabilities (cf. Pucik 1988; Teece 1987). These have to be managed (Whipp 1990c). The outcome in terms of performance can be vital. As a major project moves downstream resource acquisition and allocation decisions may in the most extreme cases threaten not only the project but the position of the whole company (Grinyer, Mayes and McKiernan 1988).

Roberts' work on the ways appropriate managerial action at both the strategic and operational level can optimize innovation is instructive here. He realizes that 'technological innovation is a multi-stage process, with significant variations in the primary task as well as in the managerial issues and effective management practice occurring among these stages' (Roberts, 1987: 4). Roberts is especially alive therefore to the array of issues which management has to confront in the translation process from invention through to exploitation. He includes the key roles of idea generators, product champions and gate-keepers relevant to different stages of the process. Others have shown how organic, less structured modes of organization are better suited to the early creative stages of the innovation process. The mechanistic or more regimented is applicable to the later distributing and servicing stages (Rothwell and Gardiner 1985).

Experts on innovation have revealed how product development occurs in cycles and now emphasize that market and manufacturing inputs need to be brought into design repeatedly. This field has also identified the contribution of customers and users, not only in revising an innovation in use but also in the way they can prompt the invention of wholly new products (Von Hippel 1988). Each stage of technological development therefore can throw up different strategic implications.

The sophistication of this area of research is amply demonstrated in its awareness of the difficulties in maintaining momentum in the innovation process. Some innovation writers have suggested the use of bridging devices to assist the transfer process. More recently attention has been drawn to the use of 'venture' techniques within firms in order to implement certain technology initiatives (Romanelli 1987). Venture approaches seek to emulate or co-opt the qualities of smaller free-standing entrepreneurial units. Gerstein's (1987) fieldwork on new technology also reminds us that the innovation process depends on the ability of a company to deploy a repertoire of facilitating techniques. These may include: project management, transition management through to staff recruitment, selection, compensation, training, development and career management (pp. 155–71)

The challenges to innovation scholars posed by new market forms and the need to develop technology which can exploit those opportunities are daunting. Yet overall their response has produced some telling insights into the problems of managing strategic and operational change. As a breed, their conclusions still lean heavily on overly rational, technical assumptions. None the less, the more skilful among them has drawn attention to the need to come to terms with the dynamics of the process, its cyclical nature, the reciprocal relationship between the strategic and operational levels and the breadth of management roles and techniques which can be employed (Keen 1986). Rothwell and Gardiner's research, for example, on the battery of techniques used to develop and operationalize a technology, might equally be applied to the implementation of a particular strategy. As will become clear, some of these results parallel our own in a number of ways.

The problem of linking strategic and operational change also appears among a band of revisionists: that is, those management writers who have attacked the formalism and certainties of the strategic planning approach which dominated the 1960s and early 1970s (see chapter 3). Although they have little to say on competition they provide useful clues to understanding the special demands of implementation.

One wing of the revisionist force has no time for the notion of any purposive relationship between strategic intent and operational outcome. Strategies and their results are seen more as accidental than intentional (March and Olsen 1976). According to this view the direction of an organization emerges from a process likened to a 'garbage can' where intentions, choices and problems are jumbled together and the outcome is extremely uncertain. At its most vociferous this perspective leaves no room for managerial discretion; management's choices are empty. In effect there are no decision makers.

Towards the end of the 1980s some management analysts, especially consultants, resurrected these anarchic notions but in a more domesticated shape. Tom Peters, after first arguing for the benefits of 'loose–tight' combinations of managerial control in the early 1980s (Peters and Waterman 1982) has recently made managing 'chaos' the overwhelming issue which corporations face in the immediate future (Peters 1988). It has also been argued that entrepreneurship, like innovation, actually thrives on conditions of chaos; the task for management is to control that chaos (Kanter 1989). The adoption of such a stance is explained largely by the climate from which it emerged. The failure of the hitherto dominant Western corporations to develop products which met market needs in the 1970s triggered off the search for alternative solutions.

The realization dawned that the giants had grown fat on positions of market oligarchy. They were too safe, too routinized and had lost many of the qualities which they enjoyed during their struggle to grow in the inter-war period. Re-creating those qualities is to be achieved by attempting a limited form of 'controlled chaos' in certain areas of the business. This in turn would require the tolerance of fanatics and experts (e.g. Sony's recruitment of non-traditional skills – Quinn 1988), or the move to flatter structures and the bringing together of senior managers with junior staff on certain projects.

One of the most articulate critiques of the strategy-as-planning approach has come from James Quinn. His work on US corporations in the 1970s (Quinn 1980) and then the later comparisons he has made with European and Far Eastern firms (Quinn 1988) has produced a rich crop of revisionist ideas. He maintains that in spite of ever more elaborate planning systems, 'executives in large corporations tend to utilize somewhat similar incremental processes as they manage complex strategy shifts.' He chides those who fall in to the 'classic trap' of seeing strategy formulation and implementation as separate sequential processes.

Quinn's later message is couched in very prescriptive terms. In his view, 'successful' managers should operate 'logically and proactively in an incremental mode'. Thereby they can build the seeds of understanding and commitment 'into the very processes which create their strategies' (Quinn 1988: 678). He goes on to recommend techniques which can empower this incrementalism. They include the use of partial or tentative solutions at early stages of the process; then 'systematic waiting' for the right option or precipitating event to occur; and later using integrating techniques such as coalition management. The examples used by Quinn to substantiate his view are convincing – as in the case of Pilsbury, Continental Group or Texas Instruments. The weakness of his position is that incrementalism is not universally applicable. As the companies in the following sections will show, crisis management for example puts a premium on swift choices and decisive action in the short term, which is then combined with longer-term approaches.

Detailed research on crisis and turnaround phenomena is helpful here. Such work has indirectly extended people's awareness of the problems which companies face in linking strategic and operational change. In fact, crises often originate from deficiencies in implementation, such as the over-reliance on fixed programmes and routines or the failure of ill-conceived and poorly monitored projects (Grinyer, Mayes and McKiernan 1988). Others have shown how dealing with a crisis and successfully effecting a recovery requires both immediate and long-term action, as well as the ability to deal with strategic and operational issues (Melin 1985).

This body of work has shown how, paradoxically, a crisis provides the space and legitimacy to effect major strategic re-orientations. It also enables managers to set in motion radically different ways of translating new postures into operational form. Some of these writers have produced highly sensitive accounts of that process. Consequently they are able to show the pervasive influence of chance in the translation process. This is especially so in the way management, unfettered by customary programmes or untied from previous one-dimensional views of implementation, has then been able to exploit the unforeseen, luck or windfalls (Grinyer, Mayes and McKiernan 1988).

The conclusions of the revisionists have been useful in a number of ways. They confirm the multi-dimensional nature of the process and they have provided telling role models for those in other fields (Beckhard and Harris 1987). Hayes and Wheelwright (1984) have gone on to uncover the 'deltaic' aspects of implementation as strategies are interpreted within individual business units. More conventional approaches to implementation, linking planning and organizational design, now recognize the revisionists' impact. Hrebiniak and Joyce

(1984) have therefore developed a subtle version of implementation seen as a cascade process down the organization of ever more detailed decisions which occur in the context of primary strategic aims.

Unfortunately the same cannot be said of the attempts by specialists to develop the strategies for individual functions within the firm. In their anxiety to increase the strategic awareness at departmental level, little space is given to the problems raised by the wider conceptualiz- ation of change provided by the technologists or the revisionists. Some advisers still argue that the strategic and operational are wholly separate spheres and emphasize the major role differences (Greenley 1989: 319). Specialists working in personnel (Carnall 1990), manu- facturing (Haas 1987), or marketing (Kotler 1984) have in recent years converged in one sense: they seem to agree that their own functions should develop a strategic perspective in their own right. They advo- cate that this view should complement the corporate strategy as a whole.

Manufacturing is a good example of the general trend. Work in both the UK and the USA maintains that companies should develop 'a manufacturing strategy – a clear sense of your production facilities backed up by detailed analysis. Above all this should be integrated with marketing and corporate strategy' (Voss 1989). Elizabeth Haas contends in the *Harvard Business Review* that 'most US manufacturers are still the slaves of operational necessity' (Haas 1987). She advises instead a 'strategic approach' with the emphasis on the integration of design, plant configuration, information systems, human resources, R&D and suppliers. The conclusion of these specialists seems to be that if manufacturing is omitted from a company's strategic decision making, then 'you leave 80 per cent of your investment and people out of synch with the market place' (Hill 1989).

Such views clearly represent the considerable headway made in the re-orientation of specialist functions in the 1980s. Yet the new posi- tions still beg many questions. How are the strategic and operational to be linked? Given what we have already established as the proble- matical nature of strategy formation, then integrating a given special- ism within that is by no means straightforward. The main problem lies in the specialists' stunted view of strategy as a process. Voss is right to warn that reliance on change programmes such as TQM or JIT in isolation is dangerous. Yet consideration by such specialists of the specific demands of implementation or the non-linear character of the translation process are rare indeed (for a useful overview see Winch 1988).

Our contrasting position sees such problems as integral to the management of strategic and operational change. This approach shares many of the concerns of the technologists and revisionists but goes beyond them in certain key respects. First and foremost, the process of translating strategic intent into operational form does not occur by single step or conversion, or even a neat sequence of steps to a logical outcome (Hall 1984). It has an especially rich set of temporal dimensions for managers. The process may need repeated attempts even to begin; it may include clusters of iterative action in order to break through ignorance or resistance; it often requires the enduring of aborted efforts or the build up of slow incremental phases of adjustment which then allow short bursts of concentrated action to take place. Separate attention is required to open up an organization to the need for change and in due course to reach closure and reinforce the changes made (cf. Pettigrew 1985a). Sustaining the pace and energy of the process has its own set of requirements (see chapter 4); the momentum cannot be taken for granted.

Secondly, the evidence from our research suggests that rigid or programmatic conceptions of the translation process are of little use in understanding how that process works in practice. As will become clear in the following examples, the process has a strong cumulative quality. Even major explosive events such as the 'Big Bang' or the 1973–4 oil crisis seldom have only an instantaneous effect. The subsequent interpretation by those affected and the myriad local adjustments are of equal importance. The translation process is the outcome of multiple actions. Sequential, linear programmes of implementation (often derived from planning software or engineering methodologies) fall down because organizations fail to fit such straitjackets (cf. Frederickson 1983: 570). In practice, attempting to carry out a given strategy or seeking to act out a plan invariably leads to its re-formulation. In the words of Karl Weick 'execution *is* analysis and implementation *is* formulation' (Weick 1987: 230, original emphasis). Putting a concept into practice leads to valuable clarification of the original (Pascale 1990). Such new knowledge may be a vital means of differentiating a firm from its rivals; it is best exploited not ignored.

Thirdly, paying attention to the iterative, cumulative and reformation-in-use dimensions of the translation process yields dividends in terms of competition. A conditional approach based on these dimensions reflects the dynamic and changing nature of the process of competition itself (see chapter 1). Matching a manufacturing function, for example, to a corporate strategy which correctly identifies the competitive bases of the industry, counts for little if that strategy is set in concrete. Examples will follow which show where firms competing in the same markets have made similar strategic choices. However, their modes of implementation have diverged considerably when set against these dimensions. Those who have adopted or assumed a linear, step-like orientation have watched the translation process collapse. They have consequently lost the often carefully conceived competitive advantage which was the object of the original strategic decision.

Fourthly, in spite of the daunting nature of the process, there are ways in which the translation of strategic intent into operational reality can be facilitated. In order to make use of the features of iteration, accumulation and transformation-in-use then a compound set of techniques is required. Strictly analytical challenges have to be met. Yet these responses are strengthened if they are linked to the resolution of educational and political problems inherent in the translation process (see figure 5.1). Thus the new knowledge and insights into a given strategy that arise from its implementation have to be captured, retained and diffused within the organization (for a more detailed exposition of the role of learning see chapter 6). Of course, the very prospect of change confronts established positions. Both formulation and implementation inevitably raise questions of power. Left un-attended such forces can provide formidable obstacles to change (cf. Pettigrew, McKee and Ferlie 1988b on the creation of receptive contexts to overcome such obstacles in the NHS). Indeed as we have already noted in the case of Jaguar in the 1970s, ultimately such forces can wreak havoc.

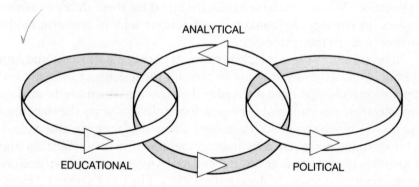

Figure 5.1 Three inter-linked aspects of managing strategic and operational change: the analytical, the educational and the political

The more successful companies in our research sample show just how extensive a range of actions can be taken to facilitate the translation process. In many ways those companies which had already developed strong conditioning features in relation to leading change had a head start. They had already justified the need for change, begun the creation of a capacity to mount the change. It was relatively more straightforward to test and build a supplementary collection of more specific mechanisms. These included the realization to not attempt to implement strategic change as a piece. Instead they broke the strategy down into smaller pieces which were more amenable to being worked on and where less risk was apparent. People were appointed with specific responsibilities for managing the change at different levels in the organization. Parallel use was also made of the reward and communications systems, often leading to their being substantially adjusted. Put together with the constant monitoring and feedback of the process such mechanisms generated valuable information. This data then enabled management to modify the original intention over time.

These means of implementing strategic change are best shown in use as the following sections will demonstrate.

Merchant banking

The evidence from the merchant banks Kleinwort Benson and Hill Samuel quickly confronts the notion of a simple translation of strategic intent into operational form. They also run somewhat counter to their reputation. While merchant banks are noted for their ability to advise others on strategy the bankers' own actions seldom conform to the orthodoxies of the textbook.

In broad terms there is a clear contrast between Kleinwort and Hill Samuel before they even began to attempt the linkage of strategic and operational change. Each differed in the extent to which a fully worked out strategic position had been developed. In this sense the merchant banks are much closer to traditional UK manufacturing and its lack of a strategic perspective by management at firm level (Elbaum and Lazonick 1986) than is generally realized. Kleinwort Benson therefore stands out progressively during the 1970s. The bank created a mode of strategic thinking during that decade which it was then able to develop in the face of the challenges of the 1980s.

By comparison, Hill Samuel did not construct an equivalent sort of corporate strategy. In fact, prior to 1980 almost the reverse was true. Indeed the bank defies the categories of the literature displayed above. It was not a case of a strategy being 'transformed-in-use'; in Hill Samuel's case the strategy as such emerged from within the balance of its operational activities. Both banks, however, confirm the importance attributed above to the cumulative aspect. In other words, Kleinwort Benson's foreign activities in the 1970s generated knowledge which was used in the global context of the following decade – even though the full exploitation of that knowledge has proved immensely difficult. At Hill Samuel the problems of the 1970s were carried forward in the shape of a more conservative mentality.

At Kleinwort the need for change had emerged from within its dominant commercial lending sphere and the imperatives which issued from its key international relationships. As was shown in the previous chapter the need for strategic change and the necessary capacity had been built up in the 1970s. These strategic intentions were then consolidated under the Hawkes regime from 1982 and the operational aspects refined accordingly. Kleinwort appears to be particularly strong in the way it proved able to adjust it supportive mechanisms such as the appointment of change managers within new structures. In view of the decade it took to develop its strategic perspective this then exposed the bank's weakness in what we have called the secondary mechanisms on a number of occasions and in different ways. Its management not only created new structures therefore but went on to rework its communications in order to tap a variety of levels and disciplines. The Hawkes generation of management, when it assumed executive responsibility from 1982, was equally prepared to adjust its strategy in the exceptional conditions of deregulation.

It is instructive that Kleinwort Benson had already gone through one cycle of thought over the need for a strategic view in the years after the merger in 1961. As we noted in chapter 3, Sir Mark Turner was anxious that the board should 'think strategically' and hence the use of Professor Rowland Smith at UMIST to run a series of seminars for the members. Although it proved short-lived, the episode was immensely instructive for junior management and the bank as a whole in the long term. Senior directors of the 1980s well remember the impact of Cyril Kleinwort (chairman from 1968) after the Smith exercise asking them to:

> get hold of the more articulate managers to meet with you and write a résumé of what we all thought we were growing to. That was a very interesting and useful exercise because for the first time I found that I

was having to say to these young Turks who were coming up with all sorts of ideas, now hold on we can't tear up the entire structure. (interview)

At the same time the attempt was a good example of the way political considerations can limit such initiatives as the exercise was 'rubbished in an effort to stop Mark becoming chairman'. More positively, the importance of the operation was recognized as a result of this early sequence. A new senior post was created in 1970 of Comptroller – someone responsible for overseeing that appropriate systems and people were in place for the bank's envisaged growth.

Kleinwort Benson during the 1970s was an excellent example of the adoption of a broad strategic position (the expansion of international banking) which then enabled a range of more operational ventures to develop. The necessary visions and values were supplied by the dominance of a commercial banking ethos among the senior managers. As one of their number puts it:

> there has been a tradition in commercial lending which has developed, to some extent, not only because of our traditions but also because those concerned, like Robin Fox and Michael Hawkes, have all traditionally come from that area. Though it is probably a misquote, the head of commercial banking once said, 'I don't know why we bother about divisionalizing the bank.' (interview)

With this sheet anchor, Kleinwort was able to expand its commercial banking abroad through a series of representative offices. One of those involved noted how the pattern emerged from within the set of local decisions since nobody said:

> 'I want to make a big push in Japan' . . . it was never really a commitment until individual transactions came off . . . there was no commitment to capital . . . the cost of marketing to Japan was seen as a variable item on the budget. (interview)

Yet it was from within this sequence of largely incremental, operational changes that the rising cohort of managers grew dissatisfied with the supportive mechanisms at their disposal. The result was that those managers put great emphasis in the early 1980s to adjusting structures and methods of communication. The committee structure of the management committee, and its three sub-committees (risk and resources, administration and accounts, and business development) has arisen in order to strengthen the link between strategic intent and practice. One of the keynotes has been the importance attributed to maximizing the use of the knowledge and experience at the operational level. The way the bank entered the interest rate swap market, for example, is instructive, as a committee member points out:

> We spent three meetings of the sub-committee of risk and resources discussing how we should analyse the real risk . . . Nobody on the management committee or its various sub-committees would feel they knew everything about everything so they would co-opt people . . . So the director who originated the idea would come to the meeting, he brought along two assistant managers who wouldn't sit there in silence all the way through waiting for their elders to decide – they would be encouraged and feel totally free to say whatever they thought was necessary to be said. (Interview)

It is interesting that this incipient unease shown by middle managers with the mechanisms which had evolved in the successful period of the 1970s was given full vent when they assumed senior positions in the following decade. The hallmark of Kleinwort Benson in the early 1980s was that it not only assessed its environment in a corporate sense (see chapter 3) but that it saw the need to alter the way it translated such choices into practice. Much like Longman in publishing, the bank was distinctive in that it (1) recognized early the climactic shifts in the nature of the sector and its competitive forces – especially the poor growth of UK merchant banks compared to overseas houses, and then (2) drove the implications of that assessment through the organization.

The Hermes exercise of 1982 is a case in point and illustrates how Kleinwort used its experience in the 1970s and improved its linkage of strategic and operational change. The failure to purchase a Far Eastern stockbroker in 1982 due to the slowness of Kleinwort's internal deliberations forced the issue. The resulting Hermes strategic review put the bank into a stronger position to act on such ventures. Yet this was not through bold one-dimensional initiatives, reliant only on senior executives. On the contrary, it did not provide any more than a broad overview of the main issues which the bank faced in the future and what appropriate responses might be. Yet what it did do was co-opt early on the managers and staff who would have to initiate and carry out those responses. None of the five who wrote the Hermes report included the senior executives of the chairman's committee.

The Hermes exercise was vital to Kleinwort's position in the 1980s. It clearly identified the threat of the international banking houses with their strong domestic base, capital size and their experience in providing 'dual capacity' – banking and securities trading. The keynote of Hermes, however, was the way in which this phase of linking strategic and operational change extended the techniques developed in the preceding two decades. A series of working parties were created in 1982 with representatives from the operating divisions. The chairman and his deputy, Pat Limerick, attended as many of the working sessions as possible. In other words, the formation of this strategic view for the 1980s already had certain secondary mechanisms built in. Monitoring and feedback was built in from the start, the change managers for carrying out many of the key changes were co-opted early given their central role in formulating the strategic approach.

The efficacy of Hermes became all the stronger as the need for more precise action in the divisions grew in response to the 'Big Bang'. This was clearly seen in the ability to take relatively swift action in February 1984 when the bank recruited a team of interest rate swap specialists to be based in Los Angeles. Six weeks later Kleinwort purchased ACLI, a Chicago-based US government securities dealer for $27.3 million. Two months later the UK stock broker, Grieveson Grant was acquired for $44 million. In February 1986 Kleinwort also attracted the top Eurobond trading team from the Chase Manhattan Bank.

Kleinwort Benson, with its strong cultural and technical base in traditional UK banking linked to a developed strategic perspective, produced one of the more successful initial expansions into securities trading. In 1987 Kleinwort was one of the few foreign securities firms to have a seat on the Tokyo Stock Exchange and 1,000 of its 3,500 employees were located outside the UK. This successful expansion during the upheavals of deregulation was a strong reflection of the bank's constant nurturing of ventures at the operational level which could co-exist within its evolving strategic perspective. This is not to argue that Kleinwort had discovered some perfect equilibrium. The problems faced in integrating Grieveson Grant, the backlog which emerged in the bank's back-room settlement work in 1987, and the eventual losses incurred dispel that notion.

What is significant is the way the management did not abandon its almost continuous adjustment at both the strategic and operational levels. In spite of the turbulence around the share crash of October 1987, Kleinwort set in motion another cycle of adjustments. These centred on the strengthening of the board both to match, in Hawkes' words, 'the complexity of our operations' and to cover any potential gap which might arise between the strategic and operational spheres. The extent of such a gap at Morgan Grenfell Group during the Guinness takeover of Distillers Corporation made Kleinwort's action all the more timely.

The previous chapter established how Kenneth Keith's approach at

Hill Samuel did not rely on first building a capacity for action or justifying the need for change. It is consistent therefore that little thought was given to the notion of an implementation process. Staff saw him as someone with exceptional talents related to the creation of deals but not those appropriate to the managerial problems to which such deals gave rise. Hill Samuel did not devolve decision making in the manner of Kleinwort. As in other respects the new chief executive in 1980 was left with too much to resolve in too short a time.

Hill Samuel's profile is immensely instructive. Kleinwort Benson accumulated a strong ability to relate the strategic and the operational over a number of cycles or iterations from the 1960s to the 1980s. Hill Samuel's experience was much more fragmented and it faced the problems of the 1980s largely without the abilities which Kleinwort had built up. As chapters 3 and 4 show, the expansion of Hill Samuel in the 1960s and early 1970s was not related to an elaborate strategy formulation process. Implementation was consequently even less considered. Keith's rationale was clear. He saw that the international spread of industry and finance at that time required 'a large group of financial and allied services under one roof'. In practice, operational changes had to catch up with the bold strategic actions of merger and acquisition taken by the Keith regime.

When problems arose in the mid–1970s the previous lack of attention to the strategic and operational link was exposed. The result was a string of problems which consumed the energies of the bank's staff. Unlike Kleinwort, Hill Samuel was unable to develop its methods of implementing change and then using the results to refine its strategic position across a series of episodes. Operational deficiencies in themselves were problematical. Hill Samuel's ignorance of its cost structures were therefore shown up by the sharp fall in property values and share prices in 1974 as the All Shares Index fell from 228 to 60. Even allowing for such difficulties Hill Samuel did not appear to cultivate the relations between senior and junior management. A divisional manager of the time notes how 'we never saw him [Keith] at our offices. He certainly never got into our business. I suppose it was the idea of delegation . . . but it didn't appear to have a strategic plan' (interview).

As with many contemporary businesses, the Hill Samuel group, aside from the banking operation, was treated as a portfolio of investments. Consequently there were no early attempts at constructing specialist communications, reward, or monitoring systems related to the implementation of change. In turn the extreme risk-aversion from 1974 militated against the kinds of experiment and progressive refinement of technique seen at Kleinwort – understandable in the face of interest rates at 15 per cent and inflation at 20 per cent. The 'interregnum' period between 1977 and 1980 (when Keith relinquished his position but retained the chairmanship) did little to help remedy the lack of integration of the strategic and operational levels. The especially poor performance of the HSIS part of the group exemplified the way senior group management were not fully acquainted with the constituent businesses. As at Associated Book Publishers these years were dominated by the need, in Sir Robert Clark's (deputy chairman under Kenneth Keith) words, to 'fire-fight'. In view of such problems Sir Robert did remarkably well to begin the introduction of some of the secondary mechanisms (such as new board roles linked to reporting and communications apparatus) which Kleinwort had been refining for over a decade.

It was immensely difficult for Hill Samuel by 1980 to follow Kleinwort Benson or Morgan Grenfell in the path of international development. It is highly revealing then that the improvements made by the new regime of Christopher Castleman rested in part on the attention he paid to providing a number of the mechanisms for linking strategic and operational change which had been absent in the 1970s.

Castleman took great trouble to justify the need for a new corporate orientation centred on acquisition. Yet he rejected the temptation to attempt bold, instant change. On the contrary, he preceded the move to growth through acquisition and the exploitation of the removal of foreign exchange controls with the construction of a much-needed set of supportive devices. He therefore reworked the personal link between the corporate and operational levels by becoming personally involved in those parts of the group he knew least (e.g. shipping). The reward system was adjusted through the introduction of divisional and unit profit sharing which supported the acquisition moves. Managers in the sub-divisions now acted as change managers, directly responsible for their budgets. Action to break the established disillusionment of junior management with the group was decisive. This took the form of Castleman's personal interrogation of the divisional managers with regard to their cost projections and variances. In due course the group management structure was adjusted in order to support the expansion process. From 1984 acquisitions were approved by the Group Executive Committee, made up of the five chief executives of the divisions and the group board of directors.

The outcome of this limited yet considered linking of strategic imperatives and implementation was highly positive. The group was better able to respond to the new opportunities of the early 1980s, as was shown in chapter 1. Staff felt that the Hill Samuel Group was no longer the banking operations plus a collection of divergent subsidiaries. The problem, however, was that Hill Samuel had in effect gone through but one relatively brief cycle of linking strategic and operational change. Indeed this relative immaturity supplies the main explanation as to why the senior management had not resolved their political differences over the best location for the group in the circumstances after 1986. The resignation of Castleman after the board's decision to offer Hill Samuel to the Union Bank of Switzerland glaringly illustrated how immature a capacity for integrating strategic and operational change Hill Samuel had compared to Kleinwort Benson.

Life assurance

The Prudential's experience helps develop the themes encountered with Kleinwort and Hill Samuel in a number of ways. However, Prudential is very different in one respect. While the merchant banks historically worked without obtrusive management structures, in life assurance the opposite is true. The Prudential offers contrasting portraits of how to move from the use of mechanistic to more organic modes of management (see earlier in this chapter) in order to implement strategic change.

The experience of the Prudential has many similarities to Kleinwort Benson. It is clear that a series of relatively small-scale operational changes were tried out in the 1970s. Their cumulative impact over time made a considerable difference to the further large-scale attempts at change in the mid–1980s. By that time it is apparent that Prudential's diversified product range and new distribution channels had been delivered by the combined use of both conditioning features and secondary mechanisms. As at Kleinwort, there remained in force a productive tension between the strategic and operational levels across the two decades.

The changes in the field staff in 1971 are a good example of the Prudential's early approach. The first alterations were kept small-scale due to field staff suspicion. Yet the low-key initiative was very much a critical release of the pressure for change which came from two sources:

> First was from Geoff Haslam who had felt that in the field staff we had an enormous resource which we were not making the most of. The

second was from the Agency management side. They felt there were better ways of running the business. This was partly in response to seeing how other life offices were doing it. (interview)

The result was a sequence of adjustment in the field staff over the decade. These extended from the introduction of Management by Objectives in 1972, through to the re-organization into two new divisions relating to the marketing and administration of the field staff operations.

As seen in the previous two chapters, the Prudential was able to achieve a major restructuring in 1978 to form the holding company – Prudential Corporation Limited. The benefit was greater flexibility in financing growth. The episode of restructuring was impelled by the alterations in the competitive pressures of the late 1970s. As with Kleinwort and Hill Samuel the need was for a central body with a strategic responsibility for all Prudential's subsidiaries. This was especially apparent after the unexpectedly large losses which emanated from Mercantile & General. The key point to note though is that Prudential's management was assiduous in carrying forward the implications of such episodes. The creation of the Prudential Corporation in 1978 was regarded not as an end result but as part of an ongoing sequence. The new form was used to propel the organization forward in three ways. This took the form of (1) access to both debt and equity markets for financing, (2) the development of a clearly identified senior management level, and above all (3) it was used to send a strong signal within the organization that further changes were to follow. As a senior executive put it:

> We could have remained with the Prudential Assurance Company but creating the corporation was a more dramatic gesture to make people realize we were actually making changes and to ram it home that this is the way we are going to manage. (Interview)

A middle manager confirms the point since he saw that the corporate restructuring provided

> a mental model of the Prudential as a holding company. It sometimes gets confused because the businesses are interlinked and share services but that is irrelevant. It is the organization, the system of management that matters. (Interview)

The Prudential derived great benefits from its series of changes in the 1970s. It was able to try out and strengthen a number of facilitating devices. These mechanisms were a major reason for the Prudential's ability to respond to the shifts in the wholesale financial sector, regulation and consumer demand from 1979. Unlike others, Prudential was able to generate much greater energy for key changes in the 1980s. Even among the more conservative sales staff, the evidence of the small-scale changes of the preceding decade pointed clearly to the need to enter new markets. The fear of such moves had been removed. In our terms, the sequence of strategic and operational change in the 1970s gave rise to a set of conditioning features; the corporate restructuring helped to establish the need for further change.

The Prudential has achieved a vital move in the 1980s. There has been a move away from its reactive stance to changes in the environment to one where management feels able to take the lead. What emerges in the 1980s is a deeper capacity to link strategic and operational change in spite of the turbulence in the Prudential's environment. Against what the manager called the broad 'mental model' of what the Prudential should be, a robust set of mechanisms was forged which could support the necessary operational changes.

The strategic move into a totally new market – via the Prudential Property Services (PPS) in 1985 – was achieved. The aim was to acquire local estate agents across the UK and become the largest national estate agency with 800 outlets by 1988. Prudential's intention was to exploit the wider consumer market for financial services by offering a range of products (e.g. mortgages and life assurance) to prospective home owners. Prudential management were concerned about a potentially negative reaction from the outdoors staff who feared retrenchment in their area. To counter this view the acquired estate agents were placed in a newly formed division. The PPS division was used to create a separate business culture independent of the established practices of the UK individual divisions. Although the initial move was successful, the long-term results were disappointing. A lack of understanding of the property market at operational level eventually overcame the strategic intention in this area.

Prudential has augmented its ability to implement change with a string of other measures. These include new change managers characterized by their professionalism, wider range of skills and often their recruitment from outside. In the words of a senior executive involved in the early 1980s:

> Brian Corby recognized that there was a need to shove and shake the organization. So he started to put some 'shakers' into place in critical positions underneath . . . he put a guy into the industrial division who had been with the company for only eight to ten years in a financial role. The very fact that you stick someone in who is bright but doesn't know too much about the detail of it, but knows the numbers, forces

them to sit down and think about things radically. This helped to create a much greater willingness to change because there wasn't the same commitment to the past. (interview)

The new entrants have in turn eroded the traditional middle-management aversion to taking full responsibility since the newcomers were specifically given targets which assumed their taking full managerial control. Such new managers refused to accept the traditional, formal systems of communication through the hierarchy. Keith Bedell-Pierce was the newly appointed general manager of operations with responsibility for the salesforce. He side-stepped the established lines of communication by not only increasing the amount of information to staff but also, as he put it:

> I didn't accept the old principles and old practices. I recognized that in order to get something accepted I actually had to market the concept first of all to the people who mattered out in the field – which were the line bosses, and once we got them on our side, then we marketed it to the field staff. Only then, after we had got the thing sold to the people who were going to distribute it, did we start to sell it to the public. (interview)

These types of moves supported and extended the restructuring of the Prudential, away from the old dominant Prudential Assurance Company to a set of divisions which could concentrate on the newly emerging market segments. Such a range of action had the additional benefits of allowing the move away from functional groups (marketing or actuarial) and their in-built friction as well as the decisive loosening of the actuarial culture's hold on the Prudential's strategic approach.

Automobiles

The automobile companies are distinctive since they have a ready-made industry model of linking strategic and operational change centred on project management. In particular they demonstrate the need to go beyond the structural emphases of such models in order to resolve the problems of implementation.

Jaguar's strength in the primary conditioning features has been well evidenced in the previous two chapters as it tried to make up the deficiencies of the 1970s. Where it has scored highly is in the set of secondary mechanisms assembled virtually from scratch in the 1980s.

The main internal problem facing Jaguar in 1980 stemmed directly from the vast chasm which had opened up between corporate strategy and operations at Browns Lane. The watchword for Jaguar managers after the Jaguar management board was disbanded by BL in 1975 was survival. Enormous efforts were made to prevent corporate management gaining effective control. Positive skills in implementing change were left undeveloped as the negative imperative of resistance prevailed. Jim Randle, a vehicle engineer at the time, puts the point well when he says:

> We were successful in keeping ourselves clear of BL. We were not successful in the aims of producing product or putting the product right: those got lost, I fear, in the sheer politics of the situation. (interview)

What is remarkable about Jaguar is the way the management from 1980 was able to bring into being a means of linking strategic and operational change – first during its break-even exercise of 1980–1 and then to refine it across the subsequent regeneration and growth phases. The company achieved exceptional results yet without the benefit of Kleinwort's, Prudential's or Longman's previous long-term sequence of developing such traits.

The crisis phase saw the combination of (1) justifying the need for change to an alienated work-force, and (2) creating the capacity for action around the re-establishment of the product identification of Lyons but alongside the construction of new functions necessary to meet the world market conditions of the 1980s. Beyond these conditioning features was an action plan which was designed to: improve communications and involve the work-force in the plan (for a 1986 version of how this scheme developed see figure 5.2), enhance quality and reliability standards in a measurable way, and reduce operating costs in every area. In other words, a compact set of supportive devices aimed at the strategic intention of breaking even.

The regeneration and growth stages are notable for the extent of the secondary actions which were created in order to secure the goals of sustained profitability and separation from BL (for a summary see figure 5.3; the structure develops an idea by Gerstein 1987: 53). Breaking the necessary changes into actionable pieces is illustrated by the wholesale creation of product planning and project management skills – anathema to the inspired yet *ad hoc* approaches of Lyons, England, or Knight in the past. As figure 5.3 indicates, by 1987 Jaguar had moved on to a much more sophisticated model whereby the full range of its departments were used. This was aided considerably by the formation of both new managerial positions and adjusted

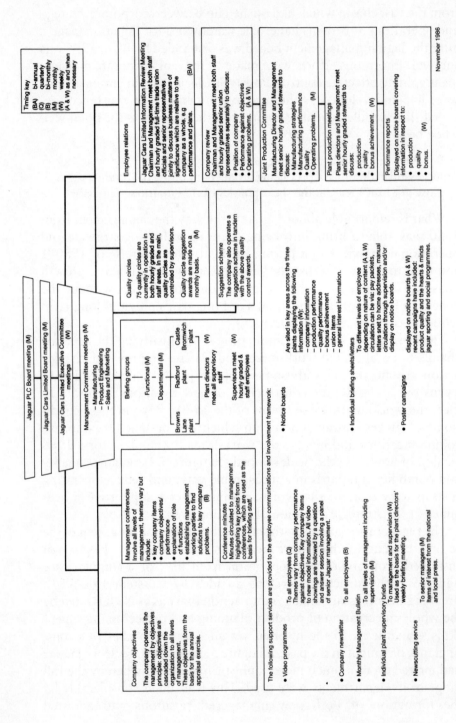

Figure 5.2 Jaguar: structure for employee communications and involvement, 1986
Source: Jaguar Cars

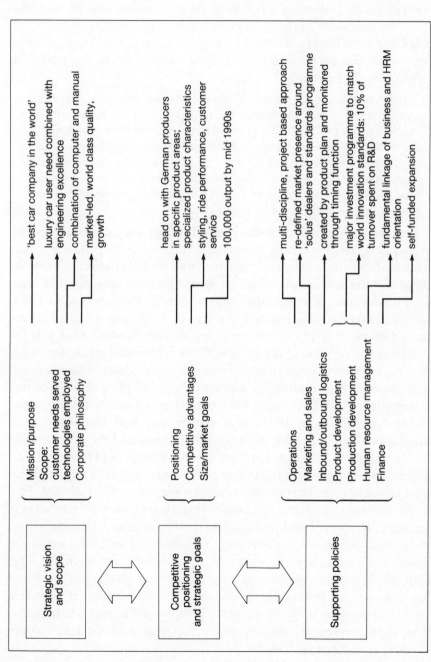

Figure 5.3 Jaguar Cars: strategic scope, competitive position and supporting policies

structures in order to facilitate the innovations which Jaguar's evolving product plan entailed. New principles were introduced of multidisciplinary project teams and the promotion of 'people to plan projects *and* run them' (interview). It was in these combinations of role and structure that some of the most entrenched political differences of the past have been broken down. The experience of a marketing planner (who now works routinely on projects with vehicle engineers) is instructive. As he puts it:

> Project teams are important. They are one of the most important generators of change in attitude we are looking for. It doesn't always work. You go to Cranfield and spend two weeks on these 'pot-boilers'. Now, what it cleverly did to my mind was to create a sort of Cranfield graduate atmosphere – and there is a bit of elitism. Now if you have all been on it and you've all had your psychology stretched across the table you are much more ready to go into team management with those people back in the company. (Interview)

Jaguar management provides one of the best instances of the use of monitoring, feedback and adjustment techniques to produce a live relationship between the strategic and operational change. We saw in chapter 3 the way feedback loops in the product development area were used as part of environmental assessment. However, since 1984 Jaguar has pushed the principle further. This was graphically demonstrated in the way the newly emerging marketing staff were able to challenge the decision to do away with the traditional interior trim on the results of their professionally run customer clinics. The resulting combination of technological sophistication and the retention of the luxury identity of the marque were critical to the successful reception of the XJ40 (XJ6) in 1986. In a similar way new technology has stimulated the relationship between the strategic and the operational. It was one thing to adopt CAD techniques for the XJ41 project, the problem was to monitor the extent of their use. The cost implications were considerable. To train and resource one user cost £100,000. The result has been a system of monitoring through the system's own software. Resources and training can then be adjusted accordingly.

Peugeot Talbot's recovery in the 1980s has seen the mobilization of similar devices – albeit less spectacularly and more incrementally. The company is possibly the strongest example of the way an organization has had to revise its strategy by use. The central feature has been the need to respond to both crisis and the position of Peugeot SA. In many ways the achievement has been the development of an implementation capacity in spite of such shifts.

The clues to Peugeot Talbot's ability to adjust its operations to meet strategic changes lie in the 1970s. Although an appalling time in terms of financial performance, CUK staff had to become adept at responding to often violent swings in corporate management's direction. The Avenger car project, although undermined by production problems was acknowledged as a technical and logistical success. Similarly CUK's engineering staff's development of the Sunbeam in 1977 won plaudits within the industry – notwithstanding the circumstances of bankruptcy, political turmoil and the removal of investment to Chrysler France.

One should not be so surprised therefore by the ability of largely the same staff at Peugeot Talbot from 1978 to respond to the switchback of strategic changes which included: an attempt to rework the CUK operation, the reduction to producer status between 1981 and 1983 and then the regeneration based on new products from 1984. In a way the staff remaining in the 1980s had been forced consistently, over a decade, to make almost continuous operational changes. It was wholly logical therefore that with greater strategic consistency under the Turnbull and Whalen regimes such a capacity for implementing change could bear fruit.

Peugeot Talbot reveals the need to break its emerging strategy into workable segments. This was exemplified in the phase of contraction during 1981–3. This entailed the reduction of its work-force by 17,000 by 1982, the closure of the Linwood and Dublin plants in 1981, the cessation of Dodge truck activities to Renault and the relocation of Peugeot Talbot's UK parts and administrative offices. What stands out is the ability of Peugeot Talbot first to carry out the major strategy of reduction and then, second, to use those same skills from 1984 to create a set of competitive bases more appropriate to the international auto industry of the 1980s.

It is intriguing to see the consistent appearance of certain mechanisms across the different phases from 1978. The appointment of change managers and the creation of suitable structures for them to work in has almost been forced on the company. Under CUK, management relied on the corporate manuals to cover operational difficulties. In Peugeot Talbot a very different answer has been found: the delegation of authority to the person best suited to carry out a given project. A clear example comes from the Triaxle bus project developed as a means of using spare capacity in the Stoke plant as the interruptions to the Iranian car kit contract worsened. Once the decision was taken to go ahead then the manufacturing director was given the clear

responsibility for implementing the change. Unlike many car companies, he had already been involved in the original simulation of the
project at the concept stage. The age-old problem of the separation
and isolation of the implementation process were therefore avoided.

As in the case of Jaguar, Peugeot Talbot has devoted great effort to
enhancing other support mechanisms such as communications. Adequate attention has also been paid to managing the political friction
inherent in the traditional specialist/departmental values of UK car
companies. Peugeot Talbot has gone against the orthodoxy and the
intense secrecy over major changes such as new car projects. The aim
of the management has been to provide a central source of information
rather than let such projects become victim to damaging speculation
and rumour. The company's communication programme now incor-
porates work-force briefings on key company performance indicators.
As part of the D60 (405) launch in 1987 every employee was taken
through a one-day course explaining the significance of the model to
the company. The approach could not have been more different than
the suffocating secrecy seen in the 1970s. According to a Ryton worker
it was all about 'getting people thinking about the car, its competitors,
the market it is competing in and how it should be presented to the
market-place . . . to the public' (interview).

Peugeot Talbot's argument is that if the work-force is to be
convinced of the relevance of managerial policies then it has to be given
the information which demonstrates it.

Book publishing

The singular aspect of the two book publishers is the differing amount
of attention devoted to the educative requirements of the translation
process. The result is seen in the relative strategic awareness displayed
at the operational level in the two companies.

Longman's ability to translate strategic initiatives into operational
form is shown with clarity in the development of its US market. In the
late 1960s it was evident to Longman (with 70 per cent of its business
outside the UK) that it was in danger of becoming too reliant on its
Commonwealth and related markets. Longman decided therefore to
expand its publishing in the developed world and particularly North
America. Longman acted early and opened a small import house in
New York in 1973. The base was then used to sell UK published books
in the USA while gradually building up Longman's own commission-

ing from New York. A senior executive was appointed in 1975 to co-ordinate an advance on three fronts: medical, college and English language teaching. The point to note is that there was no attempt to achieve major change in one jump. Instead smaller, less risky, more manageable steps were tried. The success is shown by the contribution of US sales to Longman in the 1980s, up from 2.7 per cent of total sales in 1973 to 30.2 per cent by 1987.

In the medical field the Churchill Livingstone imprint was used to sell UK texts to the USA. Subsequently, books by American medical and scientific authors were published; the added benefit was that they could in turn be sold in the UK. In college publishing in the 1970s the idea was, according to a commissioning editor, to 'build on the base of exporting from the UK appropriate books to be sold in America and then gradually publish college books locally for the American market' (interview). Here progress was slower. The mistake was in trying to publish across too wide a band of subjects. Yet this knowledge was used in the subsequent ELT and other initiatives. For example, in spite of the inviting scale of this English-speaking market Longman had learnt that it could not hope to cover the market as a whole as did native US publishers like Prentice Hall. Instead, Longman was able to exploit its strengths within further specialist niches.

In common with Jaguar, Prudential and to an extent Kleinwort Benson, Longman was able not only to deploy a spread of devices which facilitated operational change, but to refine them almost continuously. These are summarized in figure 5.4. Chapter 4 showed the importance to Longman of its move during this period from departmental to divisional and then sectoral structures. Yet within the sectoral form, for example, further innovations have been encouraged appropriate to their markets. These include the creation of highly autonomous 'publishing cells' in the scientific area, located not in the Harlow centre but adjacent to their sources and markets. Alongside these new ventures, however, there has been a constant retuning of company-wide communications. The need was felt keenly when after such expansion and innovations a questionnaire in 1983 to middle managers showed how 'little they knew about the sectors' strategic goals'. The result has been an increasing elaboration of the communications apparatus to include briefing groups, sectoral conferences and company-wide financial commentaries given to all staff.

The area which tested to the full Longman's ability to implement strategic change was its 1980s' problem child – Longman's distribution, computing and production services (LDCPS). Longman

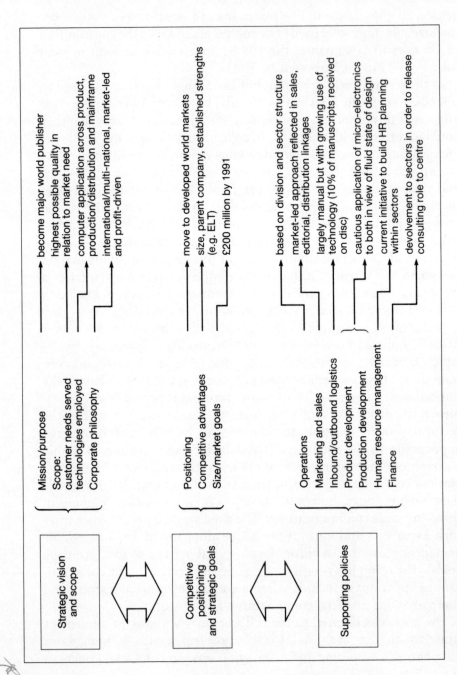

Figure 5.4 Longman: strategic scope, competitive position and supporting policies

management was forced to make use of virtually all of the secondary mechanisms we have identified. In the 1982–5 period the division was increasingly acting as a brake on the performance of the others. The aim of the board was to remove this brake. The remit of the new director of the division, Paul Blackburn, was therefore to change the division so that it could 'supply a service which enables market opportunities to be taken such that the company's business objectives may be better realized' (interview).

The basic reformation of LDCPS occurred through a set of conditioning and supporting actions which included:

- a major communications exercise to identify new commercial and service standards
- direct negotiation with the Society of Graphical and Allied Trades (SOGAT) on new working practices
- the introduction of staff from other industries to help free-up accepted yet outmoded practices and act as role models
- exposing staff to the availability of alternative supplies of their service and terminating outside contracts where the new service standards were not being met
- the creation of first, cost profiles and then, profit benchmarks
- keeping the message alive through periodic campaigns such as the 'customer care' initiatives in 1987.

The early successful impact of this programme was not then merely left in place. On the contrary, it was subsequently reworked through the application of such principles and techniques to specific projects. A case in point was the decision to adopt the VISTA computing system in 1986. February 1987 saw the first phase of the system 'go live' and by 1988 enquiry facilities to the full database were released to the whole company. What emerges is that the once laggardly LDCPS division was able to deepen its new repertoire of mechanisms to include some of the approaches seen in Jaguar's project management. These included a detailed planning phase for example involving:

- the conscious breakdown of the project into specialist groups and tasks
- the allocation of personnel and the establishment of roles
- the resolution of key organizational and policy issues with the company's finance committee.

Only when these actions had been taken was a detailed timetable confirmed. At the same time these actions were deliberately used to alter by demonstration the relationship between the computer services specialists and the staff in the sectors. The need was to break down the assumption on the part of the computing staff that they only dispensed computer know-how to sector personnel. The thrust was towards a devolution of computer use to publishing staff so that there could follow a joint development of local PC use. As in Jaguar, quite small acts (such as the use of the Cranfield course) had disproportionate effects. In the LDCPS case the moving of one of the specialists in information systems to the personnel department was exceptionally useful in demonstrating the new accessibility of such specialists. There is still a long way to go in fully breaking down what has been described as the 'we know best' attitude on the part of some computing staff. Yet without the changes which have occurred the introduction of the VISTA system would have been still-born.

It is instructive to compare the way ABP attempted to enter the US market. As the need for expansion into new product areas grew in the 1970s ABP was forced to attempt a large-scale venture in 1978. The company found itself competing head-on with established trade publishers in the USA, a product and market of which it had 'hardly any experience' (interview). The compressed nature of the attempt at change prevented the creation or use of more supportive secondary mechanisms, in comparison with Longman. The problems of almost constant fire-fighting in the 1970s precluded the previous development of such devices.

While Longman was mounting a series of adjustments to its structure to release managerial responsibility, increase market alignment and try out innovative publishing units (e.g. the cell idea), ABP was still struggling to clarify its internal form. The paradox resulted therefore of a company with world-class editorial standards yet less developed other departments. The skills of monitoring, feedback and adjustment had little chance to grow. This was acutely felt in the light of the pronounced changes in book retailing described in chapter 2. A marketing manager of the academic division saw the result was insufficient knowledge in, for example, 'exploiting certain markets'.

Management also found that the preoccupations of the 1970s had left them comparatively less familiar in using the feedback and adjustment processes as found at Longman. David Croom, a newcomer to ABP, with his key responsibility of the academic division from 1984 makes the point well. He is clear how the new growth objectives for the mid–1980s were given to the imprints. Yet in his words no dialogue, no testing or interrogation followed to develop the objectives at the operational level. The growth targets were not 'drawn out in human terms' – unlike at Kleinwort, for example, or most especially via the finance committee at Longman.

Conclusion

The importance attributed to linking strategic and operational change is because the process has both an intentional and emergent character. The need is to appreciate therefore how intentions are implemented – and hence transformed – over time. Indeed the additive effect of otherwise separate decisions and acts of implementation may be so powerful that they overwhelm the original intentions and even help create an entirely new context for future strategic decision making. Strategies so often therefore are the *post hoc* labelling of such series of 'successful' operational acts.

Unsurprisingly the conditioning features involved are similar to those in leading change. They centre on the building of a receptive context for change, the capability for action and the necessary visions and values which underwrite the chosen business direction.

Great attention is required though to the secondary mechanisms if the operational aspects are not to undermine the general strategic intentions. Not only must those intentions be broken down to actionable pieces, those components must become the responsibility of change managers, operating within appropriate structures at various levels within the organization. Clear and exacting target setting has in turn to be supported by re-thought communication mechanisms and adjusted reward systems. The modification of overall visions in the light of local conditions is a major requirement, as is the construction of human resource capabilities which can support such a raft of related changes.

The management of strategic and operational change is one of the sharpest illustrations of simultaneity. It places a premium on the ability to cope with the linked analytical, educational and political dimensions of the process – together. Indeed the benefits accumulated through analysis of the environment, and its integration into all levels of the organization through leading change, can be neutralized by inability to handle the associated political problems. The example of Jaguar in the 1970s is striking. Even more revealing is the differences within senior management at Hill Samuel in the later 1980s, and the eventual departure of the chief executive. This was in spite of the enormous strides which had been made in systematic analysis of the changing environment and an especially sensitive mode of generating collective learning in the re-shaped group structure.

The evidence from Longman, Prudential and, in particular, Kleinwort Benson, strongly suggests that the politics of managing strategic and operational change has to be consciously addressed. Nor is this just a matter of resolving the differences between senior management (see chapter 7, under 'Coherence'). Even if agreement and commitment is secured at that level, then the translation of a given strategy into operational form can fracture if attention is not paid to the issues of power and vested interest at lower levels. At Kleinwort Benson, therefore, the success of the Hermes exercise relied on the way junior staff were incorporated into the generation of the report; they were correspondingly able to understand and commit themselves to the operational actions which resulted.

Similarly at the Prudential, the new senior managers of the Corby regime in the 1980s facilitated the development of vital new products through attention to the needs of middle-ranking staff: the opposite, of course, of the actuarial and hierarchical structure of relations in the 1960s and early 1970s. In the case of both existing staff and, above all, new entrants, a climate was created which encouraged risk-taking and accepted the prospect of failure.

The examples covered in this chapter also point to the need to appreciate the time element. This appears in a number of ways. If the issue of managing the politics of strategic and operational change is taken seriously, then management has to accept differences in the time ordering of such changes across the organization (Whipp 1987: 216). As Longman shows, wide variations in the timing of the initiatives in its different business sectors was tolerated. The intention was to reflect the different competences and confidence of say the powerhouse of ELT versus the fragility of the new staff in the business publishing area.

Perhaps the strongest conclusion to be drawn with respect to the time element is the often uneven yet cumulative character of the process of managing strategic and operational change. What stands out in the case of ABP, Rootes/CUK, and Hill Samuel at certain times, is the way they were unable to maximize the operational revisions which they were forced into. By contrast, their counterparts drew tremendous benefit by transforming their strategies in use – made possible by their development of an appropriate learning capacity. In other words, Prudential, Kleinwort and Longman were able to convert a sequence of many short-run adjustments into a newly emergent strategic posture. Jaguar had done remarkably well in this respect, through the events of 1980–1, 1982–4 and 1984–7. As the problems of 1988–90 show, Jaguar did not have the benefit of such accumulation across the 1970s; indeed, it was constantly working against that disadvantage in virtually every department. It is not so surprising therefore that the company's ability in this respect was overtaken by the external intervention at both the global industry and UK government level.

Up to now implicit use has been made of the contribution of human resources to the management of strategic change. The use of new compensations systems at Prudential, in order to create the climate for risk-taking seen in this chapter, is one example. Now is the time to examine that contribution in its own right.

6

Human Resources as Assets and Liabilities

Authoritative reports have highlighted the low skill and training levels in the UK work-force compared to other countries (Handy 1987; Constable and McCormick 1987). The enthusiastic reception given to these findings is somewhat confusing; contradictions abound. To take a general example: if, as virtually any manager will say, 'people are our most important asset', then why does British management devote so little to educating its staff? A more specific instance comes from the remark of a personnel manager just before the MSC and BIM reports appeared. Working for a major international corporation in the UK he bemoaned the way his company 'spends millions of pounds on developing and testing new products yet gives "peanuts" to developing the people who produce and sell those products'. The apparent contradiction does, however, serve a useful purpose. The paradox contains some of the core problems in managing change and competition: how to maximize the effective use of the human and other resources of a firm in pursuit of competitive advantage; how to exploit both tangible and intangible assets; and to treat human resources as an investment rather than just a cost.

In many ways the divergence between managerial rhetoric and action in this area can be explained by reference to the existing bodies of knowledge that serve the subject. Social analysts have been thrown into some disarray by the impact of new technological and societal upheavals. Beyond that the contact (in the UK) between such writers and practitioners has been at best intermittent. Acute concern with national competitive performance in the late 1970s within Western economies has had its effect on the subject. The approach here though has been a partial one and the results not readily linked to managers' problems.

The growing body of specialist human resource management commentators has been more helpful. A library of working examples is
emerging and genuine insights have resulted. New benchmarks of good
HR practice have been enthusiastically proclaimed. The problem has
been the lack of attention to key issues. The blind spot in such work
has been its superficial resolution of the problems of how such new
practices and standards are created, introduced and sustained (for an
exception see Pettigrew, Hendry and Sparrow 1989). Few writers in
this field demonstrate empirically the link between human resource
management and competitive performance.

The purpose of this chapter therefore is twofold. The first task is to
suggest that the gap between rhetoric and practice at the level of the
firm is partly explained by the emphases of the commentators. The
second objective is to show how a processual analysis of the problem
is a vital step forward in both conceptual and practical terms. How
such changes are managed is of the utmost importance. The evidence
from the four sectors in the study confirms this approach and goes
further. The more accomplished firms indicate that conventional
attempts to move from a traditional personnel to a human resources
orientation by managers will be severely weakened if they ignore the
problem of learning.

Control, capital and knowledge

In spite of the efforts of novelists such as David Lodge (1989), even
the more reflective manager has a largely negative image of social
analysts. In the unlikely event that an executive considered the output
of such writers, he or she would see the relevance of those findings to
their work as remote. Even if heavy-handed sociological jargon is
condemnable this should not obscure the contribution which the
discipline has made to the understanding of industry and most
especially its human component.

Interest in the subject of management and in particular its ability to
control labour has been long-standing. The issue was of course a
burning one during the maturation of the British industrial economy
in the nineteenth century (Hobsbawm 1974). During the present
century the interest has been maintained. A number of schools of
thought have arisen, each attempting to address what was seen as the
essential problems of their time. The earliest approaches related to the
problems of regulating factory production in a supposedly 'scientific'

way (Merkle 1980) in the 1900s. A rather different emphasis was seen in the attempt to develop a 'human relations' orientation based on the techniques of social psychology in the 1920s.

A review of the succession of approaches reveals a pattern. Each variant reflected the social and economic conditions from which it emerged. Detailed studies (Ramsay 1980) covering the period 1860 to the 1970s have shown how participative managerial styles have flourished when economic conditions tightened the labour supply. Employers in the auto industry altered their forms of work organization from direct control to responsible autonomy according to the strength of the market for cars (Whipp and Clark 1986: 19).

The identification of such patterns is significant for a number of reasons. It not only helps to explain the appearance of new initiatives such as human resource management in the 1980s, it also puts them into perspective. Rather than being seen as somehow the ultimate or most highly developed form of managing the work-force, such innovations are attempts to meet particular historical circumstances. The similarities with earlier periods are often strong: one example is the parallel between the arbitration and conciliation movement of the 1880s and the more well-known industrial relations machinery of the 1970s (Clegg 1979). This long-term perspective also indicates (as the cases below will show) just how fragile and perishable such initiatives are given that they are designed to address specific conditions. The conciliation apparatus of the 1880s and 1970s were both overturned by the onset of marked economic recessions.

A further strength of the long-range analysis of management attempts to control work is the way this genre has revealed the extent of the influences in operation (Whipp 1990a). Studies of industrial conflict alone have uncovered a complex set of interlocking factors in their explanations (for a useful overview see Thompson 1983). Rick Edwards' work on US industry in the twentieth-century drew attention to the interplay of: the speed of technological change; the impact of government policies; the extent of trade union organization; the level of class-consciousness; and the centrifugal forces within the external labour market (Edwards 1979: 15).

Others have gone on to widen the investigation to include, for example, the issues of gender (Milkman 1987), the internal labour market (Loveridge 1983), the role of the state and regional character (Sabel 1982) or community structure (Whipp 1985). Any assumptions therefore of some straightforward resolution of the problems of work-force control and direction are inappropriate. The difficulties facing any study of such issues are well summarized by the conclusion of Burawoy (1985) resulting from his international comparative research on industrial relations. As he put it, the production process is not just about the production of objects, it involves the creation of social relationships.

In the late 1960s and the 1970s work on the management of the work-force was dominated with the concern of conflict and control. Market dislocation combined with the growth of unofficial shop-floor organization and attempts by governments across Europe to manage their economies produced record levels of industrial unrest. In the 1980s the climate had altered dramatically after the world-wide recession at the beginning of the decade and levels of unemployment not seen since the 1930s. Commentators have rightly drawn attention to other profound changes which have produced an entirely different context for both managers and employees.

Previous assumptions about the progress of the automation of production were overtaken by the possibilities of computerization. Now micro-electronics could be applied to not only manufacture but also design, distribution, office administration and communications together (Kaplinsky 1984). Such technological innovation was partly in response to international product market changes; subsequently the new technology itself impelled those changes even further. Long-term increases in living standards for those in work allied to the changes in the variety of consumer tastes led to a breakdown of previous patterns of mass demand. In addition the increasing international mobility of capital and the temporary saturation point reached in certain Western markets indicated that the principles of mass production were no longer dominant.

Many have argued (see Sabel 1982) that new industrial forms of organization are required to meet these circumstances. In view of the passing of the largely US auto industry model of mass production, the label post-Fordist has been used to denote the new principles of organization. The keynotes include the division of large corporations into multiple internal businesses; greater use of temporary employment contracts; the retention of a small core of highly skilled employees; extensive contracting-out of services; and the further separation of research, design and production. Unsurprisingly, new modes of work-force management have been advocated, heavily influenced by the outstanding success of Japanese companies in Western domestic markets (Pascale and Athos 1981).

There is a problem with such writing in relation to national context.

Britain is a case in point. Differences in legal, institutional and political frameworks quickly dilute the accuracy of the post-Fordist notion. More fundamentally, the deeply embedded characteristics of the firm and its management in the UK cannot be dismissed lightly. As we have already seen, the late emergence of large corporations and equally professional management has coloured the reaction of firms to the upheavals of the 1980s. After all, British management has been recognized as failing to adopt the US principles of mass production and corporate organization in the post-war era (Marginson et al. 1988). It is entirely logical therefore to expect a distinctive response on the part of UK management to the technological and market changes of the past decade. Nowhere has this been more apparent than in the area of human resource management.

The distinctiveness of the British position has been further underlined by the revival of interest in the concept of a national human resource or capital. The argument that the UK has experienced lower growth than its main competitors due to the shortcomings in managerial techniques and the training of employees is hardly new. The point was made forcibly by Royal Commissions during the great depression of the 1880s. More recently the problem of economic retardation has been attributed to the choice made by UK employers and managers to retain their imperial and specialist markets (Elbaum and Lazonick 1986). Consequently they did not need to develop corporate organization on the US scale. Above all they could maintain the largely nineteenth-century employment arrangements of piece-work and indirect control of labour (Gospel forthcoming).

Debates among economists over the precise nature of UK growth in the late 1980s have led to interesting results in the area of human resources. Crafts (1988) argues that macro structural problems (such as the growth of the public sector crowding out investment) do not explain the low growth of the UK economy. Instead he points to supply side defects. These include inappropriate plant size, a shortfall of research and development and inadequate education and training allied to problems with the structure and conduct of industrial relations. On the evidence of the 1980s there has been little reduction of this historic 'training lag'. Crafts concludes that these features supply the critical reasons why 'Britain has not yet transformed itself into an economy that is capable of rapid growth in the long term'. These findings are important in their own right but combining them with the work of other social scientists gives them even greater force. Both sets of writers confirm the long-term weakness of work-force management in the UK. They supply a useful yardstick with which to judge the attempts of the firms in our study to make the transition from a personnel to a human resource management (HRM) approach in the 1980s.

A second body of research pitched at the national level has received far greater public attention. The reports of Handy (1987) and Constable and McCormick (1987) on management education and training form the centre-piece of this work. Their main observations have been well publicized. British managers are woefully under-educated by international standards. Apparently only 24 per cent of the UK's senior managers have a degree, while in the USA and Japan the figure is 85 per cent. Half of the USA's top companies give their managers five days, off-the-job training each year. In Britain the average is one day of formal training per year. Handy's dismal conclusion is that 'management training in Britain is too little, too late, for too few'. The reports show a particular gulf between Britain and its European competitors. In France companies are obliged to spend 0.5 per cent of their wage bill on initial training and 1.1 per cent on continuous training. In practice they devote 2.14 per cent, of which just under a third goes on management training. Germany, like Japan, recruits university graduates who then receive extensive in-house training from their employers.

The findings of the economists interested in national human capital and the management education reports provide the vital national context in which UK firms operate. However, the picture they produce is a partial one. Their concern is with national aggregates, not the differences in company performance. They concentrate on outcomes at the expense of explaining how such a poor profile results from action taken at the level of the firm. Such problems will be tackled directly later in this chapter.

The 1980s have seen the appearance of an extensive literature grouped around the banner of human resource management. In the light of the manifest shortcomings of work-force management in the UK and the severe tests applied by successful overseas competitors, it was to be expected that a new 'best practice' should appear in print. The characteristics of this literature owe a great deal to their origins in the USA: that is, amidst the managerial soul-searching of the mid–1970s touched off by the poor performance of their industries (see chapter 1). The general concern in the USA was the imbalance within its managerial objectives. Attention to the needs of mass production in the post-war period had resulted in high levels of manufacturing productivity but at the expense of product innovation, marketing and the management of people (Scott and Lodge 1985). The demonstration effect of Japanese entry to US domestic markets was outstanding. As Jones and Womack (1986) observed, it was patently obvious in the light of the techniques of these competitors that US industry had devoted too much attention to its hardware and insufficient to its human 'software'.

A stream of writing and breast-beating followed into the 1980s around certain main issues. These included: the striving to achieve an improved 'fit' between strategic planning and a range of functions (see chapter 5 under 'Innovators, sceptics and specialists') but especially with the difficult areas of people management (Beer et al. 1984; Walton 1987); the notion that excellent businesses depended in part on corporate culture (Peters and Waterman 1982); and the recognition by Porter (1985) that HRM was an integral part of the value chain at firm level. In due course a specialist body of writing developed which has elaborated the contribution which personnel and industrial relations policies could make to strategy (for a comprehensive treatment of these developments see Guest 1987).

The major differences in economic and social circumstances notwithstanding, evangelists for the US-based HRM approach have been numerous in Britain. The rhetoric of HRM has slipped relatively easily into managerial parlance alongside the 1980s' vocabulary of mission statements, computer integrated manufacture (CIM) and total quality. To be sure, there have been clear indications of the way companies have attempted to link their personnel and reward systems to a longer-range strategic perspective, or in the way management have sought to integrate, say, manufacturing and personnel planning. Leading edge examples have been celebrated in the specialist business press and sometimes in greater depth. Bassett (1986), for example, produces a detailed account of the way IBM (UK) has made extensive alterations in its manpower planning, performance assessments, salary research, and communications in relation to what it sees as the projected changes in the industry and market.

It is here that a word of caution is required. The main problem with this growing literature is the way that it accepts the new HRM rhetoric but fails to question its conceptual assumptions or tackle the gulf between the US and British contexts. Given what we have already established in terms of the persistent underdevelopment of employment and personnel practices in the UK, one should at least be wary of the claims of some the more extreme HRM zealots. Substantial evidence is to hand, however, which confirms the scale of the task if HRM is to become firmly rooted in UK business.

Work done in the late 1970s showed just how alien was the notion of strategy in the industrial relations (IR) and personnel functions across different industries. Subsequent survey and case study research in the 1980s has deepened our knowledge. There have been marked changes in certain aspects of work. One example is flexibility. A study of four sectors in 1986 showed that two-thirds of the firms were attempting new pay structures, a fifth using more self-employed and 90 per cent had introduced various forms of contracting-out (Atkinson and Meager 1986; Curson 1986). Other research suggests that beyond these fragmented actions the development of full-blown personnel planning is still rare.

In 1988 an Institute of Personnel Management report (Darling and Lockwood 1988) showed that six out of seven companies had seriously underestimated the apparently well-known demographic trend in the UK labour market; a trend that will see 30 per cent less young people available to join the labour force in the 1990s. Another cross-industry survey in 1988 showed that although a majority of companies claimed to have an overall policy for the management of people, much less than half had put that policy in writing. Only a third of companies with over 1,000 employees in the UK have a board director concerned with personnel (Marginson et al. 1988; Sisson 1989). The abiding impression therefore is the persistence of a deeply ingrained short-term approach (Darling and Lockwood 1988) and the limited adoption of an HRM approach in practice. Some have gone so far as to argue that many older features of British industrial relations reasserted themselves in the late 1980s (MacInnes 1987). However, caution is required as survey techniques are not suited to capturing emergent HRM changes.

In spite of these obstacles HRM specialists have continued to work on the major objective of integrating human resources into strategic management. Guest (1987) suggests that the main aim of human resource management is to foster commitment from individuals to the success of the company through a quality orientation in the performance of individuals, departments and the total organization. Human resource management relates to the total set of knowledge, skills and attitudes that firms need to compete. It involves concern for and action in the management of people including: selection, training and development, employee relations and compensation. Such actions may be bound together by the creation of an HRM philosophy (Hendry,

Pettigrew and Sparrow 1989). This entails a shift from the emphasis found in traditional personnel management. This is summarized in table 6.1.

As the subsequent pages will show, the way in which the people within a firm are managed is a central contributor to competitive performance. Yet the difficulties within that relationship are manifold both in theory and practice. As table 6.1 implies, there is no simple direct connection between the HRM and competitive performance. The human resource is but one of the potential assets within the ensemble of capacities of any one firm. Given what we have established of the multiple bases of competition in any industry then there are many ways which the human resources of a company can help or hinder the creation of those bases. Indeed the HRM literature is constrained in understanding this relationship precisely because of its lack of attention to the concept of competition and its ready adoption of the structural models derived from the IO field.

Our research at firm level in four sectors of the UK economy

Table 6.1 Personnel management and human resource management – an outline

Element	Personnel management	Human resource management
Employee relations	Adversarial	Developmental and collaborative
Orientation	Reactive and piecemeal	Proactive and business focused
Organization	Separate functions	Integrated functions
Client	Management	Management and employees
Values	Order, equity, consistency	Client and problem focused, tailored solutions
Role of specialist	Regulatory and record keeping	Problem sensing, facilitating, changing
Role of line management	Passive ownership	Active ownership
Overall output	Compartmentalized thinking and acting	Linking various human resource levers to business needs

Source: Shell International, 1989

confirms the findings of the critical school of writers – that in practice the development of an HRM approach within a firm cannot be assumed. In the same way its positive contribution to competitive performance cannot be taken for granted. The dimensions which the vast majority of writers in the field minimize we see as paramount: the process by which human resources are developed such that they can contribute to the ability of the organization to accomplish strategic change and generate competitive bases.

Previous chapters have indicated, in a number of ways, the importance of certain human resource aspects in creating a capacity for change (see especially chapters 4 and 5). Here we isolate that contribution and the conditioning features and supportive mechanisms which have been used in the companies studied. The attempts to move directly to the HRM approach summarized in table 6.1 are often condemned to failure both for their inherent difficulty but even more so within the context of British practice. Companies in our research who have developed such an approach and used it to achieve strategic change and generate competitive advantage share a central quality. The common denominator is the extent of the attention they devoted to conditioning those concerned both prior to and during the introduction of such techniques.

Jaguar in 1980 for example was a classic case of the negative inheritance of UK engineering companies. It was forced to create a personnel function virtually from scratch. In view of the work-force's resistance to change resulting from over a decade of intense adversarial relations a series of preparatory actions had to be taken. This included the use of the survival crisis of 1980–1 to indicate the need for both business and people change, the years to 1984 to reveal the full extent of the huge gaps in the companies' knowledge base, and all the time the use of a variety of opportunities to raise an identification with HRM techniques among both work-force and management.

The national attention which Jaguar subsequently received among HRM professionals was due not so much to the creation of its HRM approach. What was critical was the way the management mobilized a set of secondary features which ensured the capacity to achieve change through the sustained use of its HRM techniques. This included the acknowledgement of such practices as a means of accomplishing commercial projects. Jaguar did not fall into the trap of raising up HRM as a new god to replace the old engineering deity which had so distorted the company's vision in the past. What stands out is the amount of action taken across the company outside of the HRM department to ensure the progressive acceptance and demonstration of its efficacy.

The results of this study go further than the majority of the HRM literature in one major respect. We see the role of knowledge as paramount in the way an HRM approach can create differential advantage among firms. Learning becomes the central means of generating, maintaining and regenerating that knowledge. An HRM approach can be a vital means of developing that learning capacity.

Writers from a variety of backgrounds have given support to the importance of knowledge in economic relations in general (Loasby 1976; Hodgson 1988). Others have recognized the role of specialist techniques and tacit knowledge in explaining technological innovation. One of the strongest versions of this research is the work of Nelson and Winter (1982). Recent results (Winter 1987: 161, 171) emphasize the great difficulty of exposing the knowledge contained within the procedural repertoires of organizations.

From our research we see two things must be stressed. First, any company develops over time its own distinctive knowledge base. That base contains both technical and social knowledge. The ability to produce books in ABP, for example, came to rely on a mixture of technical information on the specialist markets it served, the production process, and the skills necessary to put such knowledge into practice – in commissioning or desk editing. There were also the implicit notions of the standards by which such activities were practised. Furthermore, there were the values and beliefs which informed such action and helped, for example, to account for the status granted in practice to legal publishing.

What becomes critical is the extent to which the knowledge base of a firm matches changing competitive conditions. Altering such a composite base is not simple – an area where the work of the institutional economists are silent. The ability to learn is crucial. Previous work on organizational learning (Jelinek 1979) is only partially helpful here since these earlier studies did not address the importance of learning for competition. Our conclusions confirm Pucik's (1988) observation that such collective learning can indeed be a vital 'invisible asset' to a company.

Learning is seen here as not just the acquisition of new knowledge by the individual (cf. Garratt 1987). Rather, it refers to how those within firms collectively change their knowledge, values and shared mental models of their company and its markets. Learning therefore does not preclude training, it simply goes further. The head of planning at Shell International supports the case well (de Geus 1988). Educational experts have shown how fallible conventional teaching/training regimes are. Only between 25 per cent and 40 per cent of the intended knowledge is ever conveyed (Holt 1973: 72). The need is for a much broader approach which embraces the themes of structural adjustment, the use of 'play' or experimentation, the development of appropriate language, and the reshaping of attitudes and values.

The second major requirement concerns the assumptions behind the process of learning. Piaget's fundamental notion of learning as a spiral is extremely useful. As Kolb (1979) and Boissot (1987) have shown, learning for the organization involves cycles of observation, reflection, hypothesizing, experimentation, action and 'hands-on' experience (see chapter 5 for the way the link between strategic and operational change was developed in this way in the case examples). Knowledge in the minds of the experimenters, then, has to be codified and diffused within the organization through behaviour and support. Often overlooked is the necessity for breaking down entrenched knowledge and beliefs – what Hedberg (1981) called 'unlearning'. The importance of the spiral metaphor is the way it allows for movement both upwards and downwards and respects the existence of blockages to the process which may produce immobility or even regression. Examples of both the extent of learning activity necessary and the sharp relevance of the spiral will be shown later in the chapter.

Those company examples will show how it is the ability to shed outmoded knowledge, techniques and beliefs as well as learn and deploy new ones which enables firms to carry out strategies. The ability to do so faster and more effectively than your competitors becomes an almost priceless competitive advantage (cf. de Geus 1988: 71; Pascale 1990).

Automobiles

Jaguar of course supplies a striking example of the direct linkage of HRM to business needs and changes. HRM was a core concern of the survival, regeneration and growth strategies. Jaguar's ability to assess the environment, lead change (in the collective sense) and implement change would have been still-born without that link. Less well known are the situational and *ad hoc* features and the role they played. These included the realization from 1982 that world-class engineers were unable to assess purchase costs in relation to their projects. The mobilization of external influences such as the constant comparisons with competitor training and skill levels is equally overlooked by others. The linking of HRM activities with existing and emergent institutions is shown in the range of complementary activities (e.g. 'open-learning' education programmes, J-days devoted to launching a new model to the work-force and their families and a range of 'hearts and minds' social activities).

Jaguar's ultimate problem has been in its lack of capital resources to release the full potential of its technical and human assets by comparison to world standards. Peugeot Talbot's example is a sharp one since it did not have a fraction of Jaguar's capital and therefore was forced to rely on the contribution of HRM *in extremis*. The position is well-evident in Whalen's background and emphases which supplied the conditioning features. The secondary mechanisms are no less clear in, for example: mobilizing of the external comparisons with the European competitors, other UK dealers and most especially other Peugeot SA plants; the devolution of HRM concern, practice and responsibility to the line (seen in an exceptional production regime compared with CUK); and the integration of the HRM tenets throughout the 'Lions Standard Programme' and the training of dealers at Ryton.

In the 1970s Jaguar was the epitome of UK manufacturer with both poorly developed personnel management and a weakened knowledge base. Minimal formal management systems under Lyons had done little to develop the reliance on piece-work, spot bargaining at shop-floor level and personal regulation by Lyons of the salaried staff. The assumption of responsibility for industrial relations management by BL from 1975 created further problems. The IR problems of BL have become legendary. BL was faced with the task of rationalizing 25 manufacturing companies employing 80,000 people across 60 plants. All had previously been competitors. While attempting such a huge feat the company was faced with unprecedented levels of inflation and a resurgent shop-floor-based unionism. The problem for Jaguar workers was that their traditional wage differentials flew in the face of the corporation's need for wage comparability between plants.

Equally damaging was the way the conflict between Jaguar and BL did nothing to improve the growing weaknesses in the Browns Lane knowledge base. Although still sound in product design, the limitations in production, project management, quality and marketing were deepening. Action by BL exacerbated the deficiencies. Sales is a clear instance. Jaguar had relied heavily on Henleys and its dealers in the south of England to handle certain difficulties associated with new products. This knowledge was lost when divisional sales took away the Henley's franchise with the assumption that luxury and volume models could be sold equally well in the mass market Austin and Morris showrooms. Starved of major investment Jaguar simply didn't have the resources to develop its repertoire of basic techniques. It was this neglect which forced the Jaguar management under Egan to replace virtually every building on the Browns Lane site in the 1980s.

The attempt by the Egan regime to move away from the traditional UK IR approach and to build up an HRM orientation had a central source. As in the case of Peugeot Talbot, it was the chief executive who championed the move. Given his experience in introducing such techniques at Massey Ferguson both the commitment and the practical knowledge were there to guide such a process. As in other respects, such as environmental assessment, the approach was a long-term one. It was based on the wholly realistic recognition of the entrenched values and behaviour patterns of decades. Once through the survival year, the chief executive set an apparently extreme goal: 'to become the finest car company in the world'. The statement was designed to shift the standards and sights of the company above the preoccupations of the UK car industry. World standards were now to be applied in all spheres from engineering through to human resources.

This provided a vital means of raising HRM consciousness among senior management and demonstrating the linkage between business and people change. The problem which the senior management realized was that these conditioning features would not legitimate nor establish an HRM style in one go. It has been a constant feature of the work of the board and the newly created personnel function after 1981 that they have had to rework the message and apply it regularly, albeit in different ways. Each phase of survival, regeneration and growth has contained short-term targets to advance the application of HRM in practice. As the personnel director recognizes, there was no assumption that the adversarial mentality would disappear overnight as the series of shop-floor disputes between 1985 and 1988 confirmed. This is part of the reason for the elaborate communication structure which has been built up since its first vital role in the 1980 survival phase (see figure 5.2). The same attitude to adversarial relations was true in interdepartmental terms. A personnel manager notes how

> . . . friction, conflict, disagreement is healthy in any organization. The word objective is the one that has been missing. You have conflict in achieving results. What we have worked on is ensuring that behind all

the debates and disagreements, we all know what the end result should be. What we have enabled ourselves to do is actually develop a healthy rivalry based on a common goal as opposed to individual camps looking at their own results rather than the company's results. (Interview)

It is entirely consistent with this recognition of the difficulty of moving progressively from an IR to an HRM orientation that such extensive effort has been expended under what we categorize as secondary supportive activity. Action taken during the regeneration phase illustrates how Jaguar management did not raise HR development as an end in itself. The reverse was true. Specific HR initiatives were justified by reference to the business objectives which they could serve.

The BL board had voted £200 million to the XJ40 car and AJ6 engine projects in February 1981 on the strength of the company's improved performance. Jaguar's aim was to use this investment to begin the transformation of the company's technology base. This in turn required a major recruitment campaign of engineering staff if there was to be any long-term possibility of competing with the German luxury producers' technological strength. The 450 engineering force of 1980 was insufficient. So began the recruitment of staff in the product and manufacturing areas which by 1986 had added 500. The problem of integrating such a large number of new employees was considerable and hence the introduction of selection tests and induction programmes in Jaguar after years of stable numbers in engineering. The programme of investment meant that engineering staff now had to spend large sums of money. Their inexperience, given the starvation of funds under BL, necessitated a training initiative in commercial and negotiating skills.

Given that the company's main goal was to be free-standing, then a series of human resource changes which would support this objective were required. New treasury, legal and company secretariat functions were added which were needed to mount the privatization initiative. Other individual appointments were made to improve planning capacity. The overhaul of the company salary structure was required in order to meet current market rates.

The human resource approach was deepened in a number of ways. Manpower planning, in the light of the profound changes in the company's commercial approach, was developed with a five-year horizon. A 'hearts and minds' programme was initiated. The aim was to organize a range of events for employees and their families to revive the pride in belonging to Jaguar. An open learning scheme was introduced covering a range of specialist and more general education subjects. The commitment was to each employee receiving five days of training a year. The basic formula in developing the human resource was one of:

- making changes in the human resource area which were required by the capital investment programme of 1981, which at the same time would
- facilitate the structural changes necessary for improved competitive performance beyond privatization.

As the evidence of the open learning scheme and the hearts and minds programme indicates, Jaguar has had to develop a rich mixture of human resource changes and linked institutions. Central to the regeneration strategy was the adjustment of the payment system. The adoption of measured day-work by BL was a disaster. The scheme was disliked by management and work-force alike. It destroyed worker responsibility and in Jaguar's case resulted in a loss in productivity of around 20 per cent. Instead, the new management introduced a bonus scheme for both hourly paid and staff employees. This was not on an individual but a plant and company basis. The use of bonus payments consolidated into higher basic pay levels led to a tripling of productivity and the movement of Jaguar's pay rates towards the top of the UK car industry. An employee share scheme and profit sharing, linked to PAYE, were developed as an integral part of the privatization plan.

As we have seen in earlier chapters devoted to environmental assessment and implementing change, the ability of Jaguar to retain the knowledge generated by such periods of intense change is a prize asset, as other car companies have sometimes found to their cost. The way GM observed the mistakes of Ford in relying on mass-production techniques alone in the 1920s and then went on to combine successfully assembly line manufacture with multidivisional management is a classic case of such learning. The need for Jaguar has been to capture and maintain the major improvements in its business during a sequence of accelerated and intense transformation. The danger is that the pressures of such a process could mean that new techniques or approaches are lost along the way: they are then especially costly to rediscover and recreate at a later date. The company is achieving this, and not always consciously, by a combination of:

- values sponsored by the chief executive
- new internal relations which facilitate learning

- the use of formal development programmes.

At the highest level the chairman clearly espouses a personal learning philosophy. This comes out most clearly in the way he has drawn on techniques and devices learnt from his time with General Motors and Massey Ferguson. This was particularly evident in the way he created his senior management team *before* attempting to tackle the horrendous problems that Jaguar faced in 1980: a direct outcome of his previous experience. Even more important has been the way he has sought to create a learning philosophy at all levels of the organization.

In many ways the pressures of the survival and regeneration phase of Jaguar's development made learning a necessity. People had to be able to learn new techniques and assume whole new areas of responsibility across the break-even period and, for different reasons, during the re-creation of Jaguar's full complement of departments. The career of a human resources manager is indicative in the way he returned to Jaguar as head of the training function in 1980, went on to assume responsibility for internal communications and then embraced office services and special facilities. In his view this was entirely consistent since 'the chairman does believe that most people can learn most things'.

The greater problem has now arisen of how to sustain this general approach to learning through the growth stage. This is especially relevant when the company has so many new entrants, notably in engineering. Individual and group learning seems to be advancing by use of both the new interdepartmental relations and formal development approaches.

Since product quality has become of paramount importance to Jaguar's policy it is an excellent illustration of how the new structures and relations within the company are being used to ensure that hard-won improvements are not squandered. The barrage of activities to improve quality between 1980 and 1984 served their purpose in order to re-establish Jaguar back in the luxury car market. Thereafter the problem has been one of sustaining the requisite high levels of attention to quality appropriate to the ideal of the 'world's best car company'.

The use of what Rex Marvin, a senior vehicle design engineer, calls 'feedback loops' is one answer. In his view the need in vehicle engineering is for 'constant repetition of the message' of quality. Yet this has to be kept fresh as a message if it is in effect to be constantly re-learnt by those in post and by new entrants. It is here that the new web of relations with those at other points in the production chain assumes such importance. In other words, engineers are exposed to dealers who are best able to demonstrate the lesson of what quality failings mean in the eyes of the customer. The visit of the UK and Continental dealers to Browns Lane in September 1986 prior to the launch of the XJ40 was a case in point. The quarterly meetings of Jaguar's service managers from around the world (known in house as the 'hottest, coldest, fastest and largest') is particularly instructive. Their continual dialogue with the engineers, in Marvin's terms, closes the feedback loop very directly.

Post-project audits and follow-up exercises between departments are similar devices to achieve the same end. New technology, such as computer-aided design and manufacture (CAD/CAM) or the computer programs used in critical path analysis also have an in-built potential for recording vital information associated with certain new techniques and projects.

Running alongside these new relationships is of course a major investment in a human resource development programme which is an integral part of Jaguar's business policy. At the heart of that approach is a commitment to formal off-the-job-training. £10 million of the £15 million per annum HRM budget is spent on training. Moreover the combination of business and human resource planning has meant that steps have been taken which avoid the disruption which can dilute the benefits of wider group learning. Examples include the ability to plan recruitment initiatives which balance hiring outsiders with the training of in-house employees; similarly staff development programmes have been designed to build succession paths and minimize turnover (in 1989 the current rate was 3 per cent).

The industrial relations problems of Chrysler UK in the 1970s were legion. US management found the fragmented British bargaining structure and the collection of myriad, small independent suppliers bordering on the incomprehensible. As inflation hit record levels in the early 1970s and workers sought to match wages to prices, disputes reached similar peaks in both the vehicle makers and the component suppliers. Contrary to the general orthodoxy it was the undeveloped nature of CUK's and other car companies' industrial relations structures which underlay the widespread disruption and the continual inability to meet production targets, not union strength alone.

In CUK the lack of written agreements or centralized bargaining (not fully operational until 1980), the transfer to measured daywork from piece-work, together with the unfortunate interventions of

Detroit at one remove, resulted in a process of constant 'fire-fighting' by the local IR management. There were 57 negotiating groups in 1970. No formal framework for negotiations existed. The changeover to measured daywork by management in such a defensive position meant the agreement contained basic flaws. Without an incentive element or direct revision of mutuality, bargaining over the price under piece-work now became haggling over the man loading under measured daywork. The situation was exploited to the full by workers faced with conditions of inflation, interrupted production and no lay-off pay. The covert understanding that the company would always match the Coventry tool-room rate was, to quote a negotiator for the Midland plants, 'a time bomb. It blew up in our face', and most spectacularly in the tool-makers' dispute of 1973. The problem was compounded by IR and manufacturing management reporting separately to their respective superiors in central staffs. The vital joint solution of what were sometimes disputes running into double figures each day did not emerge. The Department of Trade-inspired planning agreements of 1976 failed in the short term under the weight of their own internal contradictions.

A similar set of weaknesses among Chrysler UK's suppliers was a major factor in the failure to meet production targets. Of the 390 suppliers, 185 had no 'labour agreement'. In October 1971, 150 essential components had to be 'dual sourced'. The dispute record of Chrysler UK spoke for itself (see table 6.2). The effect on performance was biting. In July 1970 the MD made it quite clear in his board report minutes that having to spend a quarter of a million pounds on alternative glass supplies due to a strike at Pilkingtons for example meant that, 'until the company can be assured of regular and stable supplies, the month to month profit performance will always be in jeopardy'.

The distinctive feature of Peugeot Talbot in the early 1980s was its ability to use to advantage the difficult circumstances it faced. In other words, the management began the development of an HR consciousness. They used many of the individual problems of 1970–83 to

Table 6.2 Hours and vehicles lost: Chrysler UK 1970–1973

	1970	1971	1972	1973
Man hours lost	556,458	497,029	1,599,271	1,751,103
Vehicles lost	23,152	37,914	43,358	90,541

Source: CUK Industrial Relations Department

demonstrate the need for a change from the IR mentality of the previous decade. We saw in chapter 5 the drastic steps which Peugeot Talbot had to take to reduce the company in the UK between 1981 and 1983. Managers describe the period as an appalling low for them. The importance of managerial persistence across a number of short-term problems in order to build a long-term HRM capability was shown in 1984–5. In Geoffrey Whalen's words:

> Throughout 1984 we were saying to ourselves . . . how good it would have been if we had been producing the 205 at Ryton, instead of having yet another year, 1985, where we were still having to produce the old Talbot cars in diminishing volumes and not being able to make money, knowing that the plant was good, that the atmosphere was good, and that the quality was good. (interview)

What is interesting is the way the extreme business problems were tackled and used as a means of effecting marked changes in the old IR regime. The continued losses in 1980–1, the disastrous contraction in demand of 12 per cent in the UK market from the Iran–Iraq war, Peugeot Talbot's fall in market share to 3.73 per cent in 1982, and the dislocation of the Iran contract were clear. Yet these were used along with short-time working, for example, to demonstrate the need for a profoundly altered approach. The whole point is that it becomes difficult in practice to separate out the commercial and the human resource issues since they were born of the same crisis and were worked out as part of the same change programme.

In simple terms the UK company, during the rigours of contraction, had made sound improvements in the key problem areas which dogged Chrysler UK throughout the 1970s, namely: productivity, costs, industrial relations and quality. These included:

- productivity gains through not simply reduction of head count but from the combined effect of an incentive-based pay scheme, competitive manning levels and consistent achievement of output targets to match French plants (see figure 6.1)
- cost reductions by consolidation, e.g. closing the Bagington packing operation and the reduction of break-even point from 2,500 to 1,500 units
- an industrial relations approach which not only reflected current market and productivity norms but which also relied on a thorough change in management style and communications policy; result: no major dispute throughout the period of work-force reduction

- quality improved to become as good as anything in the Peugeot Group's European plants due to the practical linkage of IR and manufacturing initiatives and practices. Peugeot Talbot is the only volume producer to perform 100 per cent road testing on its vehicles.

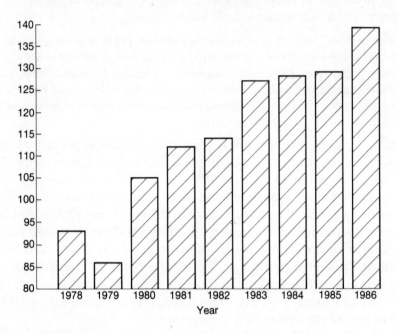

Figure 6.1 Productivity Index Peugeot Talbot Motor Company 1978–1986
Source: Peugeot Talbot
Note: Constant index of performance measured by comparing actual versus authorized output and time taken

The combined reinforcement of commercial and HR pressures for change has, then, been sustained into the growth period from 1983. As in other aspects of Peugeot Talbot's strategic management it was able to convert the energy and knowledge generated during the period of contraction to more positive use. It was during this phase from 1983 that a number of secondary mechanisms were tested and applied in conjunction with this central combination. A good illustration comes in the alteration of the Peugeot Talbot culture and the way quality and employee relations initiatives have been used to support one another.

The pursuit of quality in order to meet new sectoral standards has been most beneficial. In spite of a certain nervousness, production workers welcomed the opportunity to be responsible for the quality of their product rather than under CUK where the problem was merely passed on to the inspection department. In other words, by concentrating on quality 'we lifted the production operation up in its influence, in its standing in the factory' (interview). Indeed the contrasts with CUK and the exhortation to attain volume production at all costs could not be greater. Raising quality raises self esteem it appears.

However, the mere exhortation to the shop-floor to improve quality would have differed little from a whole string of previous attempts by successive generations of management across the UK car industry. The key difference was Peugeot Talbot's combined approach. The application of funds, albeit modest by international standards, to the Ryton plant to introduce new paint equipment and computer-based information systems demonstrated the seriousness of the company's intention. Even more important though has been the reversal of past practices. Now the old priority of keeping the track flowing has been placed second to ensuring that all faults in cars are eradicated.

At the same time, the new linkage of the industrial relations and production departments has paid off: the whole range of communications apparatus which has developed in-house has been used to reinforce the quality imperative. Alongside the red and green communications documents, are the halting of the tracks during working hours to allow discussions of problems between supervisors and their teams; the production of, by now, several generations of video films on aspects of quality (with all now made by employees). The exhibitions of Ryton-built models in Coventry and at the 1986 Motor Show by Peugeot Talbot employees is further evidence of the translation of the acceptance of the need for quality into a commitment. The reduction in warranty costs by 50 per cent or the use of Ryton videos in French plants is further testimony to this combined approach to achieving production quality. In the words of the personnel director:

> We believe that the benefit of this philosophy is felt in almost every aspect of our business – stable industrial relations; pride in workmanship and consequent quality improvement; cost and productivity consciousness; job flexibility and mobility of labour. (Interview)

The clear demonstration of the responsibilities of management in the 1979 dispute has provided the basis for a progressive reworking of many features of employee relations. Yet the quality initiative was decisive in that it began the transformation of the status of production. The overall aim has been to move away from the immensely costly adversarial stances of the 1970s and instead enhance the status of production workers and to rescue the differences between shop-floor and other staff. Peugeot Talbot is ahead of Ford therefore in the introduction of cashless pay, harmonization of hourly paid and staff conditions, notably in terms of sickness and absence pay and pensions – one of the long-standing grievances of the car industry work-force since the war. Two-year pay agreements have aided stability greatly. Moreover, Peugeot Talbot's record in this area could well be seen as a competitive advantage in its own right when compared with the serious loss of production through disputes at both Ford and Vauxhall in 1987 over precisely these issues.

Since 1985 Peugeot Talbot has gone on to augment its fundamental linkage of business policy and human resource innovation with further supportive mechanisms. The fact that the production director has assumed a clear operational responsibility for the HR issues within production has been vital. That way his managers can reverse the position they found themselves in under CUK where they constantly had to rely on an 'expert from the centre'. As Colin Walters (the production director) pointed out in 1986, much of this was driven by necessity, since, 'If you look at our factory here we have no new major technology. We have put new equipment in, we have updated technology but all our improvement has come through man management changes' (interview).

The managing director summed up the HRM achievements of Peugeot Talbot well in 1988; at the same time he confirms the view presented above of the deep-seated difficulties in creating that approach. He stated that

> our task, to put it simply, is to continue to manage people effectively, keep good co-operation, keeping good cost effectiveness . . . all very obvious things but things which we haven't been very good at in this industry in the 1970s. (interview)

Book publishing

The experience of Longman is useful in two main respects. First the company is an excellent example of the way HRM can be used to develop an appropriate knowledge base. Second, Longman reveals one of the more difficult issues confronting the successful company: how to shed outmoded features of that knowledge base.

At the core of Longman's growth from the 1970s has been the creation of an understanding of its own competitive base. Previous chapters have shown the way the company has evolved a strong definition of its business purpose involving considerable innovation. Although developed more unevenly, by the mid–1980s Longman's strategic position was underpinned by a growing HRM approach. An internal financial report addressing the issue of 'the publishing group we want to be', circulated widely to employees, is a neat example. It dwelt on:

- providing the best possible service to the consumers of Longman's products
- being market leaders/major players in all of the chosen areas of publishing
- providing the best possible service and care to authors and contributors
- obtaining the highest possible quality in relation to market needs
- responding effectively to changes in markets and technologies while remaining market not technology driven.

Longman has teased out the human resource requirements which such objectives imply as part of its attempt to increase the depth of its business planning. In that sense Longman demonstrated the need for human resource change as a result of its own maturing strategic thinking across the 1970s and early 1980s.

In an industry which relies heavily on people at every stage of the publishing process Longman has augmented its competitive base in its emerging approach to its human resource. The heavy weight of the traditional publishing industry culture of committed yet relatively low paid editorial staff has not been noticeably lifted across the industry. By publishing standards, Longman has been active in a number of ways, which, if sustained, could grow into an even greater competitive advantage as the information industry's labour market becomes more closely integrated and staff turnover rises accordingly.

In one sense Longman was forced to consider its work-force management. Longman during the 1970s became much more centralized and professional in its personnel and IR approach. In many ways this was forced by the growth of the Association of Scientific, Technical, and Managerial Staffs (ASTMS) in the publishing divisions (recognition was given in 1975) and the flow of national employment legislation. The keynote in the company was the centralization of negotiation and information, the attempt to develop a new salary structure based on job evaluation. Many of the larger publishers have not moved much beyond this phase of development.

Longman, and even more so Collins, have tried to break away from the dominant mode of IR management in the 1970s. There had been relatively few major disputes after the 1973 strike by SOGAT members in distribution over GPO staff packing parcels into mailbags on the premises. Turnover in the distribution area (see chapter 5) had been low. The problem was the accumulation of work practices, the operation of the post-entry closed shop and management which came to restrict the efficiency of the section. Since 1983 most of the existing structure and practices have been changed. The weak supervisory system has been overhauled, new values have been instituted in the bonus scheme and a totally new procedure agreement was negotiated with SOGAT across 1987 which led to Longman leaving the PA national negotiations.

Yet Longman has gone further than only reforming its industrial relations arrangements. From 1982 and with the appointment of the director of personnel to the board of the UK company, a new phase of policy has been initiated. The general aim has been to make clear throughout the company, the need for linking personnel policies much more to the strategic objectives of the business. The intention has been to diffuse the commitment to HRM beyond the senior management. Here a series of secondary actions have followed.

Devolving the HRM approach to the line was seen as imperative and to de-centralize some of the responsibility for training and development to line management. The view of the Director of Personnel was clear: in spite of the training activity which already existed, Longman's divisional method of business planning did not cover the detailed human resource needs and implications of given policies. The result was in 1987 to begin a process of developing HR plans for each division. In other words, to attach appropriate importance to people who make up 50 per cent of the UK company's overhead bill. As the managers in the divisions assume more responsibility for HR management so the central personnel staff can develop as a more forward thinking advisory/consultancy unit. The potential benefits are considerable given the slowness of other major publishers to move to such orientations.

The HRM approach has not been allowed to become a programme or end itself. Rather, its relevance has been shown to the contribution it can make to Longman's commercial objectives. Nowhere has this been better demonstrated than Longman's need to alter its knowledge base. The senior management and personnel staff have been working consistently since 1982 to alter both editorial techniques, values and standards of professionalism. The aim has been to align those more closely with the requirements of diversification. Without such a shift Longman's strategic moves to the USA and the Far East would not be possible.

One of the major needs derived from the business objectives of the company has been the creation of a more commercial consciousness among all staff but most especially on the publishing side. One publisher sums up the change neatly when she draws the distinction between 'being interested in the product for its own sake and being interested in the product as a means to developing the business' (interview).

If one takes these two types of approach as extremes then the publishers at Longman have exhibited a behaviour across the range. In general, though, the collection of commercial pressures which Longman faced in the 1980s has meant that there has been a swing very much towards the entrepreneurial business developer. The shift clearly has been necessary in order to mirror the decision to be market- rather than product-led.

It would be entirely inaccurate to suggest that there has been a simple switch somehow from one type of publisher to another. Rather, as a result of the competitive pressures in the market, the more stringent financial requirements of the company and the need to re-position Longman in new markets and growth areas, there have been new demands placed on the editorial function. Editors/publishers are still regarded as 'the creative focus of the business . . . if they aren't bringing in the authors and the books, everything else collapses'.

The major task has been to ensure that such people do not become so engrossed in their subject areas and in the nurturing of authors that they neglect the precise requirements of fast-changing markets. This can most obviously become a danger where the commitment of a publisher to a given field or subject provides the motivating force behind his or her job. In schools publishing it is apparently all too easy to be attracted to authors who write for the higher ability child and gradually to leave out the more difficult slow learner. The liaison between marketing and publishers is now expected to be much closer and more natural; it is no longer assumed that sales and marketing merely sell the product which comes from the publisher. There is a twin requirement, therefore, since to quote a sales director:

You can do an audit on a market and come up with a technical specification of a product, but then of course you need the creative ability of the publisher to interpret that into an appropriate product. (Interview)

Inertia in the change towards this new relationship has come from not only entrenched traditional views but also from the sometimes higher calibre and status of the people who used to be found as publishers when compared to certain sales people. In some sectors the change has been facilitated by the need to move into new markets, in others new financial mechanisms have demonstrated the weaknesses of certain subject areas and lists. Elsewhere the inertia has been overcome by the astute movement of staff. In sector 4 the change was assisted by the managing director moving a publisher into the position of marketing director as a vivid demonstration of the need to combine marketing and publishing approaches. In some ways it is an indictment of British publishers that such a combination should be so uncommon when in the USA transfers are routinely made between the two specialisms during a career. The issue can only grow in importance for Longman in the future.

At ABP the extent of the fire fighting required and then the slump in the company's fortunes in 1980 meant that less time was left for consideration of human resource planning compared to Longman. Most attention was given to the increasing requirements of employment legislation and the plant-based bargaining at Andover with SOGAT and ASTMS members. The smallness of the personnel function meant that there was only one training officer.

Training rested on the notions of apprenticeship inherent in the progression of editorial, sales and production staff along accepted career ladders. In the case of the editorial function this started with:

- 'secretarial'/personal assistant work, followed by
- desk editing
- junior editorial roles helping commissioning editors before becoming
- a commissioning editor in charge of a list.

Greater use was made of Book House from 1981 and their introductory and basic courses in publishing. Those making transitions to managerial responsibility faced many challenges. The conclusion of a sales manager, with experience across the divisions since 1976, is indicative:

I found that the most difficult. I went from managing a small team of people to being given something like 14 people to manage and that I found very hard . . . you do it by trial and error and it doesn't feel so good. (Interview)

When ABP considered forming a separate UK board, one of the arguments against doing so was the lack of appropriate training of the divisional directors.

Compared to Longman, ABP was unable to alter its knowledge base as extensively. The largely IR approach of its personnel department was not able to act as the catalyst for change in the same way as at Longman. The new managing director of ABP UK in 1980 noted how the principal strength of the business lay in the professionalism of its staff. There was an undoubted commitment, especially on the editorial side to their subject, their lists and their authors. The culture of ABP was founded on the quality and integrity of its publishing. The law lists through to the University Paperback series of Methuen or the Arden Shakespeare editions were united by this common denominator. The quality of the titles was widely accepted in the trade.

Yet, in relation to Longman, this adherence to editorial integrity was in danger of being maintained somewhat at the expense of increasing commercial requirements. The position is best summed up by a divisional director. He noted how 'Most of us came into publishing because we liked the idea of books or the subject behind the books. Most of us did not come into publishing because we were business people to make money' (interview).

David Croom realized the feeling behind the approach very quickly after the merger with Croom Helm in 1985. He noted how ABP editors when considering a potential book asked, 'is it worthy of my list?' Croom Helm editors asked, 'is it worthy of my ratios?'

The less accelerated development of precise awareness of other publishers' strengths and practices was apparent to the new senior management who entered from 1980. The legal division had formed, of necessity, a sharp picture of its direct competition as a result of the attacks on Butterworth and Sweet & Maxwell between 1980 and 1986 from abroad. In other words the legal editors appear to have been working with a full awareness of the incursion of Oyez and Longman followed by the American Commerce Clearing House and specialists such as Colleys in tax law. In contrast, a senior editor in the academic division in 1987 almost rejected the notion of direct competition as untenable since:

> I am not aware of the competition. How can we be? My problem is in visualizing the competition. It's so easy to get into publishing, there are so many publishers doing it that in a way you don't look over your shoulder. If it were toothpaste there are only about ten brands and you can study them intensively. . . . I'm very interested to see what other publishers are doing but by the time they've done it, it's too late because the lead time in publishing is so long. (Interview)

Other leading publishers elsewhere found it hard to construct meaningful data on competition in such a fragmented and under-researched industry.

Many of the internal characteristics of ABP were fully expressed in its culture. The hallmarks were devolvement and the pursuit of quality. In many ways the strength of these aspects of its culture tended to restrain ABP's solution to the puzzle of how to expand the total business when compared to Longman. ABP apparently did not establish ABP as a singular identity. In practice booksellers and others in the trade relate to Sweet & Maxwell or Chapman & Hall. At Longman the company name overshadows the list names (e.g. Oliver & Boyd) completely. At ABP the identification with the imprint was encouraged.

Similarly, by allowing the adherence to quality among editorial staff to become so dominant, this ran the risk of obscuring the need to develop the business. It is significant that in the reforms from 1980 quality was to remain paramount. A new structure of controls was to liberate growth. Alan Miles wished to introduce more detailed controls, but controls geared to the quality of books commissioned. He saw that the results of the business were the aggregate of the success of individual books. New routines would not of themselves solve problems but they should provide the environment necessary to encourage the growth of the entrepreneurial function. Compared to Longman there was more of a view that the system would generate growth.

In Longman's terms, ABP's ability to learn from its experience was less developed. It is interesting to compare the extensive effort made by Longman to explain not only 'what sort of company we want to be' to its staff with their relative cautious emergence in ABP. In particular Longman took great pains to lay out the rationale for its acquisition of Addison-Wesley and the implications involved. As one manager at ABP observed, 'the company's called ABP and yet the products by which it might be recognized are called something different. That has had an effect and we have been slow in correcting it' (interview).

It is clear that improvements were made in the operation of the divisions and these were retained. The reporting forms and budget systems not only gained acceptance through their immediate relevance (e.g. in revealing cash flow deficiencies), by their very nature they became self-reinforcing. Put simply, the monthly and yearly repetitions ensured increasing familiarity at editor level with the help of the divisional accountants. Elsewhere the mechanisms for learning from past successes or mistakes did emerge but did not develop over the longer term so much as at Longman. In 1979, the need was identified for 'post mortem' forms to be completed for each book. This way there was less chance of failed projects being left unrecorded or taken for granted.

Challenges to operating assumptions came through the merger with RKP and Croom Helm. The need to integrate the two organizations into the academic division did provide an opportunity for the staff to reassess their preferred ways of working. In the words of an editor of the Methuen academic list, the co-ordination of the publishing process on her list was the responsibility of the production manager,

> who spends most of her life working out how to knit these things together for better or for worse. It was really highlighted when we started to acquire other companies which caused us to reflect on how they did it and how you did it and what was the best way to make a path through these. (Interview)

The surprised reaction to David Croom's suggestion in January 1987 for a three-day seminar at Wye College for the Methuen and Tavistock imprints is interesting. Longman had been holding annual sector conferences throughout the 1980s.

Merchant banking

The importance of the set of values and assumptions within Kleinwort Benson is shown in the dominance of the banking business. Such shared understandings, as was shown in chapter 5, not only provided an anchorage for the range of the bank's business but also conditioned decisions over personnel. This was especially true for senior management. As one executive put it:

> It was an article of faith with the Kleinwort business, because it was an article of faith of the Kleinwort family that banking was the core activity. Although they would never put it this way, they would have regarded it in some ways as a superior activity to corporate finance . . . I

think in truth that it never occurred to Kleinwort that the business could have anyone but a Kleinwort as its chairman. (Interview)

The resulting career path differences were particularly strong between the banking and corporate finance specialisms of Kleinwort and Robert Benson Lonsdale in the 1960s. Corporate finance required a large number of specialist advisers such as lawyers and accountants. These required a relatively open meritocratic system. The differences were described thus:

> Kleinwort was a much more hierarchical and patriarchal business. It was run as a family business. RBL had its corporate structure. It was seen to be much more of a meritocracy. (Interview)

In this respect Kleinwort was akin to the informal managerial style of Lyons at Jaguar such that:

> Nobody talked about their salaries. At Kleinwort people were paid their base salaries . . . but then they would expect a pretty good bonus at Christmas, which was done on a completely discretionary and almost arbitrary basis. (Interview)

The reason for stressing the distinctive combination of unobtrusive personnel management and the reliance on strong underlying values is shown in the way it produced a consistent managerial cadre. As we have seen, the integrity of Kleinwort's managerial action over the 1970s and 1980s, its inherent unity, was a vital means of achieving the series of changes which it accomplished. The importance placed on supplying a necessary vision and business direction was seen in the way Kleinwort linked strategic and operational change (see chapter 5). Similarly promotion and managerial development has been facilitated and held together by the banking culture. As Michael Hawkes confirms:

> It is the yield men the big commission generators that do cut the ice. When the firm was entirely devoted to banking, I used to be the best producer in the firm. I find it rather hard to understand how a merchant bank could work if someone was brought in from outside, like Sir Peter Carey [a senior civil servant] at Morgan Grenfell. (Interview)

Of course, some might argue that a more open approach, less dependent on a commercial banking ethos would have enabled Kleinwort to develop into new areas to meet the challenge of the international, particularly US houses. In the UK, however, this knowledge base of commercial banking techniques was of great value when others such as Hill Samuel failed to attain such integrity across their diversified group. As Michael Hawkes told *Euromoney* in 1986:

We are and will remain first and foremost a bank . . . We believe in a broad spread of activities. Bullion, banking, investment management, corporate finance and treasury operations are not going to be disturbed by changes in the Stock Exchange. I am often surprised that some of our UK competitors seem to be putting banking on the back burner while they concentrate on new activities. We believe that there is a bigger revolution impending in banking than in securities markets. We intend to translate these changes into new strengths and take a lead in new developments.

In many ways the robustness of Kleinwort's knowledge base helped to ensure that a vital commercial consistency was maintained through into the 1980s. Thus Kleinwort's move to expand its international banking from the early 1980s was identified precisely because of the depth of its overseas connections which it had maintained throughout the 1970s. It was the persistence of this knowledge base which led Kleinwort's management to target the increasing threat of the international banks and securities houses. It was the maintenance of these views and values which led Kleinwort Benson to attempt to develop its international operations further.

Full corroboration came in the form of the difficulty of integrating the stockbroker Grieveson Grant. With a relatively simple personnel approach and a very different knowledge base, Kleinwort's integration of the stockbroker was constrained by the differences. From Kleinwort's perspective:

The movement from being an agency broker to being a principal is probably the thing that is the most severe shock to their system . . . whereas Kleinwort Benson was almost invariably acting as a principal in its transactions anyway. The fact that the broker was not acting as a principal did condition almost all of its thinking and probably all of its systems . . . That is what is producing the most severe culture shock. (Interview)

Characteristically more conventional HRM issues were not recognized, as the manager continued:

I don't think it is integrating people, I don't think it is salaries, I don't think it is benefits.

The contrast with Hill Samuel in terms of knowledge base has been evident. The character of Hill Samuel's knowledge base was clearly reliant on the skills of the deal makers in corporate finance. Hill Samuel's knowledge base was not allowed to deepen and provide the anchorage point for growth in the 1970s. Diversification ran counter to the idea. Sir Robert Clark goes to the root of the problem when he noted how:

> It was not too structured an idea to form a financial services company. I will say that it has only really been structured in the last 10 years where we have started to grow on these five legs [merchant banking, investment management, personal financial services, employee benefits consultancy, and shipping]. We have always in the last 15 years believed that we have a strength in the spread of our earnings . . . By combining these five things, we could spread the risk a bit. (Interview)

As in all of the other four central factors, the actions of Castleman from 1980 were certainly related to the key problems of Hill Samuel. His lengthy initiative to understand the diverse business areas of the group was an attempt to get to grips with the technical part of Hill Samuel's knowledge base. Thereafter he was able to turn to altering the broader values and standards across the group. Although it was not part of a formal HRM programme, Hill Samuel did use a number of techniques which we have identified in other sectors. As in Jaguar's share scheme, divisional and unit profit sharing was introduced throughout the group to link pay and performance. As in Longman, managers were given greater responsibility for their budgets, thus 'forcing them to manage'. After the high turnover of the late 1970s the short-term vindication of this attention to the human and managerial aspects of the bank's knowledge base was seen in the greater stability of the group's top 100 managers; at least until the enforced changes of 1991.

Life assurance

The Prudential organization provides a more conventional picture of the role HRM can play in managing change and competition. The contrast in its abilities to manage its human resources is a telling one.

The Prudential is almost a classic case of the limitations of the traditional, *laissez-faire* approach to work-force management precipitating change. The needs of business diversification simply could not be met by such a narrow orientation. This contradiction therefore provided a compelling set of conditioning features. As in the automobile companies, it was the depth of (1) the traditional employee relations approach, and (2) the company knowledge base which then necessitated the building up of supplementary action.

The bedrock of the Prudential's management before the 1980s had been its actuarial standards. In many ways this knowledge base had governed managerial careers. The Prudential, in common with other life offices, was an essentially paternalistic employer. Career-long employment was assumed to be the norm. Staff were subsidized to take the actuarial examinations. A career path was offered of slow but steady promotion related mainly to length of service. Specialist qualifications for particular functions were not required, even in, say, the head of computer services. Actuarial skills and a sound knowledge of the mechanics of life assurance were prized above all else. In a similar way, field staff emphasized their administration of their system rather than the generation of new products.

The demonstration of the need for change in such an approach ran parallel to the diversification of the 1970s. One fed off the other. The limitations of in-bred management became increasingly apparent in the 1970s. The level of sophistication in each specialist function (such as marketing, finance and data processing) grew such that the Prudential's existing management appeared less and less appropriate. The Prudential saw itself lagging behind those firms who recruited specialist personnel on the basis of the best available in the industry as a whole. Even when the Prudential brought such outside experts in, the problem was not solved. Invariably they were placed beneath the traditionally qualified managers. Status and promotion prospects appeared limited with the result that the firm was unable to attract and retain the requisite staff.

As was shown in chapter 3, the Prudential, particularly since 1980, strove to reduce its dependence on its mainstay industrial and ordinary life assurance products. Changes have included: the creation of Prudential Unit Trust Managers; the entry into real estate agency business; the offering of personal pension plans; and the acquisition of Jackson National Life as a means of entering the US market. Equally important has been the expansion of alternative distribution channels which are independent of the salesforce. These include independent intermediaries and the new high street estate agents offices.

Such commercial initiatives were vital to the existence of Prudential in the rapid changes within the sector which followed the financial legislation of 1979–86. Yet such radical changes by the Prudential were in danger of being blocked by the inability in the 1970s to alter its knowledge base. The new senior management around Brian Corby had experienced that frustration at first hand in the 1970s. They saw therefore the need to acquire new skills and knowledge which had been neglected. It was decided to short-circuit the established procedures, determine where skills were needed and then seek them out both internally and externally. A good example was the appointment of Geoff Keeys as general manager of personnel who came from the manufacturing sector. In the light of the past emphases, special attention was given to computer systems, finance and investment management and personnel itself. The fact that the organization was forced to alter its traditional compensation policies to attract senior outsiders was a massive demonstration of the linked need for business and HRM change. In contrast to the old progression by seniority, salaries had to be offered which matched the external labour market.

Already in taking these basic actions Prudential management was starting to generate a flow of subsidiary means of extending and reinforcing the contribution of an HRM approach. In order, for example, to retain such new specialists they had to be offered a commensurate share of responsibility and authority. Managers were given greater decision-making responsibility in their area, including the development of their own staff. Alongside these changes therefore was the appearance of a collection of supportive acts. Greater general emphasis was placed on management development with a new training centre, Hunton Park, acquired. More reliance has continued to be placed on non-actuarial expertise, particularly in the area of marketing. Attention to the optimum marketing mix of product development, design, advertising, distribution and pricing became a major feature of Prudential's new knowledge base in the 1980s.

The dominant quality of this spread of activity is that they have been mutually reinforcing and have had a cumulative impact over time. The linking of the commercial and human resource issue in the mid–1970s did not solve the problem by itself. The first attempts at change failed. This partly explains why the broader set of actions was undertaken in the 1980s. The deployment of a wider collection of primary and secondary mechanisms was decisive in two respects. First in their own success and second in their making possible the product and market innovations which the Prudential so desperately needed.

Conclusion

Human resource management relates to the total set of knowledge, skills and attitudes that firms need in order to compete. It involves concern for and action in the management of people, including selection, training and development, employee relations and compensation.

Such actions may be bound together by the creation of an HRM philosophy.

The differential ability of the seven firms to recognize and carry out a version of Human Resource Management is very evident. This has considerable impact on their relative competitive performance. Yet on reflection the disparity is less surprising when one considers the time it takes to develop such a capacity and its fragility. An HRM approach cannot be constructed overnight. What is involved is a much longer-term learning process which requires the creation of successive episodes of development.

The route to such learning is more promising first through a group of conditioning features. This involves the raising of a general consciousness of the benefits of HRM in relation to the business needs of the firm, by those prepared to champion the cause. A highly situational collection of features can create a positive force for HRM change. Enforced alterations in both business and people aspects of the organization are fundamental to producing a receptive context for HRM change.

Thereafter, the mechanisms for confirming and stabilizing such HRM initiatives are less programmatic and more often *ad hoc*. When added together, such practical actions can be highly conducive to the survival of the initiatives. These acts embrace the mobilizing of external influences which confirm the link between business needs and the means HRM can supply, through to the creation of linked institutions and structures which reinforce the existence and credibility of HRM policies.

A vivid example of the need for such extensive action comes in the TSB, the eventual owners of Hill Samuel. Its difficulties in 1990 notwithstanding, the TSB's early move in the 1980s from a traditional savings to a broader retail bank relied on just such a spread of HRM changes. Those alterations included, for example, mass training, followed up in due course by more focused attention to personal development, new modes of internal selection and not least a radical shift in the pattern of recruitment. In many ways, the TSB provides a parallel instance of the breadth of HRM changes needed to facilitate commercial transformation, as seen in the Prudential.

This chapter has also offered a critical reading of the current literature on HRM. Above all, the evidence presented here alerts academics and practitioners alike to the distinctive circumstances of Britain. Taken together with other survey and industry data, the findings of the four sectors here confirm the centrality of the UK's historical inheritance. The case of Jaguar is instructive. As late as 1980 it was forced to create a personnel function virtually from scratch, overcoming decades of neglect. Much of the recent enthusiasm in the UK and elsewhere for an HRM approach would be wise therefore to recognize such constraints in full.

Our second concern is with the formidable difficulties which have to be overcome in making the transition at firm level from a conventional IR/personnel orientation to an HRM philosophy. Securing that transition begs enormous questions of both managerial thinking and practice, hence the trouble taken in this chapter to suggest the multiple actions required. Nor in terms of competition should that transition become an end in itself. The results of this study go beyond the majority of the HRM literature in one major respect: it identifies the role of knowledge as paramount in the way an HRM approach can help create competitive advantage. That knowledge has both technical and social components. What becomes critical is the extent to which a company's knowledge base matches changing competitive conditions through learning. Learning here is seen as not just the acquisition of new knowledge. It also relates to how those within a firm collectively change their values and shared mental models of their company and markets (shown graphically in Kleinwort Benson). Indeed, it is the ability to shed out-moded knowledge, techniques and beliefs, as well as to learn and deploy new ones, which enables firms to carry out given strategies. To do so faster than one's competitors is likely to become one of the cardinal determinants of competitive strength in the 1990s.

The need to link that knowledge with the other central factors identified in the previous chapters – that is to maintain coherence – will be extreme. The following chapter addresses that issue in its own right.

7

Coherence

Arguably the most common yet elusive concern of those with the responsibility of managing change in the firms in this study is the problem of coherence. Given the extent of the activities required to develop the company capacities and competitive bases we have identified in the preceding chapters, this overriding anxiety is understandable. Their concern presents a major challenge.

This unease with how the composite process of strategic change and competition holds together, is seen outside the industries of this study. The breakdown of standard notions of the modern corporation has occurred at seemingly break-neck speed. The spread of internal and external contracting, the appetite for management buy-outs, not to mention the handiwork of the junk-bond finance predators, have threatened to redraw the corporate landscape in the 1980s. The rise of corporate identity consultancies speaks volumes for the way management has become acutely worried about their firm's *raison d'être* (Olins 1990). The renaming of Woolworth Holdings to Kingfisher in the UK, for example, has been matched by similar alterations at Burroughs, Sperry, US Steel and International Harvester (Rawsthorn 1989).

Little immediate help is at hand from either the academic or practitioner literatures. In the past, commentators have considered the problem of managing change largely in terms of an internal integration and as an end in itself. The issue of competition did not arise. Specialist research into inter-firm relations has been more helpful, yet it still leaves large tracts of the problem uncharted.

In our view, the problem of developing a wholeness or consistency in managing strategic change and competition has to embrace both thought and action, intra- and inter-firm relations. Such coherence is not easily acquired nor is it a steady-state which is simply maintained. Attaining coherence places a heavy emphasis on the ability to solve the analytical, educational and political problems posed within the process of managing strategic change and competition.

The dangerous reliance on fit?

In the wake of the growth of the US-inspired multi-divisional form, the problem of integration became of paramount importance (Chandler 1962). Indeed, the strength of the form rested on the potential economies of co-ordination which it promised. An extensive set of literatures developed, each addressing different facets of the structural problems (for an overview see Daft 1986: 467). Attention to maintaining that co-ordination, in the sense of managing the processes of change involved, is more of a rarity (cf. Greenwood and Hinings 1988).

Where the process of change and innovation has been addressed the emphasis on technical linkages has been pronounced. In the finance area experts have devoted much attention to the relationship between corporate planning and budgeting. They have argued that ineffective integration within the planning process of the firm is often caused by weak budgetary systems; corporate plans therefore become increasingly remote (Piercy and Thomas 1984). Behavioural scientists took an early interest, producing revealing critiques. Their examinations exposed the problem of the divergence in practice between official goals and more routine decisions (Perrow 1961). This stream of inquiry had its expression in the 1980s in the work of Bourgeois (1980) who argues that more attention should be paid by firms to integration in the means of implementing such goals. Other organizational analysts have examined personnel systems as a method of co-ordination in the multinational firm (Edstrom and Galbraith 1977).

One of the more striking examples of attempts to deal with the problem of integration comes in the area of resource planning. The importance of resource planning is seen to lie in the linkage between resources and the value chains of suppliers or customers. The more sophisticated variants stress the need for a fit between resource identification, existing resources, and required resources. Johnson (1987: 239) uses the examples of Burtons and Next in retailing. Their success in the early 1980s was based upon product differentiation underwritten by careful resource planning. The procurement of merchandise, the hiring of shop staff, shop design and layout were apparently treated as just as important as the product range, pricing and promotion policies. In his words 'the fit between these various resources was critical to their success'.

The increasingly fashionable attraction of managing corporate excellence in the 1980s placed great store on securing a match between corporate culture and planning. Both the management literature and business press, 'after Japan' or 'post-"Excellence"', appear to see the impact of culture on competitiveness with something approaching missionary zeal. Some examples include: the frequent citing of IBM's success based on a culture which integrates 'respect for the individual, service to the customer and the pursuit of excellence' (Bassett 1986). Perhaps the most recent instance of the faith in culture's competitive potency comes from an article in *Long Range Planning* which highlights the necessity of achieving a 'fit' between corporate culture and strategy itself (Scholz 1987).

The problem of achieving innovation in the less secure corporate form of the 1980s produced some interesting conclusions. However, one of the common assumptions of this work is that there exists a potentially systematic, integrated approach to innovation. The keynote is that such processes cannot be left to chance. Furthermore, the phases of invention, incubation, and introduction are said to share common features.

Conversely, Kanter (1983) generated her own set of 'rules for stifling' innovation. These include multiple layers of managerial approval for new projects; intensive control and counting; secretive decision making; and suspicion of new ideas. In other words, contradictions within corporations are shown to prevent change. This aspect of her work, though less reported than others, is intriguing and stimulating. Besides throwing welcome light on explaining failure it alerts one to the formidable obstacles which any form of integration or fit must overcome; problems to which other literatures give little consideration.

The network

One of the most attractive notions in the face of the problems of integration and co-ordination of the modern corporation has been the network. The concept of the network has a distinguished pedigree in both economics (Marshall 1920) and sociology (Grieco and Hosking

1987). The aim here is to draw on both in order to illuminate the complex relations by which a firm operates; relations which are highly relevant to the problem of coherence and managing change and competition.

In the broadest sense the operation of the firm and a market may be considered as a network of relations. These include relationships based on knowledge and institutions within which problems are framed and criteria evolved. As Loasby (1976) notes, a firm's strategic decisions are likely to be shaped by the decision maker's perceptions of the constraints and opportunities which these networks offer. A group of Swedish economists (Johanson and Mattsson 1987; Mattsson 1987) have employed the general concept to good effect as a way of understanding the market and strategic management. Instead of arms-length exchanges, firms may be joined by a variety of technical, social or legal links which evolve over time. A simple contract offers little to cope with market changes. Instead firms can invest in network relations in order to build up, for example, the vital set of complementary assets which it needs to exploit its knowledge base (see chapter 6 under 'Control, capital and knowledge').

Our own work has gone beyond the Swedish approach by differentiating between two sets of relationships: what we call the primary and secondary networks. The primary network refers to those relations between a firm and others which are directly concerned with generation of new knowledge bases. The secondary network describes the wider collection of relationships of the firm which affect its process of generating and altering its knowledge base indirectly.

An important feature of such network relations is that they can lead to competitive advantage through co-ordination. Not only can they strengthen given value chains, they can also contribute to changing the competitive position of firms and industries. As Cash (1985) has found, such inter-organizational systems can, for example, develop technology which will:

- improve efficiency and scale in production and distribution; just-in-time (JIT) systems are a fashionable example of such technological and managerial links
- the primary network may help generate a special service that differentiates the product or the firm as in the case of companies who lock their customers in to their systems by giving them microcomputers linked to the focal firm's host computer.

When the bases of competition are changed by such networks then restructuring of the competitive forces in an industry can occur. New network relations can lead to shifts in buyer, supplier and industry rivalries together with the creation of substitute products. One of the vital yet unnoticed assets of the network for the focal firm is the way it facilitates the informal trading of knowledge.

This theme is also echoed in the current international business literature's interest in the ability to co-operate (Contractor and Lorange 1988). Buckley and Casson (1988) outline both the benefits and the standards which both parties must recognize as well as the need to see the importance of multiple joint ventures (JV) over time. However, they highlight the contrasting approaches to JVs in different countries related to varying business cultures. They are clear that 'more empirical evidence is required'. However, Buckley and Casson note the need to build commitment, for example, in JVs and the potential role of training. As Lyles (1988) notes, the uncertainty and ambiguity of many joint ventures is 'uncomfortable for the firms'. Pucik (1988) suggests though that there are aspects of such co-operation which can be learnt. These include: local cultural and market conditions, techniques of partner relations development, negotiation skills related to joint ventures, and structural arrangements specific to collaboration. The specific competences which collaboration requires are often truly invisible assets (Teece 1987), they cannot be so readily purchased and controlled.

Coherence

A reliance on the notion of fit, with its connotations of constancy and rigidity, is inappropriate to managing strategic change and competition. The need appears to be not to lock the character of an organization and its strategic direction together in some timeless fashion. On the contrary, a more searching requirement is posed – the ability to hold a firm's strategic thinking together, while at the same time carrying out the reshaping and adjustments which new or emergent strategies demand. The ability to maintain such coherence is only demonstrated over time; it is tested by the multitude of unanticipated alterations which occur within the strategic change processes outlined in the preceding chapters.

The findings of this study point to the immense importance of coherence in three main senses: (1) in the strategic position adopted by the firm, (2) in the internal and external relations of the firm, and (3) in the way that the integrity of (1) and (2) are developed over time.

Coherence in the strategic position adopted by a firm can be generated by attention to four elements of strategic thinking: consistency, consonance, advantage and feasibility. These elements can take on the role of conditioning the strategic orientation of a firm in two respects. In other words that the strategic position is directed towards (1) creating identifiable competitive bases, and (2) that in creating that position it does not impair its likelihood for being implemented as a whole. Here we are in close agreement with the conclusions of Rumelt (1988). The four conditioning features are simple yet their joint effect is potent.

The first element concerns consistency. The basic requirement is that a given strategy does not contradict itself. The concept which Chrysler had of acquiring the Rootes group in 1963 was fatally flawed in this respect. CUK ended up attempting volume production in a company which had not yet mastered specialist production. The second element relates to consonance, meaning that the strategy in question should represent a tangible adaptive response to the environment. It should not therefore become the victim of the strength of its own entrenched, partial construction of the environment, as in the case of Hill Samuel in the 1970s. Though it may appear obvious, the strategy should, third, clearly seek to create a competitive advantage. Elaborate attention to the mode of implementation, or traditional beliefs (e.g. Longman's editorial standards in the late 1970s is a case in point) should not obscure the competitive purpose of strategy. Fourth, as was shown in chapter 5, the strategy should not be so demanding to implement that it overwhelms the resources of the organization, for example, the problem of Jaguar in its need to rush for growth in the late 1980s.

A strategy conditioned in such a way has also to pay attention to the secondary mechanisms which can support it. These are vital in sustaining the coherence of the changes which the strategy implies. The key mechanisms involve the need for appropriate leadership and the development of the senior management team; the way that intent and implementation are united; the extent to which an apposite knowledge base is generated; and the capacity of the firm to maintain interorganizational linkages. Creating and applying these mechanisms implies that a series of interrelated changes must be managed, not single episodes or initiatives. Above all, management has to solve the joint analytical, educational and political problems thrown up as they attempt to apply such mechanisms.

The best way to reveal the combined impact and the profound demands of sustaining such coherence is by reference to an extended working example in the form of Longman.

Longman

The extent of the action which Longman has taken in maintaining coherence in its management of strategic change and competition is summarized in figure 7.1. The figure provides a guide to the processes described in the following sections. The way in which it has responded to the problem of coherence is as follows.

Primary conditioning features

Consistency

After having assimilated the effect of the Nigerian market's collapse, Longman's strategic aims for the 1980s centred on growth, internationalism and the construction of a broad, sustainable competitive base.

Longman's overall aims were:

- to become a major world and the leading British-based publisher in business, professional, reference and information publishing
- to exploit fully its competitive advantage as the leading British and British-based educational publisher.

This would lead to the doubling of Longman's business in the 1980s, i.e. from £100 million in 1981 to £200 million in 1991. The strategy of expansion was based on the conviction that in the market conditions growth gives the benefits of not only scale but also enabled Longman to ride out market fluctuations and provide a base for a wide range of developmental activities. Longman therefore wished to be:

- 'genuinely international' by exporting its products all over the world and publishing and producing them internationally
- the leader in each of the publishing areas in which it is active
- to meet customers' needs through the adaptation of the house's publishing skills to the creation of appropriate information technology-based products.

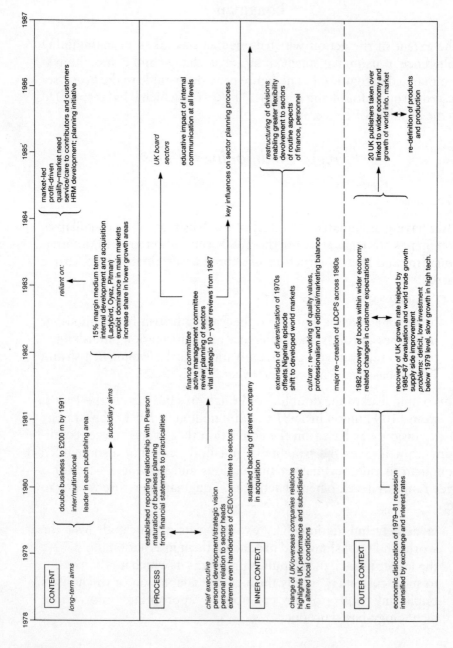

Figure 7.1 Longman strategic and operational change 1978–1987, an overview

The following is the content within the figure, organized by timeline (1978–1987) and rows:

CONTENT

long-term aims

double business to £200 m by 1991
inter/multinational
leader in each publishing area

subsidiary aims

15% margin medium term
internal development and acquisition
(Ladybird, Oyez, Pitman)
exploit dominance in main markets
increase share in lower growth areas

reliant on:

market-led
profit-driven
quality–market need
service/care to contributors and customers
HRM development; planning initiative

PROCESS

established reporting relationship with Pearson
maturation of business planning
from financial statements to practicalities

chief executive
personal development/strategic vision
personal relation to sector heads
extreme even handedness of CEO/committee to sectors

finance committee
active management committee
review planning of sectors
vital strategic 10 – year reviews from 1987

key influences on sector planning process

*UK board
sectors*

educative impact of internal
communication at all levels

restructuring of divisions
enabling greater flexibility
devolvement to sectors
of routine aspects
of finance, personnel

INNER CONTEXT

sustained backing of parent company
in acquisition

change of *UK/overseas companies* relations
highlights UK performance and subsidiaries
in altered local conditions

extension of *diversification* of 1970s
offsets Nigerian episode
shift to developed world markets

culture : re-working of quality values,
professionalism and editorial/marketing balance

major re-creation of LDCPS across 1980s

OUTER CONTEXT

economic dislocation of 1979–81 recession
intensified by exchange and interest rates

1982 recovery of books within wider economy
related changes in customer expectations

recovery of UK growth rate helped by
1985–87 devaluation and world trade growth
supply side improvement
problems: deficit, low investment
below 1979 level, slow growth in high tech.

20 UK publishers taken over
linked to wider economy and
growth of world info. market

re-definition of products
and production

These general aims gave rise to a set of more specific objectives. These include:

- accelerated growth by both internal development and acquisition, especially in the USA
- increased market share in lower growth areas where Longman has a significant competitive advantage
- full exploitation of Longman's dominant competitive position in the English language teaching markets
- maintaining presence in Third World educational markets in order to cover demand arising from international lending agency activity
- fully develop the strength of the Pitman and Ladybird acquisitions in the light of their reputations and market positions in the business education and children's publishing areas.

The financial objectives comprise a medium-term target of a trading profit margin of 15 per cent – the margin necessary to achieve a positive cash flow on a continuous basis exclusive of the financing of acquisitions; sales growth in real terms of a minimum of 5 per cent per annum; and a return on capital employed of 20 per cent each year.

Feasibility: multinational/international

Building on its post-war growth and expansion around the world, Longman has aimed to be both international and multinational. In other words, the company exports products from the UK all over the globe but also publishes and produces them in a wide range of overseas locations, importing into the UK where necessary. Longman is multinational in the sense that it owns a series of local publishing houses world-wide tied by global sourcing. It is sometimes described as operating from a UK domestic base but on an international scale. The UK company (Longman Group UK) derives 60 per cent of its sales revenue from overseas. The world-wide sales of Longman Group by the late 1980s had reached over £150 million (£44 million of which was in the UK and £45 million in North America). The highest contributors to group profits came from the UK company and Longman Group USA.

The major change in attitude which this multinational/international approach required was in the way the overseas companies were regarded. As a result of the post-war expansion the overseas companies had been seen as developed from the UK. Now the UK company is but one among the foreign companies, albeit an important one in terms of size. The overseas companies report to the board of Longman Holdings Limited made up of the chief executive and managing director, deputy managing director and financial director. This delegation of authority to the overseas companies was a natural outcome of their growth and the rise of local publishing activities.

On the other hand, the benefits of internationalism for those in the UK company have been considerable. We have already noted the gains which the company made from obtaining print and production requirements on a world-wide basis in an industry where paper accounts for 35–50 per cent of the cost of a book. UK company divisions have also had to become more flexible in their relations with overseas operations. An apt example would be in the ELT area.

Here the division is able to combine a range of linkages in world markets according to the stage of development of the local operations. So in Latin America the ELT business is run more directly from the UK given the relatively recent growth of English language teaching and the preoccupations of the Longman Inc. management in the USA with their own growth in North America. In Hong Kong the position is quite different. The UK ELT division acts more multinationally in that it sells UK products to Longman's Hong Kong company, because of the integrated sales and production set-up in Hong Kong. In the words of an ELT sales manager, 'we bind in with their local sales and marketing structure'.

The sales profile of Division A of the UK company for 1987 exemplifies the benefits to total sales of the international approach to markets. Over 50 per cent of sales are derived from outside the UK. Longman's medical list enjoys its position as the largest British medical publisher. It has the critical advantage over other UK publishers of being the only major UK publisher with its own bases in the USA, Australia and India. English is medicine's international language and Longman is well positioned therefore to supply both English language medical books and journals and draw on authors and editors from centres outside Britain.

At the same time those in the UK company are, for example in sector 3, able to offer consultancy advice to the overseas companies on production and sales organization and even provide training where necessary (see figure 4.2 for details of the Longman sector structure). According to Julian Rea, 1986 managing director of sector 3, the object was to 'try to prevent them from making mistakes which are avoidable in the light of the experience which we actually have'.

Consonance: market-led

Longman's overall growth targets and the ambition to become a leading world publisher in the business and professional areas has forced the need for the company, in its own words, to become market-led. Longman has not merely adopted one of the vogue phrases from the current popular business lexicon. The term is particularly tuned to the company's position. The abiding concern with the integrity and quality of the product among editors and publishers had long been one of the business's prime assets. Such a position can be dangerous if, as markets change, publishers fail to alter their quality product to meet the needs of new sources of demand in novel locations. In other words, the product does not determine the approach to the market but vice versa. The implications of the simple term 'market-led' for Longman are not only profound but are applicable across the whole business.

Most directly the extent and speed of the changes in even the traditional Longman markets had made it imperative that publishers are as closely in touch with those alterations as possible. The sudden movement in curriculum reform and examination at the secondary school level from 1984 to 1987 after 15 years of debate and inertia is a relevant example. Changes in demand can also occur particularly fast in those areas of growth such as English language teaching. The upsurge in demand for ELT and American English products in Latin America and Japan was met by significant alterations in the ELT division in the past decade. In the case of Japan, sales and marketing specialists were sent to cover the new market and then to work with publishers *in situ*. In order to exploit the rising demand for American English in the South Americas the person who was Latin American regional director was brought back to the UK to deploy his market knowledge as international sales and marketing director for the division.

Similar approaches have been used in the recent establishment of the subsidiaries in Spain and Italy. Structural change was made to facilitate the ability to meet the shifts in the market. People with sales backgrounds were appointed to direct the two units. The words of the sales director in the division are instructive when he says how the publishers do not dominate. There is an 'integrated range of functions where the market leads and where our type of product is defined essentially in the market' (interview).

The same principle is being applied across Longman. Perhaps the main common denominator is the drive to break down the assumption that any particular function has developed a complete and stable assessment of what the market wants. The aim instead is to recognize how the nature of demand is constantly shifting and therefore has to be continuously monitored and appropriate action taken to adjust Longman staff's behaviour. Three examples stand out:

1 The way sales reps have been sent on training courses by the Longman training manager. The keynote has been their exposure to sales experts from other industries who refuse to regard the book as different from any other product in terms of how it is sold.
2 The LDCPS division at the end of the 1980s saw a major initiative to clarify for the production staff just exactly who their customers were and thereby establish what were their specific needs and what were the commercial consequences of them remaining unfulfilled as a result of production's service. The wider importance of this orientation to the market was shown most clearly in the 'Customer care' training programme which began in 1987.
3 New and experimental forms of organization have been used in order to ensure staff can be in the closest possible touch with the needs of the market. In the higher education and medical area publishing 'cells' have been established in order to develop niche opportunities in a very concentrated way. One is in New York, the other in Cambridge, England. The aim is to separate this activity from the general administrative load of the division as well as enabling the publishers to be as close as possible to the professional market where growth potential exists.

Advantage

Longman's overall growth strategy, outlined above, is predicated on its assessment of its own competitive strengths and potential assets. In broad terms this rests on an expansion into professional and business publishing while maintaining the company's historic leading position in the educational field. This general assessment by senior management is well represented in table 7.1, taken from the business plan of 1987 and showing the nine principal publishing segments of Longman Group's business.

Internal reports to employees point to Longman's competitive strengths when they portray 'the kind of publishing group we want to be'. Reports have dwelt on:

Table 7.1 Longman Holdings Limited: Competitive position of business units/publishing segments 1987

Sector	Business unit/ Publishing segment	Sales % of total 1987 (Budget)	1986 (F'cast)	Growth	Profit- ability	Competitive position
1	North America					
	– Business and Professional	19.1	19.7	xxx	xx+	xx+
	– Academic	5.2	5.1	xxx	x+	x+
2	– Agency	0.8	0.9	x	xx=	xx=
	Australia and New Zealand					
	– Schools	4.0	4.3	xxx	xxx=	xxx+
	– Business Education	1.5	1.7	xx	xx=	xx+
3	– Agency	0.5	0.6	x	xx–	xx–
3	Far East – Schools	1.9	1.9	xx	xxx=	xxx=
	Malaysia/Singapore			(M) xxx		
	– Schools	2.1	2.2	(S) x	xxx=	xxx=
3	Africa and Caribbean					
	– Schools	4.7	5.4	x	xxx–	xxx=
	– Higher Education	0.5	0.5	x	xx=	xx=
3	Arab World					
	– ELT and Other	1.9	1.8	x	x+	xxx–

4	ELT	11.3	11.1	xxx	xxx+	xxx+
4	Home Education,					
5	Reference Dictionary	2.3	2.2	xxx	x+	x+
6	Business and Professional	8.2	6.6	xxx	xx+	xx+
	UK Educational					
7	– Schools	8.5	8.6	xxx	xx=	xxx=
7	Higher Education	3.4	3.4	xx	xx=	xx=
	Medical					
	Churchill Livingstone					
7	– UK	5.8	6.3	xx	xx=	xxx=
	– USA	3.2	3.2	xx	x+	xx+
	Business Education					
7	– Pitman	4.3	4.4	xxx	xx+	xxx=
	Ladybird					
8	– Children's Trade	8.9	8.2	xxx	xxx=	xxx=
9	Examinations	1.9	1.9	xxx	xxx=	xxx=

xxx = above average xx = average x = below average trend + – =

Source: Longman

- providing the best possible service to the consumers of Longman's products
- being market leaders/major players in all of the chosen areas of publishing
- providing the best possible service and care to authors and contributors
- obtaining the highest possible quality in relation to market needs
- responding effectively to changes in markets and technologies while remaining market and not technology driven.

The list requires explanation and expansion in order to appreciate the full dimensions of Longman's competitive strength.

Authors The importance of the author or contributor is so often taken for granted. Yet when talking to the staff of Longman the competition for authors comes across consistently as of overwhelming importance to the performance of the group. A publisher in the Africa and Caribbean division makes the point persuasively when he describes how he has to compete with Macmillan's and Nelson's editors for the single local author of secondary maths textbooks in Jamaica. Moreover it is not simply a case of securing the services of the best authors. If the Longman product and reputation is to be sustained then it is often necessary to commission and even train authors in what Longman requires in certain specialist areas. This is especially true in the ELT area. It is not enough to recruit good textbook writers since the materials and approach in English language teaching can be very specialized. A publisher in the ELT division describes the position with heavy understatement as:

> The ability to go out into the market and specify authors and then bring them in and then re-create them, reconstruct their authorship into the image of what a Longman author is, is quite important. Therefore they're not just sitting out there obviously to be picked off by one publisher or another, you go out and assess if that person has the potential to become a Longman author. (Interview)

Quality The importance of quality to Longman's leading position is not simply a matter of tradition. A cursory review of the awards collected by Longman products in 1987 indicates the strength of the Group's output in this respect. Longman authors collected awards such as the Commonwealth Writers' Prize, The Astra Prize for the year's best medical textbook, *The Times Educational Supplement* Schoolbook Award and the Duke of Edinburgh English Language

Book Competition. Yet the emphasis is not on quality-for-quality's-sake, or quality in the product at the expense of market relevance, or editorial autonomy to promote products which do not meet market needs. Instead, product quality and commercial relevance go hand in hand. Marketing therefore is not confined to sales promotion but rather 'sales and marketing has a very close relation with editorial. They are defining the market opportunity and then feeding that back into a prescription for the editorial product' (interview).

Although quality and market integrity are continuous objectives for Longman the role of tradition and reputation should not be underestimated as a significant contribution to the Group's competitive position. Longman's position in languages world-wide has therefore helped the entry of other product areas into new overseas markets. The new entrant 'slip-streams', as an editor in the higher education division put it, behind the wider reputation of the company in another area.

Scope Although something of a commonplace to those inside Longman the international scope of its operations contains major potential competitive benefits. Many of these were touched on in describing the international growth of the group across the post-war period and the advantages of scale. What is so often overlooked by commentators on the industry is that a world-wide operation which requires competent staff to travel extensively leads to vital opportunities for market and competitor intelligence. The reworking of the production department at Longman owed much to the impetus given by publishers and sales staff as they compared the lead times and prices found in the UK and other parts of the world.

New technology The competitive advantages that Longman might have in its use of new technology is considerable. Broadly speaking, Longman is well placed to exploit new technological possibilities because of the range of its publishing product markets, its own market-led approach, reputation and its valuable experience in key areas such as dictionary text processing. This combination could be decisive in competitive terms but the lack of industry standards, dominant designs and the general volatility of the information processing industries make prediction notoriously difficult.

Any view of Longman's competitive strength must also be tempered by a realistic assessment of its relative weaknesses or those forces which create inertia in relation to the company's overall objectives. These may be grouped logically in the following way:

- the decline in the school age population in the Western economies and the reduction in public spending on education and libraries
- the vulnerability of demand in developing countries to import substitution and the inability to fund foreign purchases
- the impact of fluctuating exchange rates
- the comparative advantages of some US publishers in their scale and spread across international markets.

Secondary mechanisms

Managing a series of interrelated changes over time

The previous section outlined what amounts to a sequence of considerable transformation within Longman in the 1980s. The combined impacts of such changes has been critical to the company's performance. In the broad sense this is readily apparent in the key decisions made with regard to diversification or restructuring. Yet it would be totally wrong to see the changes in Longman as a list of actions taken to effect immediate shifts in performance. The picture we have tried to present in the preceding chapters is far more complex.

First, many of the major internal changes have been carried out over the long term, often across more than a decade. This has involved the adoption of general goals which require a range of subsequent detailed action. As the following pages will show, care has been taken to hold the system together while a set of incremental often *ad hoc* changes are made. An example would be the two different phases of expansion in North America which followed the basic decision to move away from reliance on Longman's Third World markets.

Second, although we have identified the origins and bases of the decisions made in relation to each of the four key changes – diversification, restructuring, culture and technology – we have also been at pains to indicate the multiple connections between them. The need to enter new markets and develop different products would have proved increasingly impossible with the original divisional structure. Equally these two changes could have been severely damaged if no corresponding adjustment was made in the values and orientation of publishing staff. Once that change began, the new requirements for a market-led and thoroughly commercial approach to product development raised the demands on the supply of relevant information via the company's computer system. In other words, it is important to recognize the extent of the linkages involved: some intended, others equally valuable but purely unintentional.

While laying out these key internal innovations in Longman it has been apparent where failures have occurred. The intricate web of connections and relations which these main changes have generated has involved tensions. These include: the difficulties of the computing service, the loyalty to divisional sub-cultures, or the unforeseen overlaps between the interests of certain lists from different sectors as each seeks to extend its product lines. All are expressions of the forces unleashed by the four central internal changes undertaken. Above all, the balance of the changes has been positive and has facilitated the chief strategic aims of Longman. The obvious, yet often overlooked, role of success has provided a vital confirmation and means of sustaining the change process.

However, these strategic and internal transformations could so easily have been obstructed by the tensions and technical problems to which they naturally gave rise. How the process of change has been held together therefore provides a central component in explaining Longman's performance; the following section examines the issue in its own right.

Coherence in the process of managing change and competition: solving the analytical, educational and political problems

The process of change within Longman has been managed so that it complements rather than competes with the strategic objectives of the company. This has meant uniting a robust commercial analysis with the less obvious or generally recognized features of such processes of corporate change. In other words, business decision-making has been supported by attending to the educational and political aspects which arise with such changes. Uniting these three areas has ensured that a core analytical, commercial coherence has gone a long way to anticipating and driving the linked changes at the operational level which the preceding section has described.

Analytical coherence There is no single arena for decision-making within Longman and the UK company. Instead there are three settings involved: the relation between Pearson and Longman, the finance committee and the UK board. These are in turn linked to the way decisions are then translated into action at the business sector level. In order to appreciate the character of the decision-making process it is necessary to review its main constituents and how they are related.

The source and responsibility for the formation of the company's strategic direction lies with the chief executive. The relationship with Pearson was largely a reporting one through Tim Rix, the chairman and chief executive, in the light of Longman's performance. Besides routine contact on a monthly basis with Pearson's London office, financial meetings are held quarterly. Pearson's policy has been to allow 'maximum managerial autonomy to Longman'. The relationship has developed in recent years through a member of the Pearson board (the financial director) being appointed as a link man. He has played a notable role in briefing the UK board for example on the strategic thinking of the parent company.

Within the Longman Group the member companies report to the holdings board. The same three people on the holdings board make up the finance committee of Longman UK. The finance committee meets weekly, the UK board monthly. The intention has been not to run the finance committee as a remote executive body but much more, as the financial director describes it, as a management committee which can then relate to the UK board and the senior management of the sectors. The finance committee has grown into a body which takes decisions (notably over financial targets), oversees the planning activity of the sectors and can enable accountability to be devolved to their senior management.

Before examining the relationship between the finance committee and the sectors in more detail it is important to appreciate the central role of the chief executive. It is impossible to understand how both the direction and the momentum for the main business changes in Longman have been sustained without reference to the facilitating role played by Tim Rix. On a personal level his own commitment to strategic planning marked him out among his counterparts in many other publishers. He devoted considerable effort on his own development with the results widely recognized within the company. He provided a strong example of how a learning organization benefits from a learning chief executive.

Beyond this, great attention has been devoted to the progressive elaboration of the role of chief executive. One of the strongest features of this chosen style has been the heavy emphasis on visibility and communication. The chairman therefore travels extensively among the overseas companies. He speaks to each division virtually every year. Nor is this perfunctory. Often he is explaining in some detail the reasoning behind major business changes. It is interesting how easily managers seem to refer to the 'dream' put forward by Tim Rix when pressed to articulate their own planning. Some describe the role of the chief executive as supplying the source of this dream or vision for the whole group which the senior management can then relate to, so that

> in so far as there is a group vision, it's Tim's vision and Tim is trying to make it happen. It's not a collective vision. What he is trying to do is ensure that we share his vision and to that extent it becomes a collective vision. But it's quite clearly his. (Interview)

The development of the executives on the UK board in the 1980s alongside the chairman (he assumed the position of chairman and chief executive in 1976) has also had its benefits. The forging of relaxed consultative and advisory relationships between the chief executive and the sector heads, outside of formal reporting lines, has been immensely beneficial to the smooth progression of business planning. In the 1970s Robert Duncan as head of the medical division saw the usefulness. He was in

> no doubt that there was a two way movement between Tim Rix and myself . . . it appeared to me there was a lot we could do [outside our traditional markets], a lot of opportunities open to us, particularly in America. His feeling was that we should do something to get us out of the dependence on Africa and therefore he encouraged it. It was undoubtedly me and Tim, a joint version. (Interview)

Such personal contact has provided a focal point for the thinking of the divisional and sector MDs as well as easing the task of the finance committee. It has also helped to generate the shared *but challengeable* assumptions on which the coherence of the change process has rested.

Running alongside these maturing relationships, technical planning within Longman has developed markedly across the past decade. In the early 1970s the yearly group business plans submitted to Pearson were almost wholly financial documents: these were quite dense and apparently more detailed and advanced than in any other part of the Pearson group. Under the influence of Tim Rix and the four-year reporting relationship with Pearson's James Lee (an ex-McKinsey man) down to 1975, the plans were made more practical. A classic case of learning-by-doing, of precision developed not instantly but through action. A direct expression of this change was the introduction of more commentary on the significance of the figures, diagrams and explanation of how the plan was to be used.

This progression has then been mirrored by similar changes at the

UK company and sector level. Each sector now has a business plan which covers the current year and looks ahead into the two succeeding years. This plan is then discussed by the finance committee in conjunction with the senior management of the sector. The session usually lasts a whole day. Yet just as the group business plan has needed enhancing so have the sector plans. It became clear that the day's review held each year was essentially confined to the financial and numerical content of the plan. The wider strategic and long-term aspects were not being discussed even though the one-day sessions were referred to as 'strategic reviews'. One sector MD saw the problem in this way: 'They weren't really strategic, they were more of an operational review I think in so much as they were too short-term. It wasn't discursive.' Another MD felt: 'The format was mechanistic, it didn't really provide the option to learn or debate on priorities and opportunities and problems.' From 1987 this was remedied by taking two days for each sector and changing the content of the review, with the intention of forcing each sector to think ahead to 1995 and for the management involved to ask themselves such questions as:

- Where will the sector be in 1995?
- What are the key milestones along the way?
- How are they to be reached?
- What acquisitions might be involved?
- What are the implications for management?

The result now is a 'more sophisticated dialogue' between the sector management and the finance committee. Most important has been the chance to secure 'islands of progress', essential to such a long-term learning process. The new ten-year reviews could also assist UK board discussions by enabling members to participate in that forum with a better grasp of their sector's strategic direction in relation to the company as a whole.

As sector business planning and strategic thinking have deepened, so planning within the sectors has been affected. 'Top-down' plans have engaged with 'bottom-up' action. The most direct impact has been the need for each function to raise its strategic consciousness and develop its plans so that they complement the longer-term focus of the sector plan. This need is imperative if the business expansion and market changes which Longman envisages are to be achieved. Indeed the strength of such a strategic orientation within the sectors could become a major competitive asset; without it Longman runs the risk of generating ever more accomplished company and sector plans which are not reflected in action and thinking at a lower level.

A relevant example of what a strategic orientation involves, comes from sector 4. One of the main aims derived from the sector's business planning is to expand in the Japanese market. This has resulted in the bringing together of this aim with the five-year publishing cycle. The clearest manifestation of this linkage has been the joint work of the sales and editorial directors. The keynote is the combination of each function's strategic requirements in a joint planning process. Coherence has been achieved through networks not hierarchies. The marketing director describes the arrangement:

> I and a senior editorial colleague have the responsibility for developing that market and we work in close tandem on it, so that his product development cycle and my human resource and organizational development cycle are absolutely, wholly bound together. (interview)

In 1987, therefore,

> we have introduced what I see as a seminal contribution to the planning cycle, which is now the absolute touchstone – the introduction of strategic planning both in the product area and in the market area. (interview)

The major outcome has been a document which defines the key areas of operation in the market over a five-year period. It is

> an attempt to audit our market in some detail but also provide a current year operational plan so that the whole of our function areas know exactly what's going on in the market over a year. It then provides a market development plan which matches up with the product development plan. (interview)

The result in the eyes of the marketing director is that the sector is then 'planning strategically for the market in a very co-ordinated way'. It is also a considerable means of uniting the strategic and the operational components of corporate change through network relations rather than formal reporting requirements.

Having traced the planning architecture down to the functional level, one important feature has been omitted: the policy groups or working parties. The innovation was a small but significant one even allowing for their only having been set up in 1986. There were three groups looking at new markets in the developed world, acquisitions and electronic publishing. Their remit was to examine these three subjects in relation to the planned 'strategic growth and development' of Longman. In themselves the groups have clearly been a means of pursuing a focused exploration of the three policy domains (an example was given in chapter 5 of the work of the computing review). Yet the groups have also provided a vital safety-valve to the overall planning process. Given the extra requirements which were being placed on the planning process at all levels, space for the sustained consideration of such major issues was fast disappearing. The danger was that individual senior managers could feel that they had little chance to understand or discuss such subjects in the detail they deserved; there was simply insufficient time within the existing framework.

The educational One of the distinctive features of the extensive changes which have taken place in Longman is the amount of supportive action involved. Changes in policy have not been implemented in isolation. Arguably the most noticeable action which has been taken to facilitate coherent change is what might be termed 'educative'. Although the management of Longman do not espouse a formally defined theory, their actions make it quite clear that there is an appreciation of the need to manage long-term strategic changes by assisting people to understand the need for change and hence the learning which must occur if that type of change is to be successful.

Although it may sound a truism, the simple communication of the major aims of the company has been vital to the programme of strategic change which has been attempted. As the divisions and then sectors have been reshaped in order to meet external demands so the complexity of the organization has increased. The clear articulation of the developing competitive bases of Longman's publishing and, in due course, the reasons for a given success, have been especially necessary. Such action has been fundamental to the reinforcement of the more localized learning which has gone on within the sectors.

The need to convey not just the changes in direction but the reasoning behind them and the analytical basis has therefore been paramount. It is in this respect that the presentations made by the chief executive, mentioned above, have assumed such importance. The degree of professionalism and elaboration which has been reached in the company's internal publication of its results is a direct response to the need to educate staff on the logic behind the aims of the company. This move was given added impetus in 1983 by the finding of a questionnaire given to middle management in Longman that there was 'insufficient information on where the Company is going'.

It is in the sectors where some of the most telling learning can occur. In dealing with the development of the analytical and planning approach we saw how sector 4 combined the strengths of the marketing and editorial functions. The interesting point is that while the conceptual 'leap' was made by two senior managers working together, the process did not stop there. Although it was true that the new strategic market plan gave individual editors yearly breakdowns and a host of detailed information on the objectives, it did not explain the plan or its underlying logic. The new mode of analysis was therefore shared with others in the sector via a number of organized events. The status of the new approach grew through:

- the 1988 international conference with its keynote theme of 'planning for development'
- more extensive discussion of the theme for the sales and marketing staff, with an outside specialist brought in to lead the discussion.

A vital outcome of these events was that analysis and learning were combined at the same time that the new orientation gained legitimacy way beyond its originators. The sessions also revealed useful practical points that would aid the working of the new scheme. One simple instance was that in order for the integrated approach to work across the sector then a common format of the documentation would be required.

It is worth pointing out, however, that devastatingly simple devices can also play their part in facilitating the process of change. A candidate from the same division would be:

> the very simple system whereby they [editors] had to get the signature of people in the sales and marketing side before the publication proposal form came to the director for signature. Terribly simple little thing but of course it absolutely forced them to go and start to talk! (Interview)

Earlier chapters showed how the Longman culture has both evolved and been actively managed in order that the attitudes and basic beliefs of the company should be more aligned with its commercial objectives. Sometimes of course resistance is found where beliefs are entrenched. Here a collection of supporting changes have been needed to sit alongside the slower ongoing movements in attitude. In the case of the LDCPS reformation in the past five years there has been a combined use of at least six approaches (see chapter 5).

Clearly it has been insufficient to assume that fundamentally different approaches can be understood, internalized and carried into practice by a single initiative. The same is true of the creation of enhanced financial practices from formal training through to new relations between the sectors and the finance division (see chapters 3 and 4).

One of the detailed outcomes of the attempt to manage such a broad process of change within Longman has been the realization that the senior management might themselves be in need of some support in order to advance their own learning. This need has been highlighted most fully during the early stages of the move towards an integrated human resource planning model (seen in chapter 6). Above all, it has emerged how the demands of general management among the sector managing directors had expanded along with the shifts in market and structure which their sectors had been undergoing. The difficulty of moving specialists between sectors and the disadvantages of having a senior group who nearly all have similar career profiles within Longman has become very apparent. The first step has been to appoint an outside consultant as a development counsellor for all the senior management.

The political One of the most potent threats to the linked programmes of change which Longman has undertaken would be the kind of internal conflict which has accompanied such attempts at major strategic redirection elsewhere. The main reasons why the threat has never materialized are contained in not only the mode of leadership but also the structure and culture of Longman.

While the degree of change which the company has experienced has led to internal competition for resources, this has not been allowed to develop into conflict. The approach of the chief executive has been critical. The combination of Tim Rix's personal relationship with senior management, linked to the operation of the finance committee and the UK board, meant that disagreements and problems were not allowed to take root and grow. The safety valve of the working parties and groups has also made a more recent contribution. Board members have been able to work alongside one another on company-wide problems and those of other sectors. The extreme even-handedness of Tim Rix and the finance committee in the allocation of resources during such a period of diversification and restructuring has been widely respected.

It should also be remembered that the people in positions of power have very clearly risen through similar career paths within Longman. They also appear to have gone through a major programme of change and learning together as a board. They supply a much-needed element of continuity while major changes have been attempted. The absence of high turnover rates and the basic character of the Longman culture have helped to generate a generally stable and positive collective identity. The structure of Longman has also contributed in an indirect way to the absence of internal friction. The specialized nature of the publishing in each sector means that those from outside cannot easily comment on the details of the requirements involved in the projects or markets of those sectors (this of course has its disadvantages in that separation between the sectors may inhibit the development of hybrid interdivisional projects, for example). It is here the reviewing role of the finance committee ensures that appraisal across the sectors occurs.

Equally, the lack of major internal power struggles may be related to the very way in which Longman undertakes strategic and operational changes. We have already noted the long-term nature of some of the larger changes. Beyond that, the time and effort taken in preparing and legitimizing other objectives has been beneficial. The investigation, assessment and reporting which went into the momentous transfer to the VISTA computer system comes naturally to mind. Another example would be the introduction of the HRM initiative. Rather than being announced as a new departure by the personnel function a series of steps were involved. Nobody could say that the scheme had been imposed upon them given the lengthy sequence of board meetings, conferences and special events which had dealt with the project in 1986–7. Even more vital to the acceptance has been the manner of the scheme's introduction at sector level: in short it has been sold to the sectors in the first instance in sessions led jointly by their executive directors and the company's personnel director.

The overall lack of damaging political conflict within Longman obviously rests on a balance of internal features. The possible future challenges to that balance are considerable given the extent of the external forces for change which were identified in chapter 2.

Comparison of Longman with ABP

A brief comparison with ABP is instructive. Figures 7.2 and 7.3 use the framework developed in this chapter to summarize the way Longman has maintained coherence in its management of strategic change and competition. ABP did not benefit from such a strong set of conditioning features. As the previous chapters have shown, ABP's analysis of its competitive advantage relied heavily on its existing

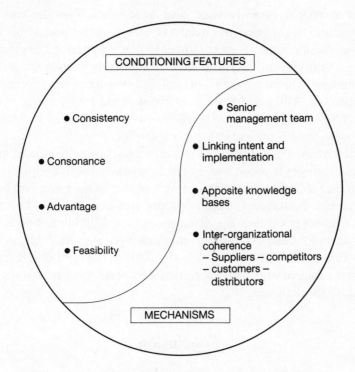

Figure 7.2 Coherence in the management of strategic change: primary conditioning features and secondary mechanisms

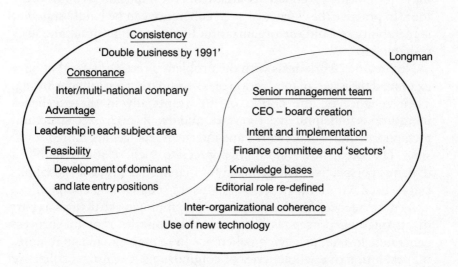

Figure 7.3 Coherence in the management of strategic change: Longman

market strengths (mainly legal and academic). Thereby the clear identification of the need and means of adapting to the changes in the book publishing markets were slower to emerge than at Longman. Its strategic thinking and actions were not as fully consonant with its environment. The result was that, unlike Longman's long-term learning approach, ABP was forced to attempt grand leaps of much higher risk to try to break into new markets – as in the case of its Magnum paperback and US projects of the late 1970s.

Similarly, ABP's capacity to achieve coherence in managing the strategic changes it chose had a certain weaknesses in comparison to Longman. Set beside Rix and the development of the Longman board, ABP's senior management appear more isolated. It could be argued that the assumption that the divisions within ABP knew best how to translate their business targets into practice, put ABP at potential disadvantage. This becomes especially clear in the light of Longman's extensive range of supportive action and its persistence in refining such secondary mechanisms.

Conclusion

The issue of coherence in managing change and competition is the most abstract and wide-ranging of the five central factors. In many ways the requirements for coherence arise from the implications of the other four. In practice the essence of such coherence can be baldly stated: it is the ability to hold the organization together while simultaneously reshaping it.

No previous work deals with the problem directly. Those that have examined the issues of integration or co-ordination are found wanting. Their reliance on the notion of 'fit' (especially in the excellence literature) is unhelpful; it is too static and dwells on a fixed structural metaphor. Studies of networks and interfirm linkages are more promising. The need, however, is to appreciate such relations within a dynamic perspective. The problem for management is how these links can be used within the process of managing change and competition.

As the evidence from Longman shows, employing structures as part of an ongoing process is but one of the puzzles that the process generates. In fact, achieving coherence in managing change requires the resolution of a whole series of conundrums. Creating a collective capacity to assess a firm's environment, lead change, link strategic and operational change and manage human resources throws up a host of dualities and dilemmas. These have to be resolved while change takes place. The four central factors outlined in the previous chapters cannot be left to function by themselves.

This chapter has suggested a twin set of actions which appear to be relevant in dealing with such apparent contradictions. As in all the other central factors the crucial need is in ensuring that the primary conditioning features are reinforced through time by a complementary set of mechanisms.

The conditioning features relate to the formation of strategy. A given strategy should therefore bear the hallmarks of: consistency – not present inconsistent goals; consonance – be a genuinely adaptive response to its environment; advantage – provide for the maintenance of competitive advantage; and feasibility – the strategy must not create unsolvable problems. Yet as the Longman example shows, how such characteristics are built up is decisive. Thus it was clear that Longman began with certain commercial insights in the 1970s (such as the need to switch to new markets). The company then took infinite pains to develop those over almost a decade. This involved: beginning with a relatively imprecise vision of what such a decision implied; using that imprecision to win over staff gradually; and maximizing the learning-by-doing which followed. The result by 1980 was a robust, well accepted strategic orientation and flexible business planning method; both have stood the test of the 1980s.

Yet in order for these qualities of a strategy to survive means that there has to be a range of complementary management action which sustains them.

There has to be a coherence of purpose and belief among the senior management team, even though individual styles and methods may differ. HRM initiatives must produce apposite knowledge bases which match the strategic conditioning features. Similarly there must be interorganizational coherence across the range of customers, suppliers, distributors and collaborators upon which the firm relies. In the case of Longman, this required parallel action in the areas of: breaking with suppliers and distributors (in the face of industry norms) who failed to meet Longman's requirements; educating authors so that they met specific market demands; using contract sub-editors to meet fluctuations in the publishing process; and forging new links with both computer hardware manufacturers, software houses and freelance designers in order to develop products which exploit new technology.

Given the scope of the actions necessary in the preceding four factors, then the ability to manage a series of interrelated and emergent changes is vital. This particular conundrum can be addressed by consciously working on the analytical, educational and political problems of the change process.

As Longman vividly shows, it was no good Tim Rix becoming ever more sophisticated at strategic analysis. His personal learning had to become generalized and taken on further within both the board and the business sectors. Nor was the company afraid to use outsiders. While this generated in time certain shared assumptions within Longman, almost equal attention was, in due course, given to the contradictions and mistakes which arose. They were acted upon and the new knowledge built in to the cycle of strategic thinking and action. The need for major alterations in markets, products or technology was met not by analysis alone, nor even by major programmes of radical change.

What stands out is the use of modest islands of progress – such as the financial planning techniques or the publishing cells idea. These tried out possible responses to a problem were non-threatening, did not raise expectations unduly, and were consequently more amenable to diffusion. Although obvious after the event, realizing and communicating such successes (but not to the point of delusion) was invaluable in sustaining the momentum of a complicated set of changes. The political implications of such actions are far reaching. Fixed, elaborate hierarchies act as a brake. The exploitation of often impermanent, less formal internal and external networks (as seen in the LDCPS division) seem far better suited to managing the necessary changes.

8

Conclusion

Managing strategic change, intangible assets and competitive performance

This book has four main types of contribution to make to the subject of strategic change and competition:

1 Relational – the demonstration of the widely assumed but seldom investigated relationship between strategic change and competition.
2 Analytical – highlighting the need to conceptualize competition and strategic change as joint processes and the way they operate at multiple levels across time.
3 Empirical – the presentation of detailed findings on how strategic change is managed and its outcome for competitive performance across a range of industrial and service sectors.
4 Practical – the implications for management practice.

Each area of contribution deserves separate explanation.

The relational

The research set out to determine if the way a firm managed strategic change made a demonstrable difference to its competitive performance. The general answer to this core problem was a resounding yes.

However, the evidence from the industries studied do not support any view of that relationship as straightforward. On the contrary, the problem turns out to be multi-faceted and not susceptible to mono-causal explanation. In broad terms, the need is first to appreciate competition and strategic change as a joint process. Second, to see that process through a multi-level, contextual perspective. This then allows the construction of a more holistic model which can account for the way firms differ in their competitive performance.

The five-factor model described in these pages (see figure 3.1) is not prescriptive. Rather it has arisen from the interplay between a given conceptual starting point and the results of empirical investigation. It is not intended to be used narrowly as a manual for managing change. No checklist of dos and don'ts is offered. Instead the term model is being used here in the way that Suppe (1977) defined it: a projection in detail of a theoretical position, which depicts a possible system of relationships, events and actions. A model offers a representation of the mechanisms by which the phenomenon under study operates.

The model depicted in the preceding chapters arises from studying firms in four sectors of the UK economy, namely: automobile manufacture, book publishing, merchant banking and life assurance. The result of that investigation has been the identification of a pattern of activity which arises from observable differences in the way the higher performing firms, in given periods, managed change from their lower performing counterparts. The higher and lesser performing firms contrasted sharply in the way they: assessed their environment, led change, linked strategic and operational change, managed their human resources, and the degree to which they achieved coherence in the management of the change process.

The key to understanding the model is its interconnectedness. No single factor among the five provides the means by itself to manage change for competitive success. The metaphor which best illuminates the model is Oriental rather than Western. According to Chinese medicine the body is governed by a number of channels of energy. Illness occurs when the body's life force fails to flow through these channels or meridians. The same by analogy is true of the five-factor model. The model attempts to capture the vital flow of energy in the change process and point to the ways by which that energy can be channelled productively or conversely blocked (cf. Roberts, N. 1985: 1,042). Jaguar is a good example. The company built totally new ways of leading change, linking the strategic and operational and managing its human resources in the early 1980s. The blockage to its energy level in managing change came in its mis-assessment of the environment and the capability to maintain coherence.

The model also stresses the subtle yet critical role of the primary conditioning features and secondary mechanisms which enable each of the five factors to operate. The essential point which the study identified here was the way the conditioning features had to be created before the specific secondary actions could have any meaningful effect.

A further general pattern is that when firms suffer lower performance, this seems to coincide with a lessened ability to combine the conditioning features with the subsidiary mechanisms over time. Organizations enjoying higher performance were able to derive the benefits which accrued from developing both aspects of each factor. In other words, during low performance firms may meet some of the necessary conditions to manage change but they do not satisfy the sufficient conditions to manage change for competitive success.

The counterpoint between the subsidiary elements within each of the five factors is paramount (see figure 8.1). That counterpoint releases its strength from the twin elements being repeatedly applied over time. Tim Rix's (former chairman and chief executive of Longman) creation of a distinctive mode of leading change arose through a series of episodes (see chapter 4). Each time the conditioning devices were adjusted in relation to the outcomes of previous secondary supportive actions. Through these repeated applications the

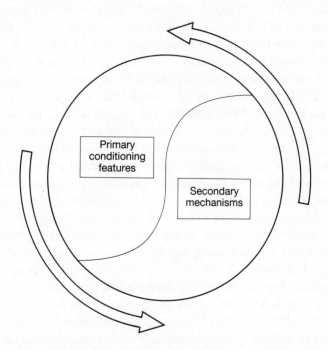

Figure 8.1 Managing change for competitive success: primary conditioning features and secondary mechanisms

robustness of the ability to lead change increased accordingly. The process might be likened to one of cumulative synthesis (cf. Usher 1954).

These conclusions do not claim universal application. None the less, the strength of their insights is confirmed by using two searching tests. That the pattern of managing change and competition represented in our model holds good across four sectors ranging from manufacturing, to service and including the hybrid, book publishing, surely commands attention. That claim is reinforced by applying a second check. The model does not differentiate between absolute high and low performers. It has also been used to explain why certain firms improved or lost their competitive position at different points over time.

Confirmation of the strength of the factors and their components comes from having studied the companies over the long term. Changes in competitive performance emerge by changes being made in each of the central factors. Peugeot Talbot therefore has registered a marked improvement in its record since 1985. This has been closely linked to a series of adjustments made in each of the five factors. In terms of coherence the company now has achieved consistency, consonance and a degree of advantage through reducing its strategic aims. At the same time a new MD has devoted far more attention to the full range of requirements for leading change outlined in chapter 4. In the area of human resources Peugeot Talbot has found the effort expended there has led to sharp productivity gains in spite of the company's relative lack of capital resources for new technology.

Any study of this kind has to make choices and in so doing compromises are inevitable. One of the central intentions of writing this book has been to combine a clear statement of the conceptual apparatus which has informed the study, together with the empirical detail from which the main themes have arisen. As linguistic scholars remind us, we are subject to the implicit rules of our discourse. One agrees that the demands of space and comparison force a degree of unnatural orderliness on a book's representation of what in real life are inherently disorderly processes. On the other hand it is not being argued that those processes of strategic change and competition are totally chaotic. There is a pattern in the process and an honest attempt has been made within these pages to reveal that pattern within the limitations of the book format.

Understanding the joint process of competition and strategic change via a contextual and longitudinal approach requires the quality and quantity of data which the project has mobilized. This strength is also a limitation. In spite of embracing the focal firms and the industries concerned the sample size is still restricted. That size is determined by the needs of intensive processual research. However, our findings now provide sturdy patterns which can be tested elsewhere. It is also the case that the original intention of using matching pairs was not totally fulfilled in that the pairs did not form perfect couples. The significance of that outcome should not be lost: in real life commercial competitors are not obligingly matched.

At this stage of what is a continuing research programme much remains to be done with regard to the immense difficulties of quantifying such change capacities. The main task here was to explore and chart such phenomena in a particular way for the first time. While we have relied on a mainly qualitative approach which the subject demands at this stage, one should not lose sight of a third intermediate mode. The study might not have been able to quantify extensively. None the less, there certainly has been a serious attempt to codify the complexities of the process of managing strategic change in relation to competition.

The analytical

The study has demonstrated that the assessment, formulation and implementation of strategic and operational change is a vital component of competitive performance. The strength of the analytical approach lies in the combination of a contextual and processual view of strategic change allied to a multi-level and dynamic appreciation of competition. Put simply this means that strategic change and competition are continuous processes not steady states. Those contexts are made up of not only the characteristics of the focal and competitor firms but also of sectoral and national/international economic structures and relationships.

Competition and the management of strategic change does not emerge therefore as an entirely rational process. On the contrary, the ability of an enterprise to compete relies heavily on: first, the capacity of the firm to identify and understand the competitive forces involved; and second, the competence of the business to mobilize and manage the resources necessary for the chosen competitive response through time.

Irrespective of the competitive response and the chosen strategy, the capacity to carry out the changes it implies is critical. Possession of the first ability by itself is insufficient: in order for a firm to compete successfully it must have both. Recognizing the full significance of the joint processes of competition and strategic change, together with the twin requirements of assessment and implementation, marks a distinctive contribution to the existing literature.

The distinctiveness of this approach to competition and strategic change at the level of the firm appears clearly when compared with other work. The main elements of that comparison are as follows:

Our research is in contrast to the neo-classical view of competition which relies heavily on the notion of rational, maximizing behaviour by all economic agents, is predicated on the absence of information problems, and is preoccupied with movements towards equilibrium states of rest. Our emphasis on the uneven capacity of management to acquire and filter information from a competitive environment, which is constantly changing its rules and assumptions, is quite different. To this extent we share the concerns of institutional economists with the way competition is not merely a matter of price mediated transactions in markets. Rather it is supported by a range of economic and social institutions which operate at each of the three levels of competition our research has identified (see figure 1.3)

The project's examination of competition clearly overlaps in some ways with the industrial organization literature. This is most obvious in the identification of the basic set of economic agents who may contribute to the competitive forces within an industry. However, we have gone much further than the conventional approaches of that body of scholars to the unique assets and capabilities of firms. That has been achieved by recognizing the significance of managerial action and the varying capacities of firms to cope with the internal process of managing change. In common with Schumpeter (1950) our conception of competition pays due attention to not only the uncertain processes of creative destruction which are at the heart of the competitive process, but also the way management can only imperfectly anticipate changes in products, markets and technologies.

Our conclusions on the nature of competition as a process and the centrality of management action have certain similarities to the North American writers dealing with what they call the 'new competition'. This project and the research in the USA discussed in chapter 1, have common features in so far as they both connect competitive performance with the bases which underlie them. In common with the North Americans we recognize the need to alter not just discrete products or production systems but also fundamental management orientations in order to improve performance. The major extension to the US work which this project offers is a means of deciphering the complex pattern of management techniques and behaviours which are involved in the joint process of competition and managing change (cf. Huff forthcoming).

There are many points of difference between ourselves and the populist general business publications which include the so-called 'excellence' and 'turnaround' books. The most obvious would be their overwhelming concern with prescription and our emphasis on empirical integrity. A more fundamental contrast arises in the way we maintain that competition and managerial action can be fully understood in relation to the their multiple contexts only over the long term. A further key difference lies in the way one regards performance. All the cases in this study show, in differing ways, how firm performance is not simply an outcome. Nor can it be regarded as just a resulting state. Performance is differentially constructed and perceived even within the same organization. Performance results therefore have their own impact on subsequent behaviour.

One of the major outcomes of this research is that understanding relative performance requires a more extensive approach than is commonly found in the business literature. The need is not only to pay attention to discrete outcome indicators (such as profits) but to examine these in the light of (1) the bases of competition on which a firm competes (such as price), and (2) the various capacities which it can develop (such as knowledge) to underpin those bases (see figure 8.2).

---

1 Performance as an outcome state
   for example:
   • profits
   • market share
   • turnover
   • various financial ratios

---

2 Bases of competition which are multiple at any time,
   and change over time
   for example:
   • price
   • quality
   • production capacity and efficiency
   • distribution networks

---

3 Creating and maintaining various layers of capacity over time
   for example:
   • apposite knowledge
   • capacity for continuous learning

Figure 8.2 Assessing relative performance

In other words, to regard performance only in terms of outcome states is insufficient; performance must be understood as a process.

This is not to argue that the more conventional outcome indicators are of little value. Rather their value can be enhanced by being used in conjunction with the broader set of features shown in the list above. The outcome indicators are but a starting point in understanding performance. A fuller appreciation of an organization's competitive position comes from paying attention to (1) the way it meets the bases of competition over time, and (2) the extent to which it has developed appropriate capacities which enable those bases to be met.

This research has particular relevance to strategic change. The previous chapters demonstrate strategic management to be far more demanding than the mastery of planning techniques, however sophisticated. Although many writers have moved away from the base camp of strategy as planning, many rational assumptions still act as their compass and route-finder. The sources of strategic thinking, the conditioning of this formulation and the way it is subsequently 'transformed in use' (see chapter 5) make it at once the most elusive yet taxing of phenomena. An uncritical acceptance on the supposedly objective character of decisions over investment, resource allocation or technology as a means of comprehending strategy is of little worth.

Great pains have been taken to show how strategic change is an organization-wide activity, with all that implies for the influence of the commercial, social and political character of the firm. It is not the preserve of the executive suite, even though so many behave as if it were. Attempts to write about strategy ignoring such considerations is rather like those management groups who go off-site for a meeting in the hope of ridding themselves of their preconceptions as easily as barring the interruptions of the telephone – it simply does not reflect reality.

Strategy as a process has to be taken seriously. Strategic change implies streams of activities across time. The specific requirements of formulation through to implementation not only account for the length of time such changes take but also the many opportunities for reversal, collapse or plain inertia which constantly appear from the firm's internal and external environment. Given that the motive force for a given strategic position may be an amalgam of personal, economic and accidental forces, the direct outcome of such processes cannot be taken for granted. The argument of Burgelman (1983; 1985) has great bearing on the issue. He sees the emergence of new knowledge within the firm as developed through an experimentation and selection process. In that sense we believe that this research has assembled some of the key determinants of that selection process in the five-factor model.

The project has also underlined the fundamentally creative character of the strategic change process. It is the impermanence of given strategic positions and the fragility of bases of competition which make the process so unpredictable (Langlois 1986: intro. *passim*). It is this unpredictable quality which leads the more successful firms to develop learning processes at all levels of the organization. Such learning is seldom through orderly progressions. As was emphasized in the linking of the primary and secondary features of the five factors, the use of the resulting knowledge occurs through a process of untidy iterations and learning spirals (see chapter 6). Such a process may be better served by not necessarily punishing apparent failures or contradictions but by using them more productively.

Prudential provides a fine example in this respect. Prudential's long-term performance stemmed not only from the way it was more adventurous in the 1970s (introducing new types of management, for example), but also in the way it was able to learn from the internal contradictions and failures which were generated.

One of the main surprises to emerge from the study comes from the educational dimension of the process of strategic change (Schon 1971: 180–201). As Bo Hedberg (1981) noted, in order for collective learning to take place organizations must discard old knowledge or techniques (cf. Foster 1986: 113–37). As was shown in chapters 5 and 6 and, most especially, the example of Longman, such 'unlearning' may for some point to the unthinkable. The jettisoning or refashioning of a core strength may be the logical necessity if the generation of new knowledge and values appropriate to the environment is not to be baulked. At Longman this required the courage to unlearn its dominant editorial mentality; a strength which had been the pillar of its competitive success over the past three decades.

Seeing the nature of competition and strategic change as a compound process is vital in one further respect. Recognizing the levels of analysis involved, the grid of relations internal and external to the firm, and the uncertainty inherent in the process, suggests one particularly firm conclusion: the idea that there is a lone engine driving this process is untenable. There is no single logic (cf. Johnson 1987). Instead, as all the examples in this book show, the process derives its motive force from an amalgam of imperatives, shifting with time (Whipp 1987). The case studies reported here indicate that within an organization one can see the interplay of analytical, educational and political driving forces in relation to differing contexts.

Jaguar is an apt illustration even when taking into account only the 1980s. Thus in a period of growth and early development and the emergence from crisis a more functional motor (Scott-Poole and Van de Ven 1989: 645–8) may operate. This was the case at Jaguar after 1982, as the organization attempted to re-recreate itself and gain independence. From 1984 to 1987 the strategic and competitive process is better understood by reference to a more emergent motor as the company tried to translate the goals and standards of its growth programme into reality. Arguably in 1988–9 the process was overwhelmed by the consequences of a single national political decision. This in turn unleashed the full force of yet another motor: the global evolutionary process of selection and survival among international car manufacturers.

Perhaps the dominant conclusion of the evidence presented here is that the management of this compound process of strategic change and competition is a vital asset in its own right. The problems of simultaneity and continuity are immense. In other words strategic change and competition are handled in practice at the same time and on a continuous basis – hence the importance of approaching the five central factors as interdependent. Yet as the detailed exposition of the five factors in operation in chapters 3 to 7 show, these in turn imply a wide range of subsidiary mechanisms. The extent to which these are complementary will determine how far a firm solves the problem of simultaneity (cf. Teece 1987; Rumelt 1988; Whipp 1990c; Whipp and Pettigrew 1990a).

Our conviction in the importance of this set of assets is strengthened by the conclusions of others. Winter's work (1987) has provided a sound demonstration of the critical role of managerial knowledge and competence which underlies technological innovation at both the firm and sector level. Others (Zuboff 1988; Kanter 1989; Lloyd and Sveiby 1989) have come from a different direction. In view of technological changes they see the extent of such knowledge growing. Managing and maximizing such knowledge will become vital.

What these opinions have missed is perhaps the most critical characteristic of such knowledge and competences. As was noted in chapter 1, the competence to manage strategic change and competition is not readily visible; in many cases it is immanent rather than explicit. It is best described therefore as an intangible asset.

The work of Budworth (1989) is instructive here. In his view, knowledge of a company's current and likely future market and how to satisfy them, for example, is not stored in ledgers or even computer databases: 'it is largely embodied in the personnel of the company' (Budworth 1989: 2). Such knowledge is a decisive yet intangible asset as a company's reputation for quality of product/service or its brand names. Recent attention has been drawn to the decisions by a few companies to include the value of brands in their balance sheets. Cadbury put brands worth £307 million on its balance sheet in February 1990 (Waller 1990). There are also requirements in France for companies to report human as well as strictly financial balance sheets. In our view the capacity to manage the process of strategic change is equally embodied in people and one of the most important intangible assets of all. The contribution of this book to this growing area of interest lies in the way we have demonstrated such assets in use, how they are created, maintained and lost, and their tangible impact on competitive performance.

The empirical

The study has collected extensive and in-depth information on the nature of the link between strategic change and competition across both industrial and service sectors. The project has made a major contribution to comprehending how firms manage change. Such detailed and longitudinal accounts of how strategic change is managed and its competitive consequences, are still rare. Above all, the research shows that the way change is managed does make a difference to competitive performance: that process cannot be assumed as given.

It is worthwhile to dwell for a moment on what the study has revealed of the way firms demonstrating high performance at given times used the five factors in practice.

Environmental assessment

The starting point in the process of competition derives from the understanding a firm develops of its environment. In general terms the research shows that it is insufficient for companies to regard the creation of knowledge and judgments of their external competitive world as simply a technical exercise. Rather the need is for organizations to become open learning systems. In other words, the assessment of the competitive environment does not remain the preserve of a single function nor the sole responsibility of one senior manager. Nor does it occur via isolated acts. Instead strategy creation is seen as emerging from the way a company, at various levels, acquires, interprets and processes information about its environment.

There are four conditioning features which help to explain the degree of openness of an organization to its environment and its receptiveness to the changes in its environment. These are:

1 the extent to which there are key actors within the firm who are prepared to champion assessment techniques which increase the openness of the organization
2 the structural and cultural characteristics of the company
3 the extent to which environmental pressures are recognized and their associated dramas develop
4 the degree to which assessment occurs as a multifunction activity which is not pursued as an end in itself but which is then linked to the central operation of the business.

However, even if this set of primary conditioning features existed within an enterprise then that would be no guarantee of the survival of its environmental assessment capacity. In order for it to endure then a set of secondary actions are required in order to stabilize and impel the assessment capacity forward. Incorporation of those responsible for planning and marketing is critical, as is the availability of purposive networks which link the firm with key stakeholders and interest groups. The use of specialist task forces or teams, beside their technical relevance, can often reinforce the importance attributed to the assessment process, especially if they are drawn from across functions.

Leading change

Our central finding in relation to leading change is that there are no simple universal rules which arise. In fact the reverse is true. Leadership is acutely context sensitive. This is manifested in a number of ways. The very choice of leader clearly relates to those who make the choice and the circumstances in which they do so. The immediate problems which the incoming leader faces are largely supplied by the situation which the leader inherits. The zones of manoeuvre open to the new leader in deciding what to change and how to go about it are bound by the context within and outside the firm.

The critical leadership tasks in managing change appear to be much more fragmentary and incremental than the popular preoccupation with business wizardry in the 1980s allow. Leading change requires a flow of actions which are appropriate to their context. Put simply, different eras produce the need for different types of leadership (see the example of Jaguar in chapter 4). Such requirements do not necessarily imply a single leader. The need may be for more than one leader over time if performance is to be maintained. Equally important may be the creation of collective leadership at a senior level (as in Longman) which may then be supported by the development of a sense of complementary leadership at lower levels. Leading change involves action by people at every level of the business.

Nowhere among the five central factors is the set of primary conditioning features so important. Moving directly to bold actions can be costly. Instead, the prior need is to build a climate for change while at the same time raising energy levels and setting out the new directions to be followed *before* precise action is taken. Subsequently, the maintenance of energy levels and the prevention of regression become major tasks in leading change. Such an approach means that leading change involves dealing with interwoven problems and dilemmas at all levels of the organization.

The primary conditioning set here includes: (1) the building of a climate within the firm which will be receptive to change, which involves justifying why the change should take place; (2) similarly, there is little point attempting change without first building the capability to mount that change; and equally, (3) establishing a change agenda which not only sets the direction of the business but also establishes the necessary visions and values is by no means simple. It is a process in itself which may take a series of attempts before completion.

Once these conditioning features have been attended to then a more direct set of mechanisms can be put to use. These extend from the breaking down of broad strategic intentions into manageable pieces (in, for example, policy initiatives or projects) to the articulation of successful outcomes in order to build confidence.

Linking strategic and operational change

The importance attributed to linking strategic and operational change is because the process has both an intentional and emergent character. The need is to appreciate therefore how intentions are implemented – and hence transformed – over time. Indeed the additive effect of otherwise separate decisions and acts of implementation may be so powerful that they overwhelm the original intentions and even help create an entirely new context for future strategic decision making. The more successful companies in our study appear to have not only appreciated this but to have used it as an opportunity. Those enjoying less success meanwhile regarded the situation as a constraint.

The management of strategic and operational change places a premium on the ability to cope with the linked analytical, educational and political dimensions of the process. Indeed, the benefits accumulated throughout the analysis of the environment can be neutralized by an inability to handle such internal problems.

What stands out in the case of ABP to an extent, or Rootes/CUK, is the way they were unable at certain times to maximize the knowledge generated by the operational revisions which they were forced into. By contrast, their counterparts drew tremendous benefit by transforming their strategies in use – made possible by their development of an appropriate learning capacity.

In other words, Longman, Prudential and Kleinwort were able to convert a sequence of many short-run adjustments into a newly emergent strategic posture. Jaguar had done remarkably well in this respect, through the events of 1980–1, 1982–4 and 1984–7. As the problems of 1988–90 show, Jaguar did not have the benefit of such accumulation across the 1970s. Thereafter it was constantly working against that disadvantage in virtually every department. It is not so surprising therefore that the company's ability in this respect was overtaken by the external intervention at both the global industry and UK government level in 1989.

Unsurprisingly the conditioning features involved are similar to those in leading change. They centre on the capability for action and the necessary visions and values which underwrite the chosen business direction.

Great attention is required, though, to the secondary mechanisms if the operational aspects are not to undermine the general strategic intentions. Not only must those intentions be broken down to actionable pieces, those components must become the responsibility of change managers, operating within appropriate structures at various levels within the organization. Clear and exacting target setting has in turn to be supported by re-thought communication mechanisms and adjusted reward systems. The modification of overall visions in the light of local conditions is a major requirement, as is the construction of human resource capabilities which can support such a raft of related changes.

Human resources as assets and liabilities

Human resource management relates to the total set of knowledge, skills and attitudes that firms need to compete. It involves concern for and action in the management of people including: selection, training and development, employee relations and compensation. Such actions may be bound together by the creation of an HRM philosophy.

The differential ability of the firms, over time, to recognize and carry out a version of HRM is very evident. Yet on reflection the disparity is less surprising when one considers the time it takes to develop such a capacity and its fragility. An HRM approach cannot be constructed overnight. What is involved is a much longer-term learning process which requires the creation of successive positive spirals of development.

The route to such learning is first through a group of conditioning features. This involves: (1) the raising of a general consciousness of the benefits of HRM in relation to the business needs of the firm, by those prepared to champion the cause; (2) there appears to be a highly situational collection of features which can create a positive force for HRM change; (3) there usually has to be enforced alterations in both business and people aspects of the organization which help to produce a receptive context for HRM change.

Thereafter, the mechanisms for confirming and stabilizing such HRM initiatives are less programmatic than *ad hoc*. When added together, such practical actions can be highly conducive to the survival of the initiatives. These acts embrace the mobilizing of external influences which confirm the link between business needs and the means HRM can supply, through to the creation of linked institutions and structures which reinforce the existence and credibility of HRM policies.

Coherence in the management of change

The last factor in managing change for competitive success is at once the most abstract and wide-ranging of the five central factors. In many ways the requirements for coherence arise from the implications of the other four. The essence of coherence appears to be not the simple fit between an organization and its competitive environment. On the contrary, the skill relates much more to the ability to hold the business together as a totality while simultaneously changing it, often over lengthy periods of time. Over-reliance on a particular short-term fit (say of market and structure) is more likely to prevent management from embarking on the range of interrelated actions shown in the case of Longman in chapter 7.

These are represented in the primary conditioning features reinforced by a complementary set of secondary mechanisms. They relate both to ways of thinking about competition and strategy and to the type of practical action which follows.

The conditioning features relate to the formation of strategy. A given strategy should therefore bear the hallmarks of: not presenting inconsistent goals; being an adaptive response to its environment; providing for the maintenance of competitive advantage; and neither over-taxing available resources nor creating unsolvable problems.

Yet in order for these qualities of a strategy to survive means that there has to be a range of complementary management action which sustains them.

There has to be a coherence of purpose and belief among the senior management team, even though individual styles and methods may differ. HRM initiatives must produce apposite knowledge bases which match the strategic conditioning features. Similarly there must be interorganizational coherence across the range of customers, suppliers, distributors and collaborators upon which the firm relies. Given the scope of the actions necessary in the preceding four factors then the ability to manage a series of interrelated and emergent changes is vital.

The four individual sectors

The study has added to the knowledge of the four sectors in their own right. The contribution to the understanding of the auto industry is distinct. In spite of the deluge of commentary on *the* mass production industry of the twentieth-century, detailed, empirical examinations of how its managers cope with competition are few and far between. The alternative picture given here to the prevailing accounts of Jaguar Cars in the 1980s stands out in this regard.

In financial services and book publishing the exploration of the strategic management process offered here is notable given the dearth of such accounts. A number of received views have been demolished. The image of book publishing, for example, as a cottage industry run entirely according to vocational ideals is revealed as caricature. Conversely in merchant banking, the almost suffocating attention given to the short-term responses of the city to the 'Big Bang' in the mid–1980s has been rebalanced. Reconstruction of the development of Hill Samuel and Kleinwort Benson in the post-war era was especially rewarding. Problems of the 1970s for instance, which were left unresolved, became acutely relevant to the ability of a bank to cope with the choices offered by deregulation in the 1980s and 1990s.

It is also worth stressing an indirect outcome of the longitudinal study of these firms in their sector and national contexts. As the journalistic first draft of the history of the 1980s has been completed, the 1970s have taken on the role of the villain of the piece. The decade is described in almost universally negative terms, all the better to affirm a resurgent view of the 1980s. The problems which came to a head in the preceding decade are clear. Yet it would be wholly misleading to let such an image stand unqualified. What this study has shown is the way some firms were able to put the experience of handling such an era to positive use. This was true of Longman's response in print sourcing in relation to the economic dislocation of the twin oil crises. The same point could be made in connection with the vicissitudes within the commercial banking markets of Kleinwort Benson.

The project raises important methodological issues for the study of competition. If the joint process of competition and strategic change is a continuous one which occurs in given contexts, then it should be studied accordingly. This means that the iterative and uncertain nature of the process should be fully recognized. Looking for clearly defined episodes of competitive assessment, strategic decision making and operational implementation is misguided. The need is to explore the cumulative and unpredictable effects of the interplay between managerial decisions and changing contexts.

It is imperative therefore that full attention is given to the impact of not only management's analytical techniques (which are never entirely objective) but also to the vital acts of learning and adaptation which have to occur. The range of linked political actions involved should also be included. By their very nature such compound processes can only be fully understood as they emerge over time. One of the clearest methodological outcomes is that the process of competition demands longitudinal techniques of study which may need to cover decades rather than years. There are a particular collection of procedural and craft skills required for the practical conduct of such work. (For a fuller account see: Pettigrew and Whipp 1989; Pettigrew 1990). One of the most useful is the visual 'mapping' of processes of strategic change and competition seen in chapter 7.

The experience of this study leads to a firm endorsement of Utterback's (1986) call for more investigations of innovation where:

> A dynamic life cycle approach should be taken encompassing changes and interactions among variables and units over time as they are related to changing competitive, technical and other environments. In sum, a more holistic approach must be taken to the field through the study of large complex cases, through experimentation with practitioners, through the development of longitudinal databases, and sustained emphasis on well designed longitudinal studies.

Competitive performance

The project has a further particular contribution to make to the understanding of competitiveness. The research shows that while it is quite legitimate to inspect the outcomes of policy decisions at the level of the firm, as in the case of the business policy literature, by itself this is insufficient to explain competitive performance. On the evidence of this project more robust explanations of performance are likely to emerge from examining the three-way relationships between strategic policy decisions, the process of change they entail and the contexts in which they occur.

We conclude that in order to understand why a firm's strategic choices produce a given competitive record one has to explain how those choices and their implications are managed to discover what is the quality of these intangible assets.

Barriers to entry and success

Addressing the linkages between strategic choice and how the resulting changes are managed within given contexts can shed further light on the competitive requirements of different industries. Rather than pointing only to technical options it is possible to suggest a much fuller set of standards which must be met by individual firms (see Whipp, Rosenfeld and Pettigrew 1989b). The difference in competitive performance between firms can then be displayed by reference to the notions of 'barriers to entry' and 'barriers to success'. The nature of those barriers for the four sectors covered in this study are shown in table 8.1.

A barrier to entry is a standard device in economics to denote the basic requirements which a firm must meet before it can even participate in a market. However, from our research it appears that,

Table 8.1 Barriers to entry, barriers to success in automobile manufacturing, merchant banks, life assurance and book publishing

Barriers to entry	Barriers to success
(a) *Automobile manufacturing*	
* Compete on price	* Application of new technology
* Minimum production logistics	* Flexibility to markets by change to technology
* Universal quality standards	* Economies of scope
* Engineering – R & D	* Range of external links
(b) *Merchant banks*	
* Established client base	* Recognition of capital required
* Provide service in all sectors	* Break organization boundaries
* Close ties with competitors	* Innovation and change led from below
* Limited capital required	
* Managers = best performers	
(c) *Life assurance*	
* Concern for reputation for security	* Provider of financial services
* Conservative operations – investment policy – new business	* Innovation through delegation
* Mutualization is a safety net for management	* Recruitment of outsiders
* Success built on service and distribution	* Profit motive

Table 8.1. (*continued*)

(*d*) *Book publishing*

* Compete on price over wide product range	* Manage foreign exchange changes
* Attract best authors	* Ability to exploit use of technology
* Cost reduction through overseas production	* Forge links across traditional boundaries
* Managerial competences = editorial standards	
* Ability to publish internationally	* Develop new management skills

in time, barriers to success appear which help to distinguish high and lesser performing firms. The critical difference is that the successful firms seem able to break through the barrier by meeting not only technical and financial standards but also by supplying vital managerial competences. In simple terms the ability to manage the changes which technical and financial decisions imply is a priceless intangible asset.

The current world car industry provides sharp examples (see table 8.1). Entry for small firms into the main volume production is prohibitively expensive in terms of the capital costs necessary to reap the benefits of scale economies or the ability to supply minimum production logistics, or the means to deliver adequate R&D resources. Yet even for those firms which can meet these demands there are those who are increasingly unable to overcome the barriers to success. This barrier appears in the form of the inability of management to apply new technology in order to match diverging patterns of demand and secure economies of scope. It also refers to the inability of management to understand and cope with the set of new practices and expectations which interfirm collaboration requires. The difficulties of General Motors in the 1980s, for example, can be understood by reference to the notion of barriers to entry and success. GM is still the largest automobile producer and one of those who has defined the barriers to entry to the industry in the post-war era. Yet the US giant is struggling to match Japanese producers and their formidable array of intangible assets who have helped to establish the set of standards which form the current barrier to success.

The practical

The complexity of the change process and its relationship with performance cannot reduce the management of that process to a narrow checklist. Although the book's findings are not meant to be taken prescriptively they do contain practical implications for the way managers might approach the relationship between managing change and competition. The following points are worth emphasising.

First, as chapters 3 to 7 show, every one of the five central factors had a direct impact on the competitive strength of the firms concerned. The Prudential assessment of its environment is a case in point. The commercial benefits of the way in which Prudential's new cadre of management (1) developed its understanding of the shifts in the financial services sector in the 1970s, and then (2) created the means of diffusing the implications of that knowledge, were clearly shown (see chapter 3). Its ability to assess the environment and turn that into appropriate internal action was one of the decisive reasons for Prudential's movement away from a reliance on its traditional distribution system and the early entry into unit-linked products.

However, reliance on only one of the five factors would have been fatal. The popular notion of a single competitive edge appears at best wrong-headed and at worst downright alarming. Pinning all hopes and resources on one main ability appears very dangerous. Should any weakness arise in that position then the entire competitive stance collapses. Other firms can also replicate a single trait or technique. The originator's advantage is thereby neutralized. Dependence on a single advantage plays into the hands of competitors who seek to enter markets by first loosening such isolated props to the competitive wall (Hamel and Prahalad 1989: 70). Trying to match such a composite capacity as represented by the five-factor model would be infinitely harder.

If the study shows nothing else it is the immense demands placed on the management and firms in our cases; both in creating the detailed techniques within each of the five factors, not to mention linking and adjusting them over time. Yet developing a deeper capacity to manage strategic change is more likely to yield long-term competitive benefits (Prahalad and Doz 1987). Based on adaptation, the capacity can be used in a range of different ways to meet varying circumstances. As the higher performing organizations in this study showed at given points, such a capacity enabled them to accommodate major threats and cope with exceptional environmental jolts (cf. Meyer 1982).

Second, given what this work has discovered about the nature of competition and strategic change as a process, then managerial expectations should be framed accordingly. An attempt to somehow implant the five factors in one go would be futile. The distinctive way of conceiving of the problem should be appreciated first. It demands a way of thinking which is not natural to Western management. This would then suggest the generation of a firm-specific capacity to manage change but one crafted to the context which it addressed. Although during the time that firms experienced high performance they used all five central factors, none mastered every last subsidiary feature outlined in figure 3.2. Each firm exhibited its own mix of primary and secondary features.

Third, developing the intangible assets required in managing change and competition suggests a number of supportive actions which managers might take. Above all, the importance of such assets has to be recognized; they must be put high on the policy agenda. The ability of a company to learn should be under regular scrutiny. In other words, the ability of the organization to reconstruct and adapt its knowledge base (made up of skills, structures and values, see chapter 6) should be a key task for managers. They should also be able to apply the 'unlearning' test. In other words, is the organization capable of mounting the creative destruction necessary to breaking down outmoded attitudes and practices, while at the same time building up new, more appropriate competences?

The implications for senior management are readily apparent. The need is for chief executives and their colleagues to: (1) renew themselves in both personal and collective terms (see, for example, Longman where Rix's persona in office gave stability to the organization during the changes of the late 1970s and early 1980s, yet while he was undergoing marked developments in his own outlook and skills); (2) not see such acts as once-and-for-all but be prepared to undertake the experience of individual and collective reconstruction over time; and (3) link those transformations beneficially by carrying forward appropriate information and insights.

The fourth set of practical insights which arises from the study relates to the problem of energy. The five factor model points to the centrality of energy in the change process (see the above section on 'The relational'). However, there are three aspects of management action which can assist the flow of energy set up by the use of the five factors.

1 In contrast to much current thinking, this research does not conclude that energy generation comes only from new leaders coming
from outside (e.g. Jaguar in the 1980s). To be sure, these entrants
can have galvanizing effects in the sense of their expectations and
assumptions which confront established views. Tension thereby
creates energy. Yet as Prudential or Peugeot Talbot show, these
productive tensions can equally be generated from within by management prepared to question company orthodoxies, to use real and
constructed crises, or to benefit from deviants and, thereby, exploit
the resulting energy.

2 Sustaining the flow of energy within a change process, especially
after crises have been successfully survived, is one of the most
recurrent difficulties for management. The evidence from this study
points to the need to avoid undue reliance on a single source of
leadership. Instead, the creation of leaders at different levels in the
organization is more helpful to the maintenance of energy in managing the process of change. The role of these leaders is to problem-
sense (see chapter 3) from their vantage point, to ask fundamental
questions, and to uncover data which disturbs and confronts in-
house assumptions. Equally relevant therefore is the necessary
reworking of HRM policies, in order to recognize such responsibilities – this may require new methods of performance review,
reward and recognition and the use of internal labour markets to
encourage such behaviour.

3 The issue of preventing regression in the change process is as
important as it is so often overlooked. Demonstrating intermediate
successes or islands of progress can play a productive role by
showing what can be achieved. Attention to the lines of succession
also count heavily since its their breakdown which leads to the
leakage of energy. Yet beyond these actions we have identified a way
of thinking which is of considerable relevance to stopping the slide
into inertia. Managers should be encouraged to see change not only
in terms of episodes or events but as an ongoing, continuous process.
The keynote of this mode of thought is the ability to not only cope
with the dualities and contradictions of the strategic change process
but to exploit them. As was seen in chapter 5, the 'transformations
in use' of original strategic intentions should not be seen as failure.
The dilemmas and contradictions inherent in the translation process
are seldom amenable to being planned out of existence. Instead the
flow of questions they give rise to should be captured and their
implications confronted as a means of preventing the slump back

into conventional thought patterns – once a given challenge is considered to have passed.

Moreover, this study calls into question any easy unitary notion of managing change and competition. Quite the reverse, the research reveals the operation of a range of highly interconnected, sub-processes which are commonly overlooked or assumed. The implication for management is that it has to master not just the readily apparent need to manage the demands of business analysis but also its siblings of politics and education. This calls into question therefore the ability of those responsible not only to problem-sense but also to: raise the energy for change; justify the need for change and legitimize chosen courses of action; negotiate the pathways of change for the organization; stabilize successful programmes; set in motion processes which will lead to the generation of relevant knowledge; and resolve the many contradictions which arise between these sub-processes.

The 1990s

Many references have been made throughout the text to the implications of managerial action in the 1980s for the future. Without pretending to don the mantle of the soothsayer there are one or two broad outcomes which will have considerable relevance for the 1990s. These suggest that the ability of companies to develop such intangible assets will become ever more relevant.

The challenges which the four very different sectors studied here face within their formal boundaries have been alluded to at many points. These can be summarized in the following way:

- automobile manufacturing
  - a new era of globalization
  - over-capacity of around 6 million units world-wide
  - making profits form shorter production runs to satisfy more varied tastes
  - massive R&D requirements
- merchant banking
  - globalization of financial services
  - innovations in both market and product form
  - huge capital adequacy to finance the innovations
- life assurance
  - marked change in consumer perception of life assurance

- threats to traditional distribution channels
- ability to run multinational corporations
- book publishing

   - major redefinition of product and production due to micro-electronics
   - opportunity for further acquisition as information based products span hitherto separate industries
   - problem demographics in differing ways of developed countries and Third World.

These specific challenges will be overlain by a much wider collection of problems or opportunities, applicable to almost all spheres of business.

The lead article in *Fortune* in September 1988 drew a number of these generic problems together (*Fortune* 1988). They included the speed at which product and service changes are made and will increase, citing Japanese camera manufacturers alongside Citibank's ability to offer three new services per week. As labour shortages become widespread the pressure for alternative ways of executing tasks will intensify. According to information technologists of the Gartner group, the number of personal computers is set to quadruple over the 1990s to 46 million by the year 2000. The results of continuing advances in semiconductors and communication systems alone will lead to further breakdown of traditional organizational and industrial boundaries (cf. Handy 1989). This of course excludes the potential impact of both the response to perceived environmental problems and the possible need to respond to a real environmental crisis, say on the scale of the 1970s' oil shocks. The immediate future would seem to hold a multilayered set of challenges.

Certain management writers have taken up the gauntlet and put forward their responses to these issues. Some of their ideas help to highlight and extend the major implications arising from this study. One has in mind the work of Hayes, Wheelwright and Clark (1988) who are unafraid to go beyond their own engineering interests. Coming from an entirely different starting point from ourselves they reach a very similar conclusion: for manufacturers to respond to the demands of the 1990s will require adjustment of the whole enterprise. They emphasize the need to become a *learning organization*.

The Harvard team draw attention to actions spanning functional areas, for example, as well as information flows and new accounting techniques. This book has demonstrated the importance of learning in relation to fast changing competitive conditions in both industrial and service sectors alike in a number of ways. These include: the opening up of organizations at all levels to the external conditions in environmental assessment; the ability to take the risk of allowing learning-by-doing in order to translate strategic into operational change; and the creation of learning loops in the progressive, cyclical development of HRM institutions.

Indeed, if *Fortune's* projections that product and service development lead times will shrink are accurate, then the relevance of such learning becomes acute. The rate at which competitive bases alter may also accelerate. This has been frighteningly demonstrated in the 1980s. At the end of the 1980s quality apparently is no longer considered by some Japanese companies as a prime differentiator as it was in the early 1980s. Rather, it is now an assumed qualification for membership of an industry.

Others raise the value of learning even higher. If in the wake of globalization, marketing, financial and manufacturing techniques become ever more capable of imitation, then their competitive advantage is correspondingly diminished. According to the one-time head of planning at the Royal Anglo Dutch Shell Group, in this sort of world 'the ability to learn faster than competitors may be the only sustainable advantage.'

The results of this research, taken together with these other signals raises concerns about the assumptions behind certain government initiatives. An example appeared in January 1990. The UK Department of Trade and Industry called for sweeping changes in the organization of British manufacturing companies. The view presented was that businesses needed to see a total change in the way they perform in an era of post-Fordist, flexible specialization. As in previous national policy debates the emphasis was on the required outcomes not the process by which they might be reached.

The DTI approach is also of great concern in that it emphasized the desirability of a revolution in UK manufacturing. All our evidence suggests that such fundamental changes are less achieved through revolutionary upheavals than along an opposite path; one of long-term, cumulative, progressive synthesis. A process which develops and uses the intangible assets described in the previous chapters. They may be on the surface less glamorous but rather more likely to succeed. Such an approach runs directly counter to the less patient, short-term imperatives of many financial analysts (*Financial Times*, 1990)

Kanter (1989) has argued that the prime characteristic of successful companies in the future will be their degree of 'all-round innovation' (see also Naisbitt and Aburdene 1985: 9–45). This will embrace the restructuring to create synergies between different parts of the business, opening boundaries in the furtherance of strategic alliances and the generation of new ventures from within. Companies may be turned inside out with the even greater detachment of previous internal activities combined with less reliance on hierarchy. She concludes that more than ever before this future company will represent a triumph 'of process over structure'. If that is the case then the extension of the change capacities identified in this book may well become the key to the continual requirement for the reinvention of the 'post-modern' business at the end of the twentieth century.

The significance of such change capacities will grow rather than diminish. That opinion is strengthened by the scope of private sector shifts on an international scale. This forms the subject of our ongoing research. Those capacities will also be intriguingly tested in the novel setting of the public sector as the implications of a decade of political and legislative programmes are played out in the 1990s. Scholars of change and competition have never been so fortunate. It is a good time to be studying change.

References

Abernathy, W. J., Clark, K. and Kantrow, A. 1981: The new industrial competition. *Harvard Business Review*, September/October, 69–81.

Abernathy, W. J., Clark, K. and Kantrow, A. 1983: *Industrial Renaissance. Producing a Competitive Future for America.* New York: Basic Books.

Andrews, K. R. 1971: *The Concept of Corporate Strategy.* Homewood, Illinois: Irwin.

Atkinson, J. and Meager, N. 1986: *Changing Patterns of Work.* London: NEDO.

Bain, J. S. 1956: *Barriers to New Competition.* Cambridge, Mass.: Harvard University Press.

Ball, J. 1989: The United Kingdom economy: miracle or mirage?, *National Westminster Bank Quarterly*, February, 43–59.

Ballance, R. H. and Sinclair, S. W. 1983: *Collapse and Survival: Industry Strategies in a Changing World.* London: George Allen & Unwin.

Barney, J. B. 1986a: Organisational culture: can it be a source of sustained competitive advantage? *Academy of Management Review*, 11, 3, 656–65.

Barney, J. B. 1986b: Types of competition and the theory of strategy: towards an integrative framework. *Academy of Management Review*, 11, 4, 791–800.

Bartlett, C. and Ghoshal, S. 1989: *Managing Across Borders.* Boston, Mass.: Harvard University Press.

Bass, B. M. 1981: *Stogdill's Handbook of Leadership: A Survey of Theory and Research.* New York: Free Press.

Bass, B. M. and Valenzi, E. R. 1974: Contingent aspects of effective management styles. In J. G. Hunt and L. L. Larson (eds), *Contingent Approaches to Leadership*, Carbondale, Il.: Southern Illinois University Press.

Bassett, P. 1986: *Strike Free: New Industrial Relations in Britain.* London: Macmillan.

Beckhard, R. and Harris, R. T. 1987: *Organisational Transitions: Managing Complex Change.* Reading, Mass.: Addison-Wesley.

Beer, M., Spector, B., Lawrence, P., Mills, Q. and Walton, R. 1984: *Managing Human Assets*. New York: Free Press.

Best, M. 1990: *The New Competition: Institutions of Industrial Restructuring*. Cambridge: Polity Press.

Boissot, M. 1987: *Information and Organisations*. London: Fontana.

Bourgeois, L. 1980: Performance and consensus. *Strategic Management Journal*, 1, 227–48.

Bourgeois, L. and Brodwin, D. 1984: Strategic implementation: five approaches to an elusive phenomenon. *Strategic Management Journal*, 5, 241–64.

Bradbury, M. 1989: Silicon fen. *The Observer Magazine*, 23 April, 19–20.

Brittan, S. 1987: Traumatic if not radical. *Financial Times*, 24 March, 16.

Brummer, A. 1989: When the compass is thrown out, then financiers beware. *The Guardian*, 30 December, 7.

Bucciarelli L. 1988: Engineering design process. In F. Dubinskas (ed.), *Making Time: Ethnographies of High Technology Organizations*, Philadelphia, Pa.: Temple University Press.

Buckley, P. and Casson, M. 1988: A theory of cooperation in international business. In F. Contractor and P. Lorange (eds), *Cooperative Strategies in International Business*, Lexington, Mass: D. C. Heath, 31–53.

Budworth, D. 1988: Was Adam Smith right about companies? Paper presented to the conference on Technology, Communication and the Humanities, Edinburgh, 18–21 August.

Budworth, D. 1989: Intangible assets of companies. Mimeo, Science Policy Support Group, London, May.

Burawoy, M. 1985: *The Politics of Production*. London: Verso.

Burgelman, R. A. 1983: Corporate entrepreneurship and strategic management: insights from a process study. *Management Science*, 29, 12, December, 1,349–64.

Burgelman, R. A. 1985: Managing corporate entrepreneurship: new strategies for implementing technological innovation. *Technology In Society*, 7, 91–103.

Burgess, R. 1989: Stiff medicine. *The Sunday Times*, 19 March. D11.

Burns, J. M. 1978: *Leadership*. New York: Harper & Row.

Business International 1990: *Making Alliances Work: Lessons from Companies' Successes and Mistakes*. London: Business International.

Calder, J. 1987: The battle of Britain's books. *Management Today*, March, 39–45.

Call, S. and Holahan, W. 1983: *Microeconomics*, 2nd edn. Belmont, Ca.: Wadsworth.

Campbell, N. 1987: Competitive advantage from relational marketing: the Japanese approach. Mimeo, Manchester Business School, November.

Carnall, Colin A. 1986: Managing strategic change: an integrated approach. *Long Range Planning*, 19, 6, 105–15, 1986.

Carnall, C. 1990: *Managing Change*. London: Routledge.

Cash, J. 1985: Interorganisational systems. *The Information Society*, 3, 3.

Cassidy, J. and Williams, I. 1988: Has Jaguar stalled? *The Sunday Times*, 4 September, D7.

Caves, R. 1980: Industrial organization, corporate strategy and structure: a survey. *Journal of Economic Literature*, 18, 1, 64–92.

Caves, R. and Porter, M. 1977: From entry barriers to mobility barriers. *Quarterly Journal of Economics*, 91, 241–62.

Chaffee, E. 1985: Three models of strategy. *Academy of Management Review*, 10, 1, 89–98.

Chamberlin, E. H. 1933: *The Theory of Monopolistic Competition*. Cambridge, Mass.: Harvard University Press.

Chandler, A. D. 1962: *Strategy and Structure: Chapters in the History of American Industrial Enterprise*. Cambridge, Mass.: MIT press.

Channon, D.F. 1978: *The Service Industries*. London: Macmillan.

Child, J. 1987: Information technology, organization, and the response to strategic challenges. *Californian Management Review*, Fall, 33–50.

Clegg, H. 1979: *The Changing System of Industrial Relations in Great Britain*. Oxford: Basil Blackwell.

Clifford, D. and Cavanagh, R. 1985: *The Winning Performance*. London: Sidgwick Jackson.

Commission of the European Communities 1986: *Improving Competitiveness and Industrial Structures in the Community*, COM (86) 40 Final Report, Brussels, 25 February.

Constable, J. and McCormick, R. 1987: *The Making of British Managers*. Corby: BIM.

Contractor, F. and Lorange, P. 1988: *Cooperative Strategies in International Business*, Lexington. Mass: D. C. Heath.

Coser, L., Kadushin, C. and Powell, W. 1982: *Books: The Culture and Commerce of Publishing*. New York: Basic Books.

Cowe, R. 1989: Strong pound puts brake on quality carmaker. *The Guardian*, 17 March, 19.

Crafts, N. 1988: British economic growth before and after 1979: a review of the evidence. Discussion paper 292, Centre for Economic Policy Research, London, November.

Curson, C. (ed.) 1986: *Flexible Patterns of Work*. London: IPM.

Curwen, P. 1981: *The UK Publishing Industry*. Oxford: Pergamon Press.

Daft, R. 1986: *Organization Theory and Design*, 2nd edn. St Paul, Mn.: West Publishing Co.

Daniel, W. 1987: *Workplace Industrial Relations and Technical Change*. London: Frances Pinter.

Darling, P. and Lockwood, P. 1988: *Planning for the Skills Crisis*. London: IPM.

Dodsworth, T. 1986: The guru factor. *Financial Times*, 30 June, 14.

Done, K. 1989: The hard road lies ahead. *Financial Times*, 17 March, 25.

Doz, Y. 1986: *Strategic Management in Multinational Companies*. Oxford: Pergamon.

DTI 1989: *Manufacturing into the late 1990s*. Department of Trade and Industry, November.

Earl, M. and Runge, D. 1987: Using telecommunications-based information systems for competitive advantage. Templeton College research paper 87/1.

Eccles, R. and Crane, D. 1987: Managing through networks in investment banking. *Californian Management Review*, Fall, 176–95

The Economist 1989a: A work-out for corporate America. 7 January, 65–6.

The Economist 1989b: The planned and the damned. 18 February, 80.

Edstrom, A. 1986: Leadership and strategic change. *Human Resource Management*, Winter, 25, 4, 581–606.

Edstrom, A. and Galbraith, J. R. 1977: Transfer of managers as a co-ordination and control strategy in multinational organisations. *Administrative Science Quarterly*, 22, 248–63.

Edwards, R. 1979: *Contested Terrain: The Transformation of the Workplace in the Twentieth Century*. London: Heinemann.

Eisenhardt, K. 1988: Building theory from case study research. *Academy of Management Review*, 14, 4, 532–50.

Elbaum, B. and Lazonick, W. 1986: *The Decline of the British Economy*. Oxford: Clarendon Press.

Evered, R. 1983: So what *is* strategy? *Long Range Planning*, 16, 3, 57–72.

Fay, S. and Knightley, P. 1986: The pit and the pandemonium. *The Observer*, 12 January, 41–2

Feinstein, C. (ed.) 1983: *The Managed Economy*. Oxford: Oxford University Press.

Fiedler, F. E. 1967: *A Theory of Leadership Effectiveness*. New York: McGraw-Hill.

Financial Times 1990, Short termism of managers. 25 June, 18.

Fleishman, E. A. 1957: The description of supervisory behaviour. *Personnel Psychology*, 37, 1–6.

Foreman-Peck, J. 1981: Exit, voice and loyalty as responses to decline: the Rover Company in the inter-war years. *Business History*, 23, 2, 191–207.

Fortune 1988: Managing now for the 1990s. 26 September, 32–5.

Foster, R. 1986: *Innovation: The Attacker's Advantage*. New York: Summit Books.

Francis, A. 1989: The concept of competitiveness. In A. Francis and M. Tharakan (eds), *The Competitiveness of European Industry: Country Policies and Company Strategies*, London: Routledge, 5–20.

Frederickson, J. W. 1983: Strategic process research: questions and recommendations. *Academy of Management Review*, 8, 4, 565–75.

Fukuyama, F. 1989: The end of history? *Financial Times*, 19 October, 2.

Gamble, A. 1988: *The Free Economy and the Strong State*. London: Macmillan.

Garratt, R. 1987: *The Learning Organization*. London: Fontana.

Gerstein, M. 1987: *The Technology Connection*. Reading, Mass.: Addison Wesley.

de Geus, A. 1988: Planning as learning. *Harvard Business Review*, 66, 2, March–April, 70–4.

Gilbert, X. and Strebel, P. 1988: Developing competitive advantage. In J. B. Quinn, H. Mintzberg and R. M. James (eds), *The Strategy Process: Concepts, Contexts and Cases*. Engelwood Cliffs, NJ: Prentice Hall, 70–9.

Ginter, P. M. and White, D. D. 1982: A social learning approach to strategic management: toward a theoretical foundation. *Academy of Management Review*, 7, 253–61.

Godley, W. 1989: Why the figures tell another story. *The Guardian*, 5 July, 15.

Goldsmith, W. and Clutterbuck, D. 1984: *The Winning Streak*. London: Weidenfeld & Nicolson.

Goold, M. and Campbell, A. 1987: *Strategies and Styles: The Role of the Centre in Managing Diversified Corporations*. Oxford: Basil Blackwell.

Gospel, H. forthcoming: *Markets, Firms and the Management of Labour: The British Experience in Historical Perspective*.

Grant, W. 1983: The organization of business interests in the UK machine tools industry. IIM Labour Market Policy, Wissenschaftszentrum Berlin, 21 August.

Gray, D. 1986: Uses and misuses of strategic planning. *Harvard Business Review*, January/February, 89–96.

Greenley, G. 1989: *Strategic Management*. Hemel Hempstead: Prentice Hall.

Greenwood, R. and Hinings, C. R. 1988: Organisational design types, tracks and the dynamics of strategic change. *Organisation Studies*, 9, 3, 293–316.

Gregory, D. 1982: *Regional Transformation and Industrial Revolution*. London: Heinemann.

Grieco, M. and Hosking, D. 1987: Networking, exchange and skill. *International Studies of Management and Organisation*, xvii, 1, 75–87.

Grinyer, P., Mayes, D. and McKiernan, P. 1988: *Sharpbenders: The Secrets of Unleashing Corporate Potential*. Oxford: Basil Blackwell.

Grinyer, P. and Spender, J-C. 1979: *Turnaround: Managerial Recipes for Strategic Success*. London: Associated Business Press.

Guest, D. 1987: Human resource management. *Journal of Management Studies*, 24, 5, 503–21.

Gunn, T. 1987: *Manufacturing for Competitive Advantage*. Cambridge, Mass.: Ballinger.

Haas, E. 1987: Strategic perspectives. *Financial Times*, 13 April, 22.

Hall, R. 1984: The natural logic of management policy making: its implications for the survival of an organization. *Management Science*, 30, 8, August.

Hambrick, D. 1987: The top management team: key to strategic success. *California Management Review*, Fall, 88–108.

Hamel, G. and Prahalad, C. K. 1989: Strategic intent. *Harvard Business Review*, May/June, 63–76.

Hampden-Turner, C. and Baden-Fuller, C. 1989: Strategic choice and the management of dilemma. Working paper no. 51, Centre for Business Strategy.

Handy, C. 1987: *The Making of Managers: A Report on Management Education, Training and Development in the United States, West Germany, France, Japan and the UK*. London: NEDO.

Handy, C. 1989: *The Age of Unreason*. London: Hutchinson.

Harrigan, K. 1984: Joint ventures and global strategies. *Columbia Journal of World Business*, Summer, 7–16

Harrigan, K. 1985: An application of clustering for strategic group analysis. *Strategic Management Journal*, 6, 1, 55–73.

Harvey-Jones, J. 1988: *Making it Happen: Reflections on Leadership*. London: Collins.

Hayek, F. 1967: *Studies in Philosophy, Politics and Economics*. London: Routledge & Kegan Paul.

Hayek, F. 1978: *New Studies in Philosophy, Politics, Economics and the History of Ideas*. London: Routledge & Kegan Paul.

Hayes, R. and Abernathy, W. 1980: Managing our way to industrial decline. *Harvard Business Review*, July/August, 69–77.

Hayes, R. H. and Wheelwright, S. C. 1984: *Restoring Our Competitive Edge*. New York: Wiley.

Hayes, R., Wheelwright, S. and Clark, K. 1988: *Dynamic Manufacturing: Creating the Learning Organization*. New York: Free Press.

Hedberg, B. 1981: How organizations learn and unlearn. In D. Nystrom and W. Starbuck (eds), *Handbook of Organizational Design, Vol. 1: Adapting Organizations to Their Environments*, Oxford: Oxford University Press, 3–27.

Hendry, C., Pettigrew, A. M. and Sparrow, P. 1989: Linking strategic change, competitive performance and human resource management: results of a UK empirical study. In R. M. Mansfield (ed.), *New Frontiers of Management*, London: Routledge.

Higgins, J. 1980: *Strategic and Operational Planning Systems*. London: Prentice-Hall.

Hill, T. 1989: A holistic approach to manufacturing. *Financial Times*, 29 November, 29.

Hobsbawm, E. 1974: *Labouring Men*. London: Weidenfeld & Nicolson.

Hodgson, G. 1988: *Economics and Institutions*. Cambridge: Polity Press.

Hofer, C. 1980: Turnaround strategies. *Journal of Business Strategy*, 1, 19–31.

Hollingsworth, J. R. and Lindberg, L. 1985: The governance of the American economy: the role of markets, clans, hierarchies and associate behaviour. IMM, Wissenschaftszentrum Berlin.

Holt, J. 1973: *How Children Learn*, 1983 edn. New York: Delacorte.

Hoover, K. and Plant, R. 1988: *Conservative Capitalism in Britain and the United States*. London: Routledge.

Hrebiniak, L. G. and Joyce, W. F. 1984: *Implementing Strategy*. New York: Macmillan.

Huff, A. 1982: Industry influences on strategy reformulation. *Strategic Management Journal*, 3, 119–31.

Huff, A. forthcoming: Mapping strategic thought. In A. Huff (ed.), *Mapping Strategic Thought*, Chichester: Wiley, chapter 1.

Hunt, J. G., Baliga, B. R. and Peterson, M. F. 1988: Strategic apex leadership scripts and an organisational life cycle approach to leadership and excellence. *Journal of Management Development*, 7: 61–83.

Iacocca, L. 1985: *Iacocca*. London: Bantam.

Jain, S. 1985: *Marketing Planning and Strategy*. Cincinnati, Oh.: South Western.

James, B. 1989: *Trojan Horse: The Ultimate Japanese Competitive Challenge*. London: W. H. Allen.

Jelinek, M. 1979: *Institutionalizing Innovation: A Study of Organizational Learning Systems*. New York: Praeger.

Johanson, J. and Mattsson, L.-G. 1987: Interorganisational relations in industrial systems. *International Studies of Management and Organisation*, XVII, 1.

Johnson, G. 1987: *Strategic Change and the Management Process*. Oxford: Basil Blackwell.

Jones, D. and Womack, J. 1986: The evolution of the world automobile industry. In J. McGee and H. Thomas (eds), *Strategic Management Research*, London: John Wiley & Sons Ltd, 245–65.

Kanter, R. M. 1983: *The Change Masters*. New York: Simon & Schuster.

Kanter, R. M. 1989: *When Giants Learn to Dance*. New York: Simon & Schuster.

Kaplinsky, R. 1984: *Automation: The Technology and Society*. London: Longman.

Karnani, A. 1984: Generic competitive strategies – an analytical approach. *Strategic Management Journal*, 5, 4, 367–80.

Keegan, V. 1990: How Britain lost a decade of investment. *The Guardian*, 1 January, 11.

Keen, P. 1986: *Competing in Time: Using Telecommunications for Competitive Advantage*. Reading, Mass.: Ballinger.

Kellet, R. 1967: *The Merchant Banking Arena*. London: Macmillan.

Kimberly, J. R. 1981: Managerial innovation. In P. Nystrom and W. Starbuck (eds), *Handbook of Organizational Design, Vol. 1: Adapting*

Organizations to their Environments, Oxford: Oxford University Press, 84–104.

Kolb, D. A. 1979: *Organizational Psychology*, 3rd edn. Engelwood Cliffs: Prentice-Hall.

Kotler, P. 1984: *Marketing Management: Analysis, Planning and Control*. New York: Englewood Cliffs.

Ladurie, E. 1979: *The Territory of the Historian*. Brighton: Harvester.

Lambert, H. 1990: *True Greed*. New York: New American Library.

Langlois, R. N. (ed.) 1986: *Economics as a Process: Essays in the New Institutional Economics*. Cambridge: Cambridge University Press.

Lascelles, D. 1990: Merchant banks bounce back. *Financial Times*, 5 April, 29.

Lawrence, P. 1987: Competition: a renewed focus for industrial policy. In D. J. Teece (ed.), *The Competitive Challenge. Strategies for Industrial Innovation and Renewal*. Cambridge, Mass: Ballinger, 101–16

Lawrence, P. and Dyer, D. 1983: *Renewing American Industry*. New York: Free Press.

Leibenstein, H. 1976: *Beyond Economic Man: A New Foundation for Microeconomics*. Cambridge, Mass.: Harvard University Press.

Lenz, R. T. 1980: Strategic capability: a concept and framework for analysis. *Academy of Management Review*, 5, 2, 225–34.

Lewchuk, W. 1987: *American Technology and the British Vehicle Industry*. Cambridge: Cambridge University Press.

Lewis, G. 1988: *Corporate Strategy in Action*. London: Routledge.

Lloyd, J. and Leadbeater, C. 1986: Work: the way ahead. *Financial Times*, 24 July, special supplement, 1.

Lloyd, T. and Sveiby, E. 1989: *Managing Knowhow*. London: Bloomsbury.

Loasby, B. 1976: *Choice, Complexity and Ignorance*. Cambridge: Cambridge University Press.

Lodge, D. 1989: *Nice Work*. London: Penguin.

Lodge, G.C. and Vogel, E. 1987: *Ideology and National Competitiveness: An Analysis of Nine Countries*. Boston, Mass.: Harvard Business School Press.

Lorenz, C. 1988: Why strategy has been put in the hands of line managers. *Financial Times*, 18 May, 20.

Loveridge, R. 1983: Sources of diversity in internal labour markets. *Sociology*, 17, 1, February, 44–62.

Lyles, M. 1988: Learning among joint venture-sophisticated firms. In F. Contractor and P. Lorange (eds), *Cooperative Strategies in International Business*, Lexington.

MacInnes, J. 1987: *Thatcherism at Work: Industrial Relations and Economic Change*. Milton Keynes: Open University Press.

Manz, C., Bastien, D., Hostager, T. and Shapiro, G. 1989: Leadership and innovation: a longitudinal process view. In A. Van de Ven, H. Angle and

M. Scott-Poole (eds), *Research On the Management of Innovation*, New York: Harper & Row, 613–36.

March, J. and Olsen, J. 1976: *Ambiguity and Choice in Organisations*. Bergen: Universitetsforlarget.

Marginson, P. 1985: The multi-divisional firm and control over the work process. *International Journal of Industrial Organization*, 3, 37–56.

Marginson, P., Edwards. P., Martin, R., Purcell, J. and Sisson, K. 1988: *Beyond the Workplace: Managing Industrial Relations in the Multi-establishment Enterprise*. Oxford: Basil Blackwell.

Marshall, A. 1920: *Principles of Economics*, 9th edn. London: Macmillan.

Mattsson, L-G. 1987: Management of strategic change in a 'markets-as-networks' perspective. In A. M. Pettigrew (ed.), *The Management of Strategic Change*, Oxford: Basil Blackwell, 234–56.

Maynard, G. 1988: *The Economy Under Mrs Thatcher*. Oxford: Basil Blackwell.

Meindl, J., Ehrlich, S. and Dukerich, J. 1985: The romance of leadership. *Administrative Science Quarterly*, 30, March, 78–102.

Melin, L. 1985: Strategies in managing turnaround. *Long Range Planning*, 18, 1, 80–6.

Merkle, J. 1980: *Management and Ideology*. London: Univ. of California Press.

Meyer, A. 1982: Adapting to environmental jolts. *Administrative Science Quarterly*, 27, 515–37.

Middlemas, K. 1990: *Power, Competition and the State, Vol. 2: Britain 1961–74*. London: Macmillan.

Milkman, R. 1987: *Gender at Work*. Urbana: Univ. of Illinois Press.

Mintzberg, H. 1978: Patterns in strategy formation. *Management Science*, 24, 9, May, 934–48.

Nadler, D. and Tushman, M. 1988: What makes for magic leadership? *Fortune*, 6 June, 115–16.

Naisbitt, J. and Aburdene, P. 1985: *Re-inventing the Corporation*. London: Futura.

Naisbitt, J. and Aburdene, P. 1990: *Megatrends*. London: Sidgwick & Jackson.

NEDO 1985: *British Industrial Performance: A Comparative Survey over Recent Years*. London: NEDO.

Nelson, R. 1986: The tension between process stories and equilibrium models: analysing the productivity-growth closedown of the 1970s. In R. N. Langlois (ed.), *Economics as a Process: Essays in the New Institutional Economics*, Cambridge: Cambridge University Press, 135–51.

Nelson, R. and Winter, S. 1973: Toward an evolutionary theory of economic capabilities. *American Economic Review*, 63, 440–9.

Nelson, R. and Winter, S. 1982: *An Evolutionary Theory of Economic Change*. Cambridge, Mass.: Harvard University Press.

Nisbet, D. 1990: *Life Assurance Annual*. London: County Natwest Woodmac.

Olins, W. 1990: *Corporate Identity*. London: Thames & Hudson.

Omae, K. 1990: *The Borderless World*. London: Collins.

Ouchi, W. A. 1980: A framework for understanding organizational failure. In R. Kimberly and R. Miles (eds), *The Organizational Life Cycle*, San Francisco: Jossey-Bass, 395–429.

Oxford Review of Economic Policy 1988: Long-run Economic Performance in the UK. 4, 1.

Parkes, C. 1986: How Bosch strengthened its defences. *Financial Times*, 2 May, 20.

Pascale, R. 1990: *Managing on the Edge*. London: Viking.

Pascale, R. and Athos, A. 1981: *The Art of Japanese Management*. New York: Simon & Schuster.

Pearce, J. and Robinson, R. 1985: *Strategic Management*, 2nd edn. Homewood, Illinois: Irwin.

Perrow, C. 1961: The analysis of goals in complex organisations. *American Sociological Review*, 26, 854–66.

Peters, T. 1988: *Thriving on Chaos*. London: Macmillan.

Peters, T. J. and Waterman, R. H. 1982: *In Search of Excellence: Lessons from America's Best Run Companies*. New York: Harper & Row.

Pettigrew, A. M. 1973: *The Politics of Organisational Decision Making*. London: Tavistock.

Pettigrew, A. M. 1979: On studying organisational cultures. *Administrative Science Quarterly*, 24, December, 570–81.

Pettigrew, A. M. 1985a: *The Awakening Giant: Continuity and Change in ICI*. Oxford: Basil Blackwell.

Pettigrew, A. M. 1985b: Examining change in the long-term context of culture and politics. In J. M. Pennings (ed.), *Organizational Strategy and Change*, San Francisco: Jossey-Bass, 269–318

Pettigrew, A. M. 1986: Some limits of executive power in creating strategic change. In S. Srivastra and associates (eds.), *Executive Power*, London: Jossey-Bass, 132–540.

Pettigrew, A. M. 1987a: Context and action in the transformation of the firm. *Journal of Management Studies*, 24, 6, 649–70.

Pettigrew, A. M. (ed.) 1987b: *The Management of Strategic Change*. Oxford: Basil Blackwell.

Pettigrew, A. M. 1990: Longitudinal field research on change: theory and practice. *Organisation Science*, 1, 3, 267–92.

Pettigrew, A. M., Hendry, C. and Sparrow, P. 1989: *Training in Britain: Employers' Perspectives on Human Resources*. London: HMSO.

Pettigrew, A. M., McKee, L. and Ferlie, E. 1988a: Understanding change in the NHS. *Public Administration*, 66, Autumn, 297–317.

Pettigrew, A. M., McKee, L. and Ferlie, E. 1988b: Wind of change blows through the NHS. *Health Service Journal*, 3 November, 1,296–8.

Pettigrew, A. M. and Whipp, R. 1989: The management of strategic and operational change. End of Award Report to the Economic and Social Research Council, F20250006, January.

Pettigrew, A. M., Whipp, R. and Rosenfeld, R. 1989: Competitiveness and the management of strategic change processes: a research agenda. In A. Francis and M. Tharakan (eds), *The Competitiveness of European Industry: Country Policies and Company Strategies*. London: Routledge, 110–36.

Pfeffer, J. 1981: Management as symbolic action. In L. L. Cummings, and B. Staw (eds), *Research in Organisational Behaviour*, Greenwich, Ct.: JAI Press.

Phelps-Brown, H. 1988: *Egalitarianism and the Generation of Equality*. Oxford: Clarendon Press.

Piercy, N. and Thomas, M. 1984: Corporate planning: budgeting and integration. *Journal of General Management*, 10, 2, 51–66.

Porter, M. 1980: *Competitive Strategy*. New York: Free Press.

Porter, M. 1981: The contributions of industrial organisations to strategic management. *Academy of Management Review*, 6, 4, 609–20.

Porter, M. 1985: *Competitive Advantage: Creating and Sustaining Superior Performance*. New York: Free Press.

Porter, M. 1987: The man who put cash cows out to grass. *Financial Times*, 20 March, 18.

Porter, M. 1989: *The Competitive Advantage of Nations and their Firms*. New York: Free Press.

Prahalad, C. K. and Doz, Y. 1987: *The Multinational Mission*. London: Macmillan.

Prowse, M. 1987: A decline which may have gone too far. *Financial Times*, 30 March, 12.

Pucik, V. 1988: Strategic alliances, organisational learning and competitive advantage: the HRM agenda. *Human Resource Management*, Spring, 27, 1, 77–93.

Quinn, J. B. 1980: *Strategies for Change: Logical Incrementalism*. Homewood, Illinois: R. D. Irwin.

Quinn, J. B. 1988: Managing strategies incrementally. In J. B. Quinn, H. Mintzberg and R. M. James (eds), *The Strategy Process: Concepts, Contexts and Cases*, Engelwood Cliffs, NJ: Prentice Hall.

Ramsay, H. 1980: Participation: the shop floor view. *British Journal of Industrial Relations*, XIV, 2, 128–41.

Rasanen, K. 1989: Sectoral roots and strategic change: the case of Finnish corporations: 1973–1985. Paper presented to the 9th EGOS Colloquium, WZB Berlin, July.

Ravenscraft, D. and Scherer, D. 1987: *Mergers, Sell-offs and Economic Efficiency*. Washington, DC: Brookings Institute.

Rawsthorn, A. 1989: Fishing for a new corporate image. *Financial Times*, 24 February, 23.

Riddell, P. 1987: An instinct not an ideology. *Financial Times*. 23 March, 12.

Roberts, E. B. 1987: Managing technological innovation – a search for generalizations. In E. B. Roberts (ed.), *Generating Technological Innovation*, New York: Oxford University Press, 3–21.

Roberts, N. 1985: Transforming leadership: a process of collective action. *Human Relations*, 38, 11, 1,023–46.

Robinson, D. 1976: The strategy and structure of some major merchant banks and their financial performance. Unpublished MA thesis, Manchester Business School.

Rogaly, J. 1989: Audit of evolution. *Financial Times*, 4 May, I.

Romanelli, E. 1987: New venture strategies in the minicomputer industry. *California Management Review*, Fall, 160–75.

Romme, A. G. 1989: The dialectics of closing and opening in strategy formation. Paper presented to the Workshop on Making History/Breaking History, European Institute for Advanced Studies in Management, Leuven, 28–9 September.

Ropo, A. 1989: Leadership and organizational change. *Acta Universitatis Tamperensis*, A, 280.

Rosenfeld, R., Whipp, R. and Pettigrew, A. M. 1989: Processes of internationalisation: regeneration and competitiveness. *Economia Aziendale*, vii, 1, April, 21–47.

Rothwell, R. and Gardiner, P. 1985: *Innovation: A Study of the Problems and Benefits of Product Innovation*. London: Design Council.

Rumelt, R. 1988: The evaluation of business strategy. In J. B. Quinn, H. Mintzberg and R. M. James (eds), *The Strategy Process: Concepts, Contexts and Cases*, Engelwood Cliffs, NJ: Prentice Hall, 50–6.

Sabel, C. 1982: *Work and Politics*. Cambridge. Cambridge University Press.

Scholz, C. 1987: Corporate culture and strategy – the problem of strategic fit. *Long Range Planning*, 20, 4, 78–87.

Schon, D. 1971: *Beyond the Stable State*. New York: Norton.

Schotter, A. 1981: *The Economic Theory of Social Institutions*. Cambridge: Cambridge University Press.

Schumpeter, J. A. 1950: *Capitalism, Socialism, and Democracy*, 3rd edn. New York: Harper.

Scott, R. and Lodge, G. C. 1985: *US Competitiveness in the World Economy*. Boston, Mass.: Harvard Business School Press.

Scott-Morton, M. 1986: Strategy formulation methodologies. Sloan School, MIT, *Management in the 1990s* series.

Scott-Morton, M. and Rockart, J. 1983: Implications of changes in information technology for corporate strategy. *Interfaces*, 14, January/February, 84–95.

Scott-Poole, M. and Van de Ven, A. 1989: Toward a general theory of innovation processes. In A. Van de Ven, H. Angle and M. Scott-Poole (eds),

Research on the Management of Innovation, New York: Harper & Row, 637–62.

Shearman, C. and Burrell, G. 1987: The structures of industrial development. *Journal of Management Studies*, 24, 4, July, 325–45.

Simpson, D. 1986: Where hearts and minds are in the front seat. *The Guardian*, 21 August, 18.

Sisson, K. (ed.) 1989: *Personnel Management in Britain*. Oxford: Basil Blackwell.

Skidelsky, R. (ed.) 1988: *Thatcherism*. London: Chatto & Windus.

Smith, C., Whipp, R. and Willmott, H. 1988: Case-study research: methodological breakthrough or ideological weapon. *Advances in Public Interest Accounting: A Research Annual*, New York: JAI Press, 95–120.

Snoddy, R. 1988: A chapter of acquisitions. *Financial Times*, 3 October, 28.

Suppe, F. 1977: *The Structure of Scientific Theories*. Urbana: University of Illinois Press.

Taylor, B. 1983: Turnaround, recovery and growth: the way through crisis. *Journal of General Management*, 8, 5–13.

Taylor, B. 1986: Corporate planning for the 1990s: the new frontiers. *Long Range Planning*, 19, 6, 13–18.

Teece, D. J. (ed.) 1987: *The Competitive Challenge: Strategies for Industrial Innovation and Renewal*. Cambridge, Mass.: Ballinger.

Thirlwall, A. 1989: Myth of Thatcher's miracle. *The Guardian*, 26 April, 15.

Thomas, H. and McGee, J. 1985: Making sense of complex industries. Mimeo, University of Illinois at Urbana-Champaign.

Thompson, A. 1983: *The Nature of Work*. London: Macmillan.

Thompson, A. A. and Strickland, A. J. 1980: *Strategy Formulation and Implementation*. Dallas: Business Publications.

Tichy, N. 1983: *Managing Strategic Change*. New York: Wiley.

Tushman, M. and Romanelli, E. 1985: Organizational evolution: a metamorphosis model of convergence and reorientation. In T. Cummings and B. Staw (eds), *Research in Organization Behaviour*, Greenwich, Connecticut: JAI Press.

Usher, A. P. 1954: *A History of Mechanical Invention*. Cambridge, Mass.: Harvard University Press.

Utterback, J. 1986: Innovation and corporate strategy. *International Journal of Technology Management*, 1, 1/2.

Van de Ven, A. 1986: Central problems in the management of innovation. *Management Science*, 22, 5, May, 590–607.

Von Hippel, E. 1988: *The Sources of Innovation*. New York: Oxford University Press.

Voss, C. 1989: A holistic approach to manufacturing. *Financial Times*, 29 November, 29.

Waller, D. 1990: Cadbury ignores ASC plan on brands. *Financial Times*, 1 March, 1.

Walton, R. 1987: *Innovating to Compete: Lessons for Diffusing and Managing Change in the Workplace*. San Francisco: Jossey-Bass.

Waters, R. 1989: Identity crisis threatens balance sheet values. *Financial Times*, 27 April, 35.

Weick, K. E. 1987: Substitutes for corporate strategy. In D. J. Teece (ed.), *The Competitive Challenge: Strategies for Industrial Innovation and Renewal*, Cambridge, Mass.: Ballinger.

Weiner, M. 1981: *English Culture and the Decline of the Industrial Spirit 1850–1980*. Cambridge: Cambridge University Press.

Wheelwright, S. 1987: Restoring competitivenes in US manufacturing. In D. J. Teece (ed.), *The Competitive Challenge: Strategies for Industrial Innovation and Renewal*, Cambridge, Mass.: Ballinger, 83–100.

Whipp, R. 1984: 'The art of good management': managerial control of work in the British pottery industry 1900–1925. *International Review of Social History*, XXIX, 3, 359–85.

Whipp, R. 1985: Labour markets and communities: an historical view. *Sociological Review*, 33, 4, November, 768–91.

Whipp, R. 1986: Democracy and the design cycle: the Rover Company and BLMC. In J. McGoldrick (ed.), *Behavioural Science for Business Studies*, Wokingham: Van Nostrand Reinhold, 1–17.

Whipp, R. 1987: A time to every purpose: an essay on time and work. In P. Joyce (ed.), *The Historical Meanings of Work*, Cambridge: Cambridge University Press, 210–36.

Whipp, R. 1988: Work and social consciousness. *Past and Present*, 119, May, 132–57.

Whipp, R. 1990a: *Patterns of Labour: Work and Social Change in the Pottery Industry*. London: Routledge.

Whipp, R. 1990b: Crisis and continuity: design and innovation in the British automobile industry 1896–1986. In P. Mathias (ed.), *Innovation and Technology from the 18th Century to the Present*, Oxford: Basil Blackwell.

Whipp, R. 1990c: Managing technological changes: opportunities and pitfalls. In M. A. Dorgham (ed.), *International Technology Management*, Geneva: Inderscience, 90–108.

Whipp, R. and Clark, C. 1986: *Innovation and the Auto Industry: Product, Process and Work Organisation*. London: Frances Pinter.

Whipp R.and Pettigrew A. 1990a: Managing change for competitive success: bridging the strategic and the operational. Paper presented to the 10th International Conference of the Strategic Management Society, Stockholm, 24–7 September.

Whipp, R. and Pettigrew, A. 1990b: Leading change and the management of competition. Paper presented to the SMS Workshop on Leadership and the Management of Strategic Change, University of Cambridge, 11–14 December.

Whipp, R., Pettigrew, A. M. and Sparrow, P. 1989: New technology, competition and the firm: a framework for research. *International Journal of Vehicle Design*, 10, 4, 453–69.

Whipp, R., Rosenfeld, R. and Pettigrew, A. M. 1987: Understanding strategic change processes: some preliminary British findings. In A. Pettigrew (ed.), *The Management of Strategic Change*, Oxford: Basil Blackwell, 14–55.

Whipp, R., Rosenfeld, R. and Pettigrew, A. M. 1989a: Culture and competitiveness: evidence from mature UK industries. *Journal of Management Studies*, 26, 6, November, 561–86.

Whipp, R., Rosenfeld, R. and Pettigrew, A. M. 1989b: Managing strategic change in a mature business. *Long Range Planning*, 22, 6, 92–9.

Williamson, O. E. 1975: *Markets and Hierarchies: Analysis and Anti-trust Implications*, New York: Free Press.

Winch, W. 1988: The implementation of CAD/CAM: concepts and propositions. Warwick Papers in Management, No. 24, September.

Winter, S. 1987: Knowledge and competence as strategic assets. In D. J. Teece (ed.), *The Competitive Challenge: Strategies for Industrial Innovation and Renewal*, Cambridge, Mass.: Ballinger, 159–84.

Wolf, M. 1988: Is there a British miracle? *Financial Times*, 16 June, 27.

Wong, V., Saunders, J. and Doyle, P. 1989: The barriers to achieving stronger marketing orientation in British companies: an exploratory study. Proceedings of the 22nd Marketing Education group Conference, 3, Glasgow Business School

Yamazaki, T. 1989: Corporate investment. *Financial Times*, 29 November, 18.

Young, H. 1989: *One of Us*. London. Macmillan.

Zan, L. 1987: What's left for formal planning? *Economia Aziendale*, VI, 2, 187–204.

Zenter, R. D. 1982: Scenarios, past, present and future. *Long Range Planning*, 15, 3.

Zuboff, S. 1988: *In the Age of the Smart Machine: The Future of Work and Power*. New York: Basic Books.

Index

intrinsic merit. Elsewhere his position becomes still less certain: 'The respect paid to men on account of their titles is paid at least to the supposal of their superior virtues and abilities, or it is paid to nothing.'[1] Since 'superior virtues and abilities' would be entitled to respect in any case, Fielding implies that title *per se* is a meaningless distinction.

The inconsistency to which he is tending may seem a small one, but its implications are far-reaching. In a sense his dilemma is a product of the basic intellectual ambiguity mentioned at the beginning of this chapter. Reason was made the ultimate criterion, but old forms of thought were still instinctively preserved. Hence in this case Fielding retains his belief in the validity of rank, though he can neither justify it in practical terms, nor derive it from supernatural dispensation.

The effect of this kind of uncertainty is to impair the objectivity essential to his role as moral commentator. For example in both *An Inquiry into the Causes of the Late Increase in Robbers* and *A Proposal for Making an Effectual Provision for the Poor*, he draws a distinction between the idle rich man and the idle beggar. The former is a useful member of the community because his very luxury provides employment and promotes the circulation of money. The latter, however, having only his labour to offer to society, is a useless member, and must legally be compelled to work. Similarly the rich are to be allowed their trivial entertainments, 'their masquerades and ridottos; their assemblies, drums, routs, riots, and hurricanes',[2] while the poor are to be debarred them, since in their case such pleasures are likely to lead to crime: 'In diversions, as in many other particulars, the upper part of life is distinguished from the lower.'[3] When Fielding is discussing the dispensation of charity in *The Champion*,[4] he at once excludes beggars from any benefit, because these 'deserve punishment more than relief'. The chief beneficiaries should be gentlefolk who have impoverished themselves through over-spending.

[1] *An Essay on Nothing*, Henley ed., xiv.316.
[2] *Inquiry*, Henley ed., xiii.27.   [3] *Inquiry*, Henley ed., xiii.28.
[4] Henley ed., xv.203 ff.

Fielding's work. On occasion he implies that even the Church is tainted with this materialism.[1]

The result of this venality is that virtue and merit are at a discount:

A very virtuous man may starve in Westminster Hall, or among the fair traders in the city, while the gentleman who would take fees in any cause, or sometimes on both sides of the same cause; and the trader who swears solemnly that he gets nothing by his silk at a crown a yard, and sells it afterwards for four shillings, will be pretty sure of growing rich.[2]

In the sphere of literature 'true wit and genius' are 'in a manner deposed, and imposters advanced in their place'[3]: '. . . for I think I may affirm with truth, that there is no one patron of true genius, nor the least encouragement left for it in this kingdom.'[4] There is a similar lack of encouragement for military merit. Fielding refers to: '. . . an acquaintance of mine, who, after he had served many campaigns in Flanders, and been wounded in Spain, with a generous heart and an empty pocket died in the King's Bench . . .'[5] Even marriage has become a way of making money. A pretty girl is a marketable property, disposed of to the highest bidder, and must resign herself to a loveless marriage.[6] Understandably such unions frequently lapse first into hatred and then into adultery. Altogether Fielding's writings imply a society that is decadent, frivolous, and often brutal.

It is by comparison with this gloomy picture of the town that his constant ideal of a peaceful country existence gains in persuasiveness. In one of Fielding's contributions to his sister's *Familiar Letters*, a Miss Lucy Rural, having received her friend's account of the delights of the city, replies that she is: ' . . . convinced of the impertinence and stupidity of a town-life; and that we are not only more innocent, but much more merry and happy in the country.'[7] No doubt, as Battestin suggests, this theme partly derives from poetic

[1] (e.g.) *The Champion*, Henley ed., xv.273.
[2] *The Champion*, Henley ed., xv.172.
[3] *Familiar Letters*, Henley ed., xvi.28.
[4] *Familiar Letters*, Henley ed., xv.31.
[5] *The Champion*, Henley ed., xv.78.
[6] (e.g.) *The Champion*, Henley ed., xv.192.   [7] Henley ed., xvi.43.

tradition; but with Fielding the attitude is not purely a philosophical one. The country was preferable to the town not necessarily in absolute terms, but because the contemporary values of the town happened to be particularly vicious and inane. In any case the superior happiness of rural life is a constant theme in Fielding.

This rough categorizing of the social comments and criticisms which recur most frequently in Fielding's work probably makes them appear too unoriginal and miscellaneous to form a serious part of a didactic writer's material. But while it is true that Fielding was often repeating strictures previously passed by Steele, Gay, and others, he no doubt felt that he had an ethical justification for doing so. It was the moralist's task to be effective rather than original. Some critics have been puzzled that Fielding should find Dr. South 'wittier than Congreve'; but he was probably thinking of South's own definition: 'Wit in Divinity is nothing else, but Sacred Truths suitably expressed.'[1] Fielding shared this belief in the importance of apt new formulations of familiar ideas. He suggests as much in *An Essay on the Knowledge of the Characters of Men*:

> Neither will the reader, I hope, be offended, if he should here find no observations entirely new to him. Nothing can be plainer, or more known, than the general rules of morality, and yet thousands of men are thought well employed in reviving our remembrance, and enforcing our practice of them.[2]

Since the specific social evils he was concerned to criticize flourished throughout his life it is not surprising to find the same particular targets attacked again and again.

More notable in its effect on Fielding's work is the miscellaneousness of much of his satire. His didacticism tends to take two distinctive forms. The positive side, the propagation of the ideal of Charity, provides a constant point of reference, even when left tacit and only implied through irony. The negative side, the condemnation of various vices, and more particularly of various social practices, finds expression in a host of self-contained, usually satirical, attacks.

[1] *Thirty Six Sermons and Discourses*, ed. cit., ii.14.
[2] Henley ed., xiv.283.

It is the heterogeneousness of these attacks which i other main factor conditioning Fielding's chosen lit forms. As the ensuing chapters will show, the multiplic: minor didactic comment has a marked effect on the herence and the continuity of both his dramatic and narrative writing.

3

Since the corruptness Fielding censured extended to political and legal administration of the times his s naturally tended to imply flaws in the system. In his years, when working as a magistrate, he criticized var specific weaknesses in the law. Yet it never occurs to hi question the system as a whole. He has complete faith in current social order, and attributes any failings in it sole the corruptness or inadequacy of individuals. For him malaise in society can be no more than the sum total o symptoms.

This implicit confidence in the existing order of things a special significance for Fielding's didactic position in he derives from it certain assumptions which do not q square with his moral beliefs. The slight contradiction volved may be observed in some of his comments on rank *An Essay on Conversation* he states: 'Men are superic each other in this our country by title, by birth, by ran profession, and by age . . . '[1] Later in the essay he con his belief in birth, saying that he would not withhold it 'that deference which the policy of government assigned it'.[2] But at another point he admits:

> . . . birth . . . is a poor and mean pretence to honour, when su with no other. Persons who have no better claim to sup should be ashamed of this; they are really a disgrace to those cestors from whom they would derive their pride . . . [3]

There is clearly a clash here between Fielding's accep the idea that birth can confer social superiority practical view that superiority must depend on som

[1] Henley ed., xiv.257-8. [2] Henley ed., xiv.266
[3] Henley ed., xiv.265.

In all these cases, granted Fielding's confidence in the social system as a whole, his conclusions are very sound; but he has reached them at the expense of introducing an extra-moral premise into what he assumes to be a purely Christian theory of life. Moreover the very system he endorses he is constantly convicting of corruption in practice. Throughout his work, therefore, he is liable to make attacks on the workings of society which cut deeper than he realizes, or to preach absolute moral attitudes which his social preconceptions make it impossible for him to sustain. Where the novels falter it is often due to the fact that though they are didactic works concerned with social morality, the moral and social views of their author are slightly at odds.

III

DIDACTICISM IN FIELDING'S PLAYS

IT seems dangerous, at first sight, to generalize about Fielding's dramatic work, since in his busy theatrical career he wrote not only several kinds of comedy, but also farce, ballad-operas, burlesques, and rehearsal plays. But the diversity is more apparent than real. Fielding's work reflects an Augustan tendency to intermingle the various genres. As Allardyce Nicoll points out: 'Even his best plays show the power of diverse schools—manners, intrigue, humours and sentiment meeting in one.'[1] What is significant, therefore, to a consideration of the forms Fielding had to deal with, is not the particular demands of each individual category, but rather the important factors common to all.

The several current types of comedy were characterized above all by artificiality. Plots were compounded of coincidence, deception, impersonation, and 'discovery'. The leading characters were aristocrats, miraculously freed of any concerns irrelevant to the courtship or intrigue in hand. Their dialogue was epigrammatic in ordinary exchanges, stiltedly emotional in romantic scenes.

But whereas Wycherley, for instance, had exorcized almost every distracting suggestion of real-life emotion or real-life morality, his successors had begun to reinfuse these elements into the artificial context. The sentiment which Steele and Cibber introduced into their plays had automatically a moral implication. Easy's promiscuities, in *The Careless Husband*, cannot be treated as comic once the Steinkirk scene has demonstrated his wife's devotion to him.

Yet *The Careless Husband* illustrates the incompatibility of Cibber's comic and serious intentions. As Bateson comments: 'The fundamental confusion remains; it was beyond Cibber's power to reconcile the artificial values of the

[1] *A History of English Drama 1660-1900*, Cambridge, 1955, ii.158.

Restoration comedies and the ethics of "sentimentalism".[1] In many plays of the period this duality of motive is blatant. For every true drama of sentiment there are several basically immoral comedies brought to a pious conclusion by an unlikely conversion.[2]

The Augustan comic dramatist, however, did not invoke ethical judgements only with respect to the conduct of his chief characters. A certain amount of general social criticism was filtering into the drama. In Mrs. Centlivre's *The Gamester*, for instance, there is a significant little scene in which the hero, for once in funds, lies his way out of paying a long-standing debt to a tradesman who needs the money for his wife's lying-in.[3] John Gay's *The What D'Ye Call It* contains an episode in which three country justices are haunted by the ghosts of five people they have wronged. Primarily it is a parody of the Shakespearean ghost-scene, but the spirits' accusations have a realistic flavour:

> I was begot before my mother married,
> Who whipt by you, of me poor child miscarried.[4]

Where the moralizing grows more serious, however, the limitations of the mixed genre become apparent. Steele's *The Conscious Lovers* is quite heavily didactic; it was avowedly written to attack the practice of duelling,[5] and it contains a number of moral reflections, such as Isabella's dictum on men: 'They have usurped an exemption from shame for any baseness, any cruelty towards us. They embrace without love; they make vows without conscience of obligation; they are partners, nay, seducers to the crime, wherein they pretend to be less guilty.'[6] Yet although the play is ethically relevant to everyday life, its plot depends on several wildly romantic improbabilities, and its dialogue is often lavishly melodramatic: 'No, 'twas Heaven's high will I should be such; to be plundered in my cradle! tossed on the seas!

---

[1] F. W. Bateson, *English Comic Drama 1700–1750*, Oxford, 1929, p. 26.
[2] See Nicoll, *A History of English Drama*, ii.183–4 ff.
[3] 4th ed., London, 1734, p. 33.
[4] *The Poetical Works of John Gay*, ed. G. C. Faber, p. 348.
[5] *Richard Steele*, Mermaid Series, London, 1894, p. 269 f.
[6] Ibid., p. 303.

and even there an infant captive! to lose my mother, hear but of my father! to be adopted! lose my adopter! then plunged again into worse calamities!'[1] The structure and style of the comedy, that is to say, are too formalized for its simple ethical content.

The comedy form which Fielding was to use, then, had already been a vehicle for moral comment; but it was clearly an unsuitable didactic medium for two reasons. First it was essentially an amoral form, at least as far as sex was concerned. Secondly its technique, both of plot and of diction, was too artificial readily to embody moral ideas concerned with the practicalities of ordinary living.

I

Twenty-two of Fielding's twenty-five dramatic works appeared between 1730 and 1737. In 1732 alone he staged five new plays and had a hand in a sixth, one of these, *The Mock Doctor*, being written and produced in three weeks.[2] Fielding had to make money from an unpredictable audience, and his work was conditioned by their reactions: *The Mock Doctor* was completed in such haste in order to fill the gap in the repertory left by the failure of *The Covent-Garden Tragedy*. Not only was Fielding compelled to write plays fast and frequently: he often found it necessary to adapt them during their run, expanding a success or cutting a failure. A well-known player such as Mrs. Clive might have a part created or enlarged for her. Topical references, social and political, were introduced to gain easy laughs.

It would therefore be pointless to expect too much of the plays: there were obvious commercial reasons why they should be inferior. The brief period in which Fielding could turn out a play contrasts strongly with the 'thousands of hours' he claims to have spent in the composition of *Tom Jones*.[3] Nonetheless he asserts in the Prologue to *The Modern Husband* that the Stage:

> . . . was not for low farce designed,
> But to divert, instruct, and mend mankind.[4]

---

[1] *Richard Steele*, Mermaid Series, London, 1894, p. 354–5.
[2] See Cross, i.129–31.   [3] Henley ed., iv.246.   [4] Henley ed., x.10.

and he often claims that his plays have a moral purpose.[1] Such claims, of course, were a literary commonplace of the time. How far they had real justification in Fielding's work can be shown by an examination of *The Temple Beau*, which provides a good example of the way in which Fielding's dramatic writing was genuinely modified by a didactic intention.

Allardyce Nicoll classes *The Temple Beau* as a comedy of intrigue. Certainly part of the play stems from this tradition. Wilding, the thriftless law-student of the title, conducts simultaneous affairs with two sisters, one of them married, surviving a succession of imminent exposures through desperate resourcefulness. Yet the characterization in the play derives largely from the Comedy of Humours. Wilding's lovers, Lady Lucy Pedant and Lady Gravely, are types, respectively, of coquette and prude. Young Pedant, and his father Sir Avarice, as their names imply, are also Jonsonian personifications. Fielding, as often, was mixing two kinds of artificial comedy.

There is a sub-plot, however, which belongs to neither genre. It tells how Veromil wins Bellaria, Lady Lucy's niece, despite the treacherous rivalry of his friend Valentine, who is already engaged to Clarissa. It is a serious story, seriously treated; none of the three main characters is a type, nor are they concerned in intrigue.

This need not have meant more than that Fielding wanted to instil some romantic interest into his play: the various lovers could have described a sentimental, as the intriguers a frivolous, pattern. But clearly Fielding is aiming at more than this, for he involves Bellaria and the rest in a number of direct conflicts. There is a scene where Veromil persuades Valentine to put friendship before his lust for Bellaria,[2] and another where Bellaria forces her lover to believe her protestations of innocence at the expense of his trust in Valentine.[3] In what is admittedly a clumsy way, Fielding causes his characters to face moral decisions. Characterization,

---

[1] Cf. the Prologues to *Love in Several Masques* (Henley ed., viii.11), and *The Coffee-House Politician* (Henley ed., ix.75), and the dedication to *Don Quixote in England* (Henley ed., xi.7).

[2] Henley ed., viii.162 ff.   [3] Henley ed., viii.148 ff.

motivation, and dialogue are on a different level from that of the main plot.

The difference might have remained largely implicit, the worthy behaviour and rather solemn speech of Veromil and Bellaria not being sufficient of themselves to impair the unity of the play. Fielding, however, makes these characters explicitly condemn vice and extol virtue. Veromil, for instance, assures a repentant Valentine: 'The innocent, the perfect joy that flows from the reflection of a virtuous deed far surpasses all the trifling momentary raptures that are obtained by guilt.'[1] This is a straight expression of the latitudinarian idea of 'laudable epicureanism'. When Valentine is tempted, his friend challenges him: ' . . . would you sacrifice our long, our tender friendship, to the faint, transitory pleasures of a brutal appetite? for love that is not mutual is no more.'[2] Such pronouncements disclaim the cheerful amorality which makes Wilding an acceptable and even likeable figure: the play becomes slightly at odds with itself. Yet the disparity between romantic and comic plots need not have been drastic had the moralizing been merely the by-product of the serious situation. Much of the sententiousness, however, far exceeds the scope of the immediate context. It is for no obvious personal reason that Bellaria condemns the fashionable sexual code: 'Inconstancy, which damns a woman, is no crime in man. The practised libertine, who seduces poor, unskilful, thoughtless virgins is applauded, while they must suffer endless infamy and shame.'[3] Veromil, with almost equal inconsequence, denounces the age at large:

Surprised at villainy, now-a-days! No, Valentine, be surprised when you see a man honest; when you find that man whom gold will not transform into a knave, I will believe it possible you may find that stone which will change every thing into gold.[4]

Not only, then, has Fielding strained the framework of his play by introducing a serious sub-plot, with the discordantly realistic morality which that entails: he has made the

---

[1] Henley ed., viii.164.   [2] Henley ed., viii.163–4.
[3] Henley ed., viii.149.   [4] Henley ed., viii.145.

characters in it mouthpieces for some of his own social and moral views. Yet he never suggests that the ethics of the romantic plot should cross-refer to the comic plot. Veromil's virtue is rewarded by Bellaria's hand and the restoration of his rightful inheritance; but equally Wilding, cheerfully unregenerate, not only lives to intrigue another day, but extorts a five-hundred-pound annuity from his father.

In short *The Temple Beau* represents the inconsistencies typical of the moralizing comedy of the period. What is unusual is the number and severity of its strictures; Fielding is at least as critical of society as Steele. Veromil, like Bevil in *The Conscious Lovers*, rejects a challenge to a duel;[1] but he also indicts the whole fashionable conception of honour—'Just the reverse of Christianity'[2]—and on occasion attacks the general shallowness of the age: 'Virtue may indeed be unfashionable in this age; for ignorance and vice will always live together. And sure the world is come to that height of folly and ignorance, posterity may call this the Leaden Age.'[3] *The Temple Beau* is particularly significant of Fielding's didactic intention in that it was only the second of his plays to be performed. Right at the beginning of his dramatic career he was prepared to introduce a number of moral ideas into his work, and they were substantially the same ideas as he was to advance in his journalism nearly ten years later.

2

Not all Fielding's plays contain as much ethical material as *The Temple Beau*, but all include a certain amount. Farce and artificial comedy give him little scope for recommending his positive ideals of beneficence, but a good deal for attacking the manners and morals of society. In his first play, *Love in Several Masques*, the hero talks of the Town as: ' ... that worst of wildernesses! where follies spread like thorns; where men act the part of tigers, and women of crocodiles; where vice lords it like a lion ... '[4] Even in amoral comedies such as *The Letter-Writers* and *The*

---

[1] Henley ed., viii.163.   [2] Henley ed., viii.131.
[3] Henley ed., viii.131.   [4] Henley ed., viii.63.

Universal Gallant there tends to be criticism of fashionable life. Fielding follows a current trend in genteel comedy by infusing into the portrayals of beaux and courtiers, prudes and coquettes, who figure in these plays, an element of serious satire. The diversions of the Town also come in for slighting comment: in *The Modern Husband*, one of the harshest plays, virtually a whole scene is devoted to an attack on card-playing.[1]

Above all, however, Fielding censures the venality of fashionable marriage dealings. In *Love in Several Masques* he makes Merital remark: 'In short, beauty is now considered as a qualification only for a mistress, and fortune for a wife',[2] and the point is made again frequently in his later plays. He also suggests some of the results of basing marriage solely on money. Sir Apish Simple, for instance, assures his unwilling bride: ' . . . I'll engage we shall hate one another with as much good-breeding as any couple under the sun',[3] while Lady Lucy Pedant inquires of her niece: 'And have you the assurance to own yourself in love, in an age, when 'tis as immodest to love before marriage, as 'tis unfashionable to love after it?'[4] Fielding's plays depict a number of such 'fashionable' marriages, thriving on mutual detestation. The natural corollary, he demonstrates, is that adultery has become taken for granted. He makes the point even in the farce *An Old Man taught Wisdom*, where the naïve Lucy asks a suitor:

LUCY: Ah, but there is one thing though—an't we to lie together?
BLISTER: A fortnight, no longer.
LUCY: A fortnight! That's a long time: but it will be over.
BLISTER: Ay, and then you may have any one else.[5]

Fielding exposes, in *The Modern Husband*, a particularly unpleasant way in which society marriage was being made a source of income: needy husbands sometimes prostituted their wives to rich lords. Bellamant, the hero of the play, sums up the contemporary situation: 'It is a stock-jobbing age, every thing has its price; marriage is traffic throughout;

---

[1] Act III, scene vi. Henley ed., x.50–51.
[2] Henley ed., viii.25.   [3] Henley ed., viii.81.
[4] Henley ed., viii.124.   [5] Henley ed., x.335.

as most of us bargain to be husbands, so some of us bargain to be cuckolds . . .'[1] The practice condemned in *The Modern Husband*, then, is only an unusually gross example of the general corruptness.

The tendentious comment in the plays, however, is not limited to the concerns of the Town. In *The Author's Farce*, *Pasquin*, and *The Historical Register* there is literary and theatrical satire. Avarice is a frequent subject of attack, most notably in *The Temple Beau* and, of course, *The Miser*. The medical and legal professions earn a spate of incidental jibes:

> Mongst doctors and lawyers some good ones are found;
> But, alas! they are rare as the ten thousand pound.[2]

runs a chorus in *The Lottery*. In *The Coffee-House Politician*, a play bordering on farce, there is a good deal of serious criticism of the law. The villain of the piece, Justice Squeezum, is shown rigging juries and taking protection money from brothels; he warns a prisoner: 'Well, sir, if you cannot pay for your transgressions like the rich, you must suffer for them like the poor.'[3] Worthy's indignation in the last act reflects the underlying earnestness of the play:

. . . by Heaven it shocks me; that we, who boast as wholesome laws as any kingdom upon earth, should, by the roguery of some of their executors, lose all their benefit. I long to see the time when here, as in Holland, the traveller may walk unmolested, and carry his riches openly with him.[4]

It would be superfluous to try to list here all the topics on which Fielding comments didactically in his drama; as the last chapter suggested, they are too many and too heterogeneous. Only three of the plays embody an overall didactic theme: *Don Quixote in England*, *The Modern Husband*, and *The Fathers*. Don Quixote is made a mechanism for condemning a series of evils: arranged marriages, the tyranny of country squires, and election bribery. The moral purpose of the play is made clear by Fielding's prefatory letter: ' . . . I fancy a lively representation of the calamities brought on a country by general corruption might have a very sensible

---

[1] Henley ed., x.35.   [2] Henley ed., viii.296.
[3] Henley ed., ix.104.   [4] Henley ed., ix.146.

and useful effect on the spectators.'[1] *The Modern Husband* not only anatomizes the current state of matrimony in society, but also makes a calculated attack on the law of criminal conversation.[2] *The Fathers* is a study in contrasted ways of bringing up children, and, as the sub-title implies, an examination of Good-nature. In all the other plays the didactic elements, though recurrent, remain scattered and largely disconnected.

The quality of this didacticism is not particularly remarkable; very often, especially in his attacks on doctors, lawyers, and politicians, Fielding is merely restating contemporary commonplaces. What is significant is the ubiquity of his moral comment and its consequent effect on his form.

Much of it is absorbed conveniently into the text; into the songs, for instance, of *The Author's Farce*:

> The lawyer, with a face demure,
> Hangs him who steals your pelf;
> Because the good man can endure
> No robber but himself.[3]

This is the social paradox which *The Beggar's Opera* had helped to make familiar; although it is close enough to Fielding's general attitude, the idea is expressed too conventionally to be disturbing. Equally such observations can merge satirically into the dialogue. When Constant is under arrest in *The Coffee-House Politician*, Staff brings in a second prisoner, and announces his crime: 'A rape, Captain, a rape —no dishonourable offence—I would not have brought any scoundrels into your honour's company; but rape and murder no gentleman need be ashamed of; and this is an honest brother ravisher . . . '[4] Much of Fielding's didacticism, however, is bluntly imposed on an alien context. In *The Modern Husband*, for example, a Captain Merit appears at Lord Richly's levee, reluctantly compelled to plead for preferment: 'Shall I, who have spent my youth and health in my country's service, be forced by such mean vassalage to

---

[1] Henley ed., xi.7.

[2] See C. B. Woods, 'Notes on Three of Fielding's Plays', *PMLA*, 52 (1937), 359 ff.

[3] Henley ed., viii.245.   [4] Henley ed., ix.111.

defend my old age from cold and hunger, while every painted butterfly wantons in the sunshine?'[1] Having voiced his protests he disappears from the action, his only function being to state Fielding's views about the injustice of the current system of military promotions and rewards. In the same play Fielding devotes a whole scene to satirizing the fashionable enthusiasm for Italian opera,[2] and another (mentioned above) to attacking the vogue for cards.

One more example of Fielding's didactic intrusiveness may be quoted as especially revealing. In *The Grub-Street Opera* Owen Apshinken, an effeminate beau, is bent on seducing Molly Apshones, the daughter of one of his father's tenants. Mr. Apshones assures his daughter that Owen has no honourable intentions, and makes the usual Fielding generalization: 'Poor girl! how ignorant she is of the world; but little she knows that no qualities can make amends for the want of fortune, and that fortune makes a sufficient amends for the want of every good quality.'[3] Later he assails young Apshinken himself:

I desire not, Mr. Owen, that you would marry my daughter; I had rather see her married to one of her own degree.—I had rather have a set of fine healthy grandchildren ask me blessing, than a poor puny breed of half-begotten brats—that inherit the diseases as well as the titles of their parents.[4]

He continues in this full-blooded idiom to the end of the scene, concluding his final speech: ' . . . and if you should prevail on her to her ruin, be assured your father's estate should not secure you from my revenge.—You should find that the true spirit of English liberty acknowledges no superior equal to oppression.'[5] Yet the wretched Owen has been shown in his first speech to be no great menace: ' . . . when once a woman knows what's what, she knows too much for me.—Sure never man was so put to it in his amours— for I do not care to venture on a woman after another, nor does any woman care for me twice.'[6] Apshones's vehement denunciation is wasted on so ineffectual a seducer. In any

[1] Henley ed., x.20.   [2] Act III, scene ii. Henley ed., x.46.
[3] Henley ed., ix.236.   [4] Henley ed., ix.250.
[5] Henley ed., ix.251.   [6] Henley ed., ix.216.

case Owen, rebuffed by the two servant-maids he attempts, ends by marrying Molly. Not only, therefore, do the two scenes in which Apshones appears run counter to the light mood of the ballad-opera, they are quite irrelevant to the plot.

What is more, it seems certain that in the original version of the piece (entitled *The Welsh Opera*) Apshones did not appear at all.[1] This is a clear case of Fielding inserting didactic scenes for their own sake, regardless of their irrelevance to the play as a whole.

Fielding worked over, and added to, many of his plays. *Tom Thumb* went through a series of versions; *Don Quixote in England* and *The Wedding Day* were both refurbished after an interval of years. It was not only in the case of *The Grub-Street Opera* that the additions were didactic. One of his most trenchant attacks on contemporary social standards is an insertion in *The Author's Farce*:

> What does the soldier or physician thrive by, but slaughter? The lawyer, but by quarrels? The courtier, but by taxes? The poet, but by flattery? I know none that thrive by profiting mankind, but the husbandman and the merchant: the one gives you the fruit of your own soil, the other brings you those from abroad; and yet these are represented as mean and mechanical, and the others as honourable and glorious.[2]

Fielding's willingness to adapt and enlarge his plays suggests that form was not very important to him. Certainly his

---

[1] The play went through three versions. It was first acted on 22 April 1731, as *The Welsh Opera*. From 19 May it was performed 'with several alterations and additions'. During May Fielding rewrote the piece, expanding it from two to three acts and renaming it *The Grub-Street Opera*. There were also three published versions in 1731. In the first of these (*The Welsh Opera*, two acts) Apshones does not appear. In the second (*The Genuine Grub-Street Opera*, three acts) he has one scene with Owen. The third (Fielding's authorized version, entitled *The Grub-Street Opera*, three acts) allots Apshones a second scene, with Molly. Although the published *Welsh Opera* was denounced by *The Daily Post* as not a true copy (see Cross, i, 111) it seems strong evidence that Apshones's two appearances were among Fielding's extensive additions to the original play.

[2] Henley ed., viii.205. This speech seems to be one of the additions Fielding made when revising the play for production in 1734. It does not appear in the published versions of 1730.

insertion of speeches and episodes solely for their didactic content implies that he subordinated form to his moral intentions. It is not surprising then, to find that his later dramatic work was becoming totally formless. *Pasquin, Tumble-Down Dick, Eurydice, The Historical Register,* and *Eurydice Hiss'd,* his last five pieces before the licensing act virtually ended his dramatic career, were all rehearsal plays. Fielding used the genre very freely, breaking it down to such an extent that what he was really writing was a species of revue, in which all kinds of moral, social, and political points might be made. In *The Historical Register,* for example, the auction, the attack on Cibber[1] and the political scenes are all, in effect, self-contained episodes.

The implication is that Fielding was moving towards a construction so loose as to be able to accommodate any incident he needed to make a didactic point. It is a tendency understandable in a writer whose moral concern generates such a miscellany of practical comments, but it clearly has a limiting effect. *Pasquin* and *The Historical Register* are two of the wittier plays, but they are almost totally lacking in continuity of interest. Moreover the fragmentary style they exemplify, while ideal for attacking particular practices, or even particular personalities, cannot embody those of Fielding's ethical ideas which are expressible only in terms of human relationships. He remains a didactic writer in these plays only to the extent that his satire has a serious purpose. In the novels, where he is concerned both 'to recommend goodness and innocence' and to evoke a picture of life sufficiently coherent and realistic to justify his claim to be a 'historian', this inclination towards the self-contained satirical episode was to be, to some extent, a drawback.

3

It was suggested in the preceding chapter that Fielding was essentially a practical moralist, concerned less with moral doctrine as such than with its application in everyday life. That being so, he was at a great disadvantage in working through a medium which was by definition at a remove

[1] See Cross, i.212–13.

from reality. Sometimes he solves the problem by implying that the amoral world of his comedy is an accurate representation of London Society; the intriguing and cuckoldom not being wholly insulated from real-life moral standards. Sir Simon, in *The Universal Gallant*, may be a ridiculous figure, but his reaction to his wife's unfaithfulness involves a serious reflection on the morals of the Town: 'A man that robs me of five shillings is a rogue, and to be hanged; but he that robs me of my wife is a fine gentleman, and a man of honour.'[1] This special attitude of Fielding's means that there is a logical connexion between, say, the satirical portraits of prude and coquette in *The Temple Beau*, and the denunciations of fashionable life in the same play. But the element of comic exaggeration in both characterization and action rather smothers the moral implication.

The nature of eighteenth-century society gave Fielding's comedies another potential which he sometimes exploits. The people whose fatuity, immorality, and corruptness he was portraying were also the wielders of power. They could rig elections, grant or withhold preferment; they were above the law. If Fielding had consistently applied his identification of the amoral comedy world with the contemporary society world, he would have been permanently constrained to the deep pessimism he only sometimes shows. Captain Merit looks in disgust at Lord Richly's coterie:

'Sdeath, there's a fellow now—That fellow's father was a pimp; his mother, she turned bawd; and his sister turned whore: you see the consequence. How happy is that country, where pimping and whoring are esteemed public services, and where grandeur and the gallows lie on the same road!'[2]

It was a point Fielding could not afford to make often. If, for didactic purposes, his comedies were sometimes a means of attacking society life, for commercial purposes they had always to be entertaining, and therefore to observe the traditional standards of artificial comedy. The clash of values in *The Temple Beau* is only one example of the anomalies resulting from Fielding's duality of purpose. *The Wedding Day*, another comedy of intrigue, contains a scene in which

Millamour, the philanderer-in-chief, is won to virtue by Heartfort, who preaches Fielding's Good-natured brand of chastity:

> My practice, perhaps, is not equal to my theory; but I pretend to sin with as little mischief as I can to others: and this I can lay my hand on my heart and affirm, that I never seduced a young woman to her own ruin, nor a married one to the misery of her husband.

> . . . what can be more ridiculous than to make it infamous for women to grant what it is honourable for us to solicit . . . to make a whore a scandalous, a whoremaster a reputable appellation![1]

Here the traditional amorality of the genre and Fielding's real views on sex are in head-on collision. In the same play there is a character named Mrs. Useful, who is at first depicted as being in the comic tradition of bawds. Millamour calls her 'the first minister of Venus, the first plenipotentiary in affairs of love'.[2] Later he cries: 'Oh, thou dear creature! suppose I gave thee worlds to reward thee!'[3] Yet at the end of the play he fiercely condemns her:

> Thou art a more mischievous animal than a serpent; and the man or woman who admits one of thy detestable character into his house or acquaintance, acts more foolishly than he who admits a serpent into his bosom. A public mark of infamy should be set on every such wretch, that we might shun them as a contagion.[4]

So complete a volte-face demands a selective moral judgement which will condemn Mrs. Useful, but not act retrospectively against Millamour himself.

It was suggested at the beginning of this chapter that fifth-act conversions were fairly frequent in Augustan comedy. Usually, however, they were simply a convenient rounding-off device, by which the rake was abruptly reformed in the interests of a happy ending. Fielding condemns the practice in *Tom Jones* (book viii, ch. 1),[5] but, as *The Wedding Day* shows, was prepared to go much farther than most of his contemporaries towards attempting to

---

[1] Henley ed., xii.130–1. Heartfort's formulation of Fielding's ideas about chastity is very similar to that of Tom Jones (book xiv, ch. 4; Henley ed., v.108).
[2] Henley ed., xii.72.   [3] Henley ed., xii.78.
[4] Henley ed., xii.139.   [5] Henley ed., iv.65.

4—T.R.

introduce a positively reformative element into the intractable artificial comedy. Even his lightest works were liable to
be manipulated for this purpose. For instance *Miss Lucy in
Town*, 'a farce with songs', flows along cheerfully as it
shows the bucolic heroine of *An Old Man taught Wisdom*
swiftly acclimatizing herself to city life: ' . . . for if all the
gentlemen in town were in love with me—icod,—with all
my heart, the more the merrier.'[1] But at the end of the play
there is a complete change of mood. Lucy's husband
Thomas, an ex-footman, challenges the lord to whom she has
light-heartedly sold herself: 'I have as good a right to the
little I claim, as the proudest peer hath to his great possessions; and whilst I am able, I will defend it.'[2] He takes
charge of the reluctant Lucy: 'Come, madam, you must
strip yourself of your puppet-show dress, as I will of mine;
they will make you ridiculous in the country, where there is
still something of Old England remaining.'[3] Lucy's father
draws the democratic conclusion: 'Henceforth I will know
no degree, no difference between men, but what the standards of honour and virtue create: the noblest birth without
these is but splendid infamy; and a footman with these
qualities, is a man of honour.'[4] The crux here and elsewhere
is that real-life morality cannot be relevant unless the
characters involved are more realistic than was possible in
artificial comedy. Millamour's conversion and the condemnation of Mrs. Useful only make sense in the light of
ethical standards which would make nonsense of *The
Wedding Day* as a whole. If Thomas's final outbursts are to
be taken seriously Lucy must be seen as not comically but
sinfully frail.

Obviously such sudden shifts of attitude are incongruous,
but even where Fielding tries to be consistently earnest there
is a dissonance. The fact is that there was no machinery for
stage representation of characters real enough to embody
persuasively Fielding's realistic morality. The dialogue, for
instance, was too inflexible. F. W. Bateson remarks: 'It is
one of the curious features of the sentimental comedies of
the eighteenth century that the writing always deteriorates as

[1] Henley ed., xii.53.   [2] Henley ed., xii.61.
[3] Henley ed., xii.62.   [4] Henley ed., xii.62–63.

the emotions are intensified.'[1] But it is not, after all, so very curious. The playwrights of the time were using the artificial idiom of the Restoration theatre for their comedies. When they chose to introduce emotional scenes they had to sacrifice the wit which gave that style its effectiveness, and were left with an inexpressively rhetorical mode of speech, lacking any pressure of real feeling. Veromil, in *The Temple Beau*, cries out in the throes of love: 'Eternal transports, agonies of joy delight thy soul. Excellent, charming creature!—But ah! a sudden damp chills all my rising joys; for oh! what dragons must be overcome, before I gather that delicious fruit!'[2] Veromil, however, for all his moralizing, is primarily a romantic character. Bellamant, in *The Modern Husband*, undergoes a much more real conflict, but uses the same stylized manner of address. Torn between his mistress, Mrs. Modern, and the wife he still loves, he soliloquizes at one point:

> What a wretch am I! Have I either honour or gratitude, and can I injure such a woman? How do I injure her! while she perceives no abatement in my passion, she is not injured by its inward decay: nor can I give her a secret pain, while she hath no suspicion of my secret pleasures. Have I not found too an equal return of passion in my mistress? Does she not sacrifice more for me than a wife can? The gallant is, indeed, indebted for the favours he receives: but the husband pays dearly for what he enjoys. I hope, however, this will be the last hundred pounds I shall be asked to lend. My wife's having this dear note, was as lucky as it was unexpected—Ha!—the same I gave this morning to Mrs. Modern. Amazement! what can this mean?[3]

The ideas in this speech could form the basis of an emotional conflict: Bellamant is balancing the duty he owes his wife against the duty he owes his mistress, trying to convince himself that an unperceived injury is no injury. But there seems little emotion in the soliloquy because the expression is too formal. The conventional exclamations, the rhetorical questions, the neat antitheses are inimical to the kind of feeling the situation seems intended to generate.

The conclusion of the speech points to another aspect of the artificiality which suffuses the play: the devices by means

---

[1] *English Comic Drama 1700–1750*, p. 28.
[2] Henley ed., viii.129.   [3] Henley ed., x.56.

of which Bellamant's conflict is to be dramatized are those of the comedy of intrigue. This stylization of both plot and dialogue is damaging to *The Modern Husband* because Fielding is illustrating certain moral imperatives in the story of the Bellamants, which seem more forceful as the relationship embodying them is made convincing and moving. When this is rendered lifeless by formalism the moral content of the play also droops.

The Fathers represents a similar kind of clash between manner and matter. Since Fielding is comparing, in the play, two opposed methods of bringing up children, much of his effect depends upon the plausibility with which he depicts the relationships within the contrasted families. If the result is distinctly unconvincing, it is only partly because the dialogue is as stilted, and the plot nearly as artificial, as usual. In order to make his point Fielding has reduced most of his leading figures to personifications. Mr. Boncour becomes the type of the good-natured parent, while Valence represents miserly self-interest. The result is that although the characters go through the motions of full relationships, the absence of real-life complexity and ambiguity makes their attitudes almost meaningless. The schematic approach and the realistic are clearly irreconcilable.

Since the basis of the schematic approach here is the technique of personification used in the Comedy of Manners, it seems reasonable to relate the inadequacy of *The Fathers*, too, to the limitations of the contemporary dramatic formula. Bateson writes of the drama of the period: 'Its history is that of the strangling of a tentative, still embryonic realism by an obsolete technique.'[1] He is talking of the crude lighting and stage conditions of the time, but his remark is true in a wider sense. It goes far towards explaining Fielding's comparative failure as a playwright.

[1] *English Comic Drama 1700–1750*, p. 150.

IV

JONATHAN WILDE
AND
A JOURNEY FROM THIS WORLD
TO THE NEXT

Jonathan Wild and *A Journey from this World to the Next*
formed part of the *Miscellanies*, which first appeared on
12 April 1743, more than a year after the publication of
Joseph Andrews. There are good grounds, however, for
supposing that both works were written, at least in part,
before Fielding's first novel.[1] In any case it is convenient to
consider them apart from the novels, since in neither case is
the author concerned, in the sense he was later to be, with
telling a story. *A Journey from this World to the Next* is an
imitation of Lucian's *Dialogues*, and his *True History*;[2]
Jonathan Wild has marked affinities with the popular
criminal biographies of the eighteenth century.[3] In both
cases Fielding's form is non-fictional and extremely tractable.
The two works, however, provide further evidence of the
kind of views Fielding was anxious to communicate, and
suggest how his didactic intention was likely to condition a
narrative form.

I

A Journey from this World to the Next falls naturally into
three parts. In the first of these the 'author' describes his
journey to Elysium and his initial experiences there. In

[1] On this point see *Henry Fielding*, by F. Homes Dudden, Oxford, 1952,
i.445–6 and 483.
[2] See L. R. Lind, 'Lucian and Fielding', *The Classical Weekly*, 29 (1936),
84 ff.
[3] W. R. Irwin describes the genre in *The Making of Jonathan Wild*, New
York, 1941, pp. 81 ff.

the second, rather more than twice as long, Julian the Apostate gives an account of his various transmigrations. Finally, in a fragment possibly written by Fielding's sister Sarah,[1] Anne Boleyn tells her story.

In the opening section Fielding finds occasion to stress the importance of good works, as against mere professions of faith and dignity. Minos always makes charity his chief criterion when judging the writer and his fellow spirits. After rejecting a duke he is addressed by a shade:

... who with fear and trembling begged he might not go to the bottomless pit: he said, he hoped Minos would consider, that though he had gone astray, he had suffered for it, that it was necessity which drove him to the robbery of eighteen pence, which he had committed, and for which he was hanged: that he had done some good actions in his life, that he had supported an aged parent with his labor, that he had been a very tender husband and a kind father, and that he had ruined himself by being bail for his friend. At which words the gate opened, and Minos bid him enter, giving him a slap on the back, as he passed by him.[2]

Another candidate, who 'had constantly frequented his church, been a rigid observer of fast-days' and 'never been once guilty of whoring, drinking, gluttony, or any other excess', is turned back for disinheriting his son.[3] A poet who pleads the merit of his plays eventually gains admittance only because 'he had once lent the whole profits of a benefit night to a friend'.[4] An honest and industrious family, 'starved to death through poverty', are allowed to enter; their grave parish priest, a pluralist, is refused because he

[1] Fielding comments in a footnote at the beginning of the section (Henley ed., ii.325): ' ... this chapter is, in the original, writ in a woman's hand: and though the observations in it are, I think, as excellent as any of the whole volume, there seems to be a difference in style between this and the preceding chapters; and as it is the character of a woman which is related, I am inclined to fancy it was really written by one of that sex.' Fielding appends a rather similar footnote to a letter in *Joseph Andrews* (Henley ed., i.122), and critics agree that he is there almost certainly referring to his sister. For further discussion see Aurélien Digeon, 'Fielding a-t-il écrit le dernier chapitre de *A Voyage from this world to the next?*', *Revue Anglo-Americaine*, 1931, pp. 428 ff.

[2] Henley ed., ii.243.   [3] Henley ed., ii.240–1.   [4] Henley ed., ii.241.

failed to give them help: 'for no man enters that gate without charity'.[1]

This emphasis on benevolence is central to Fielding's beliefs, as Chapter II showed. But the moral outlined in his Introduction to *A Journey from this World to the Next* is a rather different one. He claims there that 'our author' (for the work is alleged to survive only as an abandoned manuscript by an unknown hand):

... everywhere teaches this moral, That the greatest and truest happiness which this world affords, is to be found only in the possession of goodness and virtue; a doctrine, which as it is undoubtedly true, so hath it so noble and practical a tendency, that it can never be too often or too strongly inculcated on the minds of men.[2]

This axiom, another of Fielding's basic tenets, is negatively illustrated by the experiences of Julian. In a variety of self-centred and dubiously-virtuous incarnations he never finds contentment. As a miser: ' ... between my solicitude in contriving schemes to procure money, and my extreme anxiety in preserving it, I never had one moment of ease while awake, nor of quiet when in my sleep.'[3] Yet as a rich heir, wildly extravagant, 'in the midst of plenty I loathed everything'.[4] He finds the role of statesman 'subjected daily to the greatest danger and inquietude, and attended with little pleasure, and less ease'.[5] When a soldier he endures horrors 'not to be described, or perhaps imagined'.[6] Both as a fool and as a poet he pines himself to death, and as an alderman ends his days 'in universal contempt'.[7]

It is significant that though Fielding's chief purpose is to promulgate two of his fundamental moral beliefs, he introduces many of the particular subjects he has already discussed elsewhere. He attacks avarice,[8] the medical profession,[9] arranged marriages,[10] beaux,[11] coquettes,[12] and duelling.[13] Even Julian's account of his experiences as a

[1] Henley ed., ii.244.
[2] Henley ed., ii.213.
[3] Henley ed., ii.262.
[4] Henley ed., ii.266.
[5] Henley ed., ii.304
[6] Henley ed., ii.307.
[7] Henley ed., ii.320.
[8] Henley ed. (e.g.), ii.223–4.
[9] Henley ed. (e.g.), ii.219.
[10] Henley ed., ii.228.
[11] Henley ed. (e.g.), ii.267.
[12] Henley ed., ii.241.
[13] Henley ed., ii.219.

Thracian general is made to contain a reminder of the current corruption in military preferment; the emperor Zeno, Julian relates: ' ... gave me the command of a cohort, I being then but fifteen years of age; and a little afterwards, before I had even seen an army, preferred me, over the heads of all the old officers, to be a tribune.'[1] Fielding is enabled to introduce such points because his narrative is almost infinitely expandable and adaptable. He can touch on any topic he chooses by invoking a suitable spirit, or allotting to Julian an appropriate incarnation. In fact, like the later rehearsal plays, *A Journey from this World to the Next* is practically formless. Eventually Fielding breaks off, declaring that the rest of the manuscript is missing. By this time, after the long stories of Julian and Anna, the original narrator has been forgotten and all sense of continuity has been lost. On the whole Fielding seems to have used his hybrid form merely as an excuse for assembling a number of his usual didactic themes.

2

Jonathan Wild is a more integrated work than *A Journey from this World to the Next* partly because the biographical formula imposes shape and development; the story has a beginning, a middle, and an end. But equally relevant to this coherence is the fact that the underlying ironic attitude, which equates 'Greatness' with villainy, comprehends a number of moral views which in Fielding's earlier work remain scattered. Ambition, selfishness, hypocrisy, cruelty, and cunning are all subsumed under the term 'Greatness' as used in *Jonathan Wild*. If Walpole is attacked it is as the representative of these various characteristics always condemned by Fielding. With the qualities he most detests conveniently summed up in the character of Wild, and exemplified in his career, Fielding can afford to be single-minded and pursue his case in terms of generalization. If he glances at particular practices, in the course of his main narrative, it is usually only by way of a more detailed application of the comparison that is all the time implied: 'Is not

[1] Henley ed., ii.263.

as much art, as many excellent qualities, required to make a pimping porter at a common bawdy-house as would enable a man to prostitute his own or his friend's wife or child?'[1] Most of the time he neglects such specific themes, and lets his contrast of tone and subject-matter speak for itself.

The ethical content of the book, however, is not limited to the moral ideas latent in Fielding's irony. There are two sources of additional and often more positive, statement. One of these, of course, is the account of the Heartfrees. It is in this part of the story that Fielding expresses the positive side of 'the doctrine which I have endeavoured to inculcate in this history', namely that Goodness is more conducive to happiness than is Greatness:

> The same righteous judge [i.e. conscience] always annexes a bitter anxiety to the purchases of guilt, whilst it adds a double sweetness to the enjoyments of innocence and virtue: for fear, which all the wise agree is the most wretched of human evils, is, in some degree, always attending on the former, and never can in any manner molest the happiness of the latter.[2]

This idea involves a set of standards alien to those ironically adopted by Fielding in narrating the exploits of Wild. Heartfree himself, therefore, is made the mouthpiece for the many passages of pure moralizing. For instance, he tells Wild:

> There is one thing the loss of which I should deplore infinitely beyond that of liberty and of life also; I mean that of a good conscience; a blessing which he who possesses can never be thoroughly unhappy; for the bitterest portion of life is by this so sweetened, that it soon becomes palatable; whereas, without it, the most delicate enjoyments quickly lose all their relish, and life itself grows insipid, or rather nauseous, to us.[3]

Elsewhere he persuades himself into a contempt of death in a soliloquy that takes up a whole chapter,[4] and in another harangue to Wild makes explicit one of the moral views implicit in Fielding's irony: '" . . . to me baseness seems

---

[1] Book i, ch. 5; Henley ed., ii.17.
[2] In the Preface to the *Miscellanies*, Henley ed., xii.244.
[3] Book iii, ch. 5; Henley ed., ii.112.
[4] Book iii, ch. 2; Henley ed., ii. 99 ff.

inconsistent with this rule, OF DOING NO OTHER PERSON AN INJURY FROM ANY MOTIVE OR ON ANY CONSIDERATION WHATEVER. This, sir, is the rule by which I am determined to walk ... "'¹ Such direct statements of ethical doctrine certainly weaken the ironic force of the narrative as a whole. That Fielding should impair the stylistic consistency of his book by inserting them is evidence of the seriousness of his didactic purpose. It is also a reminder that although as a moral commentator his chief talent was for satire, he was also by instinct something of a preacher.

The other source of additional didactic comment in *Jonathan Wild* is the unobtrusive, but regular, introduction, independent of the main narrative, of some of Fielding's favourite topics. The fourth chapter of Book I includes a concise exposure of the system of imprisonment for debt,² so often assailed in his writings. The tenth contains an attack on beaux.³ When in prison, Heartfree quite gratuit-ously voices to the ordinary the latitudinarian view that a sincere Turk might win salvation.⁴ Typically, one of Mrs. Heartfree's helpers during her unlucky journey is a lieu-tenant described as: ' ... a virtuous and brave fellow, who had been twenty-five years in that post without being able to obtain a ship, and had seen several boys, the bastards of noblemen, put over his head.'⁵

Although *Jonathan Wild* is much tauter in construction than *A Journey from this World to the Next*, then, Fielding contrives to work in a variety of local didactic matter. That he does so is significant both of the importance of the didactic motive in his work, and of his attitude to form.

3

At a deeper level *Jonathan Wild* sheds more light on Fielding's moral position. There is an inconsistency in it which illustrates that clash between his ethical views and

¹ Book iii, ch. 10; Henley ed., ii.128.
² Henley ed., ii.12.
³ Ibid., 32–33.
⁴ Book iv, ch. 1; Henley ed., ii.144. Parson Adams makes the same sug-gestion in *Joseph Andrews* (book i, ch. 17; Henley ed., i.96).
⁵ Book iv, ch. 7; Henley ed., ii.171.

his social preconceptions outlined in Chapter II. Since this discrepancy derives from the inclusion of the Heartfree chapters, it is worth recalling Digeon's plausible suggestion that these were an insertion into an original version which was unremittingly ironic.[1] None the less, whatever the processes of composition, Fielding's final judgement sanctioned a work which combines a ferociously satirical narrative with a bourgeois romance of married life.

In the satirical portion of the book Fielding's method is ironically to approve and recommend all the anti-social attitudes which a gang-leader is likely to have in common with a dictator. The procedure involves, of course, the tacit endorsement of the public-spirited viewpoint which is apparently decried. Naturally the satire gains in scope and power when the moral positions concerned are absolutes, and the irony is unimpaired by the need for qualification.

The most successful parts of *Jonathan Wild* derive authority from just such a lack of compromise. In some of the most striking passages in the book, Fielding shows Wild's philosophy to be a rationalization of the conduct of society's leaders:

'Is not the battle gained by the sweat and danger of the common soldier? Are not the honor and fruits of the victory the general's who laid the scheme? Is not the house built by the labor of the carpenter and the bricklayer? Is it not built for the profit only of the architect and for the use of the inhabitant, who could not easily have placed one brick upon another? ... Cast your eye abroad, and see who is it lives in the most magnificent buildings, feasts his palate with the most luxurious dainties, his eyes with the most beautiful sculptures and delicate paintings, and clothes himself in the finest and richest apparel; and tell me if all these do not fall to his lot who had not any the least share in producing all these conveniences, nor the least ability to do so?'[2]

Much of the book's point derives from the fact that Wild's immoral creed is founded on his accurate observation of various existing social practices. Fielding is condemning any custom or institution which he makes his hero use as a precedent. Here his absolutism has betrayed him into an

---

[1] A. Digeon, *The Novels of Fielding*, London, 1925, pp. 115 ff.

[2] Book i, ch. 8, Henley ed., ii.26–27.

unlikely premonition of Marxism; he is implying a fundamental criticism of the existing social system, which he
would not dream of advancing in practical terms.

If *Jonathan Wild* were purely a work of irony, Fielding's
implied denunciation of capitalism might serve, as it was
presumably intended to do, merely as a convenient moral
reference point. But thanks to the Heartfree chapters the
existing context is too uncertain to accommodate it.

Wild has ironically been shown to be a 'Great Man', in
that, like the corrupt political leader, he takes advantage of
a fallible system. Clearly the system itself is to some extent
condemned. Yet Heartfree, who has been introduced into the
book to represent the positive values which the narrator
purports to scoff at, though appropriately Wild's antithesis
in private morality, founds his life on the same system which
has produced Wild and is exploited by him. In the romantic
part of the book the moral values of the system remain un-
questioned—the emphasis is restricted to the moral values of
the individual. Since Fielding has apparently elected to
affirm his own views as well as to attack false ones, his failure
to state how far he does support the system leaves the criticisms implied in Wild's speech unanswered.

Moreover the Heartfree section further emphasizes the
weaknesses of the existing regime. As Arnold Kettle (who
has admittedly a Marxist axe to grind) shrewdly points out,[1]
Heartfree is quite passive and defenceless in face of Wild's
implacable treachery. When his happiness, and even, it seems,
his life, have been destroyed by Wild, he is obliged to retreat
into religious consolation. Only sheer chance brings redress.
The social order which Heartfree accepts and Wild manipulates provides no protection, still less reward, for the virtuous.

In one sense the confusion involved is a kind of elaboration of that in *The Temple Beau*, where Fielding's sound
workaday morality cast a harsh light on the code of artificial
comedy. In *Jonathan Wild* this morality is itself exposed, by
the absolute ethical standards implied in Fielding's irony, as
enfeebled by the social system.

No doubt this book reveals a failure of literary judgement.
It is notable that the Heartfree story disturbs its whole

[1] *An Introduction to the English Novel*, London, 1954, p. 49.

ironic focus. Ironically speaking, Wild's zenith should be the peak of his material fortune, when his gang is at its most powerful and his income at its greatest. But from the narrative point of view it has to come when he seems most nearly to have destroyed Heartfree, a negligible achievement by Wild's standards. Again, Mrs. Heartfree's long account of her travels slows down the narrative just when it should be gathering speed in approaching the climax, Wild's death.

The inconsistency in *Jonathan Wild*, however, is not primarily the result of literary misjudgement, but of a defect in Fielding's thought. A Marxist might accuse him of being too timid to draw the conclusion of his social observations. But the point is rather that he has not realized just how fundamental is the variance between the Christian morality he is everywhere concerned to recommend, and the practice, if not the theory, of the current English social system. In the light of the contemporary belief in subordination no doubt Fielding could have worked out his own theoretical reconciliation of the eighteenth-century oligarchic system with Christian precept. But he nowhere establishes the requisite fundamental compromise. The result is that often in his work, as in *Jonathan Wild*, there is an underlying moral uncertainty. Only in *Amelia* does Fielding explicitly face the fact that the society he is living in is infinitely remote from the Christian ideal.

V

THE INFLUENCES BEHIND THE NOVELS

Iᴺ his plays and early narratives Fielding was manipulating an existing form in the interests of his didactic intention. When he came to write his first novel the position was changed; he was free to design a new form expressly to embody his moral ideas.

Yet although Fielding regarded himself as 'the founder of a new province of writing', he clearly had certain preconceptions which helped to determine the nature of his novels. Various literary genres offered precedents for plot, characterization, dialogue, and style. Moreover a gradual intermingling of these genres had already produced a number of novels of a kind, both in England and in France. There was, then, no abrupt conflation of forms, but rather a merging. Fielding himself, for all his careful theorizing, is no great innovator.[1] If his novels achieve a particularly balanced synthesis it is less the result of an individual feat of imagination than a combination of learning and experience able to profit from the current fusion of techniques and carry it a stage further.

But even though Fielding is combining existing methods it is hard to trace in his novels examples of indebtedness to individual writers. Just as he was steeped in the thought of his age, so he was steeped in its literary experience. In *Joseph Andrews* he pays tribute to Marivaux, Scarron, and Lesage, but he rarely draws upon them directly. G. E. Parfitt, in a detailed study of the French influence on Fielding, remarks: 'On doit se rappeler que Fielding, plus qu'aucun autre auteur se sert surtout de sa mémoire en

---

[1] In this connexion see A. L. Cooke's 'Fielding and the Writers of Heroic Romance', *PMLA*, 62 (1947), 984 ff. Cooke shows that Fielding's theoretical programme was almost identical with that of the romance-writers he professed to despise.

écrivant ses œuvres, ce qui a comme résultat que l'on a souvent une idée des auteurs qu'il a lus, sans pouvoir la préciser.'[1] *In The Covent-Garden Journal* Fielding claims to have 'formed his Stile' on that of Lucian.[2] Yet L. R. Lind, who explores the relationship, can trace only a few minor correspondences. His view resembles Parfitt's: 'Like all great writers ... Fielding borrowed much which was completely absorbed into his own work, so that accurate identification of the borrowing is next to impossible.'[3] But even if such 'accurate identifications' must be few, it is helpful to gain some idea of the general influences behind the novels. For although Fielding did not have to invent a new genre from scratch, he did have to assemble a kind of narrative adapted to his purpose. He was rejecting, for instance, both the epistolary form of Richardson and the autobiographical convention of Marivaux and Lesage.

To gain an insight into the way in which Fielding evolved his form, therefore, it is essential to consider, if necessarily in general terms, what other genres and authors seem to have influenced the novels. The rough divisions to be made in this chapter isolate a few important trends for the sake of definition. In practice these trends overlap, and interact with, a number of others less easily sensed and much less easily traced.

I

It has often been noted that the characters of Fielding's novels derive from the tradition of the Comedy of Humours. Certainly he carries over into the novels the general idea of using a quirk of speech or behaviour to provide both entertainment and a useful identification mark. Slipslop's malapropisms, Partridge's Latin tags, and Mrs. Western's political pronouncements all suggest the dramatist's hand. In some cases it is even possible to find among Fielding's plays

---

[1] *L'Influence Française dans les Œuvres de Fielding*, Paris, 1928, p. 99.
[2] *The Covent-Garden Journal*, ii.50.
[3] L. R. Lind, 'Lucian and Fielding', *The Classical Weekly*, 29 (1936), 84 ff.

the antecedent of a particular character. Sir Harry Wilding in
The Temple Beau, Squire Badger in *Don Quixote in England*,
and Sir Gregory Kennel in *The Fathers* all serve as proto-
types for Western. Politic in *The Coffee-House Politician* is a
fore-runner of Mrs. Western.

But Fielding's debt to the drama here is even greater than
at first appears. In fact he takes from the artificial comedy his
entire system of characterization. In a typical comedy of the
period the *dramatis personae* consisted of a hero and heroine
or two and a group of minor figures. The leading roles would
be straight romantic parts, the lesser rules 'humorously'
comic. In *Love in Several Masques*, for instance, Fielding's
first play, there are six main figures: Wisemore, Merital,
and Malvil, together with their eventual brides to be, respectively Lady Matchless, Helena, and Vermilia. The
minor characters are Lord Formal, Rattle, and Sir Apish
Simple, whose names give some idea of their personalities,
Sir Positive Trap, who exemplifies snobbery, and Lady
Trap and Catchit, respectively prude and resourceful ser-
vant-maid. In practice, then, the doings of the romantic
characters in the plays furnished the sustaining interest of
the action, the 'happy ending' being the successful outcome
of their various love-affairs. The minor characters, on the
other hand, served only to provide comedy and carry on the
plot.

At least in Fielding's first two novels the balance of
characterization is substantially similar. There is a pair of
romantic lovers, who dominate the story, and a host of
friends, relations and chance acquaintances who occupy the
peripheral position of the lesser figures in the comedies.

Without doubt this technique contributes certain valuable
qualities to the novels. The numerous minor characteriza-
tions, for instance, derive from it their unusual definition
and vitality. Moreover the machine-like intricacy of plot
largely depends on the absolute predictability of the simpli-
fied characters. If Western were capable of reason, or Blifil of
remorse, the whole course of *Tom Jones* would have to be
different; in this respect, too, the 'humorous' manner
supplies clarity of outline. It can also, as in the plays, have a
didactic usefulness, the humour being equated with a ruling

passion that can hence be satirized. Thus the immensely touchy Colonel Bath is often ridiculed by Fielding, and through him the whole practice of duelling.

This Jonsonian technique, however, also has its limitations for the narrative writer. In a novel which is partly realistic no character appearing with any frequency can plausibly be limited to a single emotion. Thus Mrs. Western, for example, is made a compendium of several humours. She is not just an amateur of politics but also a woman of society and a Beauty *manquée*; virtually all her actions spring from one of these three sources. Similarly Partridge is given alternative motives of cowardice, inquisitiveness, and superstition. Yet somehow this aggregation of humours does not produce a 'rounded' character, on a plane with, say, Tom. In the plays a figure such as Sir Positive or Sir Apish was not permitted the slightest normality of feeling, and so ceased to exist as a moral agent. The lesser characters in the novels, even those who are not confined to a single reaction, are equally devoid of complexity or power of moral choice. There remains, consequently, an absolute division between major and minor figures.

The result is that there can be no very realistic relationship between a leading character and a lesser one; they exist on different levels. Tom's 'love' for Molly Seagrim is thus instantaneously and totally dissipated when he discovers her to be promiscuous. Altogether the influence of the Comedy of Humours produces a formula of characterization in which the leading figures, theoretically at least, are subject to the emotions and morality of real life, while the minor figures remain stylized, and out of touch with normality. This disparity existed in the plays themselves, of course, but it is greatly heightened by the length and circumstantiality of the novels.

It is not only in characterization, however, that Fielding is indebted to the drama. He uses a number of theatrical devices in the novels. The discoveries of Square and Honour[1] in their hiding-places, for instance, recall the similar predicaments of Wilding in *The Temple Beau* and Rakel in *The*

[1] *Tom Jones*, book v, ch. 5, and book xv, ch. 7; Henley ed., iii.226, and v.174.

Letter-Writers.[1] As in Fielding's first play masks are used to further intrigue in two of the novels.[2] Tom Jones and Amelia, like Valentine in *The Temple Beau*, are deprived of an inheritance by a scheming relative.

The latter correspondence suggests a more fundamental relationship between the plays and the novels. It is hardly surprising that a few incidental devices for puzzlement or entertainment should have been borrowed from the drama. What is significant is that Fielding, as his reliance on the malevolent relative implies, should have been obliged to take the plot structure of his 'true histories' from the artificial comedy. In fact there can have been no obvious alternative at the time. Fielding's concern for epic regularity demanded a clearcut action to which the incidents of his story could contribute. The novels had to have a resolution which was not simply the result of marriage (as in *Pamela*) or of death (as in *Don Quixote*). Accordingly Joseph Andrews is saved from the seemingly impossible predicament his poverty has brought upon him, by the discovery of his true parentage. Tom Jones is redeemed into solvency and happiness by the unmasking of Blifil's deceit. Booth and Amelia are restored to fortune by the providential news that a large legacy has been treacherously withheld. In the novels, in fact, as often in the plays, traditional variations on loving, losing, and regaining are finally resolved by a comfortable economic solution.

As in the plays this solution is imposed from without. The problems of Joseph, Tom and Booth all stem from lack of money, yet none of them is given the chance to repair his fortunes by work. The truth is, of course, that except by a good marriage there was no obvious way for a gentleman to make money for himself. All Fielding's heroes, therefore, have to be enriched by Fortune; their destiny is never in their own hands. Once again there is clash between formalism and realism: Fielding can invent characters and incidents to embody realistic moral problems, but he can only develop them within a conventional plot, essentially amoral in its separation of effort and reward.

[1] Henley ed., viii.157 and ix.173.

[2] *Tom Jones*, book xiii, ch. 7; *Amelia*, book x, chs. 2–4; Henley ed., v.61 ff. and vii.185 ff.

Another obvious symptom of Fielding's experience as a dramatist is the extensive use of dialogue in the novels. In *Joseph Andrews*, for example, only eight of the sixty-four chapters are completely lacking in direct speech. Moreover the idiom used is in general that of the contemporary theatre. That is to say that the comic dialogues reveal the element of caricature implicit in the Humours tradition, while the emotional episodes are written in the rhetorical style of the stage sentimental scene. Since the novels depict personal relationships more realistically than do the plays, this mannered speech has to encompass more nuances of feeling than it can comfortably express. Ultimately most of the serious relationships in the novels are impaired by the stylization of the dialogue in scenes of emotional crisis.

Altogether, then, Fielding's experience as a dramatist influenced his narratives to the extent that characterization, plot, and dialogue all derive largely from the artificial comedy. The gain in terms of incidental liveliness and a certain formal discipline is obvious. On the other hand it was this same artificiality of technique which smothered a potential realism in several of the plays, and with it their didactic effectiveness.

2

Professor A. R. Humphreys[1] also ascribes to Fielding's training in the theatre his method of emotional analysis by means of personification—the process used, for instance, in the description of Lady Booby's feelings after she has dismissed Joseph: 'Love became his advocate, and whispered many things in his favor. Honor likewise endeavored to vindicate his crime, and Pity to mitigate his punishment. On the other side, Pride and Revenge spoke as loudly against him.'[2] Yet Marivaux had already used such a device in *Le Paysan Parvenu*: 'But on the other side, this Honour pleaded his Cause in my Heart, which was in a perfect Uproar, whilst Ambition pleaded his . . . Said Honour to me, stand your Ground firm . . . Ambition answer'd all this by

[1] In 'Fielding's Irony: Its Methods and Effects', *RES*, 18 (1942), 183 ff.
[2] *Joseph Andrews*, book i, ch. 9; Henley ed., i.55.

only a Word or two . . . '[1] The fact that this kind of emotional analysis had already filtered into the novel, illustrates the difficulty, for the critic of Fielding, of separating a specifically chosen, from an unconsciously accepted, technique. Fielding was familiar with various literary genres and with works involving an intertwining of genres. It was open to him to draw either on sources or on adaptations of these sources. Almost certainly he did both.

It is this ambiguity which discourages an assessment of the kind of help he derived from his familiarity with previous novelists. All that can be demonstrated is that he had a respect for certain writers of this kind, and that he was influenced by certain details of their work.

In *Joseph Andrews* (book iii, ch. 1)[2] he refers respectfully to four writers who might be classified as novelists: Cervantes, Lesage, Scarron, and Marivaux.[3] Since the title-page of the first edition bore the sub-heading 'Written in imitation of the Manner of Cervantes', it might be thought that Fielding had made a large number of specific borrowings from *Don Quixote*. But his debt seems, on the whole, to have been limited to an adaptation of the central formula, much of the substance of his novel consisting of the involuntary exposure of hypocrisy by the quixotically innocent Parson Adams. There are a number of similarities of detail, but these, while suggestive in quantity, are individually trifling.[4]

Lesage's *Gil Blas*, like *Don Quixote*, relates the various adventures of a single vagabond and involves a prolixity of incidents and characters. But its particular influence on

---

[1] *Le Paysan Parvenu* (anonymous translation), London, 1735, 30–31.

[2] Henley ed., i.212–14.

[3] Fielding frequently pays tribute to Cervantes, of course. He praises Marivaux again in *Tom Jones* (book xiii, ch. 1; Henley ed., v.33) and refers to Scarron's *Le Roman Comique* in *The Opposition*; *A Vision* (Henley ed., xiv.323). *Don Quixote* had been frequently translated, and Fielding's library included a copy of Jarvis's rendering (1749 edn.). Unlike Richardson Fielding could have read the four French novels principally concerned in the original, but in any case *Gil Blas*, *Le Roman Comique*, and *La Paysan Parvenu* had all been translated by 1735, and *Marianne* was translated in instalments between 1736 and 1742.

[4] Battestin lists a number of these (*The Moral Basis of Fielding's Art*, p. 176).

Fielding seems to have been slight. Scarron, however, made use of at least one specific device later to be found in *Joseph Andrews* and *Tom Jones*: the mock-heroic descriptions of time. *Le Roman Comique* begins:

> Bright Phoebus had already perform'd above half his Career; and his Chariot having past the Meridian, and got on the Declivity of the Sky, roll'd on swifter than he desir'd . . . To speak more like a Man, and in plainer Terms; it was betwixt five and six of the Clock . . . ¹

It is Marivaux, however, who seems to have had the most direct influence on Fielding. Early in *Le Paysan Parvenu* he begs leave to digress:

> . . . for it's proper I should accustom my Readers betimes to my Digressions; I am not very positive whether I shall be guilty of many, perhaps I may, and perhaps I may not; I can answer for neither; only this I am resolv'd, not to confine my self . . . ²

Fielding claims a similar licence in *Tom Jones*:

> Reader, I think proper, before we proceed any farther together, to acquaint thee that I intend to digress, through this whole history, as often as I see occasion, of which I am myself a better judge than any pitiful critic whatever . . . (book i, ch. 2)³

Again, Marivaux's use of the story of the fallen Mlle. du Bois as what Crane would call a 'negative analogy' to Marianne's, is paralleled in *Tom Jones* and *Amelia*, where the histories of Mrs. Fitzpatrick and Mrs. Atkinson show the fates which the respective heroines of these novels might have incurred had they succumbed to weakness. Within such reported stories Fielding often explains an implausible exactness of detail in the kind of terms Marivaux uses: ' . . . I lost not a syllable of what she said; for it made such an impression upon my mind, that, I believe, I have repeated it word for word.'⁴

---

¹ Scarron's *Whole Comical Works* (translated by Brown, Savage and others), London, 1700, p. 1. Compare, for example, *Joseph Andrews*, book i, ch. 8; Henley ed., i.47.

² p. 6.

³ Henley ed., iii.22.

⁴ *The Virtuous Orphan; or, the Life of Marianne* (anonymous translation), *The Novelist's Magazine*, 16, London, 1784, p. 15. (This is the earliest

These minor similarities of technique suggest that Fielding was fairly closely acquainted with the work of his Continental predecessors. It seems reasonable to suppose therefore that he derived from them certain broad narrative effects that his novels have in common with theirs. It may be noted, for example, that all the five novels concerned proceed chronologically through a series of brief, intrinsically entertaining, and virtually self-contained episodes. The unifying principle in each case is that the adventures all centre round a single character or group of characters. All five stories range over a wide cross-section of society.

One more particularly significant point is that all four authors use interpolated stories to diversify their main narrative, and in fact show a general willingness to introduce extraneous matter. It is assumed that part of the narrative-writer's business is to keep up a commentary on manners and morals. The common attitude seems to be fairly, if light-heartedly, expressed in Scarron's *Les Hypocrites*, where after a burst of sententiousness he concludes:

> And now methinks I see some malapert Critick cock his Hat, toss his Wig over his Shoulders, look fierce, and ask how these Moral Aphorisms come to be thus brought in hand over head. Why, pray Sir don't be so cholerick; make use of them, or let them alone as you see fit; 'tis all a case to your humble Servant, I'll assure you; but under favour, Sir, methinks you ought to thank the man who gives you them for nothing.[1]

Marivaux and Cervantes go a stage further, and even insert passages of literary theory and criticism.[2] The scope for digression perhaps depends on the fact that all the novelists except Scarron are recounting adventures seen from a distance. The autobiographers are looking back on youthful adventures from a serene middle age; Cervantes appraises

---

English translation available in the Bodleian Library.) Compare, for example, *Amelia*, book iii, ch. 1; Henley ed., vi.111. Cervantes, however, uses a similar technique.

[1] *The Whole Comical Works*, 'The Hypocrites', p. 70. (Owing to an error in pagination 'The Hypocrites' contains two pages 70. This is the second of them.)

[2] (e.g.) *Don Quixote* (trans. Jarvis), London, 1749, i.372 ff., and *Le Paysan Parvenu*, 262 ff.

Quixote's exploits from an ironic height. In each case the result is a certain disengagement from the action. Marianne may be more deeply committed to stirring the reader's feelings, but even she can always withdraw sufficiently from her past to point a moral, or to generalize about human nature.

As far as tone is concerned, however, Fielding was probably at least as much influenced by his work as a journalist. Like Steele and Addison, of course, he had made his editorials exercises in polite didacticism, and he had often adopted the widespread practice[1] of stating a general ethical premise, illustrating it by an example, and then drawing the moral. A typical *Spectator* essay begins: 'The most improper things we commit in the Conduct of our Lives, we are led into by the Force of Fashion.'[2] Fielding opens many of his articles with a similar kind of generalization: 'The conquest of one's self is justly preferred by wise men to that of armies and kingdoms.'[3] It is not surprising to find him carrying over this aphoristic style into the novels. A chapter in *Joseph Andrews* starts: 'Habit, my good reader, hath so vast a prevalence over the human mind that there is scarce any thing too strange or too strong to be asserted of it' (book iv, ch. 7).[4] The recurrence of this gnomic manner suggests Fielding's didactic concern in the novels. In the above instance, as in many others, he proceeds from his opening statement to an illustrative anecdote which leads into a generalized discussion. Finally the issue is narrowed down to the effect on Lady Booby of a habitual pretended aversion to men. As regularly happens in Fielding's novels, the local incident has been made to point a moral.

The aphoristic habit also helps to fix Fielding's tone as narrator. 'My good reader' is the typical vocative of polite journalism; the authoritative but informal tone of Fielding's occasional essays is also to characterize his manner in the

[1] Described by I. Z. Sherwood in 'The Novelists as Commentators', *The Age of Johnson, Essays presented to C. B. Tinker*, New Haven, 1949, pp. 113 ff.
[2] No. 64.
[3] *The Champion*, Henley ed., xv.177.
[4] Henley ed., i.339.

novels. Since the French novelists have a similar approach
to the reader it is impossible to guess whether narrative or
journalistic tradition has the greater influence here. But the
question is hardly worth deciding, because the similarity of
manner in the two genres represents a common attitude to
matter, an attitude which Fielding shares. 'He asks that the
reader should survey life, rather than experience it', comments Kettle.[1] If this is true, however, it is not because
Fielding's detached, well-mannered, generally ironic tone
accidentally discourages the reader from too close an involvement in the action. Style and content both stem from an
assured, objective mind, confident of a capacity to interpret
experience, to derive rules of conduct from it, and to create
incidents and characters which will embody those rules
unambiguously.

Much has been written about the influence of classical
epic on Fielding, but Ian Watt plausibly dismisses such
influence as 'very slight' and 'mainly retrograde', useful
chiefly in setting him an exalted standard.[2] This last point,
however, is more important than Watt seems to suggest.
Without a consciousness of classical precedent the cultivated
Fielding might well have hesitated to involve himself with the
novel at all. And his awareness of tradition provides him with
criteria for scale, variety, and formal discipline. Finally it
has its own effect on Fielding's tone within the novels.

Epic precedent demanded a certain dignity of style and
incident. Since Fielding was writing comedy the heroic
manner would have been incongruous. Like many of the
Augustans he reconciles comedy and dignity by means of a
mock-heroic manner. This is most evident in such totally
stylized scenes as that of Joseph's fight with the hunting-
pack, or the churchyard battle in *Tom Jones*. Elsewhere,
however, this tone is generally diffused. There are mock-
heroic descriptions of time, probably borrowed from Scarron;

---

[1] *An Introduction to the English Novel*, i.80.
[2] *The Rise of the Novel*, London, 1960, p. 259. In general Watt's summary
seems to me much more realistic than such tortuous investigations as E. M.
Thornbury's *Henry Fielding's Theory of the Comic Prose Epic*. Fielding's
pronouncements about the requirements of prose epic are usually only
grandiose formulations of the current practice of many narrative writers.

Slipslop becomes 'this fair creature', Mrs. Partridge 'this Amazonian heroine', and Tom 'our hero'. The touch of pedantic humour harmonizes both with Fielding's usual ironic tone, and with the formalized dialogue. It helps to reduce personal involvement with character or story to a minimum.

There is one more major influence on Fielding's novels, however, which is almost antithetical to this stylization: his concern with truth to life. Cervantes had suggested the programme in general terms: 'All it [i.e. *Don Quixote*] has to do, is, to copy Nature: Imitation is the business, and how much the more perfect that is, so much the better what is written will be.'[1] Marivaux carries the idea even further; he writes in *Le Paysan Parvenu*: ' . . . this I dare assure the Reader, that the Facts are all really true, it's not a History forg'd for Diversion, which I imagine will easily be discern'd.'[2] In eighteenth-century England Truth to Nature was in any case a conventional literary principle in all genres. Fielding, however, interprets the idea much more narrowly than most of his contemporaries, claiming in his preface to *Joseph Andrews* that:

. . . every thing is copied from the book of nature, and scarce a character or action produced which I have not taken from my own observations and experience, yet I have used the utmost care to obscure the persons by such different circumstances, degrees, and colors, that it will be impossible to guess at them with any degree of certainty . . . [3]

In the last book of *Joseph Andrews* he justifies an extraordinary comment of Didaper's in a footnote: 'Lest this should appear unnatural to some readers, we think proper to acquaint them that it is taken verbatim from very polite conversation' (book iv, ch. 9).[4]

There is evidence at all levels of this realistic bent in Fielding. *Tom Jones* is based on an exact scheme of time and geography, worked out with almanac and map. In common with *Joseph Andrews* it includes some real inns and real innkeepers. Models have been found for certain characters. Parson Adams seems without doubt to have been drawn from the Reverend William Young, and Peter Pounce from

---

[1] *Don Quixote*, book i, Author's Preface, penultimate paragraph.
[2] p. 3.   [3] Henley ed., i.24.   [4] Henley ed., i.357.

a miserly lawyer named Walter; Fielding admits that the portrait of Sophia is based on his own first wife.[1] Sporadically the dialogue develops a real-life vitality; in the blunt vernacular of Mrs. Tow-wouse's 'Common charity a fart!' for example, or the righteous indignation of Mrs. Miller's ' . . . if any other person had called him villain, I would have thrown all this boiling water in his face'.[2]

The inference seems to be that Fielding saw no discrepancy between the Truth claimed by previous fiction-writers, and the Truth of Life itself. As a result he inserted raw fragments of his personal experience and observation into novels which various other literary influences combined to make formal in plot, characterization, and style.

3

With the exception of this concern for verisimilitude, then, the various literary tendencies mentioned in this chapter are fully compatible with each other. They are also well adapted to at least part of Fielding's didactic intention.

It was suggested earlier that Fielding's later plays resolved into a series of sketches, each one making a distinct moral or social observation. The picaresque formula of the Continental fiction-writers offered him the chance again to disperse his views in self-contained incidents. A concern for classical regularity makes him impose some unity on these incidents by relating them to an artificial plot, and he calls the result a 'Comi-prosai-epic'; but it is essentially a *loose-leaf* epic. Granted a slight functional link with the chain of events composing the action, an episode designed to embody any of Fielding's views could be inserted into his novel. In any case the narrative manner he had adopted gave him scope for a large measure of direct comment. It was even open to him to digress from his story altogether in order to make a point.

In other ways, too, didactic and literary requirements could be identified. The 'flat' minor characters derived from

---

[1] Most of these points are elaborated in the chapters on the individual novels.

[2] *Tom Jones*, book xvii, ch. 2; Henley ed., v.249.

the Comedy of Humours not only added life to the picaresque story but could readily be manipulated into patterns
illustrating a didactic view. They could also be made to
represent distinct attitudes to be defended or attacked,
especially since the stylized idiom of current literary dialogue made elaborate formal statements of moral ideas a
possibility. Even the current tone of essayist or narrator was
appropriate, in its detachment. Fielding could evaluate for
his readers the characters and incidents he created and
manipulated, interpreting the patterns he himself imposed.

If this had been the whole story the resulting works must
surely have been 'moral fables', such as *Candide* or *Animal
Farm*. As the ensuing chapters will show, there are incidents
in Fielding's novels which have a comparably schematic
quality; but the total effect of the narratives derives to a
great extent from their closeness to ordinary human experience. One reason for this has been suggested in this chapter:
Fielding's pursuit of Truth to Life leads him to introduce
into his novels all kinds of material drawn directly from his
personal observation. He could hardly reduce a heroine
based on his beloved Charlotte to the status of a Cunégonde.

The other reason has been put forward earlier in this
book. Fielding is naturally drawn to realism by the nature
of his moral beliefs. What he regarded as vices could be
adequately represented by the 'two-dimensional' figures of
the tradition of humours, but the 'good' he preached was an
everyday charity and sympathy which was not to be so glibly
personified. Heartfree and Allworthy, who come closer than
any of his other characters to being 'types' of virtue, remain
lifeless and insipid. Good-nature can only be felt as real when
invested with the human warmth and absurdity of Adams,
or the human gaiety and faultiness of Tom Jones. Moreover,
since one of Fielding's themes is the contrast in practical
results between this positive goodness and the theoretical
virtue of the hypocrite, he naturally requires a realistic
setting to provide his perspective. It is because Black
George's family are shown suffering 'all the misery with
which cold, hunger, and nakedness can affect human
creatures'[1] that the generosity of Tom, who tries to help

[1] Henley ed., iii.137.

them, and the meanness of Blifil, who tries to prevent him doing so, are vividly realized. Increasingly in his narratives Fielding defines a good or bad action by means of a circumstantial context.

The general conclusion must be that there was a fundamental ambiguity in Fielding's approach to the novel. He was trying to produce work at once formalized and realistic. It is quite remarkable, therefore, that he achieved such comparatively harmonious results. Criticisms levelled against particular limitations in the novels are often an involuntary compliment to the skill with which he had compromised. Those who complain, for instance, that certain characters are 'two-dimensional', or that, say, the episode of Tom's encounter with the gypsies is irrelevant, imply that the characterization in general is realistic, or that most of the episodes which compose *Tom Jones* have been adequately fused into the plot. In other words they are accepting Fielding's form as a consistent whole, with an internal logic abrogated only by certain details. As this chapter has tried to suggest, it was really a conflation of various literary methods into a medium for his didacticism. The surprising thing is that the resulting syntheses should have sufficient breadth, vitality, and consistency to warrant assessment as coherent pictures of eighteenth-century life.

The tension between realism and formalism, however, is not resolved in the same way in all three novels. In each case the emphasis is different, and the component elements are rearranged. As Fielding's didactic intention grows progressively more sophisticated his novels develop in seriousness and complexity.

VI

JOSEPH ANDREWS

Joseph Andrews is not only the shortest of Fielding's novels, but also the simplest in form. Indeed the whole structure of the book can be fairly explained in terms of its three main constituent parts. The story begins as a parody of *Pamela*, develops into an adaptation of Cervantes's picaresque formula, and concludes with the kind of happy ending characteristic of the artificial comedy. It is, moreover, a very light-hearted novel, containing a much greater proportion of pure comedy than *Tom Jones*.

Nonetheless Fielding's literary intention is plainly serious. He claims to be attempting a new kind of writing, the comic prose epic, 'which I do not remember to have seen hitherto attempted in our language' (Preface).[1] Carefully he distinguishes this genre from Romance and Burlesque. He numbers himself with Cervantes, Lesage, Scarron, and Marivaux as a historian, recording fundamental truths about human nature. A book such as *Don Quixote*, he suggests: '... is the history of the world in general, at least that part which is polished by laws, arts, and sciences; and of that from the time it was first polished to this day; nay, and forwards as long as it shall so remain (?)' (book iii, ch. 1).[2] Fielding consequently lays great stress on truth to life, asserting that in *Joseph Andrews* 'every thing is copied from the book of nature, and scarce a character or action produced which I have not taken from my own observations and experience' (Preface).[3]

But in addition to this formal aim Fielding has a moral aim. He is concerned to expose vanity and hypocrisy: '... to hold the glass to thousands in their closets, that they may contemplate their deformity, and endeavour to reduce it, and thus by suffering private mortification may avoid

[1] Henley ed., i.17.   [2] Henley ed., i.214.   [3] Henley ed., i.24.

public shame' (book iii, ch. 1).[1] He reconciles this programme with his new form by making the picaresque
adventures embody a succession of the particular attacks on
affectation which he had made many times before in his
writings. The novel becomes a sequence of didactic episodes,
its plot being so loosely knit that Fielding can insert an
adventure in dialogue illustrating any idea he chooses.

There remains, however, some conflict between Fielding's
literary and didactic intentions in *Joseph Andrews*. His
concern to shape his incidents into a series of neat moral
comments naturally militates against the realism and continuity of the book. None the less critics have always judged
it, like any other novel, in terms of character and plot. Such
an approach is clearly inappropriate to a story constructed
largely as a sequence of self-contained episodes, contributing
to the action only in their narrative concentricity. Digeon,
Cross, and Dudden all describe at length the various adventures in which Parson Adams is embroiled, but chiefly for
the light these shed on the characterization. In fact it would
almost be true to say that Adams is created as a necessary
condition of these incidents, rather than that they are in-
vented to illustrate different qualities in him.

This chapter will try to show how far *Joseph Andrews*
was designed as a series of didactic episodes, and how far as a
picture, arbitrarily stylized, of real life. Finally it will suggest what sort of whole these discordant aims produce.

I

Battestin claims that *Joseph Andrews* shows the specific
influence of the latitudinarian homilists. In defining the sum
of a Christian's goodness as 'chastity . . . with respect to
himself, and charity with respect to society', they regularly
instanced Joseph as epitomizing the former quality, and
Abraham the latter; hence the parallel exemplification in
Fielding's novel.[2]

The representation of virtue in *Joseph Andrews* is
therefore twofold; and this dichotomy is reflected in the

---

[1] Henley ed., i.214.   [2] *The Moral Basis of Fielding's Art*, pp. 26 ff.

narrative form. In effect the first ten chapters of the first book and much of the last book constitute a romance of which Joseph is the hero, while the rest of the novel comprises a variety of picaresque adventures in which Adams is the central figure. Joseph's story begins, at least, as a parody of *Pamela*; Adams's justifies the book's sub-heading: 'written in imitation of the manner of Cervantes'.

The history of Joseph, however, provides the formal framework for the adventures of the book's long central section, and has consequently to include all the paraphernalia of introduction, plot, and discovery. Even so it occupies less than a third of the novel. Only one important moral point is made: the sincere, uncomplicated relationship between Joseph and Fanny embodies an attitude towards love which is in deliberate contrast to that in *Pamela*. The element of parody dilutes but does not disguise this moral intention. On the whole, however, this part of the book has little bearing on the general didactic purpose.

The substance of *Joseph Andrews*, both quantitatively and thematically, is the account of the journey from London to Adams's parish. Functionally it is independent of the rest of the story. Apart from the encounters with Mr. Wilson and the pedlar, nothing happens on the journey which affects the outcome of the novel. The chapters in question consist of a succession of episodes which are self-contained, but for a certain amount of narrative coupling, and which almost invariably make some moral point. (Those fights and comic dialogues included solely as entertainment are the only exceptions.) When Joseph sets out for home the plot has come to a complete standstill. The ensuing happenings are relevant to this plot only because they delay his arrival.

Perhaps Joseph's first mishap supplies the clearest guide to Fielding's intentions, since with his action at a halt the author is free to exert any kind of fresh impetus he chooses. What he does choose is to retell the parable of the Good Samaritan in contemporary terms. Joseph is robbed and stripped, and his naked body flung into a ditch. A stagecoach stops when the postillion hears his groans, and the passengers debate whether to assist the injured man.

An old gentleman is for hastening away at once, for fear of

a second robbery. A lawyer counsels assistance, but only because he fears the consequences to himself should Joseph die through lack of aid. The only woman occupant of the coach, however, is firmly against admitting a naked man, and in any case the coachman refuses the extra passenger till won over by bribes and threats. Like the travellers and the lady's footman he declines to lend the victim any kind of garment, and it is left to the postillion—'(a lad who hath since been transported for robbing a hen-roost)'—to provide Joseph with a greatcoat.

The author makes Joseph's injuries continue to produce moral repercussions right up to the end of Book I. Not only the reactions of the coach-party are scrutinized, but also those of Mr. Tow-wouse, Mrs. Tow-wouse, Betty, a clergyman, a doctor, and Parson Adams. In all, the goodwill of a dozen people is tested by Joseph's misfortune, in each case with a different and plausible result. The robbery initiates a series of events clearly designed to form an elaborate little commentary on charity and hypocrisy at a variety of social levels.

The extent to which the didactic aim takes priority is underlined by two facts. The episode is self-contained, since not only does Joseph make a complete recovery from his wounds, but the one robber who is captured is allowed to escape, and none of the coach-passengers reappears in the novel. Fielding's manner of narration also makes it quite clear where he wants the emphasis to fall. Joseph's injuries are never described or even specified, and the attack itself is introduced perfunctorily in mid-sentence: 'He had not gone above two miles, charmed with the hope of shortly seeing his beloved Fanny, when he was met by two fellows in a narrow lane, and ordered to stand and deliver' (book i, ch. 12).[1] Joseph is so stylized and idealized a figure that there is no personal involvement in his plight. The robbery and its consequences are interesting not as part of Joseph's story, but for the reactions they evoke from various people.

Within the parable Fielding is able to re-express a number of his stock prejudices. The squeamish woman who looks at the naked Joseph through the sticks of her fan but refuses

[1] Henley ed., i.62.

to allow him in the coach is typical of the hypocritical prudes Fielding constantly satirized. The lawyer and Mrs. Towwouse represent the self-interested Hobbesian philanthropy he detested. The quack who attends Joseph at the inn is of the kind Fielding exposes in *The Mock-Doctor* and elsewhere, and he talks the same jargon: ' "The contusion on his head has perforated the internal membrane of the occiput, and divellicated that radical small minute invisible nerve which coheres to the pericranium ..." ' (book i, ch. 14).[1]

The first episode in *Joseph Andrews* not dependent on the *Pamela* parody, then, shows Fielding resorting to the picaresque pattern of summary incident, but infusing the incident with moral significance. The particular misadventure with which he begins is used to link a group of seven chapters; the subsequent episodes, though briefer, fulfil the same kind of piecemeal didactic purpose. He moulds the adventures of his travellers into a series of short satires which embody many of his views on social morality.

These wayside incidents and dialogues illustrate what Fielding considered to be common attitudes of meanness or hypocrisy. If this were all, *Joseph Andrews* would be no more than a sequence of parables. The separate episodes are linked, however, by the presence of Parson Adams who, in his consistent innocence and humanity, represents Fielding's ideal of Good-nature. Adams's presence gives the novel an obvious advantage in construction over *The Historical Register* or *A Journey from this World to the Next*. In the play the various self-contained points were only perfunctorily linked by the rehearsal plan. Like Fielding's other rehearsal plays it amounts to no more than the sum total of its episodes. *A Journey from this World to the Next* collapses into an even more aimless consecutiveness. In *Joseph Andrews*, however, the adventures have an Odyssean unity in that they all involve one central figure. Moreover this figure, Parson Adams, represents the permanent standard of goodness which exposes the falsity of the hypocrites encountered in his travels.

In short, *Joseph Andrews* provided scope, theoretically at least, for a complete embodiment of Fielding's moral

[1] Henley ed., i.76.

views. The positive side of them could find expression chiefly in the characterization of Parson Adams, the negative side in the attitudes exemplified by various of the people he meets.

A corollary of the method is that the characters of these people must emerge as two-dimensional, since each one represents some moral standpoint. Fielding himself admits as much in the introduction to Book III: ' . . . I describe not men, but manners; not an individual, but a species.'[1]

What the central section of *Joseph Andrews* primarily consists of is Parson Adams's introduction to a series of such semi-allegorical figures, on whom, implicitly or explicitly, he passes judgement. Many of these encounters are very brief and many are entangled with the purely burlesque or purely functional incidents. It would therefore be too intricate a task to trace the whole series of didactic episodes from the beginning of the journey to its end. But a number of examples will illustrate the general method.

Adams hears two vastly different accounts of a certain squire. It transpires that the speakers have been winner and loser of an action decided by the man in question. ' "God forbid!" said Adams, "that men should arrive at such a pitch of wickedness to belie the character of their neighbor from a little private affection, or, what is infinitely worse, a private spite" ' (book ii, ch. 3).[2] After a fight at an inn a stranger slily suggests to Adams that with a little distortion of the facts he might gain legal damages from his opponent:

'How, sir,' says Adams, 'do you take me for a villain, who would prosecute revenge in cold blood, and use unjustifiable means to obtain it? If you knew me, and my order, I should think you affronted both.' (book ii, ch. 5)[3]

Unable to pay his bill at another inn he visits Trulliber, a fellow clergyman, to seek a loan, but is treated with rudeness, and dismissed with a contemptuous refusal. Adams condemns him outright:

'Now, there is no command more express, no duty more frequently enjoined, than charity. Whoever therefore, is void of charity, I make no scruple of pronouncing that he is no Christian.' (book ii, ch. 14)[4]

---

[1] Henley ed., i.215.   [2] Henley ed., i.114.
[3] Henley ed., i.141.   [4] Henley ed., i.193.

Peter Pounce, Lady Booby's steward, an inveterate miser, suggests to Adams as they are travelling in a coach on the last stage of the journey home, that 'the distresses of mankind are mostly imaginary': '"Sure, sir," replied Adams, "hunger and thirst, cold and nakedness, and other distresses which attend the poor, can never be said to be imaginary evils"' (book iii, ch. 13).[1]

The interpolated stories, and particularly that of Wilson, have the effect of expanding the cross-section of society on which Fielding (usually through Adams) is enabled to comment. Wilson's history is unconvincing as autobiography precisely because it constitutes so full a survey of the vices of London society. First he describes the kind of shallow pursuits which occupied him, and gives the diary of a typical day: 'At which Adams said, with some vehemence, "Sir, this is below the life of an animal hardly above vegetation ..."' (book iii, ch. 3).[2] Then Wilson tells of his sexual adventures, ranging through affairs with common prostitutes, a kept mistress, a seduced girl, a coquette, and a married woman. Each kind of relationship brings its own punishment—disease, betrayal, remorse, unfulfillment, legal penalties. He admits that finally: '"I looked on all the town harlots with a detestation not easy to be conceived; their persons appeared to me as painted palaces, inhabited by Disease and Death ..."' (book iii, ch. 3).[3]

The rest of his London career—his encounter with the Rule of Right, his ruin by gambling, his work as a hack-writer—has a similar kind of unlikely comprehensiveness. Once again Fielding is taking the opportunity of making as many different specific points as he can.

Many of these are the customary onslaughts. Wilson's vain pursuit of a coquette is made the occasion for a long attack on the whole class. His predictable imprisonment for debt produces an incredulous outburst from Parson Adams. The seduction of inexperienced girls, so often deplored by Fielding, is here shown carried to its logical conclusion, with the victim, diseased and debauched, ending her days in Newgate. The girl, incidentally, was:

---

[1] Henley ed., i.310.   [2] Henley ed., i.232.   [3] Henley ed., i.237.

' ... the daughter of a gentleman, who, after having been forty
years in the army, and in all the campaigns under the Duke of Marlborough, died a lieutenant on half pay, and had left a widow, with this
only child, in very distressed circumstances ... ' (book iii, ch. 3)[1]
Yet another of Fielding's stock social criticisms has been
edged into the text.

In other parts of the narrative, too, familiar points are
made. Didapper, a character quite extraneous to the action,
is introduced into the last book to provide an excuse for
Fielding's usual satire against beaux. The practical jokes
played on Adams by the hunting squire and his toadies
recall the attack on 'roasting' in *The Champion*.[2] Bellarmine
and the traveller from Italy show the fatuity of the Grand
Tour, ridiculed by the author in *The Fathers*[3] and elsewhere.

The paratactic form of *Joseph Andrews*, then, gives
Fielding the opportunity to assemble a large number of the
ideas previously disseminated in his works. He makes his
novel still more didactically inclusive by the insertion of
self-contained dialogues, dissertations, and even short
essays. Fielding himself is quite explicit about his episodic
manner. After expatiating at some length on High People
and Low People, he continues: 'And now, reader, I hope
thou wilt pardon this long digression, which seemed to me
necessary to vindicate the great character of Mrs. Slipslop
... ' (book ii, ch. 13).[4] Another chapter begins:

> Our travellers ... travelled many miles before they met with any
> adventure worth relating. In this interval we shall present our
> readers with a very curious discourse, as we apprehend it, concerning
> public schools, which passed between Mr. Joseph Andrews and
> Mr. Abraham Adams. (book iii, ch. 5)[5]

Some of the chapter-headings also suggest how far *Joseph
Andrews* was constructed as a string of self-contained adventures, dialogues, and observations. One runs: 'A discourse between the poet and the player; of no other use in
this history but to divert the reader' (book iii, ch. 10).[6] A
chapter which comprises several such fragments can reflect

---

[1] Henley ed., i.234.
[3] In the character of Young Kennel.
[5] Henley ed., i.260.

[2] Henley ed., xv.240 ff.
[4] Henley ed., i.182.
[6] Henley ed., i.293.

the fact in the title: 'Sayings of wise men. A Dialogue between the lady and her maid; and a panegyric, or rather satire, on the passion of love, in the sublime style' (book i, ch. 7).[1]

The panegyric mentioned here is, of course, presented by Fielding himself, intervening as narrator. There are several such apostrophes and interludes in *Joseph Andrews*. Sometimes Fielding comments in a more particularized way, as in the description of Didapper (book iv, ch. 9),[2] or the attack on Scout:

> This Scout was one of those fellows who, without any knowledge of the law, or being bred to it, take upon them, in defiance of an act of Parliament, to act as lawyers in the country, and are called so. They are the pests of society, and a scandal to a profession to which indeed they do not belong, and which owes to such kind of rascallions the ill-will which weak persons bear towards it. (book iv, ch. 3)[3]

More generally, however, Fielding is able to propagate his own views through the conversations of his characters. Joseph holds forth on charity, Wilson on coquettes, patronage, and vanity, Adams on the duties of a clergyman, education, faith without works, and submission to the divine will. Often, also, comment is infiltrated into the novel by means of innuendo:

> ' ... it would do a man good to see his worship, our justice, commit a fellow to Bridewell, he takes so much pleasure in it; and when once we ha'un there, we seldom hear any more o'un. He's either starved or eat up by vermin in a month's time.' (book iv, ch. 3)[4]

The loose-leaf formula of *Joseph Andrews* thus gives Fielding, within the limits of Joseph's own story, the opportunity of making almost any point he wishes, either by embodying it in some directly enacted scene or by advancing it in a passage of direct or indirect didactic comment.

Demonstrating the pervasiveness of didacticism in *Joseph Andrews* entails a neglect of the book's most obvious and remarkable quality—its humour. The humorous and the didactic intention can co-exist because Fielding chooses to make most of his points through a satire as entertaining as

---

[1] Henley ed., i.43.   [2] Henley ed., i.355.
[3] Henley ed., i.324.   [4] Henley ed., i.323-4.

it is corrective. His province, he explains in the Preface, is 'the Ridiculous'; he specifically relegates 'great vices' to the background. In any case a number of incidents are included solely to amuse. But Fielding's primary intention in *Joseph Andrews*, as in his other novels, is without question didactic, and it is the didactic intention which determines the form and nature of the work.

2

The schematic approach which derives from Fielding's moral intention has an alienating effect. It constantly puts the narrative interest at the mercy of the didactic. A clear example of the subordination of story to satire is the account of the raid on the coach carrying the injured Joseph. Fielding describes it as casually as he has described the previous attack on Joseph himself: 'The lawyer was inquiring into the circumstances of the robbery, when the coach stopped, and one of the ruffians, putting a pistol in, demanded their money of the passengers, who readily gave it them ... ' (book i, ch. 12).[1] When the passengers were deciding whether to help Joseph, an old gentleman cried 'let us make all the haste imaginable, or we shall be robbed too'. Yet in common with the other passengers he seems undisturbed by the robbery when it comes; in fact he makes no reference to it at all, but resumes chaffing Joseph. Since the incident has not the smallest narrative repercussions its only possible usefulness is that it further exposes the hypocrisy of the prude. She has just answered the lawyer's suggestion that she give Joseph a dram, by protesting that 'she never tasted any such thing'. But in the course of the robbery she hands over '... a little silver bottle, of about a half-pint size, which the rogue, clapping it to his mouth, and drinking her health, declared held some of the best Nantes he had ever tasted ... ' (book i, ch. 12).[2]

The incident is one of a number so lacking in plausible detail as to appear nothing more than means to a didactic end. The minor characters are in any case merely representatives of single moral attitudes. The cowardly braggart, for

---

[1] Henley ed., i.65.   [2] Henley ed., i.65.

example, or Miss Grave-airs, have no existence outside the one hypocritical impulse they embody. When the story seems to be most blatantly manipulated to highlight those impulses the novel takes on the air of a moral demonstration in which the characters serve only as models. The calmness with which Fielding proposes the imminent death of Joseph, or the imminent rape of Fanny, tends to reduce even his hero and heroine to this level of simple manœuvrability.

The truth to life of *Joseph Andrews* is also affected by Fielding's choice of narrative conventions; notably by the romantic tradition behind Joseph's story, and the picaresque tradition behind the account of the journey home. The portrayal of Joseph is initially influenced by the demands of parody: ' . . . he retired into his own garret, and entered himself into an ejaculation on the numberless calamities which attended beauty, and the misfortune it was to be handsomer than one's neighbors' (book i, ch. 10).[1] Subsequently, however, he emerges simply as an amiable young man, protective towards Fanny, dutiful towards Parson Adams, and valiant in face of danger. As a model youth, first idealistically and then realistically, he tends to be a rather colourless figure, though this normality if anything serves to heighten the general plausibility of the characterization. Yet this worthily ordinary hero has to find fortune and his rightful parents by means of some highly implausible coincidences and discoveries. This is to say that the romantic plot belongs on a level of stylization different from that of much of the characterization in the book. The disparity is illustrated in the behaviour of Pamela's mother. After the pedlar has told his story: ' . . . old Mrs. Andrews, running to Fanny, embraced her, crying out, "She is, she is my child!"' (book iv, ch. 15).[2] This is the formal romantic reaction. When the 'discoveries' are complete and the story is back on its normal course she is less emotional: 'Gammar Andrews kissed her, and said she was heartily glad to see her; but for her part, she could never love any one better than Joseph' (book iv, ch. 16).[3] Mrs. Andrews's snatch of rhetoric, and the events which occasion it, belong to a romantic convention which Fielding seems to invoke as the only means of

[1] Henley ed., i.56.   [2] Henley ed., i.384.   [3] Henley ed., i.388.

resolving his story. As in the plays, his formal method of organizing his material is discordantly artificial.

The story of the journey home, of course, tends to stylization in its sheer copiousness of incident. Far more important, however, is another result of picaresque influence—that the burlesque interludes, and notably the fights, seem overdrawn in relation to the rest of the action. Adams at different times is involved in four fights, getting soaked with urine in one of them and with hog's blood in a second. On other occasions he falls in the mire of a pig-sty, is attacked by a pack of hunting dogs, and finds himself in bed first with Slipslop and then with Fanny. Such incidents have a cheerful obviousness tolerable enough in itself, but clumsier than the usual manner of the incidents which help to characterize Adams.

These discrepancies of approach are worth labouring because they derive from Fielding's central problem of establishing a consistent narrative convention. His didactic scheme, and the formal pattern he constructed from the romance and the picaresque tale, could have combined to produce a consistently stylized moral fable. But he was also concerned to present a realistic picture of ordinary experience. The inadequate narrative realization of the robberies, the unlikelihood of Wilson's life consisting solely of a series of moral and financial crises, the abrupt and unexplained death of Sir Thomas Booby, all these seem inharmonious because they figure in a story where the narrative generally has a convincing life of its own. Not only are the adventures themselves credible enough (compare those of *Candide*, a moral fable proper) but the continuity between them is sustained by a great amount of trivial circumstantial detail which gives the novel an air of reality. For instance, Joseph, leaving the friend who has accompanied the first stage of his journey home, buys him a pint of wine, and thanks him for the favour of his horse (book i, ch. 12).[1] Fanny, when she hears of Joseph's injuries at the hands of the robbers:

... that instant abandoned the cow she was milking, and taking with her a little bundle of clothes under her arm, and all the money she was

[1] Henley ed., i.62.

worth in her own purse, without consulting any one, immediately set forward . . . (book ii, ch. 10)[1]

When the three travellers leave the Wilsons:

The gentleman importuned them much to stay dinner; but when he found their eagerness to depart he summoned his wife; and accordingly, having performed all the usual ceremonies of bows and courtesies more pleasant to be seen than to be related, they took their leave, the gentleman and his wife heartily wishing them a good journey, and they as heartily thanking them for their kind entertainment. (book iii, ch. 5)[2]

Such passages are more than mere random gestures of verisimilitude. Because Fielding is preaching about the morality of everyday life it is essential for him to establish a context in which the standards of ordinary courtesy and humanity are seen to be important. The amicable farewells to Joseph's friend and to the Wilsons are in strong contrast to the parting words between the travellers and a grasping landlady:

. . . they all sailed out of the house without any compliments from their hostess, or indeed without paying her any, Adams declaring he would take particular care never to call there again, and she on her side assuring them she wanted no such guests. (book ii, ch. 15)[3]

Certainly realistic details of conduct and subsistence have an important narrative function: they help to prevent the story from resolving itself into a collection of fragments. They give some impression of a continuity of behaviour and relationships extending beyond what is revealed in the text alone. And passages of credible-sounding conversation assist the illusion:

'D—n me,' says the coachman, 'I will shoot with you, five guineas a shot.' 'You be hanged,' says the other; 'for five guineas you shall shoot at my a—.' 'Done,' says the coachman; 'I'll pepper you better than ever you was peppered by Jenny Bouncer.' 'Pepper your grandmother!' says the other: 'Here's Tow-wouse will let you shoot at him for a shilling a time.' (book i, ch. 16)[4]

It is true that this particular exchange has a partly satiric intention, but its total lack of relation to the story—neither

---

[1] Henley ed., i.167.   [2] Henley ed., i.259–60.
[3] Henley ed., i.196.   [4] Henley ed., i.88.

sportsman ever has anything to do with the travellers—and still more the sense of literal accuracy which the *non sequiturs* and the narrative irrelevance underline, make it seem like something overheard, and add to the sense of life going on around and outside the adventures recorded in the novel.

No doubt it was partly Fielding's adherence to the precept of Truth to Life which occasioned this realism of detail. But often the fidelity of idiom is carried over into dialogue clearly fulfilling a didactic function. As Cross points out, Fielding characteristically worked from observation to theory rather than the other way about.[1] He was not obliged to *invent* embodiments of the relevent abstract qualities; it was part of his purpose to use specific examples of such qualities which he had himself observed. Like Hogarth, he could work out a moral plan in terms of real-life instances. The first conversation between the Tow-wouses is a case in point:

'My dear,' said Mr. Tow-wouse, 'this is a poor wretch.' 'Yes,' says she, 'I know it is a poor wretch; but what the devil have we to do with poor wretches? The law makes us provide for too many already. We shall have thirty or forty poor wretches in red coats shortly.' 'My dear,' cries Tow-wouse, 'This man hath been robbed of all he hath.' 'Well, then,' said she, 'where's his money to pay his reckoning? Why doth not such a fellow go to an ale-house? I shall send him packing as soon as I am up, I assure you.' 'My dear,' said he, 'common charity won't suffer you to do that.' 'Common charity, a f—t!' says she . . . (book i, ch. 12)[2]

The whole exchange is true to life in every expletive and inflection; and the importance of this realism of speech to Fielding's didactic purpose is considerable. He is presenting instances of meanness and hypocrisy particularly cogent because they reflect widespread and familiar attitudes. Mrs. Tow-wouse may incarnate a Hobbesian self-interest, but it is because she uses the phrases and cadences of a familiar style of selfishness that she is an effective didactic mechanism.

More than anything else, however, it is the completeness of the characterization of Parson Adams which gives the

---

[1] Cross, i.341.   [2] Henley ed., i.68.

novel an air of realism. There are two reasons for the exceptional fullness of this portrayal. One is that Fielding is clearly describing a character taken from his own circle of friends. Even in the author's lifetime Adams was identified with a certain Parson Young.[1] If Fielding's prefatory claim is accepted, that he drew nearly all the characters from his personal experience, then it is understandable that this portrayal should involve an intimacy of detail hardly present in the re-creation from memory of, say, an innkeeper or a coachman. Secondly Adams is clearly the embodiment of Fielding's positive precept of Good-nature, and as such has almost by definition to be drawn on a generous scale. The Good-natured man, as was suggested in an earlier chapter, had not only to do good, but to feel an active sympathy with all the joys and sorrows of his fellow men. In other words a positive abundance of goodness and warmth was involved, which could only be suggested in a fictitious character by extra-functional details of character and behaviour.

For both these reasons the character of Adams is developed to an extent larger than is essential to the part he plays in the action. Many of the oddities of his personality and conduct are of a kind to suggest, unverifiably, that Fielding is recalling real-life episodes. In any case they have the effect of exciting an interest in Adams for his own sake, of a kind which is not aroused by the other characters.

His absent-mindedness is depicted in a dozen extraneous incidents. The first time he is seen on his own he leaves an inn without remembering to pay for the board of his horse, wades through a stream up to his middle simply through failing to notice a nearby bridge, and finally has to ask a passer-by the way to the nearest inn, although there is one clearly visible a stone's throw away.

In conversation he is made equally self-revealing. His active sympathy finds expression in a ready concern for the characters whose stories he hears: 'At these words Adams fetched a deep groan, which frighted the ladies, who told him "they hoped he was not ill." He answered, "He groaned only for the folly of Leonora"' (book ii, ch. 4).[2] When Wilson recounts the sad end of the girl he debauched,

---

[1] See Cross, i.344 ff.   [2] Henley ed., i.126.

he gives 'a deep sigh, which Mr. Adams echoed very loudly'. Adams is 'in a rapture' to hear of Harriet's generosity to Wilson, and he weeps with his host when the latter recalls the abduction of his first child.

Such reactions might be intended specifically as lively demonstrations of Good-natured warmth of feeling; but Adams's curiosity, which can have no particular moral significance, is made just as convincing. When there is a dispute as to whether the narrator of Leonora's history should repeat two letters written by the lovers, Adams contends for it 'with the utmost vehemence'. Later he interrupts the story to demand further information: '"Madam," said Adams, "if it be not impertinent, I should be glad to know how this gentleman was dressed"' (book ii, ch. 4).[1] Even details of Adams's appearance—his torn cassock, his large fist, and his long stride—have the authority of harmony and irrelevance. Of all the characters in the book he is the only one clearly developed for his own sake, and as such he affects the whole narrative balance.

There is one more important element in *Joseph Andrews* which disturbs the schematic plan, though in an entirely different way, and that is the characterization, or more particularly the motivation, of Lady Booby. With the very minor exception of Betty she is the only character who has to make a difficult choice of any kind. It seems fairly obvious, however, that the complexity of emotion she is endowed with is chiefly the product of narrative expediency; for it is the fluctuations of her attitude to Joseph which keep the plot in motion. She has to desire him, be angry enough at his rebuff to dismiss him and regretful enough to pursue him again. She must be sufficiently humiliated by his love for Fanny to take steps to have him condemned to Bridewell, and sufficiently infatuated to contemplate marriage with him when his love for Fanny seems doomed.

Fielding is obliged to suggest some sort of motive for all these changes of heart. By means of a number of soliloquies and descriptions he plausibly adjusts and readjusts the balance between pride and infatuation. Yet he also manages to develop such passages for their own sake. He makes Lady

[1] Henley ed., i.125.

Booby's emotional plight the occasion for a 'panegyric, or rather satire, on the passion of love, in the sublime style', and for a long reflection on female sexual psychology in general. At several points in the story his inserted didactic comments are concerned rather with human nature than with ethics. His account of Lady Booby's heart, even if forced on him by the plot, may well have shown him some of the possibilities of a closer study of feeling than the general plan of his novel permitted him.

3

There was little in *Joseph Andrews* that was essentially original. Its moral attitudes are those which underlie all Fielding's serious writing, and many even of the specific points had been made in previous works. Fielding had also written an earlier parody of *Pamela* which, if ribald, aimed at a serious exposure of the book's implicit hypocrisy; and as early as 1728, when he began *Don Quixote in England*, he had used the Cervantesque formula to satirize certain aspects of English society.

In *Joseph Andrews* Fielding was employing all these elements, together with some character-sketches and dialogues drawn from personal observation, as the ingredients of a new form, the comi-prosai-epic. The chief interest of the finished book from the point of view of literary history is the fact that its author has somehow found a means of fusing his diverse materials into a coherent whole. He has done so, moreover, despite the fact that both his moral intention and his narrative intention are inherently contradictory. From a didactic point of view Fielding required an artificial convention of plot and character, which would enable him to shape the episodes into a series of parables. Yet the general tenor had to be realistic, in order to lend point to the very practical terms of the moralizing. From the narrative point of view the only available formal discipline was the artificial romantic plot; yet much of Fielding's material was taken direct from real life.

As might be expected, this ambivalence of intention gives the novel a somewhat spasmodic quality. The aspects of reality on which the author chooses to place emphasis are not consistently chosen. For instance, during the journey home, when the poverty of the travellers is the cause of most of their adventures, Fielding records their financial state in detail. When they reach their destination, however, the interest is centred on Lady Booby's machinations, and there is no explanation of how Joseph and Fanny, both of whom are destitute, find food and shelter. Again, certain minor characters are described in detail—Didapper, for example, and Mrs. Tow-wouse—but there is no direct description of Lady Booby, or, oddly enough, of Parson Adams. Above all, as the second part of this chapter tried to show, the narrative shifts between several levels of verisimilitude.

Yet critics have rarely spoken of this very experimental novel as being anything short of a balanced, articulated whole, and it is not difficult to see why. In the first place almost everything that happens in the book is ultimately plausible. All the main adventures occur in the course of a single English journey, and none of the characters is outside the range of ordinary experience.

Also important is the novel's prevailing lightness of tone. Fielding's ironic, alienating style of narration muffles any potential seriousness in the incidents. The robberies, the attempted rapes, the threatened imprisonments, are never felt as real dangers. As Fielding claims in the Preface, those 'great vices' which do figure in the novel 'never produce the intended evil'. Consequently such characters as Lady Booby or the 'roasting' squire never seem as vicious as their actions ought to make them seem, and are rather ridiculed than condemned. On the other hand, of the book's two heroes Parson Adams is a comic, and Joseph a mock-heroic, figure; without belittling them Fielding need never take either completely seriously. Even the graver dialogues and the moralizing are usually comic in tone.

What has happened is that Fielding has instinctively played down those elements which threaten to take him outside the province of everyday comic incident and everyday morality. The novel has consequently a coherence in matter and manner which has led to its being taken for granted as an assured totality. But this coherence is something less than Fielding was aiming at. The range of his material is wider than the effective range of his finished novel. The broader of the burlesque scenes, the description of Didapper, the squalid realities of Wilson's youthful career, Adams's dignified defiance of Lady Booby's threats—none of these features is subsumed under the general convention of *Joseph Andrews*. Even the moral intention of the book is partly gelded by its manner, as is shown by the way in which critics have consistently stressed other virtues in the novel: its variety, its characterization, its humour.

Fielding therefore constructs a narrative presenting a fairly consistent picture of life at the expense of writing a rather smaller novel than he intended. None the less he had shown that the prose narrative could embody moral ideas and be subjected to formal discipline. He had experimented with different ways of projecting character and motive, different ways of infiltrating didactic comment and different ways of drawing on real-life experience. It was open to him in his next novel to use the knowledge he had gained about his new form to construct a larger-scale narrative, embodying a more comprehensive set of moral views.

VII

TOM JONES

R.S. CRANE suggests in an article that the 'unifying
idea' which holds *Tom Jones* together is:

> ... the dynamic system of actions, extending throughout the
> novel, by which the divergent intentions and beliefs of a large number
> of persons ... are made to co-operate, with the assistance of Fortune,
> first to bring Tom into an incomplete and precarious union ... with
> Allworthy and Sophia; then to separate him as completely as possible
> from them through actions that impel both of them, one after the other,
> to reverse their opinions of his character; and then, just as he seems
> about to fulfil the old prophecy that 'he was certainly born to be
> hanged,' to restore them unexpectedly to him in a more entire and
> stable union of both affection and fortune than he has known before.[1]

This is an adequate statement of what happens in the story,
but it overlooks the moral significance which makes the
novel more than a romance with an artificial plot. Fielding
states, in his dedication to *Tom Jones*, that 'to recommend
goodness and innocence hath been my sincere endeavour in
this history'.[2] Although the claim seems conventional it is
markedly different from the intentions outlined in the
Preface to *Joseph Andrews*. In that book Fielding's concern
is with 'the true Ridiculous', of which 'the only source'
is affectation.[3] His aim is primarily the negative one
of exposing various vices and follies. Parson Adams, the
exemplar of his positive precept of Good-nature, is therefore
largely a passive figure, serving as a touchstone for the worth
of the people with whom he is brought into contact. In *Tom
Jones*, although it is again part of Fielding's intention 'to
laugh mankind out of their favourite follies and vices',[4]

---

[1] 'The Plot of *Tom Jones*', *Journal of General Education*, iv (1950),
112 ff.

[2] Henley ed., iii.12. [3] Henley ed., i.21.

[4] Dedication; Henley ed., iii.12–13.

the emphasis is clearly to be rather the positive one of promoting virtue.

The same basic antithesis of charity and self-interest is expounded, however. Tom's youthful generosities to Black George's family are designed to show him as essentially the Good-natured Man. In any case the author is quite explicit about the humanity of his hero:

... he was one who could truly say with him in Terence, *Homo sum: humani nihil a me alienum puto.* He was never an indifferent spectator of the misery or happiness of any one; and he felt either the one or the other in great proportion as he himself contributed to either. (book xv, ch. 8)[1]

This is exactly the kind of warm concern for others which Fielding implies in his several definitions of Good-nature, and which is embodied in Parson Adams. As was suggested in the preceding chapter, however, Adams only shares the role of hero in *Joseph Andrews.* Joseph, in other respects a rather colourless figure, is the narrative centre of the book, the fulfilling of his romantic aspirations constituting the plot. Parson Adams is the didactic centre, round whom Fielding is able to develop the series of moral episodes which compose the substance of the novel. To a great extent Tom combines these two roles. Clearly he is the romantic hero of the story, but he is also, as will be shown, the focus of didactic interest.

The negative side of the antithesis, the representation of hypocrisy, is similarly more crystallized than in *Joseph Andrews.* A variety of false values are epitomized by the single person of Blifil. The chief difference between the didactic content of the two novels, however, does not lie in the greater refinement that this more complex personification suggests, but in the fact that Fielding is less interested in displaying the falsity of Blifil than in showing the strengths and weaknesses of Tom. In the dedication he declares his intention of proving that virtue brings more rewards than vice:

For this purpose I have shown that no acquisitions of guilt can compensate the loss of that solid inward comfort of mind, which is the sure

[1] Henley ed., v.178.

companion of innocence and virtue; nor can in the least balance the evil of that horror and anxiety which, in their room, guilt introduces into our bosoms. And again, that as these acquisitions are in themselves generally worthless, so are the means to attain them not only base and infamous, but at best incertain, and always full of danger. Lastly, I have endeavoured strongly to inculcate, that virtue and innocence can scarce ever be injured but by indiscretion; and that it is this alone which often betrays them into the snares that deceit and villainy spread for them.[1]

These are stock themes of Fielding's which found little expression in *Joseph Andrews*. It is notable that they are all illustrated by the reactions of Tom rather than those of Blifil. Despite his constant deceit it is only when unmasked that Blifil shows 'horror and anxiety', and he never seems to feel that the objects of his machinations are 'worthless'. It is Tom who is overcome by remorse at his comparatively minor sins, and appalled at their consequences. And above all it is Tom whose 'indiscretions' betray him into the traps spread by Blifil's 'deceit and villainy'. This point is underlined by Fielding in Book III, chapter 7, 'In which the author himself makes his appearance on the stage.' In this very deliberate intervention he announces that Tom's adventures will:

... if rightly understood, afford a very useful lesson to those well-disposed youths who shall hereafter be our readers; for they may here find that goodness of heart and openness of temper ... will by no means, alas! do their business in the world. Prudence and circumspection are necessary even to the best of men ... no man can be good enough to enable him to neglect the rules of prudence; nor will Virtue herself look beautiful unless she be bedecked with the outward ornaments of decency and decorum. And this precept, my worthy disciples, if you read with due attention, you will, I hope, find sufficiently enforced by examples in the following pages.[2]

The point is emphasized again at other crucial moments in the narrative. Allworthy, on what he thinks to be his death-bed, puts it to Tom himself: '"I am convinced, my child, that you have much goodness, generosity, and honor in your temper; if you will add prudence and religion to these, you must be happy ... "' (book v, ch. 7).[3] When

---

[1] Henley ed., iii.12.   [2] Henley ed., iii.131–2.   [3] Henley ed., iii.243.

reconciled with Tom at the end of the novel he recalls this counsel:

'You now see, Tom, to what dangers imprudence alone may subject virtue ... Prudence is indeed the duty which we owe to ourselves; and if we will be so much our own enemies as to neglect it, we are not to wonder if the world is deficient in discharging their duty to us ... ' (book xviii, ch. 10)[1]

It is indiscretion which has by then betrayed Tom into a knowledge of the miseries which the guilty man must suffer. As the next section will show, the misfortunes Crane mentions befall Tom as the result of various imprudent deeds, and his ultimate return to favour is the reward of his true good-nature. Fielding is 'promoting the cause of virtue' by showing some of the pitfalls it must avoid: 'A moral which I have the more industriously laboured, as the teaching it is, of all others, the likeliest to be attended with success; since, I believe, it is much easier to make good men wise, than to make bad men good' (Dedication).[2]

This is an idea demanding a much more intricate narrative embodiment than that of *Joseph Andrews*, a movement away from the fairly simple personification of the moral fable. The central character must be more complex, must be allowed to do wrong, and eventually—since the book, as a comedy, is to end happily—must be shown as developing a new discretion. Moreover since the hero's active goodness, and more particularly his imprudence, can only be demonstrated through positive deeds and their repercussions, he must be shown to be much more in control of, and responsible for, his own destiny. Altogether, in fact, the didactic plan of *Tom Jones* demands a narrative projection a good deal closer to the modern novel, in its complexity, than *Joseph Andrews* was.

At the same time, however, the narrative plan seems to have become more ambitious in its own right. It is true that there are certain general similarities to *Joseph Andrews*—the plot is founded on a mystery of birth, and deals in thwarted love eventually fulfilled. Like the earlier novel, *Tom Jones* is divided into a period passed in London, a journey, and a

---

[1] Henley ed., v.346.   [2] Henley ed., iii.12.

period passed in the country, though here the order is reversed.

In *Tom Jones*, however, the plot is much more elaborate and ingenious. The final 'discovery' of Tom's parentage is brought about by a series of events to which almost every incident in the book has directly or indirectly contributed. Fielding himself several times draws attention to the relevance of even the most minor happenings. In short, this plot is far more artificial, and therefore more constricting, than that of *Joseph Andrews*.

In general structure, too, the novel is more sophisticated. It is divided into eighteen books, of which six are concerned with the country, six with the journey, and six with the town. Each book is prefaced with an introductory chapter. Not only unity of action is observed but, from the moment of Tom's banishment, unity of time, an exact scheme of dates and hours being pursued, in which even the phases of the moon tally with the almanac.[1]

Incidental entertainment in the picaresque tradition, by means of fights, mock-heroics, and comic dialogues, remains part of the intention. But *Tom Jones* is very clearly designed as a complex artifact of which almost every detail is calculated and relevant. Fielding's literary programme is thus as demanding as his didactic one, and it is not surprising that the two are sometimes impossible to reconcile.

I

Because the plot of *Tom Jones*, unlike that of *Joseph Andrews*, involves a 'system of actions', the moral argument is less close to the surface than that of its predecessor. Tom's good deeds and indiscretions do not usually bring immediate reward or retribution, but rather initiate sequences of action which prove in the long run to be advantageous or disadvantageous. Moreover they only produce these effects because of the elaborate context of Tom's unknown parentage, and adoption into a largely hostile household. In tracing the main didactic theme of the book, therefore, it is necessary to disregard much of the narrative

[1] See Cross, ii.188 ff.

which merely establishes or develops various features of the plot. Fielding has to devote several chapters even of *Joseph Andrews*, with its relatively simple story, to the foundation of his plot. In *Tom Jones* both the first two books are needed to bring the story up to date.

Even Books III and IV are largely expository; but it is to be noted that Fielding makes them serve a double purpose. Not only is the contrast between Tom and Blifil established, but four major characters are introduced—Western, Sophia, Thwackum, and Square—and the first hint is given of the impending romance between Tom and Sophia. The whole section suggests an advance in technique in that, unlike most of *Joseph Andrews*, it contributes both to the action and to the moral purpose.

The story proper displays a similar inter-involvement of action and theme, its chief didactic point being made through the plot. Perhaps the most emphatic evidence that the fluctuations of fortune described by Crane are expressly conceived as punishments and rewards for Tom's imprudence and his good-nature, is supplied by Tom's own very explicit attitude during adversity. When visited in prison by Mrs. Waters he

... lamented the follies and vices of which he had been guilty; every one of which, he said, had been attended with such ill consequences that he should be unpardonable if he did not take warning, and quit those vicious courses for the future. (book xvii, ch. 9)[1]

The nadir of Tom's ill-luck is Partridge's disclosure that Mrs. Waters, whom he slept with at Upton, is his own mother. After his first despair Tom again faces the fact that it is his own conduct which has brought disaster: 'I am myself the cause of all my misery. All the dreadful mischiefs which have befallen me are the consequences only of my own folly and vice' (book xviii, ch. 2).[2] When eventually extricated from his various predicaments and reunited with Allworthy, Tom tells him:

'... believe me, my dear uncle, my punishment hath not been thrown away upon me: though I have been a great, I am not a hardened sinner; I thank Heaven, I have had time to reflect on my past life,

[1] Henley ed., v.291.   [2] Henley ed., v.296.

where, though I cannot charge myself with any gross villainy, yet I can discern follies and vices more than enough to repent and to be ashamed of; follies which have been attended with dreadful consequences to myself, and have brought me to the brink of destruction.' (book xviii, ch. 10)[1]

Clearly the reader is meant to see Tom's story, as he himself so specifically does, as a series of follies bringing eventual retribution. Though Tom's misfortunes are not simply the direct consequences of wrong-doing, as for example was Wilson's venereal disease, they do ultimately derive from it. He commits four major indiscretions, and in each case a chain of unlucky circumstances brings about a painful result.

His affair with Molly Seagrim comes to light purely by chance. Sophia, hearing of the Seagrims' plight from Tom, sends them some money and clothes. The vain Molly wears some of the finery to church, thereby so exciting the jealousy of her acquaintances that a fight ensues in the churchyard. A travelling fiddler, injured in the brawl, applies to All-worthy for a warrant, and in the course of the subsequent inquiry Molly's pregnancy is disclosed. The outcome of the affair is not very damaging to Tom. Although Sophia resolves to stifle what she now realizes to be her love for him, circumstances soon cause her to change her mind. The worst of the repercussions is that Square is able to suggest that Tom's previous kindnesses to the Seagrims have been motivated by lust for Molly, an insinuation which 'stamped on the mind of Allworthy the first bad impression concerning Jones'.[2]

Tom's second indiscretion is his misconduct during All-worthy's illness. Meeting Molly by chance, he is making love with her when surprised by Thwackum and Blifil, and he fights them both off rather than expose the identity of his mistress. The consequences are in this case grave enough. Tom is turned away by Allworthy, thereby being 'separated as completely as possible' from his guardian. Yet these results only ensue through the malice of Blifil, who mis-represents the whole matter, and the ill-luck of the affair's

---

[1] Henley ed., v.346.   [2] Book iv, ch. 2; Henley ed., iii.190.

being revealed at a time when Tom is too upset over Sophia to defend himself properly.

Though it is Tom's expulsion from Allworthy's household which physically separates him from Sophia, she herself does not 'reverse her opinion of his character' until learning of his behaviour with Mrs. Waters. Thereupon she leaves Upton without seeing him, convinced that '"he is not only a villain, but a low despicable wretch"'.[1] (book x, ch. 5)

To punish this instance of Tom's folly Fielding has to contrive not only that Sophia shall leave home, but that she shall arrive at the same inn as her lover just after he has succumbed to Mrs. Waters. He has also to arrange that her father shall reach the same hostelry next morning, since it is his intervention which prevents Tom making an immediate pursuit of Sophia. The morally remedial outcome of Tom's weakness—that he comes later to believe he has committed incest—depends on the large coincidence of his having chanced to rescue the same Jenny Jones who had admitted to being his mother.

Tom's final error, his liaison with Lady Bellaston, depends less on contrivance of plot to produce its unpleasant results. He naturally meets her in the course of seeing Sophia, and it is not unnatural that jealousy should cause her to initiate a plan to punish her lover and her rival. But even here coincidence plays some part in the punishment of Tom. The press-gang sent to capture him happens to arrive at the very moment of his victorious duel with Fitzpatrick, and it is only through the agency of these men that he is arrested and accused of starting the fight.

Fielding makes some effort to place these misdemeanours in an appropriate light, stressing that Tom falls through folly rather than vice. It is emphasized that each of the women takes an active part in seducing him, that he thinks himself in love with Molly in the first instance, and that all his subsequent lapses occur when he seems to have no hope of gaining Sophia. None the less Tom is justified in seeing his final accumulation of misfortunes as the consequence of his previous errors. He has been turned away by Allworthy and finally abandoned by Sophia, as a result of his affairs with

[1] Henley ed., iv.217.

Molly and with Lady Bellaston; he is imprisoned and
apparently guilty of incest as a result of his affair with Mrs.
Waters. That his plight should be so appropriately punitive,
and bear out so clearly the moral that Fielding states in his
dedication and recalls at regular intervals in the narrative,
makes it plain that the plot has been designed and manipulated specifically to a didactic end. That is to say that the
whole structure of the novel, like that of *Joseph Andrews*, is
subordinated to the moral intention.

Tom's eventual good fortune is less explicitly a reward
for his good deeds. His return to favour depends chiefly on
the realization by Allworthy and Sophia of his true merit.
Nevertheless certain of his worthy actions have repercussions
which help to effect his ultimate prosperity. Mrs. Waters,
whom he rescues from imminent murder, pays tribute to his
character before Allworthy, and happens to be able to solve
the mystery of Tom's parentage. Mrs. Miller, who reveres
Tom not only for promoting her daughter's marriage with
Nightingale but also for preserving her cousin Anderson
and his family, staunchly supports him before both Allworthy and Sophia, to each of whom she tells the full story
of her obligations. It is through her agency, too, that Sophia
comes to hear of another of Tom's commendable actions, his
refusal of an advantageous match with Mrs. Hunt:

' . . . when I mentioned the young lady's name, who is no other than
the pretty widow Hunt, I thought she turned pale; but when I said
you had refused her, I will be sworn her face was all over scarlet in an
instant; and these were her very words: I will not deny but that I
believe he has some affection for me.' (book xviii, ch. 10)[1]

The incident of Mrs. Hunt relates to another tendency
in some of Tom's 'good' actions: they justify his claim to
Allworthy and Sophia that he has learned wisdom from his
past errors. Not only does he reject the rich widow's tempt-
ing offer, he also resists the blandishments of Mrs. Fitzpatrick: ' . . . for, faulty as he hath hitherto appeared in this
history, his whole thoughts were now so confined to his
Sophia that I believe no woman upon earth could have now
drawn him into an act of inconstancy' (book xvi, ch. 9).[2]

[1] Henley ed., v.350.   [2] Henley ed., v.242.

This new maturity in Tom suggests that he will now be able to foster the good fortune he has long deserved.

The plot of *Tom Jones*, it has been suggested, is designed to bring home to the hero himself, and to the reader, the dangers of imprudence. But since it is only through elaborate processes of coincidence and intrigue that retribution is made to descend, the simple moral intention is rather submerged in the complex execution. If the novel none the less shows a strong ethical concern it is because Fielding contrives to insert a great deal of local didactic comment in his usual vein.

He can do this the more easily in that *Tom Jones*, although its main theme is worked out rather in terms of character than of incident, quickly resolves into the episodic manner. When Fielding is first delineating the characters of Tom and Blifil, he resorts to a technique of direct illustration after only three paragraphs: 'An incident which happened about this time will set the characters of these two lads more fairly before the discerning reader than is in the power of the longest dissertation' (book iii, ch. 2).[1] The anecdote in question extends over five chapters. Two further chapters in the same book also contain complete episodes: 'A childish incident, in which, however, is seen a good-natured disposition in Tom Jones' (book iii, ch. 8),[2] and 'Containing an incident of a more heinous kind, with the comments of Thwackum and Square' (book iii, ch. 9).[3] After introducing Sophia at the beginning of Book IV, Fielding relates another such event: 'Wherein the history goes back to commemorate a trifling incident that happened some years since; but which, trifling as it was, had some future consequences' (book iii, ch. 3).[4]

These episodes are, of course, chiefly designed to illustrate the difference in character between Tom and Blifil, but subsidiary didactic points are also made. The pattern in this section of the novel is for incident to be succeeded by discussion, and Fielding makes the chief disputants hold views which he proceeds to satirize. Square is a deist and Thwackum virtually a Methodist; Fielding exposes what he regards as the absurdity of their beliefs by contrasting their

---

[1] Henley ed., iii.108.   [2] Henley ed., iii.132.
[3] Henley ed., iii.135.   [4] Henley ed., iii.149.

learned, but partial and wrong-headed, reactions to Tom's escapades, with the common-sense views of Allworthy, and even of Bridget, and Squire Western.[1]

Both Thwackum and Square have a part to play in the narrative—a part to which the ethical beliefs Fielding imposes on them are quite irrelevant. Characters and incidents all through *Tom Jones*, although marshalled to serve the purposes of the complex plot, are frequently used in this way to make minor didactic points. For instance when Allworthy shows the infant he has just discovered in his bed, to his maidservant, Mrs. Wilkins, she at once exclaims against it:

> 'Faugh! how it stinks! It doth not smell like a Christian. If I might be so bold to give my advice, I would have it put in a basket, and sent out and laid at the churchwarden's door. It is a good night, only a little rainy and windy . . . ' (book i, ch. 3)[2]

When both her master and mistress speak in Tom's favour she quickly changes her tune: ' . . . she fell to squeezing and kissing . . . crying out, in a shrill voice, "O, the dear little creature!—The dear, sweet, pretty creature! Well, I vow it is as fine a boy as ever was seen!"' (book i, ch. 5).[3]

The only essential narrative issue at this juncture is the introduction of Tom to the Allworthy household. Fielding enlarges on the essentials to make the kind of satirical point he makes against Mrs. Tow-wouse in *Joseph Andrews*. Similarly, although it is for a narrative purpose that Tom has to break his arm—it is because he injures himself in saving her, that Sophia begins to fall in love with him—Fielding again makes didactic capital of the situation. Square is lecturing Tom on the contemptibility of physical suffering, when he bites his tongue, and breaks into muttered oaths of pain.[4] It is the same kind of 'reversal' by which in *Joseph Andrews* Fielding shows the discrepancy between philosophical theory and practice.[5] His former didactic method is still functioning alongside the new.

---

[1] (e.g.) Book iii, chs. 3, 8, 9; book iv, ch. 4; Henley ed., iii.121, 134, 136, 155.

[2] Henley ed., iii.25.   [3] Henley ed., iii.30.

[4] Book v, ch. 2; Henley ed., iii.212.

[5] Book iv, ch. 8; Henley ed., i.349 ff.

Since the incidents in *Tom Jones* have almost always to produce some particular result necessary to the plot, they can rarely be as autonomously didactic as the loosely strung adventures of *Joseph Andrews*. But when Tom and Sophia are travelling to London the narrative demands only that they take certain routes and meet certain people, so that Fielding has reasonable scope to make his episodes fulfil a second function. Tom's encounter with the Gypsies develops into an oblique comment on the law of criminal conversation;[1] the affair of the puppet-show is a jibe at the morality of the contemporary stage.[2] It is in this section of the novel, too, that both the long interpolated stories appear. Not only do these furnish, in Crane's term, 'negative analogies' to the situation of Tom and Sophia, they constitute attacks on misanthropy—one of Fielding's recurrent targets—and the kind of repressive marriage he had already exposed in *The Champion*.[3]

The characters encountered on the journey are also put to didactic use. The worthy lieutenant who befriends Tom has gained no promotion for nearly forty years, because his wife—whose charms have presumably weathered well— refuses to sleep with his commanding officer.[4] Yet again Fielding points to the corruptness of current practice in military preferment. The surgeon who attends Tom after he has been injured by Northerton, is another of Fielding's magniloquent quacks: ' " ... the aliment will not be concreted, nor assimilated into chyle, and so will corrode the vascular orifices, and thus will aggravate the febrific symptoms" ' (book viii, ch. 3).[5]

The chapters on London contain a greater proportion of sheer plot, but even here Fielding finds opportunity to be didactic. He makes his characteristic attacks on the manners and morals of high society, and ridicules various fashionable diversions, such as drums and masquerades.[6]

[1] Book xii, ch. 12; Henley ed., v.17–18.

[2] Book xii, chs. 5–6; Henley ed., iv.321–5.

[3] Henley ed., xv.185 ff. The story told there has some close affinities with Mrs. Fitzpatrick's.

[4] Book vii, ch. 12; Henley ed., iv.31.

[5] Henley ed., iv.72.

[6] (e.g.) Book xiii, ch. 7; book xvii, ch. 6; Henley ed., v.65; 274.

These examples should be sufficient to show how Fielding manipulates the incidents and characters involved in the plot of *Tom Jones* so that they embody, as do those in *Joseph Andrews*, a series of specific ethical ideas. He also makes use of the other didactic methods of his earlier novel. Once again he moralizes both *in propria persona* and through the mouths of his characters. The chapter-headings: 'Containing a few common matters, with a very uncommon observation upon them' (book i, ch. 5),[1] and 'Consisting partly of facts, and partly of observations upon them' (book xv, ch. 10)[2] suggest, as is in fact the case, that Fielding frequently slows down the narrative in order to comment directly or indirectly on some happening in the story. His tale naturally provides him with frequent texts for homilies on Good-nature, indiscretion, the cruelty of arranged marriages, or the joys of benevolence; but he finds many other incentives to moralizing in the course of the narration. There is 'a short apology for those people who overlook imperfections in their friends'[3] for instance, and 'a short digression in favor of the female sex'.[4] Such reflections are acknowledged in the chapter-title only when, like these, they develop considerable length, but they occur everywhere in the book. As early as his second chapter Fielding claims leave to digress as often as he thinks fit, and the digressions are usually didactic. It is to be noticed, however, that many of them are merely comments on human nature:

... though envy is at best a very malignant passion, yet is its bitterness greatly heightened by mixing with contempt towards the same object; and very much afraid I am, that whenever an obligation is joined to these two, indignation and not gratitude will be the product of all three. (book i, ch. 13)[5]

By making Allworthy a virtually perfect character, Fielding has provided himself with a ready-made didactic mouthpiece, and he takes full advantage of him. Allworthy reads Jenny a full-scale sermon on chastity, and Dr. Blifil a lecture

---

[1] Henley ed., iii.30.　　　　[2] Henley ed., v.186.
[3] Book ii, ch. 7; Henley ed., iii.92.
[4] Book iv, ch. 13; Henley ed., iii.194.　　[5] Henley ed., iii.63.

on the foundation of a happy marriage. He engages with Captain Blifil on the meaning of Charity, and expatiates on Death when on his sick-bed. Tom himself is permitted a share of the moralizing. He states Fielding's own condemnation of the sort of misanthropy expressed by the Man of the Hill; and he is even made to lecture Nightingale on sexual morality. Sophia and Mrs. Miller are others who deliver moral discourses on a variety of topics.

Throughout the novel Fielding is didactic in a more general 'epic' way, introducing all kinds of information and anecdotes from both modern and classical sources: the story of Nell Gwynn's footman,[1] for example, or of the drunken Cleostratus.[2] And apart from his direct moralizing he insinuates his opinions on certain subjects in a variety of minor ways, ranging from comparison: ' ... it is certain they were no more in the right road to Coventry than the fraudulent, griping, cruel, canting miser is in the right road to heaven' (book xii, ch. 11),[3] to the use of footnotes:

This is the second person of low condition whom we have recorded in this history to have sprung from the clergy. It is to be hoped such instances will, in future ages, when some provision is made for the families of the inferior clergy, appear stranger than they can be thought at present. (book iv, ch. 14)[4]

Many of the interludes in *Tom Jones*, however, are still intended solely to entertain. Where the plot is at its thinnest, for example during the journey of Sophia, whole chapters can consist of little but brief narrative items, comic dialogues, and snippets of comment. Again chapter-titles can reveal this miscellaneous quality:

The morning introduced in some pretty writing. A stage-coach. The civility of chamber-maids. The heroic temper of Sophia. Her generosity. The return to it. The departure of the company, and their arrival at London; with some remarks for the use of travellers (book xi, ch. 9)[5]

---

[1] Book xi, ch. 8; Henley ed., iv.285.
[2] Book v, ch. 10; Henley ed., iii.258.
[3] Henley ed., iv.348.   [4] Henley ed., iii.201.   [5] Henley ed., iv.290.

for instance, or: 'Containing little more than a few old observations' (book xii, ch. 9).[1]

These various practices combine to prevent *Tom Jones* from becoming in fact what in theory it could have been: a novel whose moral significance was expressed wholly through its characters and the complex plot in which they are involved. Despite its more sophisticated didactic plan it still retains some of the loose-leaf, episodic quality of *Joseph Andrews*.

2

Both Fielding's didactic scheme and the plot in which he embodies it require that Tom should be more strongly individualized than was Joseph Andrews. His character as a good-natured but imprudent young man is essential to the action. Two other figures in the novel, Allworthy and Sophia, are based on people whom Fielding greatly revered: his patron, Ralph Allen,[2] and his first wife, Charlotte.[3] They too, therefore, are taken seriously. Fielding does not, as in *Joseph Andrews*, merely subject his leading characters to a succession of accidents, but to a great extent founds his plot on the personalities of the three protagonists.

The result is that *Tom Jones* is a much more realistic novel than *Joseph Andrews* in the sense of conveying the existential quality of people and places. Fielding buttresses this sense of reality by observing certain formal standards of verisimilitude. His hero and heroine grow up on neighbouring estates in a fairly exact Somersetshire location. Their separate journeys are described with scrupulous concern for time and geography, and their final adventures take place in a series of precisely specified locales in London.[4] Moreover real-life characters such as Mrs. Whitefield[5] and Beau Nash[6] make brief appearances, and the final two-thirds of the book is

---

[1] Henley ed., iv.338.
[2] See Cross, ii.162 ff.
[3] Book iv, ch. 2; book xiii, ch. 1; Henley ed., iii.146–7; v.31.
[4] (e.g.) Tom is imprisoned in the Gatehouse, Mrs. Miller's home is in Bond Street, and Squire Western's lodgings are in Piccadilly.
[5] Book viii, ch. 8; Henley ed., iv.92 ff.
[6] Book xi, ch. 4; Henley ed., iv, 262–3.

set against the background of the '45. Perhaps this last point is as significant as any in revealing Fielding's intentions; the invasion has very little bearing on the plot, and can therefore serve only to lend circumstantiality to the events of the narrative.

Fielding is also much freer with realistic details of travelling, eating, and drinking than in *Joseph Andrews*. When recovering from the injury he received from Northerton: 'Jones swallowed a large mess of chicken, or rather cock, broth, with a very good appetite, as indeed he would have done the cock it was made of, with a pound of bacon into the bargain . . .' (book vii, ch. 14).[1] As in the previous novel, gratuitous passages of naturalistic dialogue contribute to the sense of actuality:

'The road to Bristol!' cries the fellow, scratching his head: 'Why, measter, I believe you will hardly get to Bristol this way tonight.' 'Prithee friend, then,' answered Jones, 'do tell us which is the way.' 'Why, measter,' cries the fellow, 'you must be come out of your road the Lord knows whither; for thick way goeth to Glocester.' 'Well, and which way goes to Bristol?' said Jones. 'Why, you be going away from Bristol,' answered the fellow. (book vii, ch. 10)[2]

Fielding is interestingly explicit on one occasion about this use of realistic detail. He has described how Mrs. Miller's little girl wept to hear of the imprisonment of Jones, 'who used to call her his little wife, and not only gave her many playthings, but spent whole hours in playing with her himself'. The author goes on:

Some readers may, perhaps, be pleased with these minute circumstances, in relating of which we follow the example of Plutarch, one of the best of our brother historians; and others, to whom they may appear trivial, will, we hope, at least pardon them, as we are never prolix on such occasions. (book xvii, ch. 2)[3]

Fielding consistently styles himself a 'historian', of course, but unlike the true historian he has to fabricate his own reality. The more frequent introduction of such 'minute circumstances' as those mentioned in the passages quoted above implies that in *Tom Jones* this 'reality' will be closer to everyday experience than it was in *Joseph Andrews*.

[1] Henley ed., iv.46.   [2] Henley ed., iv.20–21.   [3] Henley ed., v.253.

That the episodes composing the plot are to some extent modified by this changed emphasis, can be seen by an examination of particular incidents: Tom's last adventure before reaching London is a convenient example.[1] He is riding towards Highgate with Partridge and a guide, when 'a genteel-looking man, but upon a very shabby horse' asks if he may join them. The four proceed for some time, making conversation, till the stranger pulls out a pistol and demands from Tom the one-hundred-pound note he knows him to be carrying. Tom, though proferring all his own money, refuses to surrender the note, and when the highwayman threatens to shoot, he seizes the pistol and soon overpowers him. His assailant begs for mercy, claiming that this is his first robbery and that he has been driven to it by the distress 'of five hungry children, and a wife lying in of the sixth'. After testing the truth of his story Tom releases him and gives him a couple of guineas. The man returns home promising never to resort to crime again.

Unlike the two highway robberies in *Joseph Andrews*, this one has a part to play in the total story. Tom's readiness to help even the man who has tried to steal from him is one of the most striking demonstrations of his good-nature. Furthermore the highwayman, unlike those of the earlier novel, is to reappear. It later transpires that he is a cousin of Tom's landlady, Mrs. Miller, and it is gratitude for this kindness to her relative that prompts her bold and effective championing of Tom before Allworthy and Sophia. So this encounter, as well as illustrating Tom's basic goodness, is instrumental in rewarding it, and therefore relevant to both theme and plot.

The actuality of *Tom Jones* as a whole is enhanced by the continuity of detail from episode to episode. Here there is a sound motive for the robbery in the hundred-pound note of Sophia's which Tom has found. Quite plausibly his possession of it is made known through the chatter of Partridge, who has been characterized throughout by thoughtless garrulity. The courage and activity which enable Tom to overpower his attacker have also been previously displayed in

[1] Book xii, ch. 14; Henley ed., v.26 ff.

the novel. These are hardly significant, being merely by-products of his status as a hero; but the sword with which he stands guard over his opponent is a notable detail in the book's continuity. Tom buys it to fight a duel with North-erton,[1] and uses it in his duel with Fitzpatrick. Altogether, then, the robbery and its result are not arbitrarily imposed on the narrative, but derive from certain pre-existent circum-stances concerning Tom.

Yet despite all this the actual narration of the robbery retains much of the diagrammatic quality of its counter-parts in *Joseph Andrews*. As in the earlier novel, the attack is introduced in mid-sentence, which minimizes the element of drama. And Tom's reaction—'Jones was at first somewhat shocked at this unexpected demand'—is inappropriately mild. This paragraph and the next—which concludes with Tom overpowering the highwayman—have an oddly unreal quality, and the reason seems to be Fielding's inadequate imaginative realization of the scene as a whole. He makes no attempt to describe the highwayman's approach to the com-plicated feat of holding up three horsemen with one pistol. Not for some time is it explained that Partridge has tried to flee, and has been thrown from his horse; while the where-abouts of the guide during the period remains vague. Field-ing's use of indirect speech almost throughout the scene is typical of his undramatic approach to it.

What all this amounts to is that the level of reality in Fielding's account of the adventure is far lower than that of such passages as those quoted at the beginning of this sec-tion. There are two reasons for this disparity. One is Fielding's concern with exploiting the local potentialities of the incident. Just as he chooses, when describing the dis-covery of the infant Tom, to highlight the reactions of Mrs. Wilkins in the interests of making a mild satirical point, so here, as arbitrarily, he highlights those of Partridge. The pedagogue is shown in confident mood before the event:

' . . . for my own part, I never was less afraid in my life; for we are four of us, and if we all stand by one another, the best man in England

[1] Book vii, ch. 14; Henley ed., iv.46 ff.

can't rob us. Suppose he should have a pistol, he can kill but one of us,
and a man can die but once—That's my comfort, a man can die but
once.'[1]

During the engagement, however, he tries to flee, falls off
his horse, and lies roaring for mercy. He afterwards excuses
himself: '"A thousand naked men are nothing to one pistol;
for though it is true it will kill but one at a single dis-
charge, yet who can tell but that one may be himself?"'[2]
This is a 'reversal' very similar to that which exposes the
Patriot in *Joseph Andrews*.[3] Here there can be no very
pungent satirical intention, since Partridge's total cowardice
is already well established, but the change of front makes a
pleasant comic point. It means, however, that Partridge's
part in the incident has been predetermined by considerations other than those of drama and truth to life.

The other reason for the discrepancy in narrative convention is one that was of only minor importance in *Joseph
Andrews*: Fielding's plot is too artificial for his material.
In many parts of the novel, and particularly in the linking
passages between episodes, he uses much realistic detail.
But the episodes themselves cannot be realistically narrated,
partly because they are too multifarious, partly because in
almost every case certain elements must be subordinated in
the interests of the points essential to Fielding's complex plot
or his didactic theme.

In the highwayman scene attention is concentrated on
Tom's conduct. He is civil to his attacker, but shows a calm
determination, even though his life is in danger, not to give
up Sophia's note. When he has overcome his assailant he
rejects Partridge's demands that he kill him, but on the
other hand he does not release him or give him money until
he has probed the truth of his claims. It will be recalled that
Fielding's Good-natured Man is characterized by 'a constant regard for desert'.

It is surely to concentrate on these various worthy reactions of Tom that Fielding has minimized the drama of the
encounter. The last chapter suggested that certain incidents
in *Joseph Andrews* seem no more than means to a didactic

---

[1] Henley ed., v.27.   [2] Henley ed., v.30.
[3] Book ii, ch. 9; Henley ed., i.156 ff.

end. The highwayman episode in *Tom Jones* is more plausibly related to the story as a whole, and serves a narrative as well as a didactic purpose, but its limited reality makes it appear similarly a mere means to an end.

Many of the episodes in *Tom Jones* are even more sketchily narrated. The 'childish incident' which shows 'a good-natured disposition in Tom Jones' is allotted a whole chapter, but the incident itself is disposed of in two sentences:

The reader may remember that Mr. Allworthy gave Tom Jones a little horse, as a kind of smart-money for the punishment which he imagined he had suffered innocently.

This horse Tom kept above half a year, and then rode him to a neighbouring fair, and sold him. (book iii, ch. 8)[1]

In Book IV Tom catches Sophia when she is thrown from her horse, and breaks his arm in the process.[2] It is afterwards accepted in the novel that he has saved her life at the risk of his own.[3] Yet both propositions seem unlikely. It is hard to imagine how Tom could have been killed in catching Sophia; in fact in the total absence of explanation by Fielding it is difficult to see how he could even have broken his arm. Later in the novel, moreoever, Sophia falls from her horse without suffering any kind of injury.[4] Fielding seems to be invoking the formula of the hero venturing his own life to save that of his lover, without inventing a convincing narrative embodiment of it.

Yet if these incidents are not retailed with much conviction, they at least produce appropriate narrative repercussions. Tom narrowly escapes chastisement for selling his horse, explains his reasons to Allworthy and is forgiven. The setting of Tom's broken arm is described, and he is afterwards shown as confined to bed for a period. Even the highwayman episode is given a suitable emphasis through the bulking out of the chapter with comment and moralizing. But there are some happenings necessary to the plot which are given almost no narrative weight at all. For

[1] Henley ed., iii.132.
[2] Chapter 13; Henley ed., iii.195.
[3] (e.g.) Book iv, ch. 13; book v, ch. 6; Henley ed., iii.196, 236.
[4] Book xi, ch. 2; Henley ed., iv.249.

instance the only reaction to Bridget Allworthy's death is that her brother drops 'a tender tear', and commits the funeral arrangements to Blifil.[1] Allworthy himself never alludes to his sister again, and Tom, who is elsewhere portrayed as above all a warm-hearted youth, shows no grief at all. The affair of Mrs. Hunt's proposal to Tom is introduced without any narrative preamble. Presumably he is supposed to know her quite well since she remarks in her letter that she has heard from the Millers 'that neither my person, understanding, or character are disagreeable to you',[2] but Fielding simply evades the task of developing this relationship within the narrative. Because he is relating the 'history' of Tom in terms of the events directly relevant to an elaborate plot, he naturally leaves a number of such gaps.

Fielding clearly borrows this plot from the artificial comedy, and he takes from the same source other features of technique equally formal. One of these is the stereotyping of reactions and dialogue. In moments of emotional crisis Sophia faints, or nearly faints;[3] when she and Tom are worried they 'pass sleepless nights';[4] Mrs. Miller 'falls to her knees'[5] to express gratitude or supplication. Partridge, bringing Tom the news of his 'incest': ' . . . came stumbling into the room with his face paler than ashes, his eyes fixed in his head, his hair standing on end, and every limb trembling'.[6] Some emotions are formalized still more melodramatically. When Tom is first turned away by Allworthy he suffers a kind of frenzy: 'Here he presently fell into the most violent agonies, tearing his hair from his head, and using most other actions which generally accompany fits of madness, rage and despair.'[7] When he finds Sophia has left Upton without seeing him he falls on the wretched Partridge, who begs

---

[1] Book v, ch. 8; Henley ed., iii.250.

[2] Book xv, ch. 11; Henley ed., v.192.

[3] (e.g.) Book iv, ch. 14; book v. ch. 12; book vi, ch. 9; Henley ed., iii.197–8, 265, 306.

[4] (e.g.) Book v, ch. 3; book xiii, ch. 12; book xiv, ch. 3; Henley ed., iii.218; v.90, 101–2.

[5] (e.g.) Book xiv, ch. 6; book xvii, ch. 6; book xviii, ch. 8; Henley ed., v.121, 272, 336.

[6] Book xviii, ch. 2; Henley ed., v, 295.

[7] Book vi, ch. 12; Henley ed., iii.318.

for mercy: '... Jones, after staring wildly on him for a moment, quitted his hold, and discharged a rage on himself that, had it fallen on the other, would certainly have put an end to his being ...'[1] All these devices are ways of establishing that a character is adequately distressed, frightened, or otherwise moved by the situation in which the plot has involved him, without introducing distracting personal detail. Sometimes Fielding goes to the extreme of refusing to describe at all: 'What Sophia said, or did, or thought, upon this letter, how often she read it, or whether more than once, shall all be left to our reader's imagination.'[2]

Fielding's rhetorical dialogue also has a depersonalizing effect. At the climax of the book, for example, Tom's reconciliation with Allworthy has clearly to be of some intensity, yet for consistency's sake it cannot, alone of the emotional scenes, be interpreted realistically. Fielding therefore avoids portraying the beginning of the meeting: 'The first agonies of joy which were felt on both sides are indeed beyond my power to describe: I shall not therefore attempt it' (book xviii, ch. 10).[3] When direct speech is used it is highly rhetorical:

'O my dear uncle, this goodness, this tenderness overpowers, unmans, destroys me. I cannot bear the transports which flow so fast upon me. To be again restored to your presence, to your favor; to be once more thus kindly received by my great, my noble, my generous benefactor.' (book xviii, ch. 10)[4]

For Fielding the important thing is that Tom and Allworthy should be reunited with appropriate emotions and acknowledgements. Nuances of personal feeling are irrelevant to his purpose.

In *Joseph Andrews*, of course, serious speech and reactions had been similarly formalized. But there the hero and heroine were not taken too seriously, and emotional scenes were in any case few. In *Tom Jones*, however, Fielding has been at some pains to describe the love between Tom and Sophia from its minutest beginnings; it serves as a context

[1] Book xii, ch. 3; Henley ed., iv.309.
[2] Book xvi, ch. 3; Henley ed., v.212.
[3] Henley ed., v.345.   [4] Henley ed., v.345–6.

in which to judge the conduct of the pair. If the reality of their relationship is impaired by formal reactions and stilted address the novel loses much of its moral cogency. It is the problem of *The Modern Husband* all over again.

Ian Watt rightly suggests that *Tom Jones* exemplifies the principle that 'the importance of the plot is in inverse proportion to that of character'.[1] The action is constantly requiring various figures in the book to behave in a manner inconsistent with what has been revealed of their personalities. Tom, as hero, tends to be the principal victim. An interesting example of Fielding's failure to realize the effect of plot on characterization occurs in the fourth book. He accounts for Tom's early indifference to Sophia by explaining that he is already in love with Molly Seagrim. Tom feels a particular concern for Molly because he believes himself to be her first lover, and thinks he is responsible for her pregnancy. Not until he catches Square in her bedroom does he guess at her infidelity, his subsequent inquiries revealing further:

... that one Will Barnes, and not himself, had been the first seducer of Molly; and that the little child, which he had hitherto so certainly concluded to be his own, might very probably have an equal title, at least, to claim Barnes for its father. (book v, ch. 6)[2]

This allusion is the only evidence in the novel that Molly has in fact produced a child. Despite Tom's sense of obligation towards her, analysed at some length by Fielding, there is no hint of a concern for what he must assume to be his offspring. The actual birth has been allowed to pass without a reference. It might be added that it is chronologically almost certain that Molly initially succumbs to Square either in the last stages of pregnancy or the first weeks after childbirth.

The reason for this inconsistency is easily guessed. Molly has to be pregnant because it is through the physical fact of her pregnancy that Allworthy and thence Sophia learn of her affair with Tom. Once this aim has been achieved not only is Fielding no longer concerned with the incipient birth, he is obliged to play it down, since it will conflict with the

[1] *The Rise of the Novel*, p. 279. [2] Henley ed., iii.232.

necessary intervention by Square, and generate a moral issue irrelevant in that Tom is to be providentially exculpated.

This is a significant lapse on Fielding's part because it blurs a moral issue about which he is trying to be particularly precise. There seems little point in his devoting, as he does, a whole chapter to Tom's mental struggle about his love for Sophia and his duty to Molly,[1] when the child, who would surely be a primary object of concern, is never mentioned.

There is a parallel suppression in the account of what has proved the most widely criticized of Tom's sins—his acceptance of money from Lady Bellaston. Fielding simply does not attempt to motivate this uncharacteristic action. He only makes the affair itself plausible by withholding, until well after the event, the fact that the lady is of advanced years and has bad breath.[2] This is surely another case where the demands of the plot have taken priority over conservation of character. It is Tom's financial obligations to his mistress which cause him to resort to a letter of mock-proposal to be rid of her. And it is Sophia's sight of this letter which leads to the renunciation of Tom required by the plot.

The problem is not quite the same with the minor characters, since Fielding borrows from stage convention not only the artificial plot but also the system of characterizing the lesser *dramatis personae* through 'humours'. This puts them on a quite separate moral level, so that their motives cannot be treated as seriously as those of the major characters.

It was submitted in the previous chapter that Fielding's discussion of Lady Booby's motives suggested a concern for conservation of character which might lead towards a new psychological realism. *Tom Jones* is filled with such passages of analysis: they take the form of direct description, soliloquy, personification, and ironic comment; yet somehow the total effect is not of a greatly increased insight. The reason

---

[1] Book v, ch. 3; Henley ed., iii.215 ff.

[2] Book xiii, ch. 9; Henley ed., v.74. There is no previous description of Lady Bellaston.

for this is the absolute moral distinction between central and peripheral characters which, it was pointed out in an earlier chapter, is the inevitable result of mixing romantic and 'humorous' conventions of portrayal. Partridge's fear of the highwayman, for instance, is purely comic: it is not set in the perspective which reveals Tom's conduct as courageous and generous. One of Partridge's humours (the characterization is a compound of several) is cowardice—Fielding does not have to justify each fresh instance of it. What 'humorous' characterization entails, in fact, is that characters are limited to one or two motives only.

The technique has its usefulness in a complex plot such as that of *Tom Jones*, since the eccentricity of a particular figure can often be made the motive for an unlikely action important to the story. Western, for example, is drawn from the pursuit of Sophia by the sight of a hunt;[1] his sister relaxes her severity when her vanity is applied to.[2] It also means, however, that these characters fall outside the moral system by which Fielding judges the conduct of Tom. It is revealed in the course of the narrative that Western is a fool and a sot, that he treated his wife like an unpaid servant,[3] and that his attitude towards his daughter's marriage is brutally wrong-headed. But since all these failings derive from a 'humorous' portrayal which is comic in intention, they are never adequately condemned. Western is freely forgiven by Tom, and soon becomes an idyllically happy grandfather. Sophia's cousin Harriet makes a rash marriage, and is at once abandoned by both her aunt and her uncle; but again Fielding avoids an assessment either of Harriet's moral responsibility in making the marriage and later deserting her husband, or of the Westerns' in rejecting her appeals for help. She is simply defined as promiscuous, being finally left living in well-paid sin, and hence exempt from both poverty and pity.

In such cases, of course, the plot requires that the character carries out certain actions—Western must insist on the marriage with Blifil; Harriet must betray Sophia's where-

---

[1] Book xii, ch. 2; Henley ed., iv.304 ff.
[2] Book xvii, ch. 4; Henley ed., v.262 ff.
[3] Book vii, ch. 4; Henley ed., iii.344 ff.

abouts to her aunt. Fielding is not concerned with their ethics. Certainly there have been novels in which the morality only of a selected character or characters was studied, with the rest of the cast relegated to mechanical status. In *Tom Jones*, however, Fielding seems unaware of any psychological distinction between his major figures and his minor ones, advancing incidental comments on various of the latter, which their limited potentiality makes it impossible for them to sustain. Mrs. Western, for example, is on one occasion described as 'a woman of a very extraordinary good and sweet disposition' with 'great affection for her brother, and still greater for her niece';[1] yet Fielding never has the chance to display these qualities in her, or indeed any outside the humours she embodies. Similarly, many of his passages of psychological analysis deal with the motives of characters as little open to moral alternatives as Black George and Sophia's maid, Honour. In such cases he invariably proves to be justifying an unlikely piece of behaviour, or making a comic point about human reasoning in general, rather than to be concerned with the ethical responsibility of the character in question. So that, while in theory he is expounding the motives of all his characters from a consistent narrative vantage-point, in fact he regards the majority of them as morally negligible, though he does not admit it. It is another aspect of the fact that *Tom Jones* is written on more than one level of reality.

3

It is a convenient over-simplification to suppose that *Tom Jones* was conceived in three stages. First Fielding decided on his moral theme, then he composed a story to illustrate it. Finally he incorporated all kinds of local incident and comment to reinforce both the narrative and the didactic interest.

The latter process is similar to that which had already produced the best of *Joseph Andrews*. This chapter has tried to show, among other things, that the moral scheme was an ambitious one, demanding a complex embodiment. But it

[1] Book vi, ch. 2; Henley ed., iii.279–80.

should also be emphasized how much Fielding's technique of story-telling contributes to the total effect of the novel. *Tom Jones* has been called 'the most lively book ever published'; and it is easy to see why. The story is told in a sequence of brief and immensely diversified episodes; the plot is full of twists and surprises; serious and comic are consciously alternated. Yet with all this the main end of the novel is never lost sight of. Fielding shows a control of pace and development far in advance of Richardson or even Marivaux. It is easy to undervalue all these qualities as being somehow independent of the literary stature of *Tom Jones*. But its remarkable readability is not unimportant or accidental; it stems from an elaborate and original technique for stimulating the reader's attention.

It cannot be denied, however, that the artificiality of this technique contrasts awkwardly with the realism of certain passages of the novel. In Fielding's lengthy description of Allworthy's house and estate,[1] for example, and of various minor details of the way of life there, he establishes a plausibly full context which he sometimes tries to draw upon; as when he describes Bridget Allworthy's growing fondness for Tom, which rouses the jealousy of Square,[2] or Tom's own relationship with Blifil: '... for Jones really loved him from his childhood, and had kept no secret from him, till his behaviour on the sickness of Mr. Allworthy had entirely alienated his heart ... ' (book vi, ch. 7).[3] Yet these associations can never be substantiated in practice because of the arbitrary demands that the plot requires Fielding to make of his characters. The household can never become an imaginable entity because Allworthy's knowledge of Tom, or Tom's of Blifil, must never be made real enough to interfere with the pattern of deception on which the action is to depend. The characters have predestined roles, which the realism of their behaviour and relationships must not be allowed to impair.

It may be that Fielding himself sometimes felt the disparity of his methods. For instance he makes a rather

---

[1] Book i, ch. 4; Henley ed., iii.26–27.
[2] Book iii, ch. 6; Henley ed., iii.130.
[3] Henley ed., iii.299.

desperate effort to explain away Allworthy's tolerance of Thwackum:

... for the reader is greatly mistaken if he conceives that Thwackum appeared to Mr. Allworthy in the same light as he doth to him in this history ... Of readers who ... condemn the wisdom or penetration of Mr. Allworthy, I shall not scruple to say that they make a very bad and ungrateful use of that knowledge which we have communicated to them. (book iii, ch. 5)[1]

This amounts to an admission that his comically exaggerated depiction of Thwackum disqualifies the character from any plausible relationship with the more realistically drawn Allworthy.

These inconsistencies not only reveal an important weakness in Fielding's narrative convention, they also help to limit the moral effectiveness of the book in several ways. First, a number of actions become less meaningful because of the diminished actuality of the context. At the simplest level, for example, Tom's generosity in giving the highwayman more than half his remaining small capital does not emerge very forcefully, because money is casually regarded throughout; none of the major characters is ever shown in hunger or want. Then, because of the different levels of characterization in the novel, the humane tolerance Fielding shows towards Nancy's pregnancy or Anderson's resort to highway robbery is never felt to be truly comprehensive. He insulates his hero and heroine from any such painful moral predicament. Finally, because he is sometimes obliged to be arbitrary about the motives of his leading character, the moral criteria he is proposing become blurred. The controversy about the 'corruptness' of the work, from the time of Dr. Johnson onwards, stems from the fact that Fielding's plot obliges him to make Tom perform actions inconsistent with his general role in the book's ethical scheme.

Tom Jones, then, is no more a coherent whole than *Joseph Andrews*. Its didactic and narrative excellences are not only independent of, but almost inconsistent with, one another. None the less it is difficult to see how Fielding could have projected his moral scheme in any other way than by means

---

[1] Henley ed., iii.125.

of the artificial plot. His concentration on Tom's morality shows up the helplessness of individual merit in the eighteenth-century social system. A more virtuous Tom who was merely the son of Jenny Jones could not have been rewarded by marriage with Sophia; a much wickeder Tom who was truly heir to the Allworthy estates, would have had her as a matter of course. The artificial plot is Fielding's means of bridging the gap between moral worth and material reward. It enables him to avoid answering the question that suggests itself so often in the course of the story: can he endorse a social system whose standards are not only irrelevant to the morality he is preaching, but often run counter to it? It is probably because his work as a magistrate compelled him to face this problem, that *Amelia* was to prove a much more sombre, cynical work, bitterly critical of many aspects of eighteenth-century society.

VIII

AMELIA

In Book IV, chapter 3, of *Amelia*, after a conversation
between Mrs. Booth and her children, Fielding comments: 'This little dialogue, we are apprehensive, will be
read with contempt by many; indeed, we should not have
thought it worth recording was it not for the excellent
example which Amelia here gives to all mothers.'[1] Such
explanations confirm what the title of the novel suggests,
that its main didactic interest is to lie in the characterization
of the heroine. Amelia is the ideal wife and mother, and a
large part of Fielding's intention is to present her conduct,
shown to be admirable in a wide variety of difficult situations,
as an example to be followed.

As Sherburn has shown,[2] however, there is another
important didactic theme in *Amelia*. Booth, the hero, is
depicted as a deist, or even an atheist, his moral courage
sapped by his belief that men always act according to their
passions, and that their conduct can therefore have 'neither
merit nor demerit'. Sherburn claims: 'It was the psychological and moral task of the novel to rescue Booth from this
mental state.'[3] He connects this weakness in Booth with
yet a third theme, that of the corruptness of the aristocracy.
All the great men who appear in the novel are worthless and
self-interested. The Church, the Army, and the legal profession are all shown to be tainted with decadence.

Oddly enough, Sherburn does not quote Fielding's own
statement of his intentions in the dedicatory letter to Ralph
Allen: 'The following book is sincerely designed to promote
the cause of virtue, and to expose some of the most glaring
evils, as well public as private, which at present infest the

---

[1] Henley ed., iv.191.
[2] 'Fielding's *Amelia*: An Interpretation', *ELH*, iii (1936), 1–14.
[3] p. 7.

country ... '¹ The first of these intentions recalls Fielding's claim in *Tom Jones* to be 'recommending goodness and innocence'. Clearly the conduct of Amelia, and possibly the conversion of Booth, is referred to, though in each case Fielding is going well beyond the mere demonstration of good-nature. The second aim, however, is a new one. Fielding's earlier writings had contained incidental comment on specific injustices, but only in *Amelia* does social reform become an important motive. A year previously *An Enquiry into the Causes of the Late Increase in Robbers* had been published,² and a year later appeared *A Proposal for Making an Effectual Provision for the Poor*.³ Clearly Fielding's work as a magistrate had made him more aware of flaws in the country's legal and social administration.

Since *Amelia* involves three major didactic themes it is not surprising to find that Fielding's theoretical ideas about narrative structure have to be subordinated. None the less the extent to which the standards outlined in *Joseph Andrews* and *Tom Jones* are neglected is fairly remarkable—sufficiently so to cast some doubt on the seriousness of the theorizing concerned. There are no introductory chapters, and many incidents have no connexion with the plot, which is in any case random and diffuse; the mock-heroic element has been altogether excluded, and the comi-prosai-epic has been practically stripped of comedy.

Apart from this, the subject-matter of *Amelia* suggests that Fielding is trying to write a new kind of narrative. The journey which plays so important a part in *Joseph Andrews* and *Tom Jones* is missing. Moreover, although the story is again about love, the hero and heroine are in this instance already married. Fielding seems almost to be discarding, then, two of the important ingredients of his previous novels—romantic interest and picaresque variety— choosing rather to rely on the intrinsic possibilities of material drawn from ordinary contemporary life. In conception at least, *Amelia* is far closer to being a realistic novel than either of its predecessors.

---

¹ Henley ed., vi.12.
² January 1751. *Amelia* appeared in December 1751.
³ January 1753.

Understandably, therefore, it presents new problems of construction. In each of the earlier books the hero's journey and, of course, his progress towards marriage, do much to provide development. *Amelia* lacks these obvious sources of continuity. The only external clue to Fielding's plans for controlling his new kind of material is the statement in *The Covent-Garden Journal* that his model had been Virgil.[1] Yet apart from the initial use of reminiscence to bring the story up to date there is little trace of this influence.[2] *Amelia* seems less to have been conditioned by the requirements of a theoretical narrative scheme than were either of the other novels.

I

Of the three main didactic themes in *Amelia* that of public corruption is the one which has most influence on the action of the story. The entire plot of the novel, from the time Booth leaves prison, derives from the fact that he cannot gain the deserved advancement which would rescue his family from their financial plight.

Booth is shown as having direct recourse to three influential acquaintances. His old friend Colonel James advises him to re-enter the Army, but soon becomes attracted to Booth's wife, and hence willing to serve him only in so far as it will assist his own chances of enjoying Amelia. Booth's other main hope, the Noble Lord, from the very beginning merely feigns a readiness to help, and merely because he, too, hopes to get Amelia into his power. Neither is in the least concerned with the merits of Booth, the sufferings of his family, or the needs of the Army. Moreover Fielding is careful to show that it would be an easy task for either of them to procure Booth a commission. The Noble Lord obtains one for Atkinson in twenty-four hours, when he is

---

[1] *The Covent-Garden Journal*, i.186.

[2] L. H. Powers lists a number of parallels in his article 'The Influence of the *Aeneid* on Fielding's *Amelia*', *MLN*, lxxi (1956), 330–6. Most of them are absurdly far-fetched. It does not seem to have been suggested that Booth's tour of the prison (book i, chs. 3 and 4; Henley ed., vi.22–24, and 26–31) might well be an ironic parody of Aeneas' trip to the underworld.

deceived into thinking that he will thereby gain favour with Amelia; James gets places for two of his footmen within a fortnight.[1]

Booth's last resource is the Great Man whom, on Bound's advice, he bribes with the fifty pounds which Amelia has scraped together at the cost of a visit to the pawnbroker. The money is at once accepted, but there is again no intention of serving Booth. Fielding comments explicitly:

> Here I shall stop one moment, and so, perhaps, will my good-natured reader; for surely it must be a hard heart which is not affected with reflecting on the manner in which this poor little sum was raised, and on the manner in which it was bestowed. A worthy family, the wife and children of a man who had lost his blood abroad in the service of his country, parting with their little all, and exposed to cold and hunger, to pamper such a fellow as this!
>
> And if any such reader as I mention should happen to be in reality a great man, and in power, perhaps the horror of this picture may induce him to put a final end to this abominable practice of touching, as it is called; by which, indeed, a set of leeches are permitted to suck the blood of the brave and the indigent, of the widow and the orphan. (book xi, ch. 5)[2]

The ingenuous appeal in the second paragraph is evidence of the directly reformative impulse behind *Amelia*. Nor does it merely represent Fielding making didactic capital out of an incident essential to his plot. The number of extraneous examples of corruption in the novel show that the attack on current methods of preferment is central to its purpose. An old soldier named Bob Bound is introduced, for example, described by Booth as 'one of the scandals of his country'. After being commissioned by Marlborough 'for very particular merit' he has received no further promotion for thirty years.[3] By contrast Sergeant Atkinson's commanding officer is a boy of fifteen.[4] The case of Mrs. Bennet's first husband shows that the injustice extends even to ecclesiastical preferment. A peer who was a friend at college betrays all his promises of assistance; the Noble Lord pretends to interest

---

[1] Book xi, ch. 1; Henley ed., vii.244.
[2] Henley ed., vii.268.
[3] Book x, ch. 9; Henley ed., vii.236.
[4] Book iv, ch. 7; Henley ed., vi, 212.

himself in the young clergyman's affairs only in order to seduce the wife. In any event Dr. Harrison makes it clear that he regards the Church as partly responsible for the decadence of the country as a whole. In his argument with the young deacon he convicts a number of the clergy of avarice, ambition, and pride.

Altogether *Amelia* suggests an enormously widespread corruption among the country's leaders. Fielding does not hesitate to draw the pessimistic conclusion of his findings, his most explicit comment appearing in a chapter which provides yet another instance of administrative dishonesty. Dr. Harrison approaches a nobleman of his acquaintance on Booth's behalf, but the peer makes any assistance conditional on the doctor changing allegiances in a forthcoming election. In the argument that follows, the peer claims that Britain 'is as corrupt a nation as ever existed under the sun'. Dr. Harrison replies:

'If it be so corrupt . . . I think it is high time to amend it: or else it is easy to foresee that Roman and British liberty will have the same fate; for corruption in the body politic as naturally tends to dissolution as in the natural body.' (book xi, ch. 2)[1]

Short of condemning the system itself—an idea which never seems to occur to him—Fielding could hardly go further. Clearly the greatest of the 'glaring public evils' he had set himself to expose was the conduct of virtually all of society's leaders.

Fielding was justified in suggesting, as he does in this chapter, that Britain was on the verge of a total moral collapse, because he believed that the standards of a nation's rulers eventually influenced the conduct of the ordinary individual. This was by no means an idea peculiar to himself; Shaftesbury for instance, asserts:

THUS in *a civil* STATE or PUBLICK, we see that a virtuous Administration, and an equal and just Distribution of Rewards and Punishments, is of the highest service; not only by restraining the Vitious, and forcing them to act usefully to Society; but by making Virtue to be apparently the Interest of everyone . . . [2]

[1] Henley ed., vii.249.   [2] *Characteristicks*, London, 1733, ii.63.

9—T.R.

In his argument with the peer, Dr. Harrison puts forward a negative statement of the same view:

'Wherever true merit is liable to be superseded by favor and partiality, and men are intrusted with offices without any regards to capacity or integrity, the affairs of that state will always be in a deplorable situation ... But, my lord, there is another mischief which attends this kind of injustice, and that is, it hath a manifest tendency to destroy all virtue and all ability among the people, by taking away all that encouragement and incentive which should promote emulation and raise men to aim at excelling in any art, science, or profession.' (book xi, ch. 2)[1]

Within the novel there is at least one example of an individual being corrupted by the decadence of society. James, who in Gibraltar is a devoted friend to Booth, in England devotes himself to the pursuit of Amelia. When discussing James's conduct with her Dr. Harrison declares:

'The nature of man is far from being in itself evil; it abounds with benevolence, charity, and pity ... Bad education, bad habits, and bad customs, debauch our nature, and drive it headlong as it were into vice. The governors of the world, and I am afraid the priesthood, are answerable for the badness of it ... I am convinced there are good stamina in the nature of this very man; for he hath done acts of friendship and generosity to your husband before he could have any evil design on your chastity; and in a Christian society, which I no more esteem this nation to be than I do any part of Turkey, I doubt not but this very colonel would have made a worthy and valuable member.' (book ix, ch. 5)[2]

It seems very likely that the moral uncertainty which Sherburn traces in Booth was intended by Fielding as a manifestation of a similar corruption of an individual. In first describing Booth as 'a freethinker—that is to say, a deist, or, perhaps, an atheist', Fielding attributes his outlook to the fact of his believing 'that a larger share of misfortunes had fallen to his lot than he had merited'.[3] Certainly Booth's experiences in seeking preferment show that he is living in a society where merit and reward bear little relation to one another. The essence of his moral position is that he dis-

---

[1] Henley ed., vii.250.   [2] Henley ed., vii.145.
[3] Book i, ch. 3; Henley ed., vi.25.

believes in 'religion and virtue' since he considers that men always act according to the dictates of their passions. His beliefs can only be confirmed by the self-interested conduct of the great men to whom he applies; at one point he answers Amelia's protests at the selfishness of the aristocracy by reminding her that everyone is bound by necessity, so that only if his ruling passion is benevolence can a man be generous.[1] He has some grounds for disbelieving in 'religion and virtue' since he sees their influence so seldom.

It may well be, then, that by the phrase 'as well public as private' Fielding was implying an endeavour to expose both the corruptness of the State and the effects of this corruption on the individual. It must be admitted that if this is the aim Fielding does not quite achieve it. Booth's scepticism is never satisfactorily shown to derive from the amorality of society; nor, despite Sherburn's reasonable inference, are his misdeeds shown to derive from his scepticism. His moral beliefs are referred to at regular intervals,[2] but they never become clearly operative in the action. Moreover it is nothing in his unfortunate experiences which eventually causes him to alter his views, but a chance reading of Barrow's sermons.[3] In fact the strongest reason for supposing that Fielding wished to establish a connexion between his hero's deism and the decadence of society's leaders is that without such a connexion Booth's moral theory seems no more than a pointless idiosyncrasy.

The uncertainty here is probably due to the fact that Booth's failure to obtain promotion renders him morally impotent. He is confined to the verge of the court, with no prospect of employment and no obvious course of action open to him. The lack of moral courage which Sherburn describes cannot, in these circumstances, be easily demonstrated.

The situation which obscures the nature of his weakness, however, serves to emphasize Amelia's moral strength.

---

[1] Book x, ch. 9; Henley ed., vii.237.

[2] (e.g.) Book i, ch. 3; book ii, ch. 2; book iii, chs. 4, 5; book vii, ch. 10; book x, ch. 9; book xii, ch. 5; Henley ed., vi.26, 71, 121, 127–8; vii.113–14, 237, 313.

[3] Book xii, ch. 5; Henley ed., vii.312–13.

Even before the story proper begins she has been shown in Booth's account of his past to be a woman of great worth. What first draws him to her is the courage with which she faces the prospect of permanent disfigurement after her nose has been broken in a coach accident.[1] As a wife she has been devoted and self-sacrificing, submitting to her husband's authority and tending him patiently when he is sick.[2]

It is in poverty, though, that her virtue is most clearly displayed. Faced with crises which dwarf anything that Sophia, for instance, has to bear, she remains undaunted. When Booth is unemployed she consoles him: '"Fear nothing, Billy; industry will always provide us a wholesome meal, and I will take care that neatness and cheerfulness shall make it a pleasant one"' (book iv, ch. 3).[3] When he incurs gambling debts, instead of upbraiding him, she pawns the last of her possessions to obtain the money. Towards the end of the book she contemplates total penury still indomitable:

'I am able to labor, and I am sure I am not ashamed of it . . . why should I complain of my hard fate while so many who are much poorer than I enjoy theirs? Am I of a superior rank of being to the wife of the honest laborer? am I not partaker of one common nature with her?' (book xii, ch. 8)[4]

Amelia's chastity is, of course, amply attested by her rejection of Bagillard, James, and the Noble Lord. She will not consider the faintest compromise even when it seems the only possible means of freeing her husband from prison.[5] The extent of her generosity is epitomized by her free forgiveness of Booth's affair with Miss Matthews. But in addition to these cardinal virtues Fielding shows her to exemplify all kinds of minor domestic excellences. He depicts her as a good mother and hostess, and shows her at work in the house:

As soon as the clock struck seven the good creature went down into the kitchen, and began to exercise her talents in cookery, of which she was a great mistress, as she was of every economical office from the

---

[1] Book ii, ch. 1; Henley ed., vi.66.
[2] Book iii, ch. 7; Henley ed., vi.134.　　　　[3] Henley ed., vi. 185.
[4] Henley ed., vii, 333.　　　[5] Book viii, ch. 3; Henley ed., vii.74–5.

highest to the lowest; and as no woman could outshine her in a drawing-room, so none could make the drawing-room itself shine brighter than Amelia. And, if I may speak a bold truth, I question whether it be possible to view this fine creature in a more amiable light than while she was dressing her husband's supper, with her little children playing round her. (book xi, ch. 8)[1]

One of Fielding's main methods of 'promoting the cause of virtue' in *Amelia* was obviously to be a demonstration of true womanly goodness. By exposing his heroine to poverty he is able to show her nobility in a variety of trying situations from which she would be protected by the possession of money.

There are also several clearly defined subsidiary themes in the novel. Fielding widens the scope of his comment on female conduct through the insertion of the stories of Miss Matthews and Mrs. Atkinson. The first of these shows how immorality, the second how even a small compromise, can betray a woman into ruin: by contrast, of course, Amelia's virtue shines the brighter. The heinousness of adultery is another point the author labours. Dr. Harrison, for instance, is twice made to hint[2] at the view later advanced in *The Covent-Garden Journal*,[3] that adultery should be made punishable by law. Finally there is an insistence that morality has no connexion with class. Booth affirms early in the book:

'As it is no rare thing to see instances which degrade human nature in persons of the highest birth and education, so I apprehend that examples of whatever is really great and good have been sometimes found amongst those who have wanted all such advantages. In reality, palaces, I make no doubt, do sometimes contain nothing but dreariness and darkness, and the sun of righteousness hath shone forth with all its glory in a cottage.' (book iii, ch. 7)[4]

Plainly this idea is focused in the characterization of Atkinson. His worthy behaviour and the purity of his silent love for Amelia are implicitly, and at one point explicitly, contrasted to the hypocrisy and lust of James and the Noble

---

[1] Henley ed., vii, 282–3.
[2] Book ix, ch. 5; book x, ch. 2; Henley ed., vii.145, 189.
[3] *The Covent-Garden Journal*, ii.114 ff.   [4] Henley ed., vi.139.

Lord. When Atkinson, on what he thinks to be his death-bed, reveals to his foster-sister his secret devotion to her, she is understandably moved:

> To say the truth, without any injury to her chastity, that heart, which had stood firm as a rock to all the attacks of title and equipage, of finery and flattery, and which all the treasures of the universe could not have purchased, was yet a little softened by the plain, honest, modest, involuntary, delicate, heroic passion of this poor and humble swain; for whom, in spite of herself, she felt a momentary tenderness and complacency, at which Booth, if he had known it, would perhaps have been displeased. (book xi, ch. 6)[1]

Since the story has so heavy a didactic load to carry, it is not surprising that its structure should be subject to strain. Narrative interest is sustained by an arbitrary alternation of hope and fear concerning Booth's financial prospects and Amelia's chances of surviving the numerous attempts on her virtue. There is nothing to parallel the elaborate relation of incident to plot in *Tom Jones*. Fielding's complex of didactic purposes compels him to resort to a loose-leaf technique rather similar to that of *Joseph Andrews*, many characters and incidents having no narrative function whatsoever. Miss Matthews's story, for instance, which occupies much of the first book, is largely dispensable, and so is that of Mrs. Atkinson, which takes up nearly the whole of the seventh. Dr. Harrison's titled friend is introduced only for the purposes of the discussion on aristocratic decadence,[2] and the young deacon only for the long disputes about charity and the morality of the clergy.[3] In another gratuitous chapter Fielding makes Booth advance various literary views, and attack the current system of literary patronage.[4] He also finds occasion to canvass a number of specific legal issues. The chapter which describes Booth's prosecution of Betty[5] can have no other motive than to call attention to an anomalous law of theft. Elsewhere Fielding attacks the law

---

[1] Henley ed., vii.275–6.

[2] Book xi, ch. 2; Henley ed., vii.244 ff.

[3] Book xi, chs. 8, 10; Henley ed., vii.160 ff. and 173 ff.

[4] Book viii, chs. 5–6; Henley ed., vii. 83 ff. The episode extends into the beginning of the next chapter, p. 91.

[5] Book xi, ch. 7; Henley ed., vii.276 ff.

of perjury,[1] the practice of imprisonment for non-payment of legal fees,[2] the powers of bailiffs,[3] the law of evidence,[4] and the conditions affecting the granting of a search warrant.[5] Such demonstrations of particular weaknesses in the legal machinery are important to Fielding's didactic intention, but they are often embodied in incidents unrelated to the main story. There are signs that the author himself was aware of the dangers of irrelevance. In the 'trial' of *Amelia* in *The Covent-Garden Journal* the prosecution suggest 'That the Scene of the Gaol is *low and unmeaning*, and brought in by Head and Shoulders, without any Reason, or Design'.[6] The first edition of the novel contains a chapter in which Booth's little daughter contracts a fever, and after sinking fast under the ministrations of an ignorant physician and apothecary, is finally cured by the real-life Dr. Thompson, who is not recognized by the medical profession. Fielding concludes the episode: 'Some readers will, perhaps, think this whole chapter might have been omitted; but though it contains no great matter of amusement, it may at least serve to inform posterity concerning the present state of physic' (book iv, ch. 10).[7] He removed the chapter when revising *Amelia*. Clearly he had inserted it only to puff Dr. Thompson and to make an opportunity for his customary satire against the medical profession.

As usual he moralizes both directly and indirectly throughout the course of the book; but there are some interesting departures from previous practice. His own comments totally lack the light-heartedness of those in *Joseph Andrews* and *Tom Jones*. Gone almost completely are the ironic equivocations and the self-deprecating manner; Fielding is oracularly direct:

Here, reader, give me leave to stop a minute, to lament that so few are to be found of this benign disposition; that, while wantonness, vanity, avarice, and ambition are every day rioting and triumphing

---

[1] Book i, ch. 4; Henley ed., vi.28.
[2] Book i, ch. 4; Henley ed., vi.29.
[3] Book xii, ch. 5; Henley ed., vii.315–16.
[4] Book xi, ch. 3; Henley ed., vii.256.
[5] Book xii, ch. 7; Henley ed., vii.327–8.
[6] *The Covent-Garden Journal*, i.179.   [7] Henley ed., vi.232.

in the follies and weakness, the ruin and desolation of mankind, scarce
one man in a thousand is capable of tasting the happiness of others.
(book iv, ch. 4)[1]

The moralizing by characters in the book tends to be equally
severe. Dr. Harrison is far blunter than Allworthy, in both
the manner and the matter of his discourse. He threatens
Colonel Bath with damnation,[2] and on one occasion even
reduces Amelia to tears.[3] His lectures to the young deacon
are typical of his uncompromising style. Concerning the
ambitious cleric he asks rhetorically:

'Must he not himself think, if ever he reflects at all, that so glorious
a Master will disdain and disown a servant who is the dutiful tool of a
court-favorite, and employed either as the pimp of his pleasure, or
sometimes, perhaps, made a dirty channel to assist in the conveyance
of that corruption which is clogging up and destroying the very vitals
of his country?' (book ix, ch. 10)[4]

The greater seriousness of theme and tone is reinforced
by a greater seriousness of incident. Besides the breaking of
Amelia's nose, there are Booth's injuries and illness at
Gibraltar, the death of his sister, the shipwreck, and the
drowning of Mrs. Atkinson's mother. These all contribute
to a total picture much more sombre than that presented by
either of the two previous novels. Fittingly there are no
mock-heroics in the novel, and virtually no comic incidents.
Altogether the pessimistic implications of Fielding's didactic
themes gain credit from his new willingness to admit the
more painful contingencies of ordinary life.

2

The characterization of Atkinson and James provides a
useful index to the increased realism of *Amelia*. In their
general role as friends of the Booths they represent a new
departure for Fielding. Joseph Andrews and Tom Jones had
been depicted almost as solitaries. It is true that Tom
eventually becomes intimate with Nightingale, but for the
first twenty years of his life he apparently lacks even an

---

[1] Henley ed., vi.194–5.   [2] Book ix, ch. 3; Henley ed., vii.134.
[3] Book ix, ch. 4; Henley ed., vii.142.   [4] Henley ed., vii.176.

acquaintance of the same age and sex, except for the wretched Blifil. The friendlessness of his heroes is one aspect of Fielding's comparative neglect of social context in his first two novels. To a great extent he isolates his leading characters—most obviously, of course, by setting them on the road—so that their adventures take place in a kind of vacuum. In *Amelia*, however, hero and heroine are given a much fuller social definition. They are a married couple with three children, compelled by debt to take lodgings within the verge of the court. Booth is a half-pay subaltern and his wife a busy housekeeper. James and Atkinson are only two of a circle of friends from all walks of life, with whom they are in regular contact.

This careful 'placing' of the Booths adds greatly to the verisimilitude of the story. In the two previous novels the lack of background had conveniently limited the repercussions of any one incident. The episodes were so varied and prolific that Fielding would have been greatly embarrassed to depict them producing the consequences which would have ensued in real life. None the less, the reality of the story was impaired in that without this contextual perspective action tended to be weakly defined. In *Amelia* there can be no such stratification of incident, since the central characters are closely involved with a stable environment. If Booth is taken by the bailiffs the children cry and have to be comforted; if Amelia quarrels with Mrs. Ellison the family is obliged to change house.

The part played by James in the novel has a further interest. It was shown earlier in this chapter that he is explicitly an example of a worthy man corrupted by society. As such, he is a kind of character new in Fielding's work: a genuine mixture of good and bad. Fielding had often before claimed to be portraying such a figure, but in practice had only produced such characters as Diana Western, whose better qualities are mentioned but never exemplified, and Mrs. Waters, whose moral position is not really taken seriously. The nearest approach to such a mixed personality in the earlier novels is Tom Jones himself, and Fielding makes it clear that he regards his misdeeds, though real enough, as relatively minor: Tom never sins against Good-nature.

James, however, is thoroughly good at one juncture, and thoroughly evil at another; and there are other characters in the novel of similar moral complexity. Amelia's saviour, Mrs. Atkinson, is willing to compromise herself to some extent to gain a commission for her husband. Booth himself, in addition to his agnosticism, and his real guilt in the affair with Miss Matthews, is shown to have an inveterate weakness for gaming. On the other hand Trent, the pimp of the Noble Lord, has been a gallant soldier,[1] and even Mrs. Ellison is allowed a certain generosity.[2] Altogether *Amelia* shows a new degree of moral realism.

Atkinson is significant as being the first proletarian in Fielding's work to be given true dignity. In *Joseph Andrews* and *Tom Jones* the author's moral views were clearly conditioned by social preconceptions: Joseph and Fanny were virtuous, but they were patronized. The morality of the lower classes was not treated with the same seriousness as that of, say, Sophia. In a novel concerned with ethical fundamentals this was a severe limitation. Only in *Amelia* does Fielding come near to an objective moral view of society.

Since James and Atkinson are developed characters in their own right as well as being friends of the Booths, they represent yet another new departure in Fielding's narrative technique. The artificial comedy scheme, whereby the *dramatis personae* are divided into a small group of 'serious' characters, and a larger group of 'humorous' minor characters, has been almost abandoned. In *Tom Jones* not only were the leading figures friendless, but those characters who did surround them were nearly all comic puppets. Even Sophia's father and Tom's mother were made respectively booby-squire and prude. In *Amelia*, for the first time, there are several supporting characters drawn 'in the round'. The absolute moral and emotional distinction between major and minor figures has been largely removed.

All these factors contribute to the fabrication of a context which has much of the complexity of real life. Each character has a distinct relationship with the other characters, and

---

[1] Book xi, ch. 3; Henley ed., vii.256.
[2] Book vii, chs. 8, 9; Henley ed., vii.51, 57.

these relationships evolve in the course of the story. Atkinson marries Mrs. Bennet; Colonel James pursues and eventually possesses Miss Matthews; his wife is attracted to Booth, but soon gives up hope of winning him. This pattern of inter-involvement makes the sequence of encounters which Fielding exhibits far more psychologically intricate than anything in his first two novels. In the dialogue between Colonel James and Atkinson, for instance,[1] all that passes is conditioned by the colonel's hope of converting Atkinson into a pimp for obtaining Amelia's favours, and by the sergeant's own secret passion for his foster-sister. The discussion between the Booths and Dr. Harrison about the advisability of Amelia's accompanying her husband to the West Indies,[2] has as an undercurrent her knowledge that James wishes to keep her in England in order to seduce her. When Booth, later in the story, fiercely accuses his wife of having concealed James's advances, the real cause of his anger is shame at having lost fifty pounds at play. The chapter concludes: 'Thus the husband and wife became again reconciled, and poor Amelia generously forgave a passion of which the sagacious reader is better acquainted with the real cause than was that unhappy lady' (book x, ch. 6).[3] For the first time Fielding is making his dialogues reveal far more than is actually expressed.

The greater emphasis on social context in *Amelia* demands an increased amount of minor realistic detail. There are the dialogues with the children, for example, and the usual references to food and drink, which have more than the usual relevance in view of Amelia's domestic proclivities. Early in the novel the Booths are seen lunching on scrag of mutton;[4] on the night of her husband's final assignation with Miss Matthews Amelia has prepared his favourite meal, 'a fowl and egg sauce and mutton broth'.[5] The Booths meet few notable adventures and their pleasures are simple ones: a few visits, a trip to Vauxhall. Fielding des-

---

[1] Book viii, ch. 8; Henley ed., vii,100 ff.
[2] Book ix, ch. 4; Henley ed., vii.139 ff.
[3] Henley ed., vii.219.
[4] Book v, ch. 2; Henley ed., vi.234.
[5] Book xi, ch. 8; Henley ed., vii.282.

cribes how they pass an evening at home after a call from
Mrs. James:

> Booth and his wife, the moment their companion was gone, sat
> down to supper on a piece of cold meat, the remains of their dinner.
> After which, over a pint of wine, they entertained themselves for a
> while with the ridiculous behaviour of their visitant. But Amelia,
> declaring she rather saw her as the object of pity than anger, turned the
> discourse to pleasanter topics. The little actions of their children, the
> former scenes and future prospects of their life, furnished them with
> many pleasant ideas; and the contemplation of Amelia's recovery
> threw Booth into raptures. At length they retired, happy in each other.
> (book iv, ch. 6)[1]

In such passages as this, consisting of small particulars
irrelevant to the main story, Fielding sugests the daily
routine surrounding the central events he has chosen to
describe. Unlike Tom Jones or Joseph Andrews, the
Booths have a way of life.

It would be possible to adduce numerous circumstances
which contribute to this sense of actuality. Dr. Harrison's
mode of speech is one example. Many critics have found his
pedantic humour rather tiresome, but in fact it represents
Fielding's first attempt to characterize a figure through a
conversational habit not intrinsically comic.

The kind of force such minor details can be given is well
illustrated by the description of Amelia's lonely evening at
home when her husband is out gambling:

> At ten then she sat down to supper by herself, for Mrs. Atkinson
> was then abroad. And here we cannot help relating a little incident,
> however trivial it may appear to some. Having sat some time alone,
> reflecting on their distressed situation, her spirits grew very low;
> and she was once or twice going to ring the bell to send her maid for
> half a pint of white wine, but checked her inclination in order to save
> the little sum of sixpence, which she did the more resolutely as she had
> before refused to gratify her children with tarts for their supper from
> the same motive. And this self-denial she was very probably practising
> to save sixpence, while her husband was paying a debt of several
> guineas incurred by the ace of trumps being in the hands of his
> adversary. (book x, ch. 5)[2]

[1] Henley ed., vi.208.   [2] Henley ed., vii.214.

This brief description defines exactly the extent of Booth's folly in being drawn into gambling. He is squandering guineas at a time when his family must think in terms of pennies. For the first time in Fielding's novels money takes on real value; in *Joseph Andrews* and *Tom Jones*, the facility with which it is given, stolen, lost, and found, reduces it to a meaningless commodity. The Booths' financial plight can eventually be stated quite exactly by Amelia: "" . . . I believe all we have in the world besides our bare necessary apparel would produce about sixty pounds . . . "" (book x, ch. 6).[1]

The realistic detail, then, though not often as directly as in the instance quoted above, helps to supply moral definition. Amelia's devotion during her husband's illness carries more weight because he is convincingly sick, spitting blood and subject to 'violent sweats',[2] not suffering from the nominal disease of an Allworthy. Similarly, if on a rather different level, Booth's infidelity to Amelia seems appropriately sinful because of the contrast provided by her own resolute chastity and Atkinson's selfless devotion. In both large ways and small the realistic context gives meaning to Fielding's moral adjurations.

To praise the greater realism of *Amelia*, then, is not to imply that this kind of writing is in some absolute sense especially commendable. It is proper to this particular novel because essential to a full realization of the book's didactic purpose. If the total effect is at all confused, it is because a number of artificial elements have survived. The plot depends on the usual coincidences and deceptions: Booth has critically important re-encounters with three old acquaintances, Miss Matthews, Colonel James, and Atkinson, in each case purely by chance; Dr. Harrison is led to prosecute him through a misunderstanding; four characters in the book—Hebbers, Bagillard, Atkinson, and Robinson —are brought to the brink of death in order to precipitate some narrative issue, and afterwards revived. There are even episodes which derive straight from the comedy of intrigue: the deceits of the masquerade, for example, and Booth's entry into Mrs. Harris's house concealed in a wine-hamper.

[1] Henley ed., vii.216.
[2] Book iii, chs. 5, 7; Henley ed., vi.129, 134.

Above all, of course, it is only through a laborious 'discovery', similar to that in *The Temple Beau*, that the Booths' difficulties are finally resolved.

The Virgilian convention by which the chief characters bring their own histories up to date is also discordantly artificial. Booth, for instance, produces relevant letters which he happens to have in his pocket-book, and several times pauses in his account to explain away his unlikely feats of memory and mimicry.[1]

But the most limiting convention in the novel is that governing the characters' speech and reactions in moments of emotion; they are as crudely formalized as those in *Tom Jones*:

'Thou heavenly angel! thou comfort of my soul!' cried Booth, tenderly embracing her; then starting a little from her arms, and looking with eager fondness in her eyes, he said, 'Let me survey thee; art thou really human, or art thou not rather an angel in human form? O no!' cried he, flying again into her arms, 'thou art my dearest woman, my best, my beloved wife.' (book x, ch. 6)[2]

Since the harshness of the story demands that the Booths face a regular series of misfortunes, such stylized reactions are invoked again and again. 'O Heavens!', repeated at every crisis, gradually loses all force; Amelia faints five times and Miss Matthews twice, while Mrs. Atkinson has convulsions; Booth sheds tears on some ten occasions. Altogether the realism of context and incident in *Amelia* cruelly exposes the lack of any available technique for dramatizing strong emotions convincingly.

There are a number of miscellaneous factors which also diminish the actuality of the novel. One is Fielding's readiness to insert extraneous didactic matter even at the expense of narrative harmony. The chapter in which Booth airs his literary views in the bailiff's house makes him appear inappropriately cheerful; that where he pursues Betty inappropriately cruel. Similarly unrealistic are many of the purely emotional passages in the story. Fielding hints at the new trend in his dedication: 'The good-natured reader, if

---

[1] Henley ed. (e.g.), vi.72, 90, 111, 135, 154.
[2] Henley ed., vii.215–16.

his heart should be here affected, will be inclined to pardon
many faults for the pleasure he will receive from a tender
sensation . . . '[1] Clearly the growing cult of sentimentalism
was having its influence. In *Tom Jones* there had been traces of
such a tendency, and even 'A chapter which, thought short,
may draw tears from some eyes',[2] but little conscious striving after pathos. *Amelia*, however, contains a number of
scenes, such as that of Booth's parting from his wife on
leaving for Gibraltar,[3] which strive for effect through
inflated expressions of feeling, and are thus false to the
emotional realism of the book as a whole.

Fielding's moral objectivity seems slightly compromised
too, in that his attitude to certain of his characters is still
affected by social preconceptions. For instance Murphy, who
forges the will giving Amelia's estates to her sister, is
hanged; but Miss Harris herself, the instigator and main
beneficiary, is allowed to escape to France and given a small
income. Atkinson, who emerges in the story as a much
nobler figure than Booth, is rewarded only by a reasonably
happy marriage with Mrs. Bennet, the quick-tempered
blue-stocking.

The considerable realism of *Amelia*, then, is not sustained
in every aspect of the work. Fielding is still hampered, even
though unconsciously, by various moral and literary conventions of his time inconsistent with the kind of story he is
clearly trying to relate.

3

There is a variety of possible reasons why *Amelia* remains
the least regarded of Fielding's novels. Certainly it lacks the
gaiety of its two predecessors, but this would count for less
if it had fully accomplished its author's serious intentions.
Of the three main themes outlined earlier in this chapter only
that of Amelia's virtue is adequately realized; though insipid for some tastes she has never lacked admirers. The
other two themes make little impact. Booth's moral uncertainty is never expressed in action, and the final abrupt

[1] Henley ed., vi.12.   [2] Book xiii, ch. 10; Henley ed., v.77.
[3] Book iii, ch. 2; Henley ed., vi.111 ff.

conversion is rendered undemonstrable and largely unnecessary by his subsequent change of fortune. The corruption Fielding was attacking was of a kind particular to his
own time, so that his exposures rather lack force today.
Moreover, as Sherburn points out, he evades the full implications of the situation he describes by arbitrarily imposing a
happy ending.

This glib economic solution enables Fielding to beg most
of the moral questions he has been concerned to raise in his
novel. *Amelia*, as usual, is a story of love and money, but in
this case it seems that the money will have somehow to be
earned. Having demonstrated, however, that contemporary
society is too corrupt for a 'gentleman' to be able to make an
honest living, Fielding is content merely to provide a conventional escape for his particular hero. Early in the book he
shows an old man unjustly dying in prison;[1] but he reserves
such bleak objectivity for the margin of his story. Since
Amelia survives unscathed where Mrs. Bennet did not,
there is even an unrealistic suggestion that perfect virtue is
unassailable. The ethics of self-preservation in a corrupt
society are left unclear. Amelia is contemptuous of the ruse
by which Mrs. Atkinson wins a commission for her husband,
but Booth's own experience shows the futility of relying on
merit for preferment. Is it legitimate to cheat the corrupt?
Fielding's negative answer is a facile one, and the retirement
of the Booths into the country represents an admission of
defeat. The best the individual can hope for is to have
enough money to be able to preserve his virtue away from
society.

Amelia makes it clear that Fielding now saw the social
system which he automatically accepted, to be in an advanced stage of moral decay. It is not surprising, therefore,
that despite its happy ending the novel shows an extreme
pessimism. Character after character seems worthy but
proves treacherous: the Noble Lord, for example, Robinson,
James, Mrs. James, Miss Matthews, Mrs. Ellison, and even
Betty the maid. Booth's fellow officers in Gibraltar refuse to
help him when he is in financial need; his fellow farmers
systematically bankrupt him. Much of the incident is

---

[1] Book i, ch. 4; Henley ed., vi.27–28.

sombre: Booth's tour of the prison, the shipwreck,[1] the trip to Vauxhall with its unhappy outcome,[2] the gratuitously wretched deaths of Booth's sister and Mrs. Atkinson's mother.[3] The conclusion of the story is suitably gloomy. Colonel Bath has been killed in a duel, Mrs. Ellison has died of drink and the Noble Lord of venereal disease, 'by which he was at last become so rotten that he stunk above ground'; Amelia's sister has also 'died in a most miserable manner', and Robinson, of whose amendment Dr. Harrison had high hopes,[4] has relapsed into crime and been hanged. The total effect of *Amelia* is undeniably depressing.

There is a good deal of clumsiness both in the construction and in the telling of the story. Fielding's use of an artificial ending means that his hero, Booth, can do nothing to help himself, and that there is no crisis for the action to work towards. The insertion of incidents solely for didactic purposes gives the narrative a fragmentary quality. Moreover the centre of gravity of the novel is uncertain. The book gets under way with the story of Miss Matthews who, it unexpectedly transpires, is to play only a very minor part in the events to follow. Later the focus of interest is constantly shifted from Booth's preferment to Amelia's virtue and back again. These vacillations contribute to the disjointed quality of the work.

All these factors are relevant to the frequent underestimation of *Amelia*. But Dr. Johnson was probably near the mark in ascribing the short-term failure of the novel to Amelia's broken nose. She was the first heroine in English fiction allowed far enough out of the glass-case of idealism to injure her beauty. Compromised as was Fielding's realism in many respects, it was far too much for most of his contemporaries. In the 'trial' of the book in *The Covent-Garden Journal* the burden of the prosecution case is the repeated charge that *Amelia* is 'low'. Counsellor Town asks the Censor to: '. . . pass such a Sentence as may be a dreadful Example to all future Books, how they dare stand up in

[1] Book iii, ch. 4; Henley ed., vi.121–5.
[2] Book ix, ch. 9; Henley ed., vii.166 ff.
[3] Book ii, ch. 4 and book vii, ch. 2; Henley ed., vi.82–83 and vii.13.
[4] Book xii, ch. 8; Henley ed., vii. 337.

10—T.R.

Opposition to the Humour of the Age.'[1] Fielding had estimated very accurately the reasons for the unpopularity of his story. In trying, about a century too soon, to write a realistic, socially-reformative novel, he was not only straining the formal literary machine beyond its powers: he was ensuring incomprehension and commercial failure.

[1] *The Covent-Garden Journal*, i.179.

IX

CONCLUSION

O NE object of this book has been to demonstrate that many of Fielding's chosen narrative techniques were incompatible. Various specific incongruities have been pointed out by means of close analysis. In concluding it seems necessary to try to answer a question arising out of these analyses but only touched on in the preceding chapters: how important is this kind of discrepancy to the overall success or failure of the novels?

It seems safer to talk about one particular case than to generalize, and *Tom Jones* seems the obvious choice. Of this book Ian Watt remarks: ' ... [it] is only part novel, and there is much else—picaresque tale, comic drama and occasional essay'.[1] In its context Professor Watt's comment is narrower in scope than is apparent here. He has proposed that the lowest common denominator of the novel as a genre is the observance of 'formal realism', and he has shown how often Fielding departs from this standard. But it is surprising, after all, that the diagnosis is not true in a general way, as well as in Watt's special sense. The various component techniques he mentions do frequently retain too much of their intrinsic character to blend smoothly into the narrative as a whole. Yet although there are passages, and even whole episodes, which stand out awkwardly, there can be no doubt that Fielding's diverse methods do harmonize sufficiently to produce an effect as a totality. *Tom Jones* may be only 'part novel' in terms of formal realism, but generally speaking readers and critics have always reacted to it as to an inte-grated whole, and not as to a collection of amusing parts.

Moreover despite the many artificial aspects of the work this overall effect is realistic rather than otherwise. *Tom Jones* has always been read as a novel, not as a moral fable. Fielding

[1] *The Rise of the Novel*, p. 288.

scholars who carefully classify and analyse the various characteristics of Tom and Sophia are only rationalizing the reactions of the ordinary reader. The book is close enough to reality for the critic to think it reasonable to accuse Tom of hypocrisy for lecturing Nightingale on sexual morality, or Allworthy of gullibility for believing Blifil's lies. And this way of looking at the novel seems to answer to Fielding's own concepts. In the course of his brief career as a novelist he learns to discard many of his more formal devices—soliloquy for instance, and mock-heroic descriptions—and to develop the realistic aspects of his stories.

At first sight this seems to be the end of the inquiry. Fielding may have mixed his narrative methods, but thanks to some mysterious process of artistic fusion a unified result emerges. Ultimately, however, this is not a satisfactory conclusion. The total effect produced, it seems, tends towards realism. But in that case what has happened to the artificial features of the novel? They are so numerous that they must surely play some part in conditioning the reader's response. How does so heterogeneous a work as *Tom Jones* come to be construed as a coherent whole? And what kind of whole does the average reader think he is accepting?

These questions would be easier to answer if more were known about the way in which novels in general make their effect. Theoretical discussion of the genre has traditionally tended to rely on detailed analysis of separate elements: characters, plot and so on. The unstated assumption is that such analysis will amplify and elucidate the general impression gained by the intelligent reader. Indeed this is an inescapable belief if discussion of the novel is to be possible at all, for the general impression itself is by definition immune from close examination. If scrutinized it ceases to be a general impression. The critic's only resource seems to be to study what gave rise to it.

But there is none the less a clear and important difference between the impression the novel produces as a whole, and the sum total of the effects it yields up to analysis. A novel is a symposium of extraordinarily diverse information, but it is not to be judged merely on the quality of this information. The major distinction between the novel and the picaresque tale is that the information provided by the former coalesces into a credible picture of real life. But the novel is a fluid genre, which has always been in some sense experimental. No author can be certain in advance that a given detail of his narrative is going to 'take'. Not even the accepted master-pieces of the genre are wholly devoid of arbitrary or random elements. Certain words, or paragraphs, or even whole chapters, could be omitted without apparent loss, in that they do not contribute to the effect made by the narrative as a whole. A novel, in other words, is both more and less than the sum total of its parts.

This point is of particular relevance to a consideration of *Tom Jones*—or any of Fielding's novels—because, as this study has tried to show, the relationship of the part to the whole here is unorthodox by modern standards. The con-temporary reader, or even critic, assumes that a novel is primarily intended as a picture of real life, and that virtually all the information provided by the author will have been included with reference to this intention. But in the case of *Tom Jones* the choice of episodes was governed by no such principle. Many of the incidents which embody specific moral points have almost no relevance to the picture of life emerging from the story proper. The traditional method of analysis therefore leads to misconstruction. It will interpret as important to the effect produced by the narrative as a whole all kinds of detail deriving solely from some local purpose. For instance Allworthy has been described as a prig because of his sententious addresses to Jenny and to Dr. Blifil. Yet these speeches are included not to demon-strate an aspect of Allworthy's character, but to instruct the reader. Again, the account of Bridget Allworthy's life with her husband is designed not to show what kind of person she is, but to satirize a certain type of marriage which Field-ing thought to be deplorably prevalent.

Naturally the difference between Fielding's practice here and that of the modern novelist is only one of degree. All-worthy has to be shown as a character capable of sermoniz-ing, and his sister as a woman capable of suppressed lust and domestic hatred. But whereas the modern writer would feel constrained to root such striking tendencies deep in the characterization as a whole, Fielding is content simply to leave the Allworthys weakly and generally defined—he as a Good Man and she as a Prude—and manipulate them in different ways for a variety of local purposes.

In the chapter on *Tom Jones* a second way was noted in which an individual episode may provide information useless, or even misleading, from the point of view of the narrative as a whole, Fielding is sometimes cornered by his plot. Allworthy's belief that he is about to die (Book V, Chapter 7), for example, is not remotely intended to imply that he is a hypochondriac. Such return-trips to the brink of death are frequently arranged by Fielding to advance his plot. Similarly, Bridget's apparent transfer of affection from Square to Tom (Book III, Chapter 6) is not significant of anything in any of their characters—it is simply included to explain the otherwise unaccountable fact that Thwackum and Square, who are at variance on every other topic, happen to be united in hatred towards Tom.

On the other hand some of the information which Fielding provides solely to enhance the illusion of reality seems unlikely to survive at all in the reader's memory of the story. In the fourth chapter there is a fairly detailed account of Allworthy's estate and the surrounding countryside—yet this never proves relevant to anything in the ensuing action. Allworthy himself has earlier been described as a widower and the father of three deceased children—but there is no further reference to his ill-starred family. It is hard to see how this kind of information can become a living part of the narrative when it bears no relation to the story which is being told.

This kind of piecemeal criticism, however, is bound to be fragmentary and subjective, and seems unlikely to lead to any general conclusion. A more comprehensive approach to the problem may be suggested by an analogy from the visual arts concerning the way in which a painter's audience is likely to interpret the information he puts before them. In *Art and Illusion* Professor Gombrich devotes several chapters to a consideration of how a picture is 'read'—how the various patches of paint on a canvas come to be seen as representations of trees or clouds or people. It is shown that the man who looks at a picture has a natural tendency to assist in the illusion that is being presented to him. He will expect to see the colours concerned as a coherent pattern, and will as far as possible relegate to the background elements which are irrelevant to this pattern or which would impair it.

It seems likely that the way in which we react to the novel is a cognate process. We are so conditioned to reading a story in terms of a sustained illusion of reality, that only the most positive efforts on the part of the author could persuade us to view a narrative disjunctively. But there is the one obvious difference between the reading of a narrative and the 'reading' of a painting, that whereas the latter is characteristically an instantaneous process, in which the various constituent elements fuse into a distinct pattern at a glance, the former procedure is necessarily linear—the illusion cannot immediately be sensed, but defines itself as it emerges.

It is impossible to state precisely, even in the case of a single work, what the illusion created by a novel consists in. But the traditional idea that the novelist 'creates a world' suggests a clue. A novelist cannot handle all the eventualities and kinds of behaviour to be found in real life, but he can produce a lifelike effect by working with a limited number, mutually consistent. In theory his readers will not be able to make a certain judgement about the range within which he has decided to work until they have read the whole of the given novel. But in practice the general tendency of the action will suggest from the first the limits the author has set himself, and the way in which he tells his story will reinforce this suggestion. The illusion created by a novel, then, defines itself by an interaction of plot and tone. This interaction provides certain criteria for the automatic sorting process which the reader carries out as he goes through the novel. He is able to 'place' each episode in terms of the emerging pattern.

The fact that the novel produces a consecutive, and not an instantaneous, effect gives the novelist an advantage which the painter does not have. If a painting contains information at odds with the prevailing illusion the observer may register it as a disturbance—may have to make a deliberate effort to disregard it. But the reader of a novel, encountering items of information successively, can have little immediate certainty about the importance of the individual item. Each episode must be filed away in his memory. If it eventually proves to be unnecessary or discordant it may well be forgotten altogether. At first it seems possible that the description of Allworthy's estate and the account of his married life will prove significant to the story to follow. But as chapter follows chapter without either subject being referred to again, the information gradually recedes. Perhaps not one reader in ten will remember by the end of the book that Allworthy is a widower.

At first sight this winnowing process seems to operate only in Fielding's favour. The information he assembles rather haphazardly, without making overall coherence a primary consideration, is conveniently pruned and shaped for him by the subconscious of the modern reader. In fact, however, there is a considerable loss entailed. The reader who is interpreting an episode as a contribution to the illusion created by the novel as a whole is less likely to notice any intrinsic point it may be making. Part of Fielding's didactic intention is therefore liable to remain unfulfilled.

The major drawback, however, is something subtler and more serious than this. Fielding has often been praised for his use of irony and ambiguity—for the way in which he leaves the reader to draw many significant conclusions for himself. Often the author passes no final judgement on a character or situation. Often he suggests several possible points of view, implying that all of them would have to be taken into account in a fair estimate. It has been claimed that much of the richness and complexity of the novels derives from unresolved tensions between conflicting ways of looking at a single character or incident.

It may be argued, parenthetically, that Fielding sometimes makes a self-indulgent use of this sort of ambivalence. He gets a great deal of broad comedy out of Western by portraying him as the familiar booby-squire of artificial comedy, but he interpolates an account of his married life that is ruthlessly realistic. It happens to be convenient to the story that is being told that Western is both a comic character and a brutish sot, but what impression of his personality does

Fielding want the reader to take away? In this case the two possible readings cannot easily be reconciled: Western must be either basically endearing or basically repellant. By posing these alternatives without further explanation Fielding is evading a responsibility.

But the real weakness of this technique only becomes apparent when *Tom Jones* is considered in terms of the way it works as a totality. It has already been suggested that the plot and tone of the book will play the major part in determining what items of information the reader is likely to register as important, and what he is likely to relegate to the back of his mind as subsidiary. What frequently happens, therefore, is that of several possible readings left open by Fielding's irony only one survives in practice since it is the only one endorsed by the working of the text as a whole. To take two examples: there are a number of passages describing the tender nature of Tom's feelings for Molly Seagrim. Yet in general the part she plays is the familiar one of the comic whore. Tom's affair with Mrs. Waters at Upton is narrated lightly enough—in fact it is made the source of a series of farcical scenes. Later in the story, however, Tom comes to believe that he was committing incest. In retrospect the episode takes on a different character, potentially horrifying. Now it can be argued that these are two cases where Fielding points to a moral complexity without trying to resolve it. From one aspect Molly may be a whore, but from another she may be an object of love or compassion. Tom's night with Mrs. Waters may have seemed good fun at the time, but it could have led to tragedy. Tom was being irresponsible.

But the narrative illusion produced by *Tom Jones* as a totality admits in each of these cases only one of the possible readings. The reason is clear—in Professor Gombrich's words: 'Ambiguity cannot be seen.' While subject to the illusion created by a painting, we cannot *simultaneously* be aware that some element in it could be differently interpreted if considered outside the context of the illusion. The plot of *Tom Jones*, incorporating so much that is artificial and far-fetched, and its tone, light and often facetious, suggest that Fielding is claiming for his work only a limited seriousness, a limited reference to real-life standards of probability and morality. Conditioned to this level of response the ordinary reader will tend towards the simplest reading to the exclusion of the others. The night at Upton will seem good fun, and nothing worse: Molly will seem a comic whore, and nothing better. To generalize a point which seems relevant to criticism of the Novel in general: traditional methods of local analysis fail to allow for the fact that the part so analysed will be modified by its relationship to the novel as a whole. And it is basic to the way in which novels are written and to the way in which we respond to them, that the effect of the whole will predominate at the expense of that of the part.

The above comments on *Tom Jones* run counter to a notable trend in Fielding criticism. Professor Crane, for example, would see the limitation in the reader's response as a tribute to the author's controlling skill. If the reader never really believes that Tom will prove guilty of incest, this is because the book is, after all, a comedy. The incident may have serious implications, but these must not disturb the comic surface of the novel. It is precisely Fielding's careful adjustment of manner and matter that gives the book its remarkable unity.

But to accept this argument is to assume a control of narrative effects unlikely in an author experimenting in a brand-new form and preoccupied with the problem of projecting certain didactic views. Fielding would scarcely have been satisfied to evoke a general response too lighthearted to take in even the basic moral of *Tom Jones*—the need for prudence—and still less the continual flow of detailed ethical comment that the novel was designed to accommodate. Yet the moral seriousness of the book was not generally appreciated for a century and a half. The harmony that Crane finds is surely not the harmony that the author planned for his novel as a whole, but the harmony of the illusion that the modern reader finds in the story: something much simpler than Fielding intended.

To answer the question posed at the beginning of this chapter: the effect of the artificial elements in the novel is to persuade the reader that the narrative functions on the level of reality of, say, a Rowlandson print. Hence the difference between the response of the critic and that of the ordinary reader will inevitably be a radical one. The local subtleties which the former can find are often inoperative in an overall reading.

It happens, then, that although Fielding's novels tacitly lay claim to a prevailing moral delicacy and alertness, this complexity of approach is in practice often vitiated by the broad artificial comedy and the complex plotting which are also fundamental to his programme. Consequently it is hardly surprising that his novels do not succeed at quite the level at which they were intended to succeed. But it is surprising that there has been so comparatively little critical awareness of the interesting gap between intention and achievement. This may be taken as a tribute to the degree of success which Fielding does attain, or as a demonstration of the extent to which the novel has come to be automatically interpreted in terms of the illusion it creates.

It would be misleading, as well as ungrateful, to close the argument here. If, as this chapter has implied, Fielding's critics have in a sense overestimated his novels, it is because they have underestimated the extraordinary breadth of his theoretical scheme. His new form was intended at once to instruct and to entertain, and it was to do both by giving full scope to the author's personality as moralist, scholar, humorist, reformer, satirist and man of the world. The novels are epic in their comprehensiveness.

Very few, even of the most eminent English novelists, could have sustained this kind of programme. Fortunately Fielding had a personality rich enough to justify such full-scale exposure, and honourable enough to survive it. But the experiment might nevertheless have proved a failure. The major risk was not that the very various constituent parts would fail to cohere in terms of 'formal realism' or 'narrative illusion', but that they might fail to coalesce into any kind of unified undertaking whatsoever. Fielding might have produced, not a novel, but a box of tricks—a kind of premature, more serious *Tristram Shandy*. But in the event, of course, he achieves this preliminary unity with complete assurance. His main story has a sustained development and animation which draws the reader into, and through, the numerous digressions. The digressions themselves, though diverse in nature and purpose, are linked not only by an underlying consistency of attitude, but also by a consistent tone of voice.

The bustling plot of *Tom Jones*, then, though in one sense inhibiting the realization of Fielding's intentions, does provide a centripetal vigour which holds the book together. The smoothness of tone that reduces the impact of certain episodes does help to blend Fielding's multifarious kinds of comment on life and human nature. The attenuation of the narrative illusion, therefore, seems almost a condition of the novel's succeeding in a simpler and more necessary way.

These unifying tendencies are of particular importance in Fielding's work because he was aiming at extensive effects, requiring a great variety of experiment. By contrast Richardson's powerful intensive effects could be achieved within a relatively restricted form. But Fielding's concern to make his heterogeneous methods of entertainment and instruction relate to a consistently unfolding story is also an advantage in absolute terms. Richardson's dropsical works, for all their remarkable qualities, only spasmodically generate the narrative energy which would be necessary throughout if they were to justify their length. The critic, as in some sense a professional reader, is the very person likely to overlook the critical significance of the fact that Fielding's novels are still read for pleasure.

INDEX